Contending for the Faith

Contending for the Faith

A History of the Evangelical Movement in the Universities and Colleges

Douglas Johnson

Inter-Varsity Press

Inter-Varsity Press
38 De Montfort Street, Leicester LE1 7GP, England

First published 1979

ISBN 0 85110 591 2

Set by Woolaston Parker Ltd. in 11 on 13 point Times
Printed in Great Britain by Billing & Sons Ltd.,
Guildford, London and Worcester

*Inter-Varsity Press is the publishing division of the
Universities and Colleges Christian Fellowship (formerly the
Inter-Varsity Fellowship), a student movement linking
Christian Unions in universities and colleges throughout the
British Isles, and a member movement of the International
Fellowship of Evangelical Students. For information about
local and national activities in Great Britain write to UCCF,
38 De Montfort Street, Leicester LE1 7GP.*

To the wives of the secretaries, travelling secretaries and other graduates, who loyally endured their husbands' repeated absences; and to the succession of clerical secretaries, whose industry made possible the growth of the Fellowship.

Contents

Preface   9

PART ONE

1 Student Christian societies   13
2 Pioneers in the universities (*1665–1876*)   26
3 The great student awakening (*1877–1892*)   44
4 Gain and loss (*1893–1918*)   66

PART TWO

5 The rebirth of the Evangelical Movement
   (*1919*)   87
6 New student initiative (*1919–1924*)   97
7 The Inter-University Conferences
   (*1919–1927*)   115
8 The watershed (*1928*)   137
9 Growth in the universities (*1929–1939*)   149
10 International relations (*1929–1939*)   173
11 The missionary volunteers (*1929–1939*)   187
12 The Second World War (*1939–1945*)   197
13 Challenge and response (*1946–1970*)   218
14 Colleges of education and technical
    colleges (*1935–1978*)   251
15 The International Fellowship (*1946–1978*)   268
16 The specialized departments   282
17 Overseas students   302
18 The Inter-Varsity Press   314
19 New environments (*1970–1978*)   333

Appendix 1 Officers and Secretaries
of the Fellowship   351
Appendix 2 The constitution   359
Bibliography   362
Acknowledgments   364
Index of subjects   365
Index of names   367

Preface

The religious societies in the universities have a fascination which is all their own. In the history of the Christian Church student initiatives and informal discussions in college rooms have often been the seed-beds from which new spiritual movements have grown to national, or international, importance.

The following pages, whilst explaining the earlier traditions from which they arose, are mainly concerned with one such movement, the Inter-Varsity Fellowship of Evangelical Unions. The history of the 'IVF' began in 1919 at the close of World War I and continued until 1975, when its name was changed to The Universities and Colleges Christian Fellowship. Over the intervening fifty-six years the Fellowship has illustrated most of the typical features and vicissitudes of student-run organizations. The author's purpose has been, therefore, to highlight the chief lessons for future student generations. He trusts that he has neither over-embellished the more interesting aspects of the story, nor unduly glamorized the leading personalities. On the other hand, he sincerely hopes that, in erring on the side of understatement, he has not overlooked due credit wherever it should have been given.

To lighten the pages a limited number of references, cross-references, memoranda and a short bibliography are given in the appendices. Three major acknowledgments, however, must be made. Important aspects of the earlier phases of the movement were discussed with the late Rev. G. T. Manley, formerly a Fellow of Christ's College, Cambridge, where he was resident during the time of the greatest influence of the Student Missionary Volunteer Movement. In later years he had special opportunities for further observation of student activities; for example, on returning from India he became one of the departmental secretaries of the Church Missionary Society.

Grateful thanks are also due to Dr. F. Donald Coggan, the Archbishop of Canterbury, for permission to quote freely from *Christ and the Colleges* (1934, Inter-Varsity Press), a volume which he edited for the student committee shortly after his graduation from St. John's College, Cambridge. Finally, of the specialist studies which are concerned with the beginnings of Christian witness among students, the most valuable proved to be *Two Centuries of Student Christian Movements* by the late Dr. Clarence Shedd of Yale Divinity School (1934, Associated Press, N.Y.). Dr. Shedd saw Chapter 1 in draft form and approved of its quotations from his authoritative survey.

It is difficult to evaluate recent history and to keep it in perspective. The true assessment is known only to God. The late Dr. John Mott, who was intimate with the early development of the worldwide student Christian movements, used to comment, 'If ever you see some Christian work which is really poor, really small, but really sincere, you may be sure that God is behind it.' The Father of our Lord Jesus Christ is, of course, neither poor nor small! The Apostle Peter provides the clue in his comment: 'God opposes the proud, but gives grace to the humble.'

D.J.

PART ONE

'What memory is to individuals, history is to
institutions.'
Sir George Clark

PART ONE

Chapter 1

Student Christian societies

Writing some twelve years after he had left Cambridge, Norman P. Grubb[1] described the inception of a student conference at the close of World War I, which proved to be the birthplace of the movement which later became known as the Inter-Varsity Fellowship. This student initiative was destined to grow between the Wars to a place of considerable influence in the British and overseas universities. 'I cannot remember the exact day, but it was sometime in the middle of the Michaelmas term, 1919, that in my room in Trinity College, God gave me a clear vision of the IVF that was to be. I saw that not only must there be this witness in every university, but that God was going to do it. Probably the fact of Noel Palmer's prompt action in Oxford at the end of the 1914–18 war in getting to work to re-start an inter-collegiate Christian Union enabled God to open our eyes to this much better thing.' (An account of Noel Palmer's initiative in Oxford will be found on page 97 ff. and the continuation of Norman Grubb's reference to the 1919 conference on pages 90 and 115.)

The background

From the point of view of those who at that time took the initiative, the 'vision' was certainly new. Yet the student traditions out of which it had emerged were far from new. Successive

13

expressions of spiritual vision in the academic world have had their prototypes in university life for over four hundred years. Particularly in the English-speaking universities there are records of such societies which have in different ways organized themselves for Christian action. Nor should this be surprising. In an environment of intimate student friendships, with ample scope for the more robust minds to indulge in limitless discussion, the dreams of the later school years very often crystallize into action. Biography is eloquent concerning the outcome of the gathering of kindred spirits in the colleges and the influence which such groups later had on their generation. It is as true in politics and various aspects of culture as in religion.

Such initiatives have certainly left their mark from the earliest days of the Christian church. In the British Isles one has only to note the emergence of such nurseries of the faith as those of the fifth to the eighth centuries in the Celtic religious communities in Bangor, Kells, Iona and Lindisfarne. Some of these were virtually embryo universities. In the 14th century there was the Oxford of John Wycliffe and his itinerant preachers. Over a century later came the secret meetings of Thomas Bilney and his friends (amongst them the martyr Bishop Hugh Latimer, and Matthew Parker, a future Archbishop) in the White Horse Inn at Cambridge. Their reading of the Greek New Testament and Luther's works was to have far-reaching effects upon the English Reformation. Perhaps the classic example is that of the 'Holy Club' of the Wesleys in 18th-century Oxford, which gave rise to the Methodist Movement. Such groups were, of course, not always 'Evangelical' in the modern sense of the term and other ecclesiastical traditions have had their comparable fountain heads. For, with different assumptions and with a somewhat different purpose, in early 19th century Oxford the Senior Common Room of Oriel College included amongst its fellows J. Keble, J. H. Newman and E. B. Pusey. Their discussions gave rise to the 'Tractarian' (later known as the 'High Church' and – with a difference – the 'Anglo-Catholic') movement in the Church of England. It was, however, in the late 19th and early 20th centuries that the Christian student movements in Britain came to their fullest expression and greatest influence.

In changing conditions

Again, in 1919 it was not new for various student societies to coalesce into larger inter-university and international associations. Such a process had been taking place throughout the late 19th century in North America, as well as in the British Isles and other parts of Europe. There were, however, two major respects in which these post-war expressions of student enterprise, such as those at Cambridge and Oxford described by Norman Grubb above, differed from their predecessors.

Throughout the last third of the 19th century, three radical changes in the intellectual climate of the universities were making themselves increasingly felt in the faculties of science, arts and theology. First came the new era in geology and biology, with the uniformitarian and evolutionary hypotheses which were in direct conflict with the church's traditional views concerning creation and miracle. Then, over much the same period, the age-long gulf between current philosophies and Christian theology greatly widened. The new tensions were felt primarily in the departments of the philosophy of religion. Third was the emergence of new fashions and schools of thought in historical and linguistic studies, and these were powerfully reinforced by the numerous archaeological discoveries throwing light on the civilizations in the ancient Near East.

The universities were naturally focal points at which the shifting of the foundations were most felt. In the aftermath of war and during the early 1920s a very different spiritual environment had begun more directly to challenge the faith of those who came up from schools and churches with a conservative Evangelical faith. The effects, first of the Higher Criticism of the Bible (along with the characteristic attitudes of the 'modernism' which usually accompanied it), together with a parallel trend in the churches towards a new ecclesiastical Catholicism, tended to force them on to the defensive. Such widespread changes in the entire intellectual climate of the universities and theological colleges could not but pose disturbing questions to many of the sincere younger Christians at that time coming up to the universities from home, churches and schools in which the older traditional views still prevailed.

At the close of World War I, spiritual conditions in most of the religious denominations were at their lowest ebb for many years. Ex-servicemen, who had served in the armed forces amidst the horrors of the trenches in Flanders and many of the workers in the industrial cities to a large extent were no longer attending places of worship. The Christian church in the British Isles, for the first time for many centuries, found itself declining into the position of a minority movement, with a correspondingly reduced influence in national life, including the universities. During former years the student leaders, as a rule, had found that their official teachers in the theological colleges were to a great extent united, in theory at least, in accepting the older 'orthodox' views concerning the inspiration and authority of the Bible as 'the rule of faith'. In the 1920s this was true no longer.

Theologically conservative and evangelistically-inclined students became uneasily aware that they could not count on official sympathy with their outlook and activities. Not only so, but they frequently met a passive, and sometimes an active, opposition from their theological college authorities, not to speak of fellow-students. The practical consequences of these new conditions on the policy of the student leaders will need little elaboration. If anything of permanent value to the church has been achieved by the 20th century student Evangelical enterprise, then it has been won by persistence in the face of a theological and ecclesiastical landslide, which went far towards carrying away with it the total birthright of the Protestant churches. To what extent the position has yet been stabilized and how far the student Evangelical unions have assisted in its recovery must be left to the church historians of the future. There can be no doubt, however, that during the period covered in these pages many students in the English-speaking universities and colleges throughout the world were – in spite of many discouragements – brought to faith in Christ and strengthened in their allegiance to Him. In addition a truly significant number – some of them amongst the ablest students of their years – were encouraged to devote their lives to the full-time service of God's kingdom.

The nature of a student Christian society

One instructive approach to an understanding of the essential features of a typical student Christian society is afforded by the inner history of the early prototypes in the universities of the United States of America. A former Dean of the Yale Divinity School, Clarence P. Shedd, has produced two well-documented books[2] in which he has analysed the characteristics of the pioneer societies. It is necessary first, however, to explain the need for initiatives of these kinds in institutions which were mostly founded on religious principles. In view of their Puritan origins, the conditions into which official religion and personal piety had fallen by the end of the 18th century might well be a matter for surprise, were it not that our own national history records a similar decline in Britain over the same periods.[3] It is a fact of history that it was not until small groups of the more devout students, especially theological students, began to meet for prayer and mutual spiritual stimulus, that a change for the better took place in the universities on both sides of the Atlantic.

The moral standards of the New England colleges at one stage became so low that the Rev. Cotton Mather, the foremost Boston preacher at that time, wrote in 1716 in his diary concerning Harvard (where his father had been Principal), 'Is there nothing to be done for the miserable College? Yes, I will commend some things unto the perusal of the more serious youths associated for piety there.' He at once began to invite some of the students, with other young people from his church, to meet with him on Sunday evenings. He adds, 'We constantly prayed (both before and after the repetition of a sermon) and sang a psalm, taking our turns in such devotions. We then had a devout question, proposed a week before, whereunto anyone present gave whatever answer he pleased and I still concluded the answer.' From this beginning other groups developed amongst students and young people in other parts of the city. Mather regarded such societies as 'incomparable nurseries unto the Church.'

The earliest extant account of a student religious meeting in America is dated 10 January 1723, and describes 'the Private Meeting Instituted at Harvard College, 1719'. At that time the group had a membership of twenty-six students. It was a secret society, as were the student societies in other universities at first. The reasons for the secrecy seem to have been, first, because of the strict laws which were constantly enforced by the state churches and the authorities of the colleges against 'conventicles' and, secondly, the irritation which any appearance of 'piety' apparently provoked in the attitudes both of academic staff and students.

In those times students had reason for remaining on good terms with their tutors who were intolerant of many aspects of student life, especially of youthful devotional exercises. The latter were virtually prohibited in the college except in the form of official services in the chapel. In 1743 two brothers were expelled from Yale for absenting themselves from an official service in order 'to attend, with their parents, religious meetings run by a layman in a private house'. The 18th century American theologian Jonathan Edwards, in his *Life of David Brainerd*, reveals that an embryonic religious society existed at Yale during his student days and that Brainerd, later to become a missionary to the Indian tribes, had been a member. Edwards writes, 'At the time of the awakening at the College, there were several religious students who associated themselves with one another for mutual conversation and assistance in spiritual things, who were wont freely to open themselves to one another as special intimate friends.' Frankness and non-conformity, however, had its dangers for it was not long before Brainerd was expelled from Yale because of some 'uncomplimentary remarks on Tutor Whittlesey's religious life and for attending a separatist meeting against the order of Rector Clap.'

The societies' beginnings at Harvard and Yale were not isolated phenomena. Well before 1800 traces are found of secret religious groups in sixteen out of the twenty-two American 'colleges' (which were, in effect, developing universities). During the expansion in higher education after the year 1800, a corresponding increase took place in the number of student Christian societies. These have left more than a trace of their existence, and Dr. Clarence Shedd has instructively condensed the results of his examination of their minute books, preserved in the libraries of the respective universities. Their names give clues to their aims. For example, 'The Private Meeting' (Harvard), 'Adelphi Theologia' (Harvard), 'The Moral Society' (Yale), 'The Religiosi' or 'The Religious Society' (Dartmouth), 'The College Praying Society' (Brown), 'The Rising Sun' (Williams), 'The Society for Inquiry concerning Missions' (Andover), 'Philadelphia Society' (Princeton), and the 'Society for Religious Inquiry' (Vermont). The primary aim in the case of some of these private societies was to promote practical ethics, that is, they required strict Christian conduct on the part of their members. The occasional minute reveals that an intemperate or otherwise too easy-going member stood a good chance of being admonished by the president. If he then persisted in such habits he could expect to be expelled from the society! When perusing the early minute books, Dr. Clarence Shedd found that a secretary, in writing the society's records, had sometimes allowed his humour to get the better of him. For example, before leaving the college for his last long vacation, one secretary closed the records for the preceding academic year with, 'The seniors took their leave this evening. May they be better members of the great society into which they are about to enter than they have been of *this*. This ends my secretaryship'(!)

In the early 19th century, several influences increased the number and size of these societies, and enabled them to pursue a more open policy. One factor was that along with the larger student intake came a greater number of convinced Christians into the colleges. There was also a relaxation of ecclesiastical regulations concerning conformity, a process which was speeded by the greater number of denominational and racial backgrounds from which the student body came. The biggest single factor, however, was undoubtedly the first wave of the great religious revivals which became such a feature in the later 19th century life of the American nation. Thousands of young people were brought into an active experience of the Christian faith and the college students were no exception.

The characteristics of a student society

The temptation to pursue the history of these American

19

forerunners of the student movements in the later years of the century must be resisted. Our purpose here is to call attention to the chief features which marked these societies. They have been set out for us by Dr. Clarence Shedd at the close of the foreword to his valuable study.[4] The following is a summary:

1. The presence of 'Christian Student Societies are indigenous to the religious and educational life of the American colleges. They are neither a "flash in the pan" nor something "outside" the life of these institutions'. If they were wiped out they would reappear in a short time under new names, but with an organization possessing the same general characteristics. The tradition is almost unbroken into the present from the years soon after the foundation of the various collegiate institutions

2. 'The urge for widest possible inter-collegiate fellowship' is a regular feature. Sooner or later a group in one college will communicate with like-minded students elsewhere.

3. 'The societies always have been interdenominational in composition.' This is to some extent inevitable from the very nature of college life. Evidence is clear that most of the groups which have started as denominational societies have, after a short time, tended 'to become more interdenominational in spirit and method'.

4. 'It has always been possible to discern main strands of emphasis in the work of the Student Christian Societies.' The earliest Unions were purely devotional. Others then appeared which met for theological research and discussions of problems in apologetics. Later unions concentrated on evangelistic and missionary inquiry. 'With the organization of the (student) Young Men's Christian Associations and YWCAs, there was added the emphasis of seeking to transform the campus life and relating students to the urgent problems of community, national and world life.' The more recent student societies tend to combine all these strands in the one organization.

5. Almost from the beginning came a desire of all student life to express itself internationally, both through the foreign missionary enterprise of the Churches and through inter-

national student organizations.

6. Although outwardly appearing conservative, there has always been the typical student impatience with academic discussion, and a desire for a programme of practical action which can be pursued with all the ardour and idealism of youth. To attempt to wrestle vigorously with the problems of temperance, slavery, social conditions, peace and war, is all part of the authentic student tradition.

7. Typically, decisions have been made by the students themselves, or on the advice of post-graduates who are in close touch with them. The more mature leading students, however, value the advice of Christian professors, ministers, chaplains and others. In the early days the influence of seniors was often apparent as, for example, that of Cotton Mather (Harvard), Professor Moses Stuart (Andover) and the Chaplain Dabney Carr Harrison (Virginia). But what the students want and what they most benefit from is to be allowed to have their 'final decisions made by students under student leadership'.

8. As in all higher education, the tendency is continually towards equality in co-operation between the sexes, though there remains the necessity for the women members to remain identified with their own sex in some of the social issues.

9. Loyalty to the college (or university) society tends to supersede other historical or contemporary loyalties. The interest is in relating the Christian message to contemporary life. This practical ambition tends to displace denominational loyalties during college life.

10. The student societies tend towards a democratic organiz-ation, towards 'catholicity' of theological and social thought, and towards being 'prophetic' and activist in their approach to the problems of the day. Repeatedly the student world has set the fashion which later has been followed in the churches and in other parts of the national life.

The above analysis, written with the earliest American Christian student societies in mind, is also mostly true of the corresponding British student societies which developed over the same period. In his account of the Student Christian Movement of Great Britain and Ireland, Tissington Tatlow has added to Clarence Shedd's list a further characteristic. When discussing the aims of the ' Brethren Society' (formed in 1806 by the students of Williams College, Williamstown, Mass.) he points out that this is the first known specifically *student missionary* organization. It also exemplifies clearly the personal note of challenge which is typical of most student religious organizations. The members did not in the first instance combine to activate *other* people, but were concerned with themselves, that is, to quote their own words, 'to effect in the *person* of its members a mission, or missions, to the heathen'.

The meaning of 'Evangelical'

The societies so far described were representative of widely varied theological traditions in British and American church life. Those with which this present study is concerned arose from what in the history of the British churches is known as the 'Evangelical Movement'. At this point the word 'evangelical' needs to be defined. In the context of today's loose theological thinking this descriptive adjective has been allowed to lose some of its distinctive meaning. It is frequently confused with 'evangelistic' (that is, active in sharing the gospel) and hence given too superficial a meaning. Its full connotation needs to be kept in mind if the subsequent story is to retain its due perspective.

The word 'evangelical' derives from the Greek New Testament's use of the word *euangelion*, of which the English equivalent is the 'gospel' or 'good news'. In England its Latin form may be traced back as far as John Wycliffe, who was known as 'Doctor Evangelicus', and who died before he had completed his last book under the title '*Opus Evangelicum*', in which he has used the term to describe the basic message of the Bible. Its first known use in English was by Sir Thomas More, who in 1532 referred – disapprovingly – to the advocates of the Reformation as 'those Evaungelicalles'. On the continent of Europe, soon after the Reformation, the name was employed to describe Protestantism in general, and more particularly the churches which followed the Lutheran branch of the Reformation. For example, in Germany and Scandinavia the official title adopted for each of the state churches was 'The Evangelical Church'.

This tends to emphasize one of the fundamental principles of Evangelicalism. For Martin Luther bequeathed to these state churches the central doctrine of justification by faith, that is, God's direct act of pardon for the individual repentant sinner without priestly mediation. The Bible states more than once that 'without faith it is impossible to please God' and that 'the just shall live by faith'. To Luther and his fellow reformers this doctrine was 'the Article of a standing or falling Church'. It is fundamental to all Evangelicals.

In the British Isles during the next two centuries, and especially in England, the term tended to take on a somewhat more limited meaning. Following the religious revivals of the late 18th century, 'Evangelical' was used to describe those clergy and their followers in the Church of England who, whilst deeply influenced by and sympathizing with the contemporary revivals, had remained in the national church at the time when the leading Methodists were being driven by the bishops and clergy, unwillingly, to form a new free church. However, with the subsequent growth of Methodism and other free churches the term 'Evangelical' was again used to embrace all those who accepted a Bible-based declaration of the gospel, together with the other doctrines of a truly Biblical theology.

In subsequent chapters the descriptive adjective 'Evangelical' will be employed, therefore, with this fuller 19th century connotation. To an Evangelical there is nothing sectarian in the word for it is as wide *and as narrow* as the Christian gospel (*euangelion*) itself. But in church history it stands for a certain clearly defined outlook. To borrow the words of Handley C. G. Moule, a former Bishop of Durham, the aim of every Evangelical must be to be 'faithful in essentials to the all-important test of the scale of Christian truth as presented in the Holy Scriptures . . . and to place "the first things first" (which the things of Salvation are) as set before us in the divine Book of Appeal'.[5] The basic principle in Evangelical belief and activity is the conviction that the essential is to give a firm and honest obedience to the plain teaching of our Lord and His apostles as this is presented to us in

23

the Bible. If Christ is to be Lord and Master and the teaching of the apostles is to be accepted then there is no place for editing their words. Whatever scientific discovery, intellectual achievement and modern cultural progress may bring, the Master and His gospel must not be transmuted by some 'doctrine of development' into something else.

The duty of preserving the incomparable treasure of the Christian gospel and of passing it on unspoilt from age to age has been achieved, and can only be achieved, in one way. It is by guarding, explaining and obeying the authentic records as they have come down to us. For the church knows virtually nothing for certain of God's self-revelation, nor about her divine Master, except what is found in the Bible. It is for this reason that the Evangelical places such emphasis upon the title deeds to his inheritance in Christ. It is one of the reasons why he originally resisted, and continues to resist those forms of biblical criticism (so called 'higher' criticism) which undermine the authenticity and authority of the Bible. Originally such criticism depended on a long chain of assumptions erected on a very narrow base. He feels justified in asking 'Is the higher criticism with its web of increasing hypotheses really scholarly?' In the absence of sufficient contrary evidence he continues to accept direction from what he is convinced is the 'word of God written'.

In the last analysis, an Evangelical orders his life by three great truths. First that sinful man can be justified before God only through faith in His grace as it was revealed and made effective in the atoning death of Christ. Second, that God has authoritatively, accurately and sufficiently revealed Himself, His will and His action in Holy Scripture. Third, that the Holy Spirit, the Lord the lifegiver, comes to the individual disciple, converting, purifying, empowering and guiding in the way of Christ. This embraces the 'evangel' – the 'good news' – and it is this that the Evangelical is concerned to spread.

This evangel came to have an increasingly powerful influence on the nation during the late 19th century. It was then that the foundations were laid for those upsurges of undergraduate initiative which it is the purpose of our later chapters to recount. Writing in later life of his home[6] the Rt. Hon. George W. F.

24

Russell gives many sidelights on the single-mindedness and zeal of his generation. 'Let me put in the very forefront of my description the happiest and deepest of all my impressions. The Evangelicals were the most religious people whom I have ever known. I was brought up among the spiritual descendents of the men and women who constituted 'the Clapham Sect'.... The fathers were gone, the children survived; and they in turn were the parents of the generation to which I belong. To those parents I look back with loving and grateful reverence, and I recall an abiding sense of religious responsibility, a self-sacrificing energy in works of mercy, an evangelistic zeal, an aloofness from the world, and a level of saintliness in daily life, such as I do not expect again to see realized on earth.'

NOTES

1   The son-in-law of the late C. T. Studd, who was a well-known pioneer missionary, first in China and later in Central Africa. Norman Grubb succeeded his father-in-law as leader of the Worldwide Evangelistic Crusade.
2   C. P. Shedd, *Two Centuries of Student Movements* (Associated Press, 1934), and *Some Early Student Religious Societies and the Inter-Collegiate Beginnings of the Student Christian Movement*. For the following pages concerning the American Movements the author is indebted to the first of the above-named volumes, and the following sections of this chapter are largely taken from it.
3   J. Wesley Bready, *England Before and After Wesley* (Hodder and Stoughton, 1937).
4   Dr. Shedd approved this summary.
5   H. C. G. Moule, *The Evangelical School in the Church of England* (James Nisbet, London, 1901).
6   G. W. F. Russell, *A Short History of the Evangelical Movement* (Mowbrays, 1915).

Chapter 2

Pioneers in the universities
(1665—1876)

The earliest known reference to a *student*-initiated religious society in the British universities occurs in biographical allusions to Henry Scougal in Aberdeen. Henry Scougal (1650–78), a son of the Bishop of Aberdeen, entered the university at the age of fifteen. On graduating he was appointed for five years as minister in Auchterarder. He had already acquired a reputation for his preaching and had written a useful devotional book, *Private Reflexions and Occasional Maxims*, when he was brought back to be Professor of Divinity at the early age of twenty-five. He died of tuberculosis two years later. But during those two years he wrote his best-known work and so bequeathed to later Christian generations one of the most influential of the early devotional books of Scotland, *The Life of God in the Soul of Man*. As will be shown below, this book was to exercise a crucial influence in the 18th century revival of religion.

From a sermon preached at his funeral, we learn that in his student days he had brought together at the beginning of the long vacation 'serious students to spend three days in prayer, Bible study and self-examination.... He was made constant president amongst his fellows, his discourses to them were so grave and becoming that they looked on them as the sayings of grey head, and thought they savoured of the wisdom of a senator.' The rules of this little society were bound up in earlier editions of Scougal's

Works and there is ample evidence of their influence in the 'praying societies' of later Scottish church history.

Eighteenth-century Oxford

Scougal's *The Life of God in the Soul of Man* became one of the favourite devotional books of that remarkable woman, Susannah Wesley. When her sons left Epworth Rectory to go to Oxford she recommended to them this 'excellent good book' and lent them her copy. They found the Aberdeen Society's rules bound up with it. Later, whilst John was back at Epworth helping his father, it was Charles who founded 'the Holy Club',[1] as it was cheerfully labelled by contemporary Oxford undergraduates.

It welcomed 'serious' visitors. George Whitefield, who at the time was disturbed by religious thoughts and seeking peace with God, became a 'visitor' to the Club and was encouraged by Charles Wesley. The latter began to lend him books. Whitefield describes how 'In a short time he let me have another book entitled *The Life of God in the Soul of Man* (and, though I had fasted, watched and prayed, and received the sacrament so long, yet I never knew what true religion was till God sent me that excellent treatise by the hands of my never-to-be-forgotten friend).' Whitefield goes on to explain how, on reading Scougal, he wondered what he meant by 'that some falsely place religion in going to Church, doing harm to no one, being constant in duties . . . giving alms to poor neighbours etc. "Alas", thought I, "if this be not religion, what is?" God soon showed me. For in reading a few lines further, that "true religion was a union of the soul with God, and Christ formed within us" a ray of divine light was instantaneously darted in on my soul and from that moment (but not till then) did I know that I must be a new creature.' The winning of George Whitefield was as crucial for the future of the later Evangelical Revival as that of John Wesley for, of the two, he was perhaps the greater preacher. It was he who first took to preaching in the market places and fields when pulpits in the churches were closed to them.

It is not altogether clear how far the rules of the 'Holy Club' and the topics discussed, were influenced by Scougal's rules. It is

27

certain, however, that they were very influential when John Wesley was drawing up the directions for the Methodist Societies and their 'class meetings' which grew out of the Revival. This can be seen from the Class Meeting Rules appended for many years to the minutes of the Methodist Conference. It is also probable that, at the time of their Oxford activities, the two Wesleys' attitude to religious duty was more in keeping with that of the later 'Tractarian' Oxford Movement of the 19th century. For John Wesley was a 'high churchman' in several respects.

We have no clear description of the actual procedures at the meetings of the 'Holy Club'. We only know that they met at first on Sunday evenings, then on two evenings a week and eventually it seems on *each* evening of the week from 6 to 9 pm.(!) Comments and circumstantial evidence make it clear that they read and discussed the Greek New Testament and pursued topics such as those which were listed by John Wesley in his introductory letter to his own final edition of the *Journal*. They then went on to discuss the next day's visits to the castle prison and 'the Bocardo' (i.e. the university prison). They ended by planning practical deeds of charity.

When the senior members had graduated and John Wesley went to America various other factors reduced the circle. 'The Holy Club' gradually faded and was eventually dissolved. It must be remembered that the university authorities were active in suppressing all signs of Methodism. When Thomas Haweis, an 'Evangelical' ('believed to be Methodist'), came as a curate to St. Mary Magdalene in Oxford, the church was put out of bounds and the university's proctors regularly arrived during the services to see that there were no undergraduates present. It showed considerable courage for James Stillingfleet, a Fellow of Merton College, regularly to entertain a small circle of Methodists, whom he steadfastly befriended. They met in the drawing room of a certain Mrs. Durbridge for united prayer and Bible study. In most of the colleges, however, an undergraduate would have had a hard time if he were even suspected of being a Methodist. The authorities allowed no 'conventicles' in college, nor did they permit the students to attend anything resembling one in the city.

Expulsion of Methodists from St. Edmund Hall

In February 1768 one of the tutors of St. Edmund Hall brought to the Principal a formal complaint that there were amongst the undergraduates 'several enthusiasts who talked of regeneration, inspiration and drawing near to God'. When the Principal took no action the tutor referred the matter to the Vice-Chancellor. A later Vice-Principal of the college, S. L. Ollard[2] tells the story. The so-called 'Court of Enquiry' was guilty of a travesty of justice. The gravamen of the charge against the undergraduates was that they were 'Methodists' and, therefore, were automatically assumed to be 'enemies of the doctrine and discipline of the Church of England'. Amongst other embarrassments, the hapless and bewildered students were suddenly given a section of the Greek New Testament to translate aloud, to the evident enjoyment of the onlookers. Their indifferent success was taken as amply proving their guilt. They were expelled from the University. The event, however, precipitated a great deal of serious public discussion throughout the country and pamphlets appeared for and against. Horace Walpole wrote exultantly, 'Oxford has begun with these rascals, and I hope that Cambridge will awake'. Many of the public, however, were less happy and more impressed by the rebuke of the pseudonymous writer 'Shaver', who addressed the Oxford 'dons' in stinging satire –

'My thanks, and the nation's, to the Doctors be given,
Those guardians of virtue, those Porters of heaven,
For their timely wise care in suppressing the growth
Of praying, expounding and hymn-singing youth.

Should praying be suffer'd by our learnèd Sages
(What has not been known in Ox...d for ages)
Instead of gay parsons, with cassock and band,
There would be none but Puritans all o'er the land.

Expounding the Scriptures! this still is more wicked,
Therefore from college be they instantly kickèd,
For Scripture and priest-craft as distant do dwell
As some parsons from virtue, or Heaven from hell.'

(There were five more verses and the pamphlet ran to twenty-five editions. It was sung to the popular tune of 'Down, down with Hypocrisy'!).

Whilst the tragic injustice of St. Edmund Hall did not end the Evangelical succession in Oxford (as biographical comment and the records of some of the city's churches show), it seriously retarded it. Evangelicalism became virtually an underground movement. It did not again emerge in any robust *public* form until Alfred Christopher, a Cambridge graduate, was appointed Rector of St. Aldate's in 1859.[3]

Other religious societies

At this point it will be relevant to return to the years following the Restoration of 1660. The rise of the better known Methodist societies a century later has tended to overshadow a remarkable movement amongst the young men of the Metropolis and big industrial cities in England. From a small book, J. Woodward's *Rise and Progress of Religious Societies*, we learn that, beginning about 1678 and going on to their greatest influence during the reign of William and Mary, many young men in the churches formed themselves into societies for mutual edification. These societies were first reported in connection with the parishes of St. Giles and St. Michael's in the City of London. Soon they are found all over the diocese of London. Members moving to take up work in midland and northern cities carried the ideas of the movement with them.

The members were all men, mostly young, and they were all avowedly loyal members of the Church of England. They originally met to discuss informally the sermons from the point of view of taking practical action, and for Bible study and prayer. They also encouraged one another in careful Christian living, in seeking the relief of poverty and in the preaching of the gospel. They were encouraged by some (not all) of the clergy, who were agreeably surprised by the way these societies increased the attendance at communion and all the other services of the church. The Society for Promoting Christian Knowledge (SPCK) traces its origin to these societies. In the movement as a whole, hundreds of young men were involved.

Later, about the year 1691, a second series of societies came into being. These were organized for 'the Reformation of Manners', and sought to take political and legal action to improve public morals. Whilst the memberships of the two series of societies overlapped, their roles and leaderships were not identical. Both movements were actively encouraged by Queen Mary, it is said, with William III's approval.

As the years passed, however, both the episcopal and political authorities proved to be unimpressed and impervious to reform. At that stage some members of these societies joined the earliest of the Methodist societies. The evidence is clear, however, that when later the Evangelicals in the Church of England began to oppose the slave owners, the exploiters of child labour in the mines and factories and evil vested interests of all kinds, the traditions and memberships of these societies brought in very strong support. There is also some evidence that they inspired a few of the individual Christians going up to the universities to form small unobtrusive student groups along the lines of 'the Holy Club'. These were unadvertised and remained small because of the attitude of the academic authorities to 'conventicles'.

Beginnings in Cambridge

Happily Walpole's hope that Cambridge would 'awake' to repress the Methodists was not fulfilled. In any case, speaking generally, the Cambridge authorities were rather more open-minded and tolerant of the milder deviations from the establishment. In the last third of the 18th century there is known to have been a zealous group of undergraduates in St. John's College. Individual students were also being influenced by Evangelical clergy, for example by Henry Venn, Vicar of Yelling a few miles from Cambridge, and by John Berridge, a Fellow of Clare Hall, and Vicar in the nearby village of Everton. In 1777 the Evangelical clergy of northern England formed the Elland Society in order to help to train young men for the ministry. This society decided to abandon further efforts to send its protégés to Oxford. After early disappointments, it was successful in gaining entry for several of its young men at Magdalene College, Cambridge. Such an outcome was possible only because of the persistent efforts of 'the gentle' William Farish, a Fellow of Magdalene and Professor of Chemistry. The Master of the college remained hostile and constantly remarked that his college was becoming 'a nest for Methodists'.

The first real change came with the appointment of Isaac Milner, a strong character of outstanding intellectual ability, as President of Queens' College. He was the younger brother of Joseph Milner, Headmaster of Hull Grammar School. The latter was (Sunday) afternoon lecturer at Holy Trinity Church, Hull, which became one of the strongest centres of Evangelicalism. William Wilberforce had been one of his pupils. When, however, Isaac Milner took over the mastership at Queens' he found that the college was in a poor way with the numbers of undergraduates and general standards falling. Against the united opposition of the tutors he determined to raise the fortunes of the college generally, to improve its academic attainments and to welcome the nominees of the Elland Society, when they were up to his standards. The opposing Fellows were offered college livings and other inducements to go elsewhere. They were replaced by those willing to work loyally for the Master's ideals. Queens' grew to be one of the largest undergraduate communities in the University.

The rising tide

Isaac Milner, however, was a very senior member of the university and, from the undergraduate point of view, somewhat aloof. The real turning point in Cambridge came with the appointment in 1782[4] of Charles Simeon as Vicar of Holy Trinity Church, a post which he held (as well as a fellowship of King's College, in which as a bachelor don he was able to remain in residence) until his death in 1836. When as a 'fresher' he had come from Eton in 1779, he was anything but Christian in his outlook. Well endowed financially and possessed of a robust physique, he was looking forward to a merry time in King's. Soon after taking up residence, however, his tutor informed him that under college rules he would be expected to attend a celebration of Holy Communion in three weeks' time. Subsequently he wrote, 'On being informed that I *must*, the thought rushed into my head that Satan himself was as fit to attend as I; and that if I must attend, I must *prepare* for my attendance there'. He at once purchased several books and one of these, in reference to the Old Testament sacrifices, contained the phrase 'the ancient Jews knew what they did, when they transferred their sin to the head of their offering'. He continued, 'The thought came into my mind, "What? Can I transfer all my guilt to another? Has God provided an Offering for me, that I may lay my sin on His head? Then, God willing, I will not bear them on my own soul one moment longer." Accordingly, I sought to lay my sins upon the sacred head of Jesus. ... From that hour peace flowed in rich abundance into my soul, and at the Lord's Table in our Chapel I had the sweetest access to God through my blessed Savour.'

The outcome of that spiritual crisis was nearly fifty years of a most influential, national ministry from the pulpit of Holy Trinity Church. Through the 'Conversation Parties' and sermon classes held in his large room at King's College, he had a unique impact on each succeeding student generation. Hundreds of young men were, over the years, won by Simeon to Christ and for the cause of Evangelical Christianity. At the height of Simeon's influence Macaulay wrote home, 'If you knew what his authority and influence were, and how they extended from Cambridge to the most remote corners of England, you would allow that his real sway over the country was far greater than that of any primate.' Opposition was not absent. His followers were soon called 'Sims', a name which stuck for many years to any students or clergy who showed signs of being Evangelical. The jealousies of the senior members, however, gradually died down, and Simeon's relations with the University became more cordial. Finally, he was on several occasions invited to preach the University Sermon. His funeral in 1836 brought together one of the largest crowds ever seen on such an occasion in Cambridge. Senior members, graduates, hundreds of undergraduates and clergy from miles around united to pay homage to this unique spiritual father.

Simeon's teaching made its impact on undergraduates chiefly through three avenues. The first was 'the Lecture' (or sermon) in Holy Trinity Church on Sunday evenings. The second consisted in the 'Conversation Parties' (or 'open tea-parties') when the students crowded his large room at the top of a staircase in King's. Here, after the meal, questions were asked and he discoursed on the relevant topics chosen at the time by his audience. The third was the 'Sermon Parties' designed for those entering the ministry. Here he would explain the art of preparing a sermon and dictate outlines, which really explained each text *in its context*. No doubt some lazily-inclined ordinands merely took notes to add to their store of ready-made sermons for future use; but the net effect of this method was that the great evangelical doctrines were imbibed by hundreds of future clergy and later disseminated all over the land. Throughout his career, Simeon was intensely loyal to the Church of England and his single repeatedly expressed aim was the spiritual rehabilitation of the national church.

Simeon's work was continued on a lesser scale by William Carus, his successor at Holy Trinity Church. This devoted worker for Christ has put posterity in his debt by editing the informative *Memoirs of Charles Simeon*. He also endowed the Carus Greek Testament prize which has in later times encouraged many clergy to follow in the steps of what came to be known thirty years later as the 'Cambridge Exegetical School', when it was led by those incomparable scholars J. B. Lightfoot, B. F. Westcott and F. A. Hort. The outstanding characteristic of Cambridge theological training in the second half of the 19th century was a careful handling of the Greek text of the New Testament and its interpretation in conformity with the 'grammatico-historical' principle of exegesis. Biographies and incidental references in mid-19th century Christian literature also suggest that Holy Trinity church – supplemented by William Farish's work at St. Giles' – continued to maintain the evangelical tradition in Cambridge to the good of many later generations of under-graduates. But the contemporaneous gradual development of student initiative grew to have a particular significance.

The Jesus Lane Sunday School

One Sunday morning in the spring of 1827 five undergraduates were walking back to their own colleges after attending the morning service in Holy Trinity Church. They sat in a summer house near St. John's College, discussing the sermon. One of them, James Wright, made the comment, 'It seems a pity that we could not spend some part of our time in Sunday School teaching'. But where? They then began to discuss the spiritual state of the small village of Barnwell on the road to Newmarket. The area at the time was in a somewhat depressed state. Its spiritual care was based on the one not too well sited church and it was receiving little encouragement. Typically the undergraduates forgot to consult the vicar (if, indeed, there was one resident at that time) and proceeded to carve up the parish between them into areas to be visited. After some difficulty they secured the loan of a suitable building for a school. It was a little used hall owned by the Society of Friends, situated in Jesus Lane, which led into the Newmarket Road near Barnwell. They then began to visit all the homes in the area, inviting the children to a Sunday school.

The response was surprisingly good. The mothers were impressed by the interest and earnestness of 'the young gentlemen'. On the first Sunday the place was almost filled by a very noisy and thoroughly curious collection of children. When some degree of order had been established these were grouped into classes and a beginning of teaching the alphabet was made. Letters were copied on to slates and they were then spelt out to form a text of Scripture. One such text was copied each Sunday and repeated, in the hope of memorization. It was then explained. In the process the children began to learn to read. The first message introduced by the hopeful undergraduates to the Jesus Lane Sunday School was that great statement in Holy Scripture, 'God so loved the world, that He gave His only begotten Son, that whosoever believeth in Him should not perish, but have everlasting life'. The records clearly show that over the years a succession of undergraduate teachers sought to include in the curriculum all the main doctrines of the faith. They also adapted their methods with increasing skill as provision for better secular elementary education in Barnwell caught up with them.

Over the years the Jesus Lane Sunday School proved to be a most influential training ground in the art of communication for many ordinands and future schoolmasters who were on the

35

teachers' roll. Many who later occupied important pulpits and posts of influence learnt to communicate clearly the truths of the gospel in teaching the Barnwell children. *A History of the Jesus Lane Sunday School (1827–1864)* was revised for the occasion of the Jubilee celebrations in 1877. The record was compiled by Charles Alfred Jones, formerly of St. John's College and later senior mathematics master at Westminster School. One of the founders, E. T. Leeke, writes, 'The week in which we visited Barnwell was one of the most pleasing weeks of my life. On the following Sunday morning 220 scholars of both sexes made their appearance at the appointed time in Jesus Lane. They were formed into classes. . . . The teachers were in the habit of visiting the parents of the children belonging to their classes.' Several others describe the enthusiasm and great industry which the founders and their successors bestowed on this school.

The list of those who as undergraduates were superintendents, secretaries or teachers in the school is most impressive. Amongst them are such names as J. C. Adam (Professor of Astronomy); A. Barry (Principal of King's College, London); T. R. Birks (Professor of Moral Philosophy); H. M. Butler (Headmaster of Harrow); W. J. Conybeare (of Conybeare & Howson's *Life and Epistles of St. Paul*); H. Cotterill (Bishop of Edinburgh); G. E. L. Cotton (Bishop of Calcutta); F. W. Farrar (Dean of Westminster Abbey); A. F. Kirkpatrick (Lady Margaret Professor of Divinity); C. F. Mackenzie (Bishop of Cape Town); T. Maxwell (medical missionary in Kashmir); C. J. Vaughan (Headmaster of Harrow and, later, Master of the Temple); O. E. Vidal (Bishop of Sierra Leone); B. G. Westcott (Regius Professor of Divinity and later Bishop of Durham). Interested by his friend B. F. Westcott, the chair was taken at the Jubilee celebrations by J. B. Lightfoot (Lady Margaret Professor of Divinity and, later, Bishop of Durham); he is described as 'always a warm friend of the school, though not himself a teacher'.

The wider significance of the Jesus Lane Sunday School in its influence on Christian activity in the University becomes apparent from occasional references in the biography and autobiography of the central years of the 19th century. There is no doubt that from its inception until 1877 it was in effect a small indirect Christian Union in the University. It drew into its fellowship and weekly activities the more zealous and outgoing of the undergraduates coming up from Evangelical homes. Then later two of the new teachers in the school in 1847 conceived the idea of the Cambridge Prayer Union. Support from 'the Jesus Lane lot' was also expected, and received in 1862, at the start of the Daily Prayer Meeting. This 'lot' also proved one of the chief centres of support for the university missions in the 1870s, on which followed the founding of the Cambridge Inter-Collegiate Christian Union in 1877. It is encouraging to be able to add that the school continued into the present century and, in somewhat different conditions, is believed to be still active.

The Scottish universities

It is not known how long the students' religious society in Aberdeen, resulting from Henry Scougal's initiative (1667–78) continued. But echoes are to be found here and there in the four Scottish universities of 'the Praying Societies of Scotland'. Writing in a series of articles on the religious revivals and the *'ecclesiolae in ecclesia'* of the 18th century,[5] Professor J. Davidson claims that the movement was far more influential in the parishes of the Lowlands and Central Scotland than has often been realized. He claims that 'Praying Societies sprang up in nearly every parish of the Lowlands'. From time to time students appear to have attempted something of the kind in their universities, that is, whenever they could find like-minded fellow students. Professor Davidson found, and has reproduced, the 'Rules for a Young Men's Praying Society' of about the year 1750. Yet usually the Scottish academic authorities were not, at that time, any more favourable to such student-organized activities than were their counterparts at Oxford. Any students who met to pray probably did so at one of the city churches where there may have been a Praying Society.

In the early 19th century, however, there is more definite documentation of direct student initiative, especially in relation to an interest in Christian missions and discussion amongst theological students. The parents of Alexander Duff, the first (officially recognized) missionary sent overseas by the Church of Scotland, had been converted through a small revival of religion which had taken place in the parish of Moulin, Perthshire. This had occurred during a week-end visit to the Manse by Charles Simeon of Cambridge when he was travelling in Scotland to convalesce after a period of ill-health. On going to St. Andrew's University, Duff came under the beneficent influence of Thomas Chalmers, who was at that time Professor of Moral Philosophy there. Chalmers kept open house for the students and was friendly to student religious initiatives. Duff records that he heard at Dr. Chalmers' hospitable table 'the emphatic opinion that religious societies should be managed by laymen, whilst Ministers confine themselves to the more spiritual duties of their office'.

Earlier, at St. Andrew's, there had been a small society of divinity students. During the session 1824–25 Duff and six friends founded the Student Missionary Society in order to study the non-Christian world and the new societies, such as the London Missionary Society, which were endeavouring to pioneer overseas missions. Neither the University nor the civic authorities would allow these students a room for the purpose and they had at first to meet in a small school in a side lane. Their main encouragement throughout came from Professor Chalmers who was, however, soon after lost to them through his appointment as Professor of Divinity in Edinburgh. A year later, in a letter to Dr. Chalmers, Duff reports that the Student Missionary Society (unlike the Town Missionary Society) was in a flourishing state. From the group, five pioneer missionaries (in addition to Alexander Duff) were destined to take a distinguished part in the epic of Christian missions in the later 19th century.

Cambridge again

For the next indubitable evidence of student initiative we must look to mid-19th century Cambridge. On arrival as a freshman at Corpus, Albert Isaacs describes how he was quickly contacted by Frederick Gough of St. John's, and informed about 'the various works which Christian young men were carrying on in the town and university. The first Sunday I spent in Cambridge I was inducted into the office of teacher in the Jesus Lane Sunday School'. When the time came for Gough to leave Cambridge for a curacy prior to going to China as a CMS missionary, Isaacs and several others discussed an idea which had been brewing for some time in their minds. It was proposed that, 'We might agree amongst ourselves to meet in the spirit of prayer in whatever part of the world our lot may later be cast'.

The resulting agreement among a few friends soon grew into the founding in March, 1848, of the 'Cambridge Union for Private Prayer for Members of the University preparing for the Ministry'. The main rule was that they should pray for each other on the second Monday of each month from six to seven in the morning or at 'the first convenient hour thereafter'. They were to pray for the church at home and abroad and for 'the increase of Christian Ministers who would be devoted to the spread of the Gospel'. They were also regularly to write a letter giving news to the secretary, who would periodically circulate it to the members in the form of a report. It is significant that far into the 20th century there continued the use and adaptation of this form of association. Several of the 'Prayer Bands', which were formed between the two World Wars have continued to be numerically strong and the members have remained in close touch with each other.

By 1850 requests were being made by undergraduates who were not ordinands to be allowed to join. Eventually there came into being what appears to be the first fully organized undergraduate Christian society in Cambridge, the Cambridge University Prayer Union. It grew in membership until, by the year 1870, it was said to have had approximately one thousand members. It must be noted, however, that this society was designed for *private* prayer and there were few, or no, corporate activities, except for a somewhat brief monthly members' meeting for exchange of views.

Following the visit of the missionary-explorer David Livingstone to the University in the autumn of 1857, an undergraduate named W. H. Mark brought together all the undergraduates whom he could contact who were especially interested in Christian missions. The number of men who, on graduation, were volunteering for overseas service was increasing. He aimed to unite those in the University who supported the (Evangelical) Church Missionary Society or the (High Church) Society for the Propagation of the Gospel. The result was that early in 1858 there was formed the Cambridge University Church Missionary Union.

A further important step of undergraduate initiative was taken in 1862 when a Daily Prayer Meeting was begun. Two freshmen, both from Liverpool College, J. F. B. Tinling of St. John's and A. Maynard of Clare, sought the approval of certain senior members of the University for the organizing of a 'short daily prayer meeting on each day of full term to ask for the outpouring of the Holy Spirit on our University'. They did not, at first, meet with the encouragement which they had expected. The dons were apprehensive that in the hands of unsupervised and inexperienced student leadership there might be unwise 'excitement' and possibly an element of 'fanaticism'. Tinling, therefore, wrote to his former headmaster at Liverpool, Dr. Howson, and Maynard communicated with Dr. C. J. Vaughan, who had recently retired from his headmastership of Harrow to be Vicar of Doncaster. The two headmasters advised 'carefulness and moderation', but did not dissuade them from their intention. Eventually on 24 November 1862, Maynard nervously stood up to lead the first Daily Prayer Meeting in a small room behind a bookshop at 20 Trinity Street (opposite the Blue Boar Hotel). This fruitful tradition of the Daily Prayer Meeting has continued in more suitable environments down to the present time.

The idea of a Prayer Union, and also of daily prayer meetings, spread in different forms to other universities and to the various centres for professional training. Oxford began a Prayer Union in 1850, and a Daily Prayer Meeting in 1867. Officers in the army and, separately, in the navy, began a similar union in 1851, (later to be united in the Officers' Christian Union, which today serves officers in all the Services). The barristers (in the Inns of Court) and solicitors formed the Lawyers' Prayer Union in 1852. Then, in London, starting as a Bible Class led by two medical Consultants, Guy's Hospital medical students had their Christian Union from 1847. This circle united with similar groups in other

London teaching hospitals to form the Medical Prayer Union of 1874. These all were harbingers of much greater things to come towards the close of the century.

Recovery in Oxford

In the early part of the 19th century Oxford did not give evidence of anything comparable to the strength in Christian witness found at Cambridge. From the time of the expulsion of the six 'Methodists' from St. Edmund Hall, the Evangelical tradition was confined to the activities of one or two of the city churches and individual clergy. The Evangelical societies, as earlier explained, were sending their candidates for Holy Orders to Cambridge. This tended further to weaken the witness in Oxford. Selina, Countess of Huntingdon (a convert of Whitefield's who was using her wealth to support candidates for the ministry) not only gave up sending her protégés to Oxford, but eventually, in 1768, opened her own college at Trevecca in Wales.

In 1773, Richard Cecil (1748–1810) went up to Queen's College, Oxford. Having definite Evangelical convictions he shrugged off the current dislike of the 'pious' and the 'precisionists' and emerged as one of the Evangelical leaders of his generation. Then came Daniel Wilson (1778–1858) who entered St. Edmund Hall in 1798 and eventually became its Vice-Principal. He was able to give a new turn to 'the rather mysterious religion of Teddy Hall' and finally emerged as a missionary statesman and Bishop of Calcutta.

The Oxford churches

The main factor which eventually rebuilt Evangelical influence in Oxford was the appointment of several definite Evangelicals to some of the city churches. The most important of these from the point of view of undergraduate Christianity have been St. Aldate's, St. Ebbe's, St. Peter-le-Bailey (later to be incorporated as the chapel of St. Peter's Hall, now St. Peter's College) and Holy Trinity (which was later combined with St. Aldate's). To these must be added St. Clement's on the far side of Magdalen

41

Bridge. To each of these churches, by the middle of the 19th century, were appointed a succession of clergy who made, in their different ways, an outstanding contribution to the spiritual life of the undergraduates. Several of these parishes, notably St. Aldate's, are provided with large 'Rectory Rooms'. These were built ostensibly as parish halls, but probably it was not without thought of providing accommodation also for undergraduate members of the colleges who wished to meet there for a special address, a study group or a prayer meeting.

In this phase of Oxford's history, the graduate leader of note was Alfred M. W. Christopher, of Jesus College, Cambridge. He was appointed in 1859 as Vicar of St. Aldate's and later became a Canon of Christ Church. On Saturday evenings he held meetings for university men in the Rectory Room (his 'Upper Chamber'), which he also lent them for the 'University Prayer Meeting'. Annually, for a number of years, he organized a large missionary breakfast, addressed by contemporary pioneer missionaries, to which he would also invite senior members of the University. In 1868 his presence was reinforced by Edward Penrose Hathaway who became Rector of St. Ebbe's. It was largely Hathaway's foresight which co-ordinated the witness and consolidated the work of 'the Quadrilateral' of Evangelical churches in central Oxford.

In 1877 F. J. Chavasse (later Bishop of Liverpool) was appointed Rector of St. Peter-le-Bailey. He started in his house after church on Sunday evenings the very successful 'Greek New Testament readings'. Many Oxford men at the turn of the century could look back with gratitude for their lessons in the accurate exegesis and interpretation of the Bible gained from this source. A later Rector of St. Peter's was Henry Linton who was outstanding as a man of prayer and enthusiasm for overseas missions. His weekly meeting on Friday evenings for missionary intercession was closely linked to the Oxford Union for Private Prayer. St. Clement's was briefly served from 1858–61 by E. A. Litton, chiefly known as the able writer of the valuable *Introduction to Dogmatic Theology*. He was followed by a succession of Evangelicals.

Student activities in Oxford

The first clear sign of student initiative in Oxford came with the beginning of the Daily Prayer Meeting in 1867. Earlier promptings in 1863 from Cambridge had been ignored for a time. But a year or two later a series of evangelistic meetings in the city led by Henry Bazely, a graduate of Brasenose College, greatly increased interest in spiritual matters. A number of undergraduates in 1867 began to meet each evening to pray for the success of these meetings. At the end of term they asked the Rector of St. Aldate's, A. M. W. Christopher, if they could continue their meetings in the Rectory Room. From that time the DPM became a tradition in Oxford. In 1870 the undergraduates, inspired by Henry Bazely, started open air services on the summer Sunday evenings at the Martyrs' Memorial in St. Giles. These continued for many years until the 1930s, when the noise, and altered control of the traffic, made the site untenable.

NOTES

[1] Other nicknames were 'the Godly Company', 'the Reforming Club', 'The Bible Moths', 'the Enthusiasts' and 'the Methodists'.
[2] S. L. Ollard, *The Six Students of St. Edmund Hall* (Mowbrays, 1911).
[3] In his *The Evangelicals in Oxford 1735–1905*, J. S. Reynolds has rendered valuable service in showing the continuity and ultimate influence of the evangelical tradition in Oxford.
[4] The date is sometimes given as 1783. The appointment was, in spite of the opposition of the parish, confirmed by the Bishop of Ely in November 1782.
[5] *The United Presbyterian Magazine* (June, 1899).

Chapter 3

The great student awakening (1877–1892)

Towards the last quarter of the 19th century there arose a series of student activities which eventually developed on an international scale. Inter-university travel became something of a fashion with the growing ease and cheaper cost of transport. Even more important, from the Christian point of view, were the growth of interdenominationalism and the greater welcome of the missionary challenge. There was also an increase of the number of cities in which there were new universities, together with an overall total increase in the student population.

Until the late 19th century, university education in England had been largely confined to the two 'older Universities' of Oxford (1249) and Cambridge (1284). Scotland had possessed four universities from the 15th and 16th centuries, St. Andrew's (1411), Glasgow (1451), Aberdeen (1451) and Edinburgh (1583), whilst in Ireland there was Trinity College, Dublin, founded in 1591. These seven older universities were joined during the 19th and early 20th centuries by Lampeter (St. David's College, 1822) London (University College in 1828 and full charter in 1836), Durham (1837), Manchester (1851), Newcastle (1852), University of Wales (1893), Birmingham (1900), Liverpool (1903), Leeds (1904), Sheffield (1905), Belfast (1908) and Bristol (1909). The student activities of the 1880s and 1890s could, therefore, take place in a much wider and more cosmopolitan environment.

Christian student initiatives now began to be recorded from other parts of the British Isles. Reference has already been made to the influence of the Praying Societies of Scotland and to the Christian societies at St. Andrew's. There were other collegiate societies, especially in the divinity faculties of Scotland. These mostly took the form of theological discussion, missionary study or debate concerning the social implications of the gospel.

In Edinburgh University a society for theological students existed from as far back as 1776. Initially its activities took place under the title 'The Theological Association', but this would seem to have become a somewhat exclusive 'club', which did not advertise for members. It concerned itself with the discussion of theological problems amongst a few who regarded themselves as a theological élite. By 1825, however, a Missionary Association came into being, but still composed mainly, if not wholly, of theological students. In 1843, following the disruption in the Church of Scotland and the founding of New College, after some hesitation, two new theological societies were formed in the University, both on a more open platform. One was known as 'The Exegetical Society' and the other 'The Theological Society'. At length, in 1864, the three theological societies united, but with an interesting and unusual provision for the election of three presidents; a senior and two junior ones to mark the threefold nature of the union. In its subsequent history the Society was distinguished by a number of ably written papers presented by members of the Society, some of which were later expanded into doctoral theses or appeared as published books. After the disruption in 1843 the missionary counterpart of The Theological Society continued as the 'New College Missionary Association'. One of its more unusual developments was that, during the principalship of Dr. Thomas Chalmers, some of its members engaged in practical home missionary work in the West Port. These activities were later continued as a student form of memorial to the late Principal, whose spiritual and social concern for the underprivileged was in advance of his time. Some of the Edinburgh graduates who were later to become distinguished pioneer missionaries 'learnt their trade' in the Missionary Association's activities in the West Port.

45

Other Scottish universities would seem to have had similar, but smaller, counterparts in theological and missionary groups. In the early 1860s there are records of a rapidly growing Glasgow University Students' Christian Association. This ably took its place in a series of inter-university Christian exchanges. By the year 1892–93 a group of some twenty-four students were meeting regularly as the Aberdeen University Christian Association in Marischal College for prayer, Bible study or 'to hear a paper read'. In 1895 a regular prayer meeting was begun in one of the professors' rooms in the Tower. It met 'for 13 minutes daily to pray', and 'from time to time an extra five minutes were added' to include a short address'.

Medical students

Similar activities were becoming common amongst the students in the university medical faculties and in the twelve London 'teaching hospitals'. The interest of medical students tended to be directed towards pioneer overseas medical missions and Christian hospitals which were penetrating ever further into the tribal areas of Asia and Africa. Some of the consultants on the hospital staffs, however, were primarily concerned to emphasize that the chief immediate requirement was a considerable increase in the number of Christian medical students who would take steps to deepen their spiritual lives by prayer and Bible study, in preparation for professional service at home. Following the lead of Guy's (1847),[1] most of the other twelve medical schools in London gradually came to have their own Christian Unions. These met for occasional united meetings at the London Medical Mission in central London, adopting the name of 'the Medical Prayer Union' (1874). Outside London, there was corresponding increase in lively zeal for Christian activity amongst the medical students, especially in Scotland. The Edinburgh University Medical Students' Christian Association (1865) was formed, to be followed shortly after by the Glasgow University Students' Christian Association in which medical students took the lead. The growth of the Edinburgh Association merits a more extended reference.

The earliest records of the Edinburgh Medical Students' Association are dated 1874, when the membership is given as only thirty-eight. But in the later years of its greatest influence the number of members in this Society seem to have been in the region of 400, that is, over half the total number of medical students in the Faculty at that time. The energetic secretary for those years, the late Dr. Rutter Williamson, has described how (during their year of office) the four main officers on the executive committee divided up the list of members between them and then interviewed personally each member, using all available times, breakfast, lunch, tea and evening meal, to complete their task! They bluntly confronted each of the members with the question whether he was prepared to volunteer for a medical mission overseas. Those industrious leaders deserved their success and must share the credit of Edinburgh's enviable record in the history of medical missions.

The Volunteer Movement

The story of the Evangelical movement at this point merges with that of the Student Volunteer Movement, which became the major factor in the great increase of graduates who subsequently offered their services in the cause of Christian missions. In the closing years of the 19th century, following in the wake of the religious revivals which had taken place in North America and Britain during the era of the transatlantic journeys of the American evangelists Moody and Sankey, there was a remarkable upsurge of missionary interest amongst the students of the entire English-speaking world. The Volunteer Movement began in the USA and was introduced to the British Isles in 1887 by the arrival of its first emissary, J. N. Forman. He was soon followed in 1889 by the gifted and saintly Robert P. Wilder. In the 1840s Wilder's father, a Presbyterian missionary in India for thirty years, had been one of the leading members in the 'Brethren Society' (1810–1872) of Andover Theological Seminary, Massachusetts. During its history this remarkable group had enrolled 372 members, of whom seventy-two became missionaries.

The Andover 'Brethren' Society had arisen from the impact of a

47

similar group in Williams College, Massachusetts, which itself
had resulted from what has become known as 'the Haystack
Prayer Meeting'. Several students of Williams College, whilst
walking one afternoon at a distance from their campus, had been
overtaken by the sudden onset of a thunderstorm. They were
sheltering from the deluge under a nearby haystack, when they
began to discuss how their society could take steps to 'evangelize
the heathen'. The discussion finished with prayer and their joining
hands, promising together that, 'We can do it, if we will'. They
returned to College to found a society in order 'to effect in the
person of its members a mission, or missions, to the heathen'.
Today, a column supporting a globe stands on the site of the
haystack in silent witness to the students' resolve, which later led
to such worldwide results. 'The fathers smiled, and the wise men
shook their heads at the dream of the youth; but now the place
where they met for prayer and the grove where they walked in
counsel, have become shrines.'[2]

The Rev. R. G. Wilder's devotion to the missionary cause
greatly influenced his son, Robert, who in 1883 with two other
Princeton students founded the Princeton Foreign Missionary
Society. It met regularly on Sunday afternoons in the Wilder
home, near the University. Robert Wilder's sister, Grace, who
was then a student at Mount Holyoke College, would frequently
be praying in an adjoining room, whilst the group of men from the
University were discussing how 'to effect *in the person of its
members* a mission, or missions, to the heathen'.

Two and a half years later, in 1886, the Student Volunteer
Movement had been organized on a national scale. At a students'
conference at Mount Hermon, Northfield, Vermont, one
hundred volunteers had signed a declaration expressing their
willingness to serve overseas as foreign missionaries. The
movement swept across North America and Northern Europe
like a prairie fire. It greatly altered the outlook of many of the
older Christian societies and led to the vast missionary outreach
at the turn of the century. Widespread progress was being made
until 1914, when World War I slowed its pace and changed its
direction.

Further developments in Cambridge
The influence on the British Isles of these 19th century developments in North America took three forms. These were the impact of the evangelists Moody and Sankey; the arrival from North America of representatives of the Holiness Movements, which placed a special emphasis upon the doctrine of sanctification by faith; and a great increase of zeal in the cause of overseas Christian missions. These three forces combined over several years to weld the earlier and smaller traditions at Cambridge into a more positive and united activity. As earlier outlined, by the 1860s three societies had come into being, the Cambridge Union for Private Prayer (1848), the Cambridge University Church Missionary Union (1858) and the Daily Prayer Meeting (1862). At last came the crucial step of their merging into a more comprehensive Christian society which would effectively continue their purposes. The Cambridge Inter-Collegiate Christian Union was formed in 1877. The story of its inception is both interesting and relevant to these records.

The first signs of something new in Cambridge followed a visit to the University by Stevenson Blackwood, later to be more widely known as Sir Arthur Blackwood. An active lay evangelist, he had already been the means of bringing to Christ his friend Algernon Coote, an engineering student at Cambridge. In October 1873, Coote wrote in his diary, 'Six of us knelt in prayer. As we rose from our knees, someone quoted the words "Launch out into the deep". We felt that it was a message to us from God.' After a brief discussion they resolved that 'they would take the largest hall in Cambridge and send for "Beauty" Blackwood.' With considerable daring they booked the Guildhall (seating 1,300) for Sunday evening, 17 November, and then awaited the day with expectancy. The hall was filled with nearly 'half of the undergraduates in the University'. At the beginning of the meeting Blackwood stood up and, without any introduction, just said 'I am going to speak to you men on the secret of happiness'. He then described clearly what he felt that he himself had missed whilst at Cambridge. At the end of his address he asked all to stand whilst he prayed simply and realistically for their

49

reconciliation with God. A great impression was made. A number remained to discuss his address with the speaker or went with their friends to discuss it in their college rooms. Stevenson Blackwood was brought back again in the Autumn of 1874. His visits set the pattern for the later practice of inviting one of the leading evangelists of the time to address both the University and City.

In the Spring of 1874, two Americans, Pearsall Smith and his wife Hannah Smith, who were leaders of what in North America was known as 'The Higher Life Movement', came to Cambridge. Their visit to Britain had resulted in the beginning of a number of conventions in various parts of the country to promote higher standards in practical Christian life. It was, however, not without considerable misgiving on the part of some of the senior fellows in the University that the students had invited these comparatively unknown visitors to speak to the undergraduates on what were regarded as controversial matters. The Bishop of Liverpool, J. C. Ryle, had already outspokenly and publicly opposed the new views. Some of the undergraduates, however, who had expressed favourable interest in what the speakers were teaching, were subsequently invited, with a small party from Oxford, to take part in a summer conference at Broadlands, the home of William Cowper-Temple, M.P. near Romsey, Hants. For several years this became a centre for such conferences and the Cowper-Temples annually invited parties of undergraduates from Cambridge and Oxford.

These annual occasions came to provide opportunity for regular consultations between the Christian leaders from the two universities. The 1874 conference was the first of such inter-university exchanges, which became an important aspect of the growing co-operation between Oxford and Cambridge students. It was in 1876 at one of these conferences that a Scottish lay evangelist, Sholto Douglas, was invited for a Guildhall meeting in Cambridge, similar to those which earlier had been addressed by Stevenson Blackwood. Sholto Douglas stayed on for a week in the University and addressed several additional smaller gatherings for those who had been most attracted by the public meeting. It was on the last Saturday of this visit that the crucial decision was taken to form a new Christian Union.

On 18 November 1876, which significantly was the anniversary of the day on which Charles Simeon had been laid to rest in King's College Chapel, a 'breakfast' in honour of their visitor was given by the Cambridge undergraduates at the Hoop Inn. Some sixty were present. Sholto Douglas, speaking very practically, urged the leaders to co-ordinate more effectively their prayer meeting, Bible study and missionary studies and evangelistic activities. He also proposed more adequate provision for regular consultation between the representatives of the college groups. His suggestions were well received and it was resolved to begin to plan for appropriate steps to be taken during the following term. Action was rather deliberate and slow but, eventually, a representative from each of the colleges was invited to come on 9 March 1877 'to meet Mr. Sholto Douglas at a social conference'. It was hinted that there would be discussion of the formation of a University Christian Union. Some of their Oxford friends, whom they had met at Broadlands, were invited and seven of them were present on this occasion.

The printed letter of invitation explained that the object of the conference was 'to promote prayerful sympathy between those who are seeking the advance of Christ's Kingdom in the University, and a more entire self-consecration to God's service; to give information generally concerning God's work in the various colleges; and to make suggestions as to the best means of carrying on the work'. It was agreed to set up an informal committee to plan details. What was envisaged was a loose affiliation in which each college would have its own unit from which a representative would be on an inter-collegiate general committee. This representative committee would then elect a president, secretary and treasurer to undertake the planning and leadership of the united week-to-week central activities.

The name which suggested itself was Cambridge Inter-Collegiate Christian Union (usually shortened to 'CICCU' and pronounced 'Kick-you'). The constitution, as it evolved, retained the basic concept of college-centred units, uniting weekly for the purpose of witnessing to the University and for united prayer meetings. Though it has had to make some adjustments to modern conditions, the original concept and planning of the Union has fitted the needs remarkably well down to the present time. The weekly activities of the CICCU have brought together each of the elements in its history, the Daily Prayer Meeting, the Sunday evening sermon in Holy Trinity Church (where Simeon's 'Evening Lecture' for students had been started in 1791), the Saturday evening Bible reading (now in the hall of the Union), breakfasts (or other special meetings) when invited missionaries on furlough speak, and the Bible readings in the colleges, arranged by the college representatives.

Developments in Oxford

Similar action in Oxford was for some time delayed. As has been earlier explained, from the date of the expulsion of the six Methodist undergraduates in the 18th century, there had been official resistance to the Evangelical tradition. Yet, by 1870, there were already present in Oxford all those elements which had combined to form the Christian Union in Cambridge. There were in being a daily prayer meeting, Sunday evening sermons at St. Aldate's, Bible studies (several years later taking the form of F. J. Chavasse's Greek New Testament readings, which were crowded), a Saturday night prayer meeting, and, in the summer, the open air meetings near the Martyrs' Memorial. The bringing together of these activities into one university society awaited the 'fiery' F. S. Webster. He was academically able, a double-first, and a strong leader. He was vibrant with practical zeal to evangelize the University. Eventually the Oxford Inter-Collegiate Christian Union ('OICCU' – pronounced 'Oyk-you') was organised in 1879[3] with a similar constitution to that of the Union in Cambridge.

From the first, however, there were several important differences between the situation in which the OICCU had to work as compared with that of the CICCU. The Oxford leaders were bound to take into consideration their good fortune in the valuable assistance which their undergraduates were already receiving through several of the churches in the city and senior graduates of the University. They were wise enough not to make unnecessary changes but to endeavour to work out a *modus vivendi.* This practical caution continued until several of the more helpful senior fellows retired or moved from Oxford, as when F. J. Chavasse became Bishop of Liverpool. Similarly, the Daily Prayer Meeting, having antedated the OICCU's own foundation, continued on an independent basis for some years.

A second factor in the more complicated policy, pursued of necessity by the OICCU, was the need to make some allowance for the considerably greater variety of opinion found within its membership. The prevailing outlook of the University was 'High Church'. Some members were attracted by the courses of sermons given by such distinguished preachers for the University as H. P. Liddon, or Charles Gore (who was a High Churchman and later Bishop of Oxford). Others were attracted by trends which, at a later date, became known as 'Liberal Evangelicalism'. The majority of OICCU members derived most help from the 'Quadrilateral' of Evangelical churches situated in the centre of the city. The clear-cut stand, which the CICCU was able to take in Cambridge in a less complicated environment, was not at first possible. In later years, however, it would be seen as a necessity, as for example at the time of the rebirth of the OICCU in 1927.

One example of the internal pressures within the OICCU is interesting. It was not until 1871 that the religious tests (which from 1662 had excluded all who were not members of the Church of England from Oxford and Cambridge) were finally abolished. Until then, it had been possible in both universities to count upon a fair degree of agreement in doctrinal and ecclesiastical matters. After the abolition of the tests, however, when members of various free churches and also undergraduates with no religious affiliation, began to arrive in the Oxford colleges, the question of the OICCU's relationship to the Established Church became a cause for anxious debate. By 1899 there was considerable pressure put on the executive committee by several very strong 'churchmen' to compel the Union to declare itself 'a Church of England body, but allowing Non-Conformists to be affiliated'. It is greatly to the credit of the leaders of the Union at the time that, after a free discussion, it was firmly resolved that 'in the membership of the OICCU all are equal, and no one is included on sufferance'. Similarly, these same leaders contrived to maintain friendly co-operation, though in practice it was not always at all easy, with the various independent circles which had antedated the OICCU's own organization. When these and the local church-based activities were in the hands of a strongly individualistic leadership it called for statesmanship of a high order from the OICCU president.

University evangelism

By this time there is evidence of a marked increase of religious interest in the other universities. At the annual inter-university conferences (*i.e.* between Oxford and Cambridge at Broadlands) representative students from Dublin, Durham, Edinburgh and Glasgow were being invited to be present. There was something of a national link-up beginning between the more strongly Evangelical students in the universities. Then occurred what proved to be the single most far-reaching step in the last quarter of the century. The first of a series of triennial evangelistic 'missions' took place in a university.

The 1882 President of the CICCU was J. E. Kynaston Studd[4] of Trinity College. At that time he was also captain of cricket in the University. Much to the anxiety of some of the college fellows, he boldly proposed to the CICCU committee that they should invite to Cambridge the American evangelist Dwight L. Moody, who in the preceding months had conducted a number of successful evangelistic missions in various large cities of the British Isles. The other committee members agreed, and Moody was invited. Moody agreed to come for a joint mission to both 'town' and 'gown' in the Michaelmas Term 1882. The first part of each day would be devoted to different parishes in the town, and then university meetings would be held in the late evening.

In fixing the dates it had been overlooked, however, that the opening night would fall on Sunday 5 November. Whilst, because it was Sunday, undergraduates were expected by the academic authorities to defer their Guy Fawkes celebrations until the next day, the more light-hearted spirits have usually found it inconvenient to do so. There was clearly a challenge! The revered and saintly Handley C. G. Moule, Principal of Ridley Hall (and later Bishop of Durham), recorded in his diary that he feared the worst! Records of what actually happened differ in detail and some versions show signs of later embroidery. The main features, however, are clear.

The large hall of the Corn Exchange, which could seat over two thousand, was fairly well filled with gownsmen. During their arrival fireworks were loudly exploding outside the building. The meeting opened to the accompaniment of a series of ribald remarks and hearty 'hear, hears'. Sankey (Moody's musical accompanist and companion) had his first solo received with chuckles and uproariously 'encored'. The platform, however, battled stolidly on. Moody preached on Daniel. His American pronunciation of the prophet's name ('Dan'l') and some of his Americanisms caused a ground swell of stifled mirth and, occasionally, loud imitations. Then, after a final solo from Sankey, the chairman stood up and calmly suggested that any who wished to do so should stay behind and pray! About four hundred did so. With this now quiet audience Moody enforced more pointedly the lessons of the life of the prophet Daniel and pressed home his appeal. The two evangelists themselves reached their hotel completely exhausted. One of the members of the CICCU committee wrote 'with heavy hearts we took our way to our respective colleges'.

The two evangelists at once gave themselves earnestly to prayer in their hotel, whilst Kynaston Studd wrote the next morning in the request book of the Daily Prayer Meeting a note that 'Special prayer is requested that God will overrule any disturbance that may take place tonight'. On this, the day of the students' Guy Fawkes celebrations, well might such a prayer be devoutly offered! On this second evening, however, there was only a small, but quiet, attendance at the Gymnasium. The next night the numbers grew and then a letter from Studd appeared in the *Cambridge Review* (the university weekly) castigating the rudeness of the hundred or so of the undergraduates, who on the previous Sunday evening had 'treated the guests of some of their fellow undergraduates, who are also visitors to our country, in such a very ungentlemanly way'. He invited them to come again to hear Moody speak and Sankey sing.

The meetings in the town were going very well. Moody there called together some hundred and fifty of 'the Town mothers' to pray for the young men ('some mothers' sons') in the University, whom he was to address later that day. On that evening the Gymnasium meeting was much better attended and there was a quieter spirit. Towards the close Moody paused and then invited any interested to come to talk with him about their souls' needs. He suggested that any who felt that he and Sankey could help them in this way should join them in the gallery, whilst the rest remained in silent prayer. Fifty-two men joined them in the gallery. The numbers at the meetings were now growing and, by the Friday night, one hundred men went into the gallery. Amongst them were a number who later gave outstanding service to the Kingdom of God, including Barclay F. Buxton, grandson of Fowell Buxton the liberator of the slaves. He later became a well-known missionary in Japan.

For the final Sunday night the meeting was back in the Corn Exchange. It was packed to the doors. By an interesting coincidence the date, Sunday 12 November, was that of the centenary of Charles Simeon's first sermon in Holy Trinity Church in 1782. During the earlier part of the day there had been sermons commemorating Simeon's ministry in most of the town churches and some of the college chapels. Moody chose for this occasion the text, 'For behold I bring you good tidings of great joy, for unto you is born a Saviour, which is Christ the Lord'. It lent itself to all that was best in his evangelistic gifts. He pulled out all the stops and gave the audience the benefit of his 'full organ'. After the closing prayer, the evangelist invited those who had received Christ during that week to rise quietly in their places. It is believed that approximately two hundred stood.

So closed the first of the full-scale university missions which, led by various visiting evangelists and at three-yearly intervals, have followed in the history of the CICCU and other universities.

A new era in overseas missions

In the aftermath of the Moody mission came a much richer response to the appeals of various missionary societies calling for volunteers to take up pioneer tasks overseas. The interest grew to merge into one of the most remarkable movements for the spread of the Christian faith in modern times. In it Cambridge graduates and those of other universities were to play a large and worthy part. Two of the main features in this world-wide movement call for more than a passing reference. First is the offer for overseas service by those known as 'the Cambridge Seven' and second, the growth in North America of the 'Student Volunteer Movement' to which reference has already been made.

Two years after the Moody mission, in the autumn of 1884, there was a stir in the University and wider Christian circles, when Charles T. Studd, who followed his brother as captain of the University cricket XI, and Stanley P. Smith, the stroke of the Cambridge boat, let it be known that they had offered to the China Inland Mission for missionary service in the Far East. They had also been joined by four other graduates, each distinguished in different ways; W. W. Cassels (later to be the first Bishop in Western China), Montagu Beauchamp (later Sir Montagu Beauchamp, Bart.), D. E. Hoste (later Director of the China Inland Mission), A. T. Polhill-Turner (at the time, a graduate theological student in Ridley Hall) and, also, his brother, C. H. Polhill-Turner.[5]

It is difficult for those reading older biographies today to appreciate the impact on students, and the public, of the announcement that such a group of graduates had volunteered for service of this kind. Until the last fifteen years of the 19th century, there had been comparatively few university men amongst those who had volunteered for pioneer missionary work. A few graduate chaplains had been employed by the East India Company to serve their fellow countrymen, in places where the latter were working overseas in any considerable numbers. But many of the earliest pioneers, such as William Carey, a shoemaker, had been drawn from social groups receiving less formal education. Now, through the offer of the 'Cambridge Seven', the attitude of many in the universities became changed and missionary service began to be regarded more favourably. During the next twenty-five years and up to the outbreak of the 1914 War, hundreds of graduates were to be amongst those who offered to the various missionary societies.

On Wednesday, 12 November 1884, the Alexandra Hall, Cambridge was crowded with undergraduates to hear Stanley Smith and 'Charlie' Studd, who had returned with Dr. Hudson Taylor (the founder of the China Inland Mission) explain why they and their friends were about to set out for China. The speakers remained for several days for further meetings, and went round during the week to speak to groups in the colleges. Interest rapidly grew. Probably one of the most remarkable meetings ever held in Cambridge was when the Guildhall was packed for the farewell meeting at the beginning of February 1885. Each of 'the Seven' spoke of the reasons which had persuaded him to take the course on which he was now embarked. None of them was really an accomplished speaker, but their transparent sincerity and evident commitment to God's will made their own strong appeal. A deep impression certainly remained in the University and during the years 1882–1894 one society alone, the Church Missionary Society, accepted ninety-five graduates from Cambridge on to its roll of missionaries. In May 1899 the SVMU reported that in the seven years of its existence '1621 students had signed the declaration; 506 of these had sailed; 687 were still in college or training; 28 had died; 136 were hindered from going abroad, and 103 withdrawn'.

Other British universities

A similar rising tide of interest was found in other universities. One of the cities in which Moody's missions had exerted their deepest influence was Edinburgh. Here the results had been effectively gathered into the churches because the American visitors had been assisted in their after-meetings by a number of the most prominent ministers of the city. Amongst others attracted to Moody and Sankey was a New College theological student, Henry Drummond who, following the Mission of 1873, went with the evangelists to other cities in order to help with the younger age groups. Drummond found himself more and more drawn into evangelistic activity and chose especially to concentrate on the needs of university students. A little later he commenced a series of popular lectures for students and wrote persuasively several books in defence of the Christian faith. In 1884 Drummond was ordained and appointed a theological Professor at New College. His first address to his new student audience was typically on 'The Contribution of Science to Christianity'.

During this time the Edinburgh University Medical Students Association was experiencing a particularly prosperous year. One of their chief advisers on the medical staff, Professor A. R. Simpson, had received a letter from the secretary of a missionary society in London to say that he was coming to Edinburgh and he hoped that there would be an opportunity to put to a student audience the needs of overseas missions. The letter added that he was bringing with him two Cambridge graduates, C. T. Studd and Stanley P. Smith. Professor Simpson showed the letter to one of the leading medical students, G. Purves-Smith. The latter, supported by the student committee, asked that, if the visit could be 'a thorough students' affair', they would like to be allowed to take over the two younger visiting graduates and to plan the whole programme. The sequel was later described in a pamphlet by Professor Simpson.[6]

'The Year of Grace', 1885

During the tercentenary celebrations of Edinburgh University on 18 April 1884 there had been a unique assembly bringing together some 2,000 graduates and students. It had been organized by the Students' Representative Council. A number of distinguished representatives of the overseas universities, including the Professors Pasteur, Virchow and von Helmholtz, had been invited and were among the speakers. A deeply reverent attitude towards the Divine Creator characterized the whole proceedings, leading up to a moving address by the last speaker, Professor de Laveleye. He ended his address with the words, 'Remember the wonderful and profound word of Jesus, which would put an end to all our troubles and discords, if it were but listened to: "Seek first the Kingdom of God and His righteousness, and all other things will be added to you".'

There were other foreshadowings of things to come during the following months. In late December Professor Henry Drummond returned from a scientific expedition in central Africa and contributed a stirring address to the students. Then, in the evening of 10 December, some 700 students gathered in the Free Church Assembly Hall to hear the two visiting Cambridge athletes, Stanley Smith and Studd. Professor Charteris was in the chair. A deep impression was made. Many students stayed late talking to the two visitors, and returned for more until at midnight or next day the latter were put on to a train at Waverley Station. The students appealed for a further visit, although the two new missionaries were already booked to sail for China early in the New Year.

Stanley Smith and Studd agreed to return to Edinburgh in January 1885 for what was announced under the title of 'a Mission to the University'. The speakers were the two Cambridge men, assisted by Professor Charteris, Professor Butcher and Sir Thomas Grainger Stewart, who was in the chair. The mission ran for three days from 18 to 20 January. 'Some were impressed with the stirring eloquence of Mr. Stanley Smith's appeals and others were attracted by the straightforward narrative of Mr. Studd's experiences.' These days proved to be the beginning of a strong new spiritual movement amongst the Edinburgh students. For the following Sunday the student leaders had booked the Oddfellows' Hall and persuaded Professor Drummond to begin a series of Sunday evening addresses for the students of the university. These soon became famous. The numbers continued to grow. Many students were confirmed in their faith and others inspired to begin Christian activity. From week to week many professed to have committed their lives to Christ. Professor Drummond would close the meetings with a comment such as, 'Now, I believe that there are some men in this Hall, who are not two yards off from a treasure greater than can be found in all the mines of earth.' He would then urge them to settle the matter that very evening.

The Edinburgh students soon regarded themselves as so much favoured by the increasing evidences of spiritual revival that they began to send deputations (six students in each) to other universities. One was led by Professor Greenfeld to Aberdeen and, shortly after, similar deputations were taken by Professor Grainger Stewart and Professor Charteris respectively to Glasgow and St. Andrew's. The small memberships of the Christian Unions already existing in these cities were soon transformed. Each of the Scottish universities felt the effects of these 'winds of God' for years and during them many Scottish graduates offered themselves for overseas missionary service. The evidence is clear that Edinburgh shares with Cambridge (with its 1882 Moody Mission) the distinction of having been chief pioneer of full-scale missions to the universities, which were later to become such a feature of the student world and to have such beneficent effects in the home churches and overseas missions.

The Student Volunteer Movement

Increasing zeal in evangelism and the growing number of missions in the universities had a marked effect upon student interest in the needs of the developing countries overseas. Appeals for reinforcements from missionaries on furlough and from the missionary societies met with a mounting response both from the undergraduates in Christian Unions and those who had recently graduated. Leading students in several of the university cities, hearing of the strong missionary interest in the United States universities, began to organize British students on similar lines to those of the Student Volunteer Missionary Union of North America, as described above, page 48.

On 15 October 1889, a 'Missionary Convention' was arranged at the Metropolitan Tabernacle, with the well known preacher C. H. Spurgeon in the chair. Over 1,500 students attended it amid much enthusiasm. A London Hospital postgraduate student preparing to leave for missionary service in China, formally proposed the formation for London students of 'the Students' Foreign Missionary Union'. At the close of the convention one hundred and fifty-two London students signed the declaration that 'It is my earnest hope if God permit to engage in foreign missionary work'. The entries in the membership book begin with, 'No. 1. Taylor, F. Howard, MD, MRCP, FRCS (England), the London Hospital'. He was the son of Hudson Taylor, founder of the China Inland Mission.

There were several similar meetings in other university cities but further organization on a national scale was not attempted in the absence of a central secretariat and a travelling secretary. When the first volunteers graduated and left the university or hospital, therefore, their lead was not always succeeded by similar enthusiasm in their successors. The expected increase in the number of volunteers did not follow. The British students had tried to induce J. N. Forman, the travelling secretary for the Volunteer Movement in the United States, to come over to Britain to assist them in a series of visits similar to those he had made in the American universities. Here, some 7,000 students had joined up to the year 1891. He was, however, unable to accept the invitation.

It looked as if the big national opportunity might be lost and that interest might begin to wane, when the British delegates to the Mount Hermon Student Conference in Northfield, Vermont, managed to obtain the ear of Robert Wilder of Princeton (to whom reference has already been made, pages 47f.). He offered to come as soon as he could be freed and sailed for Britain on 18 June 1891. The first week-end after his arrival he spent in quiet prayer for guidance at Canterbury. He felt uncertain of his reception in Britain. The sermon in the Cathedral that Sunday morning was on 'moral courage'. It warned that 'to shrink from fear of ridicule is more cowardly than to run away from battle'. The American visitor felt that the preacher's message was directed specially to himself.

On returning to London he called on the Editorial Secretary of the Church Missionary Society, Eugene Stock, to whom he had an introduction. The latter at once proved more than sympathetic to the quest of this unmistakeably sincere and attractive young Princeton graduate. He introduced him to the household of the Member of Parliament for Hexham, Mr. Miles MacInnes. Mrs. MacInnes was the granddaughter of Sir Thomas Fowell Buxton, the leader of the second phase in the campaign for the liberation of the slaves and one of their two sons was at the time an undergraduate at Cambridge. The whole family took warmly to their visitor. They invited him to accompany them to the Keswick Convention, which was due to take place a few days after his arrival in their home.

At the Convention, where the crowded time-table admitted of few additions, he was offered only twelve minutes to describe the Student Missionary Volunteer Movement to the large audience in the main tent and to request prayer on its behalf. His few words, however, had two immediate results. A Glasgow student, leaning on the ropes outside the tent, responded to Wilder's address as his own 'call' to missionary service. He was Dr. Donald Fraser still remembered for his pioneer work in Livingstonia and as a Moderator of the United Free Church of Scotland. Another student was also deeply impressed by Wilder's words. It was Rennie MacInnes, the son of his host and hostess, who at the time was President of the CICCU. He immediately asked Wilder to come up during the next term to Cambridge. He (Rennie MacInnes) was destined to become the first (Anglican) Bishop of Jerusalem.

The subsequent whirlwind tour of Robert Wilder throughout the British universities is beyond the scope of this study. A few relevant facts, however, should be given. He started his tour with a meeting in Edinburgh in January 1892. Professor Henry Drummond was in the chair, and over 500 students were present. He then went on to similar meetings in Glasgow and Aberdeen, before joining Rennie MacInnes in Cambridge in the February of 1892. Here he found that missionary interest was already very much alive and that the example of 'the Cambridge Seven' was still bearing fruit. He therefore urged that the Cambridge leaders should form a definite missionary organization, similar to that with which he was familiar in North America. A few days later in Louis Byrde's rooms in Corpus Christi College, with C. T. Horan, the recently appointed new CICCU President, supporting this step, the Cambridge Student Volunteer Missionary Union was begun.

Wilder then went on to London where he stayed with Dr. James Maxwell in the Medical Missionary Association's hostel. Here were twenty-one medical students all preparing to qualify medically in order to go as medical missionaries overseas. A number of them had joined the (London) Students Foreign Missionary Union in 1889, when it was hoped that this would be extended to other universities (page 61). The proposal that they should merge the London SFMU into a new Students Volunteer Missionary Union was warmly received and tentative steps were at once taken to plan such a movement on a national scale. Since such an interest was already present in Cambridge and known to exist in other universities, besides those mentioned above, the spread of the new movement was confidently expected.

At last, throughout Britain, it became apparent that there was a widespread desire that there should be no further delay in forming a *national* organization. At a general meeting held in London on 11 March 1892 it was unanimously agreed to appoint a pilot committee to plan a 'Student Foreign Missionary Union' for Great Britain and Ireland. A few weeks later at a conference called for the purpose in Edinburgh on 2 and 3 April, with delegates who were themselves already missionary volunteers from Aberdeen, Belfast, Cambridge, Edinburgh, Glasgow, London and Oxford, the Student Volunteer Missionary Union (SVMU) was launched, with an appropriate constitution and effective provision for the active propagation of its aims. As Robert Wilder was due to return to the States in December 1892, the first travelling secretary to be appointed was A. T. Polhill-Turner, one of the 'Cambridge Seven', who at the time was home on his first furlough from China.

The strength of the appeal of the SMVU lay in its Membership Declaration, 'I am willing and desirous, God permitting, to become a Foreign Missionary.' This was regarded as a firm commitment on the part of those joining the Union. The leaders were clearly in earnest and so, history was to prove, where the majority of its members. The challenge of the whole movement reached its peak, following the great SMVU Liverpool Conference in 1896, when after an entire night in prayer and discussion the Executive Committee adopted the (American) watchword, 'The Evangelization of the World in this Generation'. This was to serve as a rallying cry comparable with that of the *Deus Vult* ('It is the will of God') during the mediaeval Crusades. At a Convention of the Volunteers in Indianapolis in 1924, Dr. John R. Mott declared 'Next to the decision to take Christ as the Leader and Lord of my life, the Watchword has had more influence than all other ideals and objectives combined to widen my horizon and enlarge my conception of the Kingdom of God.'

Robert Speer, one of the early leaders of the missionary volunteers of the nineteenth century in his *A Memorial of a True Life* describes this movement as it was seen towards the close of the last century. He writes: 'Each generation of men restates the Christian ideals. The qualities of character, which were emphasised by our fathers are viewed in a different proportion by us. Honesty, truthfulness, integrity remain the same, but the metaphors under which the Christian life is set forth changes, and many of the characteristics of the typical Christian man of our day are unlike those of the typical Christian man of another day. Especially is this true among students. In the last twenty years a new type of college Christian man has developed, like his predecessor in sincerity, straightforwardness and honour, but fonder of Paul's military metaphors, less introspective, more joyful and merry even, with a stronger sense of the call to a life full of Christian service, because perhaps more aware of the opportunities, while scarcely more awed by the responsibilities.'

Thousands of graduates from North America, Great Britain and other English-speaking countries, together with their counterparts from continental Europe, poured into what were then commonly known as the 'Mission Lands'. This movement was developing strongly until the tragic disruption caused by the 1914 War.

NOTES

[1] A Bible class had been started in 1847 by Dr. Habershon and Mr. Golding Bird.

[2] Robert P. Wilder, *The Great Commission* (Oliphants, 1936).

[3] Sometimes given as 1881, but 1879 is the date supplied by the OICCU records.

[4] J. E. Kynaston Studd was the brother of C. T. Studd, and in later years was twice Lord Mayor of London.

[5] C. H. Polhill-Turner was not a Cambridge graduate, but at the time an officer in the Dragoon Guards.

[6] A. R. Simpson M.D., *The Year of Grace 1885 in the University of Edinburgh* (Inter-University Christian Union, London, 1886).

Chapter 4

Gain and loss (1893–1918)

With a growing number of Christian Unions in the universities and an increase in student interchanges between each other's meetings and area conferences, it was not long before proposals arose for a national college movement, as distinct from the Student Volunteer Missionary Union, formed in 1892, as described above. Steps were quickly taken in 1892 and 1893 (during a general united conference in Glasgow – and also during the annual Oxford and Cambridge conference) to plan for a united organization, which would promote *general* Christian activities in student circles throughout the British Isles. The first full inter-university conference of this kind was called in July 1893 . at Keswick, Cumberland, following that year's Keswick Convention. It made use of the more prominent of the Convention's speakers. Then again in the following year, 30 July – 3 August 1894, a second united conference was called (this time it included leaders and members of the SVMU amongst those taking part). One hundred and forty-three men and thirty-nine women students were present.

In each of the immediate subsequent years a similar annual conference was held at Keswick, following the Convention. This was the great Evangelical gathering held annually in the Lake District from 1875 to the present time. A growing number attended as the years passed. During the first conference of 1893 a constitution was drawn up and the 'Inter-University Christian Union' founded. But it was soon found that applications for places at this annual conference and also for membership of the Inter-University Christian Union were being received from student members of the theological colleges, teachers' training colleges and a number of other institutions, which were not technically constituent colleges of universities. After discussion, and some hesitation, the eligibility for attendance at conferences and membership was widened and the name of the organization changed to 'British College Christian Union'. The first office of the BCCU was rented in 1894 at the YMCA building at 186 Aldersgate Street, London. It was somewhat cramped accommodation.

The new name 'British College Christian Union' continued to be used satisfactorily until 1898, when there were new pressures for further expansion in the national organization and several mergers proposed. For example, in order to avoid duplication of the committee work, personnel and office facilities, the SVMU was united with the BCCU in the summer of 1898. It was in future to be known as the 'Missionary Department' of the BCCU. This step, however, was not taken without a good deal of strong protest from the original SVMU leaders (*e.g.* Robert Wilder and G. T. Manley) who were anxious lest their earlier distinctive missionary zeal and challenge would be obscured and weakened. They feared that the BCCU administration would become too busy with the day to day general needs of the universities and colleges and only spasmodic attention would be accorded to the world needs. History, unfortunately, was to justify their fears.

An additional department was concerned to develop the beginnings of student orientated publications. Originally the first productions were simply booklets for Bible study and missionary study groups, with other subjects of practical interest to students, for which general publishers would have small sales. This department was destined, after World War I, to be organized into the publishing company, known as the SCM Press (page 118). The latter grew to be the largest of British publishers whose catalogues are confined to theology and various forms of Christian action.

The SCM

Space precludes further detailed reference to the history of the SCM. It has been recorded at length by Tissington Tatlow in *The Story of the Student Christian Movement* (SCM Press, 1933) with its sequel by J. D. McCaughey in *Christian Obedience in the University* (SCM Press, 1958). By the time of the outbreak of the First World War in 1914 the SCM had grown into an influential and well known national organization. It enjoyed the official support of the majority of the Christian churches of the British Isles. A large staff of graduate secretaries and travelling secretaries was employed, and it came to have a 'branch' in virtually every (Protestant) university and college in the country. By 1910 it had become sufficiently theologically comprehensive, by a change of its original policy basis, to be able to include most of the wide spectrum of theological traditions of the British churches, however far to the right or left these might be.

Further, through the extensive world journeys of Dr. Robert Wilder and his friend Dr. John Mott,[1] the movement was brought into close contact with many comparable movements in other continents. In association with the journeys of these two itinerant American graduates, the British SCM served as the main base for the development of international conferences which eventually resulted in an international student federation – the World Student Christian Federation. It is interesting that 'the main line of its plans were sketched out at Keswick Convention'.[2] The link finally took shape following discussions between delegates from six student movements; Canada, Germany, Great Britain, Scandinavia, the United States and a 'Union of Christian Associations in Mission Lands', at the Castle of Wadstena, Sweden. On 17 August 1895 the WSCF was launched on its international and extensive ecumenical service to students and the churches. At its first general committee Dr. Karl Fries (of Sweden) was elected the Chairman and Dr. John R. Mott (of USA) the General Secretary. The further history of the WSCF has been fully recorded by Ruth Rouse in *The World Student Christian Federation* (SCM Press, 1948).

The records leave no doubt that it was the increasing growth of the SCM and its departments (such as the Student Volunteer Missionary Union and the Theological Department) which paved the way for the Quadrennial Missionary Conventions, which were largely the sources from which grew the modern ecumenical movement. The first great missionary convention in Liverpool in 1896, with its challenging title 'Make Jesus King', led to larger and more influential international gatherings, held at intervals of four years, for example in London 1900, Edinburgh 1904, Liverpool 1908. These in turn, because many former leaders in the SCMs and SVMUs of Europe had by then become prominent official leaders in their own denominations and in the various missionary societies, made possible the epoch-making World Missionary Conference in Edinburgh in 1910 which did so much to extend co-operation between the missionary agencies and to plan for the opening up of new fields worldwide. The former SCM leaders' experience in such conferences also helped in the planning of further international gatherings, and introduced a policy of 'comity' in many parts of the world between the respective Christian missionary agencies. After the close of World War I, the WSCF also played a big part in the development of the 'Faith and Order' and the 'Life and Work' movements which finally led to their merger in the Ecumenical Movement.

The parting of the ways (1910)

This extensive growth of the SCM and its promising overseas developments were not to be achieved, however, without a considerable and growing cost in several important ways. In the process of applying and extending its new inclusivist and comprehensive policies in various theological and ecclesiastical alliances there was both serious danger to, and finally loss of, the primary aims and original foundation principle. As was later to appear there was a gradual decrease in the type of spiritual results seen in the evangelistic work of the earliest university Christian Unions. When some of the evangelical student leaders began to demur and to ask questions, those ultimately responsible in the

Movement seemed to have taken little notice. In fact the majority of members at that time on the central committees, and the majority of the Movement's senior advisers, were wholly committed to the now full-grown policy of including all theological viewpoints (and by 1905 it was even being proposed to include Unitarians) amongst speakers in the meetings and conferences and in the membership of the Movement. They were determined not to go back on their liberal policies. Only a few of the seniors, such as the redoubtable G. T. Manley of the Church Missionary Society, seem to have given clear and explicit warnings. Evangelicals who were perturbed, especially students and some of their senior advisers, who complained or asked questions about the trends, were apt to be dismissed as 'narrow-minded', 'bigoted', 'dyed in the wool Evangelicals' and 'trouble-makers'. (The word 'fundamentalist' had not yet gained currency.) Not only were the distinctive Evangelical doctrines scarcely welcome as 'one point of view', they were being discriminated against.

In 1906 or 1907 the General Secretary of the SCM began to receive more outspoken letters of dismay from Cambridge, where the Executive Committee of the CICCU was becoming increasingly anxious about its affiliation to the SCM. Similar communications also came from some of the CUs in the London medical schools and women's colleges. Occasionally, too, they came from other universities, including those in Scotland. The letters steadily grew in volume as the months passed. The chief burden of such complaints was that fewer and fewer of the meeting and conference speakers were being drawn from the ranks of the Evangelical circles which had originally pioneered the Movement. It was rather that an increasing number of speakers and elected official leaders were being chosen from those who accepted advanced critical views of the Bible. There was a consequent and noticeable weakening of their presentation of the gospel and a muted note in their advocacy of some of the most basic doctrines. The student correspondents were quite explicit. They candidly named the speakers who seemed to them 'so lost in obscure intellectual discussions' that they were unconsciously 'forfeiting all that really matters in the Christian Faith'. They would also constantly ask 'for more speakers such as Robert P. Wilder and Prebendary H. W. Webb-Peploe'. Dr. Robert Wilder, though personally accepted and admired by all schools of thought, had been trained at the Princeton Theological Seminary in the days of its impeccable orthodoxy. He was personally a 'saint', quietly outstanding as an evangelist and filled with fiery devotion in the support of the overseas missions. H. W. Webb-Peploe (incumbent at St. Paul's Church, Onslow Square, London) was one of the contemporary leading Evangelical clergy and speakers at the Keswick Convention.

During the years 1909 and 1910 matters finally came to a head. In view of the earlier history of the movement, it was entirely fitting that the issue should be taken up by the Cambridge Inter-Collegiate Christian Union, supported by some of the London hospital (and London women's colleges) Christian Unions. It is specially important to subsequent history that the crux of this matter should be clearly understood. The facts are not in dispute.

The story is set out from the SCM's point of view by Tissington Tatlow in the SCM's official history. It is recounted from the Evangelical side in *Old Paths in Perilous Times*, a booklet circulated in 1913 in explanation and defence of what was being criticized as an unnecessarily divisive step.

The chief factors in the difference

In the first place it needs to be made clear that, over the first fifteen years of their existence, the membership of both the (British) Student Volunteer Missionary Movement and the British Colleges Christian Unions (later called the SCM) had been drawn chiefly, and in some universities almost exclusively, from the Evangelical sections of the Christian churches. Rapid changes in theological outlook were, in the meantime, affecting to a greater or lesser degree the theological colleges and official councils of all the denominations. In several of the Anglican colleges there was a growing polarization between the viewpoints of members of the High Church and Low Church wings, whilst both of these traditions equally tended to look askance at the theological Liberals and Broad Church centre. It is also relevant

71

to observe that it was not only the Evangelicals who were uneasy about welcoming radically different ecclesiastical traditions into the *one* Movement. The more extreme 'High Churchmen', if they were willing to come to SCM conferences at all, showed uneasiness about the more extreme modern criticism of the Bible and also (from their view of apostolic succession) concerning the validity of the orders of the Free Church speakers.

It was, however, in this instance the Evangelicals who were the most definite in expressing their views. For (although they ought perhaps to have anticipated the results likely to arise from the growing comprehensiveness in an open interdenominational movement) it seemed to the Evangelical 'foundation members' that a successful 'takeover bid' had been completed by the other schools of thought, especially the Modernists. What had originally been planned as an Evangelical, and evangelistically orientated, missionary movement was now in other hands and being run with an outlook and policy which were essentially very different from their own. Not only so, but it also seemed clear that the policy of the central committees now dictated that the SCM should be completely comprehensive, including, it was then averred, a welcome for Unitarians, to the increasing exclusion of Evangelical leaders and speakers. The programmes of the annual SCM summer conferences were including an undue number of new speakers from the ranks of the more extreme 'Liberal' and 'Catholic' churchmen. Some of the latter were the objects of considerable criticism even within the churches to which they belonged.

The Evangelicals who, with some reason, could consider themselves to have been the originators of the Movement, found themselves on the sidelines and their most distinctive views and methods were largely discounted and discouraged. The issue, however, was far deeper than this, being essentially a matter of the policy of the organization and its control. It was a vital matter of principle. It concerned the very nature and future propagation of the Christian faith. It is to their lasting credit that, with some notable exceptions, the Cambridge undergraduate leaders of those years were in a measure aware of what was really at stake.

In general the Christianity of the British Isles was expressed in roughly five main versions at the beginning of the 20th century. Of these at least one had begun to look like forfeiting its claim really to belong to the Christian family at all! For whilst Central Churchmanship was, in effect, controlled by its intellectual position, Anglo-Catholicism by its patristic tradition and Roman Catholicism by its papal tradition, they all three, at least nominally, acknowledged the authority of the Bible. 'Modern' churchmanship, however, having proceeded by advanced subjective criticism to cut the nerve of obedience to 'God's Word' as written, was then going on to dismantle not only the church's official doctrine of the Bible's inspiration and authority, but several of the crucial doctrines of the faith. These included the divinity of Christ and His atoning sacrifice. Whilst the full consequences were not at that time as clear as they were later to become, there were more than ample signs to alert the Evangelicals. There was a need to look to the foundations. So far as the student world was concerned, the Evangelical undergraduates in the universities and hospitals, especially those in Cambridge, began to prepare for action. They were supported by their wisest senior advisers, including the saintly Handley Moule, who had not long before gone from the principalship of Ridley Hall, Cambridge to succeed B. F. Westcott as Bishop of Durham.

By 1909 the central committees of the SCM were forced to take official notice of the position, since it was now raised in the General and other committees. There had also arisen another important consideration. Some of the junior dons in Cambridge, who were liberal in their theology, wanted to be allowed to organize a branch of the SCM which would be more open to their views, as an *alternative* to the CICCU. Also at Cambridge some of the more theologically Liberal of the Free Church undergraduates, who had not been at home in the CICCU, supported this move. This request, however, posed a constitutional problem; could two movements be affiliated to the SCM from the same university? At length the SCM committee directed their General Secretary to go to Cambridge to discuss the situation fully with all concerned and to arrive at an early solution.

In his history of the SCM, Tissington Tatlow later wrote 'I was asked to spend some time in Cambridge and to decide whether it seemed wiser to advise the breaking of affiliation, or to make a further attempt to bring the CICCU into line with the Student Movement. I spent a good deal of time there seeing individuals and attending conferences, and in the end advised disaffiliation. I was influenced in this chiefly by the fact that there was a group of determined men, only a few of whom lived in Cambridge, who exercised continual pressure on the undergraduates who led the CICCU to maintain it as an organization of Christian men with no other theology than the theology they favoured. The great facts upon which the Christian faith is based do not alter, but the history of theology has been the history of man's growing, and therefore inevitably changing, insight into the true interpretation of these facts. Theology is dynamic and not static.... The literal, verbal inspiration of the Bible, the penal view of the Atonement, and the near return in physical form to the earth of our Lord were their basic tenets.'

The grudging reference to the influence of senior advisers is, however, not fair to the actual situation. For, as is the case with any other long tradition, including the political, the sporting and the social, former student presidents and other former leading officers cannot help but retain a close interest in the fate of that which they have helped to build. They surely have a right to do so. 'Some men have laboured and others are entered into their labours.' In any case, there is the clearest possible evidence that there were also some very strong similar seniors (of the opposite outlook) behind the SCM committees both in London and Cambridge. It was reliably reported at the time that the American leader John Mott (as Chairman of the World Student Christian Federation), perhaps not altogether understanding the true situation, strongly advocated the disaffiliation of the CICCU. On the other side, Handley Moule wrote later with the student leaders plainly in mind, some notes on 'thoughtful men reading about the past'... 'They will remember that the Lord and the Apostles have amply warned us that popular drifts of religious opinion are no sure sign of divine leading; that the message of the Gospel (absolutely and with divine skill adapted to man's nature) is an "offence" to man's fallen will; that human sin is as tremendous a fact as it is a mystery, and that divine salvation is as holy a mystery as it is a supreme and vital fact. He will remember that the Scriptures carry in their very structure the profound evidence of their superhuman causation, calling us evermore to "study them upon our knees"; and that the winning of the nations to the Lord will assuredly not be done through the modification of the apostolic Gospel, and the belittling of the written Word, and an incautious optimism about non-Christian faiths.'

The doctrinal divergences

Several of the SCM's leaders had been educated in strictly evangelical circles. They were fully aware from their own training and experience of the reasons for the views of the CICCU leaders. It was, therefore, not from lack of knowledge that they prejudiced the issue by using such perjorative adjectives as 'literal', 'verbal', 'penal' and 'physical' when describing the CICCU's theology. They were terms which were being used at that time by the 'Modernist' theologians to dismiss traditional doctrine in order to substitute their own new subjective insights. Whatever else may be said for such comments as that theology is 'dynamic and not static', the fact would call for all the greater care in accurate biblical exegesis. For any theologian who desires to maintain what is to be called the 'Apostolic Faith' must come to terms with certain plain statements in the New Testament records as they have come down to us. The Bible remains the only original and divinely authorized *primary* source for Christian theology. The choice is between accepting the Bible *simpliciter* or modifying it by some 'doctrine of development', by modern rationalist conjecture or the substitution of a philosophy (or a theosophy) for biblical theology.

To take the first of Tissington Tatlow's three points (above): the Apostles Peter and Paul both make strong statements concerning the reliability of Scripture as our guide, and particularly about its being 'divinely inspired'. For example, 2 Pet. 1:16–21 and 2 Tim. 3:14–17. Paul's choice of word for 'inspiration' in the Timothy passage is *theopneustos* which literally means 'god-breathed'. Luke, after his extensive researches, uses in his prologue the word certainty (*asphaleia*; our

75

word infallibility derives from the Latin translation of this word) for the Apostles' beliefs about Christ. Evangelicals, therefore, have a particular interest in the integrity of the Hebrew and Greek texts, their careful exegesis and accurate translation. Some of them have been amongst the leading figures in the field of linguistic and textual scholarship. They have had strong reservations about, and have rejected, the so-called 'higher criticism', because of its basically hypothetical nature and its subjective methodology in relation to questions of authorship and background of the biblical books. Since most of the original hypotheses were advanced by the 19th century critical scholars, there have been one hundred years of further biblical research. No other ancient MSS have received such scrutiny. Yet accurate linguistic scholarship is compelled to accord substantially the same respect to the reliability of the sacred text as at the beginning. In spite of the current statements of some scholars, the CICCU leaders' position concerning the authority of Holy Scripture would seem to have been historically justified.

The SCM leaders constantly used the deprecating adjective 'penal' in reference to the Evangelical view of the atonement. Yet the crucial question in the whole of the history of Christian doctrine is 'Why did Christ – the Son of God – *die*?' It is a profound mystery. This is a reason why those seeking to explain it must adhere all the more tenaciously to the Bible's own descriptive terminology. Our Lord made several crucial references to His death, whilst both the Apostles Peter and Paul are much more precise in their terminology than some modern scholars, who seem anxious to explain away the meaning of the atonement. Our Lord refers to his death as a ransom (*lutron anti*), which is equivalent to the Hebrew *Kopher*, a propitiatory gift offered to an avenger, *i.e.* a satisfaction offered for a life. (See also 2 Cor. 5:20–21 and 1 Pet. 2:23–24.)

The student leaders of the CICCU in 1910 were simply continuing to witness to the gospel as handed down from the Apostles. They had learnt from Charles Simeon when in 1783 he found that 'The ancient Jews knew what they did, when they laid their sins on the head of the sin-offering'. They asked again Simeon's question 'May I transfer all my guilt to another? Has

God provided an Offering for me, that I may lay my sins on His head? Then, God willing, I will not bear them on my soul one moment longer. . . .' (see page 33). For all practical purposes the Bible's view of the sin-offering and the death of Christ and His atonement is plain enough for all who are prepared to accept it.

As for the second advent, the use of the word 'physical' (in the terminology of the Bible) is not so out of place as the SCM General Secretary's statement would imply. For the record of the statement made by the two heavenly messengers at the time of the ascension (Acts 1:11) was that Christ would 'come in *the same way* as you saw him go into heaven' – '*houtōs . . . hon tropon*'. The Greek text certainly implies that the resurrection-body of our Lord had a recognizable *tropon*, or 'form', and that this was visible to the onlookers as He ascended. He would return in a similar 'form'. This promised return of Christ certainly remained a vivid expectation in the minds of the New Testament writers. One of their chief names for Him in the Epistles is 'the Coming One'. As W. H. Griffith Thomas reminds us, 'Baptism is mentioned only nineteen times in seven Epistles. In fourteen out of twenty-one of the Epistles it is not alluded to. The Lord's Supper is only referred to three or four times in the entire New Testament, and in twenty out of the twenty-one Epistles there is no mention of it. The Lord's Coming is referred to in one verse out of every thirteen in the New Testament. In the Epistles alone it is present in one verse in every ten. If frequency of mention is any criteria, there is scarcely any other truth of equal interest and value.'[3]

It should then be no surprise that, when the SCM General Secretary sought 'to bring the CICCU into line' on such points, and when he took active steps to meet the request for affiliation (as part of the Cambridge SCM) from leaders of the new liberal Nonconformists Union, a break was inevitable.

A vital principle lay at the root of the differences. Compromise could not have papered over the gap for long. Two essentially different Christianities were confronting each other. One was endeavouring to preserve the historic Christian faith under the control of the plain statements of Holy Scripture. The other aimed to embrace all possible views and to adapt the faith into terms which 'the modern mind could accept'. Therefore the request to the CICCU to disaffiliate was essentially in keeping with the theoretical and practical facts. It was the course which was most likely to lead to the best results for both sides. The SCM was free to accept the new Nonconformist Union to become its new interdenominational and comprehensive branch in Cambridge. The CICCU was now free to continue to advance its distinctive tradition and witness. In the providence of God it has continued to do so down the years and held a Centenary Service of Thanksgiving in King's College Chapel in June 1977.

The next few years

The newly independent CICCU was destined to experience only four academic years of its activity before the immeasurable tragedy of World War I shattered the peace of Europe in 1914. At the time, however, unlimited progress in the western world seemed assured and the horizon appeared bright with the promise of further worldwide Christian advances. True to CICCU tradition, the retiring President (G. F. B. Morris) and the incoming 1911 President (H. W. K. Mowll, who became Bishop of W. China and later still Archbishop of Sydney) were not slow to turn their thoughts to evangelism. They discussed the possibility of organizing another full-scale mission to the University. They agreed together the draft of a telegram which in January 1911 they sent to the American evangelist, R. A. Torrey, asking if he would come to lead a University mission to Cambridge during the following November. Torrey immediately accepted the invitation.

When the news spread in the University the reaction amongst both undergraduates and dons was one of incredulity or even hostility, especially on the part of some of the more senior fellows. They seem to have taken the project almost as a studied personal affront by the new CICCU leadership. In the event, however, those who initially had been appalled by the prospect of 'bringing American revivalism to a university' were quickly compelled to reconcile themselves to the fact that Torrey was to prove a very different person from their impressions of an American evangelist. As soon as he had begun to speak in Cambridge he was criticized for being 'a steely-eyed intellectual'. There were those who felt uncomfortable before his piercing gaze and relentless logic about the facts of the gospel. For R. A. Torrey had been a postgraduate at Yale and then for several years at Leipzig, where he had at first embraced the 'higher criticism' of the Bible from the leading German scholars of the day. He himself read daily from the Greek New Testament and was very much at home in the Hebrew of the Old Testament. His technical biblical scholarship could not be faulted. He also spoke with clarity in a cultured and dignified style, which might well have served as a model for the less successful lecturers amongst the dons. What was more, he was essentially humble in spirit, for he was a most devoted servant of the gospel which he taught.

When the date for the mission arrived, as in the case of Moody in 1882 twenty-nine years before, the organizers realized too late that the opening meeting would again fall on Guy Fawkes' Night! On the day, however, the 'wags' all seem to have been busy elsewhere. But a plot had been laid to kidnap Torrey on his arrival and to hold him to ransom at a hotel outside Cambridge. It was only narrowly averted by a strong and alert CU 'welcoming squad', which was despatched to meet him at the station! Also, from the outset of the planning for the mission there had been veiled opposition to the CICCU's attempt to book one of the biggest halls in the city. St. Andrew's Hall was the largest that could be obtained. It was packed from the start and so was the Guildhall, which had only been available for the last night.

Throughout the meetings there was hushed attention. Many of the undergraduates went to talk to the missioner each evening or asked to see him during the intervening days. The interest grew to such an extent that Torrey was persuaded to stay on for a further week of meetings, and then for a third week, to speak to groups brought together in various college rooms. Torrey later wrote, 'I believe under God that my three weeks in Cambridge have been amongst the most fruitful of my life'. Howard Mowll (the 1911 President) looking back some years later, wrote 'I have reason to know that many of the conversions were not only real, but lasting. When, too, I look at the College War Memorials of World War I,

I find on them many names of men who came to the Lord not long before they gave their lives for their country.'

During the next two years the CICCU continued to increase in numbers. During 1912 C. T. Studd returned to Britain after a further pioneer journey in central Africa to map out a new field for the 'Heart of Africa Mission'. Once again he was invited to Cambridge and addressed a crowded meeting in the Guildhall. Like Livingstone before him, he appealed for missionary volunteers in no uncertain terms. Several prominent graduates and undergraduates at once offered for Africa. One of these caused something of a stir. Alfred Buxton, a son of Barclay Buxton, the pioneer leader of the Japan Evangelistic Band, was at the time a third-year medical student at Trinity College and was about to go on for his clinical studies to the London Hospital. He abandoned medical studies and accompanied Studd back to Africa.'

The CICCU's activities continued on into the long vacations. The annual Cambridge 'camp' (under canvas) at the Keswick Convention began to attract seventy or more undergraduates. During the Convention week many of them became committed Christians, or responded to the call to the church's ministry at home or overseas. There was also an increase in the number of informal vacation houseparties, such as those organized by the Children's Special Service Mission[5] at the seaside resorts at which an undergraduate houseparty composed the team of workers. In much the way that, in the 19th century, the Jesus Lane Sunday School had proved such an excellent training ground in the art of speaking and teaching for Christ, these summer activities proved invaluable in bringing on the beginners in Christ's service.

Biography has also illustrated the fact that the benefits of these ventures were not all on the side of the undergraduate workers. The present writer was once sent by his 'chief' to the consulting rooms of a distinguished paediatrician in Queen Anne Street, W1 to receive some case records to be transferred to the Children's Hospital in Great Ormond Street. He was about to leave, when the consultant suddenly asked: 'Are you a Christian man?' and 'Do you read the Bible?' Fortunately it was possible to satisfy him on both points, only to receive the comment 'I hope that many of our medical students at King's College Hospital are all doing the same!' He then continued 'When I was a boy of about 12 years, I was playing one morning on the sands of Sheringham. An undergraduate came up in the bright summer blazer of his Cambridge College and asked me if I was doing anything in particular? I wasn't. So he replied "Right! Come and help me to build a great mound of sand. Then we'll put a lot of white stones on it to give the public an important message." We were joined by a number of other child diggers, and soon we had built a mound, with the message "God is Love" emblazoned in white stones right across it!'

'At the end of the short religious service which followed, the undergraduate came back to me and said, "If I give you this card to show you what to read, will you promise to read a bit from this Bible every day?" I promised that I would and he gave me the Bible. I have kept that promise all these years; and from reading the Bible I soon became a convinced Christian.' This distinguished consultant (Sir Frederic Still, the first Professor of Diseases of Children, London University) then produced a current Scripture Union card from an impressive looking Bible on his desk. The original Sheringham copy, which had been well thumbed, was also still preserved in a nearby glass case. Such an incident on the sands must have been repeated many times by undergraduates all round the coasts of Britain.

With the onset of the First World War in August 1914 the colleges almost emptied. Only a few medically unfit men were still left in several of them. Later, wounded men from the services began to arrive; and some colleges, for example, Trinity, became military auxiliary hospitals. Marquees were also pitched on some of the Backs. In addition, units of the Eastern Command were billeted in Cambridge. Later in the War the need for technical training for cadet officers in the services brought a number of men back to the Cambridge colleges, particularly into the mathematics and engineering departments. All the while a valiant effort was made by the few Christian undergraduates who were still resident in Cambridge and in touch with each other to perpetuate the Daily Prayer Meeting. The attempt proved successful for it survived during all but a few months in the middle of the academic year of 1916. In 1917, with ten definite members still in the Union, the Daily Prayer Meeting was restarted and some five or six university men managed regularly to attend it. In the 1917–18 session the Sunday sermons were restarted in the form of short addresses, or Bible readings for the few undergraduates and graduates who were able to meet in the vestry of Holy Trinity Church or in the Henry Martyn Hall.

At the beginning of October 1918 the Rev. P. H. Potter returned from an army chaplaincy to be Curate-in-charge of Holy Trinity Church. He moved the Sunday evening evangelistic sermons back into the church. Numbers, however, were at first low, and the actual signed up membership of the CICCU at that time probably did not exceed fifteen. They were from time to time joined by a few Cambridge and Oxford men from amongst the wounded who were ambulant. This 'Remnant' held on just long enough to reach the Armistice of 11 November 1918 and to be ready to welcome the stream of ex-servicemen back to Cambridge in the early months of 1919. A number were those whose university careers had been cut short in 1914. Others were ex-officers who had chosen to use their military gratuities to take up any vacant places in the colleges. A new era in the history of the CICCU was about to begin.

Influence on other universities

These extended references to the Evangelical tradition in Cambridge arise from the influence which the CICCU has had on other universities at home and abroad. Not only have Cambridge men played a large part in the planting of similar Christian Unions in other universities, but historically, the CICCU must be seen to be the matrix from which eventually the Inter-Varsity Fellowship itself came to birth in 1928. As Norman Grubb had written (page 13) it was in his room at Cambridge that 'God gave me the clear vision of the IVF that was to be. . . . The immediate outcome was that we saw that the first step towards the realization of the vision would be to have an annual Inter-Varsity Conference at which we would get as many as we could from other universities, and enthuse them with the vision of starting a branch in their own universities. So the first Inter-Varsity

Conference was arranged.'

Little is known of how much of the Christian Union work survived the War in other university cities, with the exception of the London medical schools and hospitals. Several of the older and larger Christian Unions in the London hospitals were able to continue their activities on a minor key because a sufficient number of medical students were retained in training. The armed services were calling for replacements for the casualties amongst medical personnel. Several of the London CUs were sympathetic to the policy of the CICCU and had linked under the name London Inter-Hospital Christian Union. Not long before the War the earlier existing Oxford Inter-Collegiate Christian Union had gone into the Student Christian Movement and had lost its identity. No record of activity during the War years similar to that available for Cambridge has been found.

NOTES

1 The gifted Christian leader John Mott was won for the cause of Christ at Cornell University by Kynaston Studd, when at the invitation of Moody he travelled back with him to speak in the USA universities.
2 *The Student Volunteer*, Nov. 1895, p. 80 (*ref.* T. Tatlow's *History*, p. 67).
3 W. H. Griffith Thomas, *Principles of Theology*, 6th edition (Church Book Room Press, 1978).
4 Later in the 1930s, Alfred Buxton led six of the next generation of University men into Lake Rudolph Territory and later into Ethiopia, serving as a pioneer for the Bible Churchmen's Missionary Society.
5 Now under the name 'Scripture Union'.

PART TWO

'The youth of a nation are the trustees of posterity.'
Benjamin Disraeli

Chapter 5

The rebirth of the Evangelical movement (1919)

In the wake of World War I the outlook in the universities differed widely from that of 1914. War had left deep wounds on the political, religious and social life of the nation. These were deeply felt in the colleges. But not all of the changes were for the worse. For one thing, those in the less privileged social groups, the 'working classes', had become alert to the value and possibilities of higher education. They found themselves with access to increasing financial provision for the abler schoolboys and schoolgirls to enter the universities. The older universities, as well as new 'civic' ones, began to be peopled and staffed by an intellectually, socially and religiously more representative body of students. This trend has gradually increased over the years. Another feature of change was that Free Church students now entered more fully into the heritage of Oxford and Cambridge from which, until 1871, they had been unjustly excluded since 1662 by 'the religious tests' of the Clarendon Code. Before 1914 their numbers had been proportionately not very great, and most of those were Free Church ordinands in the small denominational theological colleges, which had been built in the two university cities. There was also a considerable increase in the number of undergraduates who professed no religious interests. Social life in the colleges was becoming much freer and expression of opinion to a large extent untrammelled.

Another factor exercised a considerable influence. The student body over several of the post-war years was chiefly composed of ex-servicemen. Those whose education had been interrupted by national service were granted a two-year 'war degree'. This meant that, for a time, the average age of the undergraduates was higher than it had been before or has been since (except for the similar period following World War II). To the surprise of the university authorities, however, the majority of ex-servicemen settled more rapidly and easily into the university curriculum than they had feared. For these older men were in no mood for trifling. They wanted, after the unwelcome hiatus of the War in their lives, to complete their training as soon as possible and to enter on their careers. Though occasionally their high spirits would break through academic rules, there was on the whole a commendable seriousness and determination to avail themselves of their opportunities.

These older undergraduates, however, were deeply divided on matters of religion. Many who had come through the trench warfare of Flanders had lost what boyhood faith they might have had. They had been driven to ask: 'Could there really be an omniscient and omnipotent God who was also love, as the Christians taught?' At most they could be interested in the social aspects of the gospel and in anything that realistically promised to restore mankind to sanity and to help in the reconstruction of the country. There were, however, some, a small minority, who had come to quite another conclusion. To them the War had made it now clear that rebellion against God and its consequences were deep in the heart of man. Nothing but a superhuman and spiritual power was likely to eradicate it. No other source of information, except the Bible, seemed to come anywhere near an explanation which appeared true to the facts of life. Holding firmly to their youthful faith they had emerged from the fires of war spiritually much the stronger. Their faith was now convinced, determined and purposeful. They were to prove the experienced and disciplined leaders in a new work for God.

The reconstitution of the CICCU

In 1918–19, apart from those in the London medical schools, there were no other distinctively Evangelical Christian Unions except that at Cambridge. Reference has been made above (page 82) to the 'Remnant', as it was known at the time, those who were medically unfit for combatant duties and who continued the witness at Cambridge and were just able to maintain the Daily Prayer Meetings until the end of the war. In the April of 1919 several more who had recovered from wounds began to arrive. These included Captain B. Godfrey Buxton, who had been prevented from taking up a place in Trinity College until the beginning of the Summer Term by the slow recovery from a hip wound. He was shortly after his arrival elected President of the reviving CICCU.

With the beginning of the 1919–20 session, a number of other stalwart Christians, who were later destined to give outstanding Christian service in several parts of the world, joined the Union. Amongst them were Basil F. C. Atkinson,[1] Clarence H. M. Foster,[2] Theodore S. Goodwin,[3] Norman P. Grubb,[4] Clifford A. Martin,[5] Leslie Sutton,[6] and Murray Webb-Peploe.[7] At once they united to plan increased activity. The continued Sunday evening sermons were given a much more meaningful and efficient look than had been possible for the wartime 'Remnant'. The practice *de rigueur* of personal evangelism soon became a CICCU member's primary duty, whilst Godfrey Buxton, Norman Grubb and Clifford Martin started open air meetings in the Market Square and on Parker's Piece. The number attending the Daily Prayer Meeting rose to an average of nearly fifty.

The turning point would appear to have come in the July of 1919. The leaders had persuaded several newcomers in the growing membership of the CICCU to bring interested friends to a 'house-party' during the Keswick Convention at the invitation of Mrs. C. T. Studd, wife of the famous pioneer missionary and Norman Grubb's future mother-in-law. Twenty-nine undergraduates in all were there and amongst them were two or three 'freshers' about to enter Oxford. One of them was F. Noel Palmer who was to be the intrepid founder of the CICCU's post-war counterpart in Oxford.

Norman Grubb later wrote 'About half way through the Convention, one or two of us felt that we in the Houseparty were not hearing and responding to God's voice as we should. So we arranged to meet late that evening for half-an-hour's prayer that the Lord would make the remaining days a greater challenge to us. One of the youngest present – Hamilton Wilkes – who had come to the University straight from school, began to pray. We had never heard the like before – he prayed with no self-consciousness or inhibition. We began to do the same. We realized that something was happening to us and we did not break up until the small hours. The next day the whole atmosphere seemed different. Some went out in the evening into the fields and woods to pray. There were various acts of self-dedication to God's service, which subsequent history shows to have been fulfilled in our lifetimes.'[8]

'When the houseparty broke up, most of the members of the party went off to give active spiritual service during the month of August in the re-started Children's Special Service Mission at Eastbourne. When they re-assembled at Cambridge there was a great expectation that progress would be seen. Clifford Martin wrote that the most significant sign of this was the attention that these undergraduates gave to prayer. There was 'a terrific atmosphere of prayer – the spiritual temperature was magnificent'. The results soon began to appear. A fresher just arrived from Wellington School to Pembroke College at first resisted all contact with these spiritual enthusiasts. Later he wrote that he had attended one of the sermons in the Holy Trinity Church and, then, 'I was taken on Saturday night to the Henry Martyn Hall. I had never been in a prayer meeting before, had never even heard of such a thing, and it was a revelation to hear people around me praying – not formal prayers but quite spontaneously.' Some days later, over tea in a CICCU member's room he was shown that a choice could not be avoided for or against Christ. 'As though it were only yesterday, I can remember saying to myself, "for me, it will be Christ".'

It is reported that 'a number of unusual men' were soon won for Christ. By 'unusual' was meant the more academically gifted or those outstanding in sports, types of undergraduates who are not commonly fond of 'religion'. The numbers in the CICCU steadily grew and the pattern of activities inherited from pre-war days took their shape in a modified form and have continued into the present. These were the brief Daily Prayer Meeting at mid-day on week-days, the Saturday evening 'Bible Reading' (an exposition by a visiting speaker), the Sunday evening sermon and a week-evening Bible study in every college where there was a CICCU group.

A second parting of the ways

Whilst these new revived CICCU activities were taking place, other Christian societies in the university were similarly being revived. With the support of almost all the official church leaders in the University and city, the SCM was able to restart its affairs on a bigger scale. The first of a series of special meetings was addressed by such national figures as Lord Horne (one of the outstanding generals of the War) and Mr. Lloyd George, the war-time Prime Minister. Many of the older war-hardened under-graduates at the time appeared to be attracted more by the appeal of the 'social gospel' and policies for national reconstruction, than by the CICCU's direct Christian message.

There were, however, a few of the leaders of the SCM who sincerely desired, along with the wider social appeal of the Christian faith, also to offer a more personal application of the gospel. They said that they envied the CICCU its 'more direct spiritual challenge and prayer-life'. Chief amongst dons of this outlook was Charles Raven, Fellow of Emmanuel, who was later to become Master of Christ's College, Regius Professor of Divinity and a Vice-Chancellor of the University. He spoke of a 'conversion experience' in the trenches of Flanders and appealed for a fusion of the personal prayer and personal evangelism of the CICCU with 'the wider outlook and strengths' of the SCM. His hope was that the CICCU should prove itself 'a commando unit' attached to the larger and more varied forces of the SCM.

At length it was arranged that some of the CICCU's officers should be invited to meet the SCM committee in their President's rooms in Trinity College. Norman Grubb was a member of the same college. He was accompanied by the retiring CICCU President. The meeting took place towards the end of the Summer term of 1919. Norman Grubb reports, 'There were ten of them and two of us. After an hour's talk we appeared to be getting nowhere, so I asked their president point blank – "Does the SCM put the atoning blood of Jesus Christ *central* in its beliefs?" He hesitated and then answered, "Well, we acknowledge it, but not necessarily as central". The CICCU President (R. P. Dick) and I, then, said that this really settled the matter for us in the CICCU. This set the CICCU going again on its old foundation, and from which it has not moved.' Commenting later on this, together with an account of their experience at the Keswick Convention the following month, the same writer adds, 'The danger that the CICCU would be a hard barren defensive clique was over. With the decision against reunion came *faithfulness*; at Keswick came *fire*.'

A more difficult decision was posed for the CICCU leadership a little later in the Lent Term of 1920. The 'University Mission' then held was 'official' to the extent that all the chaplains and ecclesiastical authorities in the University united in inviting the Christian societies to work together under three different 'Missioners'. These were intended to represent the three chief theological trends in the church. On this occasion the missioners were Charles Gore (former Bishop of Oxford) representing the High Church tradition, Theodore Woods (Bishop of Peter-borough[9]) representing the Liberal Evangelical tradition, and Herbert Gray (a Presbyterian) representing the contemporary Free Church tradition. The CICCU leaders were invited to co-operate and to select their own (a fourth) missioner. They did so. Their first choice was of the Rev. George Grubb, who had been the means of Theodore Wood's conversion at a student mission in 1893. They found, however, that George Grubb was abroad on a missionary tour. They finally selected a veteran pioneer mission-ary, the Rev. Barclay Buxton, the father of Godfrey Buxton, who had just become CICUU President.

A neutral critic observed: 'The success of the Mission could not wholly conceal the deep divergencies which existed even within

92

members of the same denomination.' The crowds mainly went to hear the well known speakers and comparatively few to hear Barclay Buxton the saintly, but unknown, missionary not long back from six years in Japan. The CICCU certainly did its duty in securing prayer and publicity. But the experience was not a happy one. Afterwards the Vicar of Holy Trinity wrote, 'We are all gasping with wonder and praise at the events of last week. ... All groups were an unbounded success, except the CICCU's.' The result was that, apart from one other disappointing occasion, the CICCU resolved (whilst leaving its members individually free at such times to follow the course which they believed to be right) not officially to co-operate in such joint enterprises where the differences were so marked. In later years it has run its own missions in one of the intervening years when there would be no clash with any of the 'official' events.

At the same time as the post-war recovery of the CICCU was taking place the Evangelical movement in the universities entered upon a new era of expansion in Bristol, London, Oxford, Scottish universities and finally most of the universities. It will be the task of subsequent chapters to trace the story.

Sharing the tradition

No better example could be found to illustrate the beneficent influences which have been at work during the history of the Evangelical movement than is offered by an incident in the life of G. T. Manley.[10] He was exceptionally gifted intellectually and, had he not volunteered for missionary service, would no doubt have remained in academic appointments at Cambridge or in another university. From his earliest days (1890) in Cambridge (where the famous 'Memorial' of the Student Volunteer Missionary Union was compiled in his rooms at Christ's College) until his death in 1961, he remained in close touch with the CICCU leaders. He had an intimate knowledge of the early phases of the Student Christian Movement and the post-war developments of the Inter-Varsity Fellowship. Writing later of his personal impressions he says, 'From twelve years' residence at Christ's College, Cambridge, and from many personal and official contacts since then with students of London and other Universities, I have come to regard the Christian Unions as in the front rank of the Christian forces of to-day. I do not see anywhere else, even in the Mission Field, more direct, personal and valuable spiritual work being done for the conversion of others, or for deepening the spiritual life.

I thankfully recognize that, in God's providence, I owe my own conversion and the most formative influence of my life to the Christian Union at Cambridge (the CICCU); and I possess many college friends who could say the same. I owe these blessings to the faithful witness and repeated efforts of my then under-graduate friends to get me to the various meetings, evangelistic and other, of the CICCU, and to personal talks and friendship with those who were 'in Christ before me'. Soon after taking my degree, I signed the missionary declaration of the Student Volunteer Movement, and later became a member of the Executive Committee, taking a humble share in the setting forth of its motto, 'The Evangelisation of the World in this Generation'; an ideal in which I still believe, and which has greatly influenced my life.

I have great confidence in the present generation of students, and believe that through the IVF and similar agencies, they will preach the Gospel for a witness to the nations, until our Lord and Saviour shall come again.'

The personal influence of this able and committed Christian is highlighted by one of his life-long friendships. Shortly after he had been elected to his fellowship in Christ's College, he was asked by the Master of the college to welcome and help to settle into college a South African post-graduate who was coming to do a thesis in philosophy. The guest, who was installed on Manley's staircase, proved to be Jan Smuts, later Prime Minister in South Africa and a Vice-Chancellor of Cambridge University. They became close friends, attending the CICCU Sermons, and later regularly reading together and discussing the Greek New Testament. At the end of Jan Smuts' three years' residence in Cambridge, they agreed always to carry with them a pocket edition of Nestlé's Greek New Testament and to read a portion daily. Amongst G. T. Manley's papers were found letters which had come at intervals from South Africa. The last of these read:

Prime Minister's Office,
Pretoria.
23.4.42.

My dear Manley,

I was pleased to get your note of 26 Febr. and it recalled memories of 50 years ago which are very dear to me. The books of the I.V.F. have also come through Cawston and I hope to read them with much interest.

What an epoch of history we have travelled these 50 eventful years of our lives! Something fundamental is happening in history. It is not only that wars are on such a colossal scale, but in depth they are reaching to the foundations of our social order. We are too near them and too much involved in them to realise their significance but in after centuries they may appear as one of the great transitions in our human story.

You will be interested to know that throughout these long years I have remained a constant reader of my little Greek testament, and more and more it has shed a light on developments such as no other book I have known. For our time too, as for all time, the Man of Galilee dominates our horizon. The Hitlers, Stalins, and the rest are insignificant and passing phantoms in comparison.

With kind remembrances and all good wishes,
Ever yours sincerely,
J. Smuts

NOTES

1 Under-librarian and Keeper of the MSS in the University of Cambridge Library. For many years until his retirement one of the most loyal and generous of the CICCU's friends.
2 Editorial Secretary of the Children's Special Service Mission and Scripture Union, later, secretary to the Keswick Convention Council.
3 Medical Superintendent, CMS Hospital, Ningho; and physician and ophthalmic surgeon, CMS Hospital, Hangchow.
4 After service in Central Africa, with C. T. Studd, he became leader of the Worldwide Evangelization Crusade.
5 Vicar of Folkestone, later Bishop of Liverpool.

6 After service in Central Africa, with C. T. Studd, he was on the staff of the Missionary Training Colony, Norwood.

7 Medical Superintendent, Dohnavur Fellowship, South India.

8 Communication from N. P. Grubb. Also, N. P. Grubb; *Once Caught, No Escape* (Lutterworth Press, 1969) (N.P.G.'s life story).

9 Later, Bishop of Winchester.

10 G. T. Manley resigned his Fellowship of Christ's College, Cambridge, where he had been Senior Wrangler in mathematics, to go as a missionary to India with the Church Missionary Society. On being invalided home he became one of the secretaries at CMS headquarters and later, Vicar of St. Luke's, Hampstead.

Chapter 6

New student initiatives
(1919–1924)

It was now to be the turn of Oxford and London. In the spring of 1919, after recovery from wounds in the tents of the emergency hospital pitched on 'the Backs' at Cambridge, Noel Palmer (who soon came to be known as 'Tiny' because of his height of six feet, eight inches) entered Wadham College, Oxford. He has amusingly described his experiences at the hands of his new friends amongst the Cambridge ex-servicemen, and his first efforts to witness for Christ in Oxford. A few weeks before he left Cambridge a former school friend had invited him to tea in Christ's College and, later, to one of the CICCU Bible readings. He subsequently 'graduated' to one of the Daily Prayer Meetings in the Henry Martyn Hall. He writes: I had never before in my life met anything like it! The President, P. R. Dick, when we were walking home one night, suddenly asked me if I knew my sins were forgiven! I said – in a hollow sort of way – I thought that they were. Shortly after someone prayed (at the end of one of the college Bible Studies about Elijah) that God would "bring us to the foot of the Cross". This new idea intrigued me greatly and during the following days I gave a lot of thought to what it could really mean. Then, one day, Norman Grubb asked if I would like to hear the only man whom he knew whom we could really call "Christ-like". I was, thereupon, taken to hear the Rev. Barclay Buxton, who preached on the rich young ruler. I have never forgotten the impact.

'When it was reported in Cambridge that I had been accepted for Wadham, Oxford, the CICCU men all deeply sympathized, for they clearly regarded "the other place" as "the home of really lost causes", a citadel of superstition plagued by extreme High Churchmen and Higher Critics! They gathered round me with fervent prayer before I left, so that I had the feeling that I was being commissioned by them to go to start something new in a benighted place. My first term in Oxford, however, was a spiritual flop because I began to run with the hare and hunt with the hounds. But Norman Grubb prayed that I would join them all at Keswick in the historic Cambridge houseparty run by "Mother " Studd in July. Barclay Buxton was at Keswick, being home on furlough from his work in Japan. His son, Alfred, also arrived half-way through the Convention after his amazing six years in the heart of Africa with C. T. Studd.'

'Back at Oxford in October, things began to hum. The rumour went round that Tiny Palmer had got religious mania. One day in the Junior Common Room, to those who wanted to hear, I gave a clear testimony about what the Lord had done for us during the Summer vacation. I resigned my short-lived secretaryship of the Oxford SCM. Within four weeks we had probably as many as forty men meeting in different rooms for Bible Studies and prayer, and we began a Daily Prayer Meeting under the tower of St. Mary's, the University Church. But prayer would break out like April showers at all times. My room was so often occupied in this way that an old school friend reported that whenever he came to find me, on opening the door "there was nothing but a forest of bottoms!" (We used to kneel with our faces buried in the chairs.) F. A. C. Millard – later the CSSM and SU worker in South Africa – was on my staircase at Wadham and we used to assist each other to rise every day at 6 am for a "Quiet Time". My memory is that the key to all our private and public efforts for Christ was earnest prayer for God's blessing.'

Noel Palmer goes on to describe their attempts to persuade some of the Oxford men to join with those from Cambridge at the first Inter-Varsity Conference in December 1919. With greater zeal than finesse they put up public notices describing the aims of this Conference in phrases which, perhaps, could have been better chosen. Palmer writes 'I incurred great odium all over the university by a notice which went up in all the College porches announcing the conference. A number of the Chaplains were affronted by the wording which, they thought, implied that the Gospel was not being preached at all faithfully in our University!'

Many other anxious moments awaited these intrepid witnesses for Christ. Somewhat later they were satirized at student shows, and members of one of the college rugby football clubs let it be clearly known that, if they persisted in the open-air meetings (which had been commenced in the broad space by the Martyrs' Memorial in St. Giles), 'the preachers' would be carried off and dumped in the river. It is said that some of the hefty forwards did set out, but on the way came upon a Communists' strike meeting and exhausted their energies there.

They learnt soon after this from senior graduates that as far back as 1879 there had been an Oxford Inter-Collegiate Christian Union. During the early 1900s this had been absorbed into the SCM, becoming its Oxford branch. They therefore applied for the SCM's goodwill in taking up again this title for their new activities. Palmer writes 'I remember standing on the doorstep of the SCM President – a VC from the War – and praying that we should still love him, if he declined our request! He did decline it, because – as he suggested – nothing else beside the more comprehensive SCM was needed. So we waited on for a time and re-applied. Being refused a second time, we then adopted the name Oxford University Bible Union.' The OUBU started about the middle of the year 1920. The new group continued for four years, when it again lost its separate identity (see page 130).

The London hospitals and colleges

In the London medical schools several prevailing factors have long combined to bring a greater degree of continuity in the leadership and stimulus in maintaining the tradition of the hospital Christian Unions. First, the longer duration of the courses for medical degrees, as compared with those in other faculties, preserves to some degree the influence of former leaders. The high proportion of medical students in the total body of students has certainly been of marked value to the University Christian Union. Then, over the years (as in Edinburgh), there has been a high proportion of medical missionaries in training amongst the Christian students. A further influence has also been the large number of Cambridge and Oxford graduates coming down to the London hospitals for three years for their clinical studies. In recent years this factor has been much reduced, since the extension of clinical facilities in the hospitals of both the older University cities.

Each of these influences played some part in the somewhat favourable situation in which the London Christian students found themselves in 1919. At the time that the Cambridge Union (CICCU) had withdrawn from the SCM in 1910, the older hospital Christian Unions, some of whose traditions went back to the 1850s and '60s, were faced with the same dilemma. Not only had the medical missionaries in training strongly shared the evangelical outlook of the CICCU Executive, but reinforcements constantly coming down from Cambridge tended to swell the ranks of those who wished to perpetuate the strongly evangelical traditions of the hospital Christian Unions. In any case, two of the CUs, of considerable seniority, had been from the first somewhat loosely attached to the SCM. After a good deal of discussion most of the hospital leaders came together in 1912 to found 'The London Inter-Hospital Christian Union' (LIHCU). Its membership basis, fixture card and several other features clearly show traces of the influence of the CICCU. This new Union was just gathering momentum, and potentially might have become a very strong one, when the outbreak of the War curtailed, but did not end, its activities. During the War the shortened, concentrated, medical course, left little leisure for the medical students, so that LIHCU's activities were almost entirely for prayer and Bible study in the small local units at each hospital.

With the Armistice in November 1918 and the gradual filling up of the medical schools, the LIHCU's local units recovered and several central united meetings were attempted. Towards the end of 1919 a separate women's union also made its appearance, the London Women's Inter-Hospital Christian Union (LWIHCU). The separate women's Christian Unions in London (and those in several of the other universities which were started a little later) are reminders of the difficult circumstances and virtual ostracism with which the pioneers of women's higher education had to cope in the late 19th and early 20th centuries. The prejudices against women students were specially severe in certain professions such as those of medicine and law. It was, however, in the early post-war years of the nineteen-twenties that these disabilities gradually disappeared, so that after not too many years all appropriate student activities, including those of the Christian Unions, became united.

It was indicative of the current standing of the London hospital CUs that in the programme of the first Inter-Varsity Conference in 1919 the President of the LIHCU took his place equally with the Presidents of the CICCU and OUBU in chairing the sessions. By June 1920 members of the LIHCU were in personal communication with several Christian Unions recently formed in the colleges of London University. These new ventures were in Bedford College, East London (now Queen Mary's) College, Imperial College (with City and Guilds), King's College, the Royal College of Music and Westfield College. A little later representatives were attending general committees from University College, the oldest and largest college in the University.

The inception, growth and outreach of the Christian Unions in London were from the first greatly facilitated by the exchange of student leaders and deputations between the colleges. The good public transport in London meant that there was a constant coming and going between the groups, which discovered each other with surprising rapidity. The interchange was speedily to bring together the medicals with students in the other colleges. Soon, in June 1920, there were mergers into the somewhat cumbersomely named 'London Inter-Hospitals and Colleges Christian Union' and, also, the London Women's IHCCU. To say the least, both the names and initials of the two organizations were too forbidding for the average student. Consequently, first the women, in October 1920, and the men in January 1921, adopted respectively the titles – London Women's Inter-Faculty Christian Union and the London Inter-Faculty Christian Union. The two societies developed side by side for another two years until they combined on 16 March 1923. The new LIFCU soon became by far the strongest numerically of the Evangelical Unions in the country. Reference to its important service in the attention given to the doctrinal basis of the movement will be deferred to the end of the chapter.

Growth of the LIFCU

Distances between the London colleges compelled the leaders of the Christian Unions to plan from the first as if their various units were virtually autonomous. They were driven by circumstances to hold firmly to their theological aims and basis if there was to be any hope of maintaining their identities and momentum. As a result the Christians in the London colleges and hospitals became increasingly definite about where they wanted to go. They forged strong links with the leaders in Cambridge as noted earlier. Some of the Cambridge medicals spent the week-ends back in touch with the CICCU, taking up with them one or other of the London leaders. In the following years, when more of the Oxford medicals were also coming up to London medical schools, a strong triple foundation was laid for the national and, later, the international developments of the IVF.

In the early 1920s the LIFCU grew until the greater proportion of the London colleges and medical schools came to have their own large or small CUs. Combined meetings were held from time to time in the halls of the central colleges, such as at University College in Gower Street and King's College in the Strand. For such meetings Bishop Taylor Smith, who had just retired from being Chaplain-General of the Forces, was in great demand. Also the Rev. Earnshaw Smith, who in later years was again to serve the London student world as Rector of All Souls Church, was already giving much of his time as a speaker in the colleges. At this period, he was virtually the honorary Chaplain of the LIFCU.

At intervals all-day conferences were held on Saturdays in one of the central London clubs or suitable halls. Prompted by the CICCU's proof of their value, the LIFCU also attempted 'missionary breakfasts' – with speakers drawn from the ranks of well-known missionaries home on furlough. These London 'missionary breakfasts' succeeded beyond expectations. Sited at points where bus and underground transport coverged, as, for example, Trafalgar Square, where the Mirror Hall of the Strand Corner House offered considerable possibilities, or Ludgate Hill, where Hill's Restaurant was pressed into service, London University's wide geographical spread was constantly defeated. Well over one hundred, and sometimes over two hundred gathered for these occasions.

The activity which perhaps did most to weld the London units into closer unity was the experiment in the Autumn Term of 1924 of holding a residential week-end conference at High Leigh, Hoddesdon. It was quite a bold move, for even the national inter-university conferences had not yet become residential. Initially to guarantee payment for a minimum of 65 places to reserve the full accommodation at High Leigh was somewhat daunting to the youthful and inexperienced student executive. In the event, this number was considerably exceeded, and all students who booked late had to be disappointed. This week-end proved a turning point in the history of the Union. The High Leigh conference became an annual event and of vital benefit to the unity and strength of the LIFCU. Even more, it proved the factor which finally determined the Executive Committee of the Inter-Varsity Conference to abandon the unsatisfactory London day conference and billeting methods and to attempt its first fully *residential* conference at High Leigh in 1926.

The birth of new unions

In some cases on their own initiative, but in others because of their having heard of the work of the CICCU, OUBU and LIFCU, Christian ex-servicemen and 'freshers' began to pioneer Christian Union activities in a number of other university cities. Between 1920 and 1925 eight new Christian Unions came into the movement:–

1920 Dublin; 'Number 40' Trinity College.
1921 Aberdeen University Christian Students Fellowship.
1921 Bristol Inter-Faculty Christian Union.
1922 Belfast, The Queen's University Bible Union.

1922 Edinburgh Students Evangelistic Association.
1923 Cardiff Students Evangelical Union.
1923 Glasgow University Christian Students Fellowship.
1925 Londonderry Students Evangelical Union.

The first steps in founding some of these Christian Unions called for a good deal of moral courage and initiative on the part of their pioneers. Many are the anecdotes which have been preserved of the various rebuffs received from university authorities; but sometimes there were unexpected encouragements. Space permits reference to only a few.

At Trinity College, Dublin, the room 'number forty' gave its name to the informal Union which met in it until the end of the Second World War. This set of rooms (later adapted to become the college guest rooms) were those assigned to one of the professors, whose seminars met in the large class room. Being married, he was living outside college. The post-war pressure on all available college space meant that he was asked, with all non-resident staff, to allow students into the suite. Assigned to it was P. K. Dixon, the son of the Professor of Anatomy, who, with another student, could use it so long as the Seminar Room was available for classes at all times required by the Professor. 'P.K.' had become a Christian in the trenches during the final stages of the war, through reading in a dug-out the small khaki testament sent him by a Dublin woman student. Finding himself back in college with this ideal set of rooms, he invited a number of his student year to a buffet meal, and (as he himself later reported) nervously and blunderingly told the story of, and tried to explain, his spiritual change. It was more sympathetically received than he had feared. Numbers steadily grew at the weekly meeting which he started in 'number forty'. In the following spring he organized a house party over the Whitsun week-end at a large farm house near Lough Dan, Co. Wicklow. It became an annual event. Over the first two or three years a number of the ex-servicemen amongst the medicals and several of the 'wilder characters' in the engineering faculty were converted. After qualification and postgraduate experience, four of these early TCD men – including 'P.K.' Dixon himself – were to give distinguished service in the cause of medical missions.

Both at Bristol and Aberdeen there had been some pre-war beginnings of evangelical witness, which had subsequently become absorbed into the Student Christian Movement. But as far back as 1910, a surgeon, Mr. A. Rendle Short of the Bristol Royal Infirmary, with his friend Dr. Frank Bergin, Radiologist at the Bristol General Hospital, had organized successful student meetings in the Victoria Rooms on Sunday evenings. These Sunday meetings were restarted as soon as the University filled with students again in 1919. In 1921 the student leaders asked if they could take over for themselves the responsibility of choosing the speakers and running these meetings. The two senior graduates readily agreed. With such prominent speakers as Professor Albert Carless – one of the editors of the well-known Rose and Carless' text book of surgery – speaking on 'Christian hygiene', and others on challenging subjects, the Sunday evening meetings attracted full attendances.

Soon the Bristol Inter-Faculty CU emerged with a full range of student activities. The seniors stood behind the Union in several ways. For example, the Rendle Short household allowed the students the free use of their drawing room at 9.45 am before church each Sunday morning in term-time. Dr. Bergin provided the 'pitch' for informal student parties on summer Saturday afternoons, and occasionally for a week-end conference (with neighbours offering beds for a generous overflow of students), at his large bungalow on the coast near Portishead. 'Bergo's Bung' and its rose gardens became quite a BIFCU institution and proved a most valuable gathering point up to the beginning of World War II.

In 1892 Aberdeen students had started a Christian Union, affiliated to the SCM, first at Marischal College and later in the University buildings. Following the war, interest began to revive in the winter of 1921 and it first arose in the medical faculty. Two second-year medical students and several women students in the arts faculty started a Bible study in the YMCA building not far from the University. From this small beginning the Aberdeen University Christian Students Fellowship gradually emerged. It proved to have considerable vitality. For the leaders were soon attempting some evangelistic meetings for students and inviting to

105

address them such well known speakers as the Rev. A. Douglas Brown and the Rev. Alexander Fraser from Edinburgh. An application to the Principal for permission to meet in the University was at first refused on the ground that an Aberdeen branch of the Student Christian Movement was already at work. A few years later the Union, having demonstrated clearly its different outlook and methods from those of the SCM, succeeded in obtaining recognition. The membership and influence of the Union were then much increased.

Some time during 1921, two freshmen in the medical faculty of the Queen's University, Belfast agreed together 'to consecrate their lives to Christ's service and to meet regularly to pray for their fellow-students in the University.' Early in January 1922 they found four others who were interested in the project and willing to join them in a prayer meeting weekly. Soon the members of the group all agreed that they would begin to discuss with any of their individual fellow-students who would show any interest in their Christian beliefs. The immediate result was that to their surprise they stumbled on the fact that there were far more committed Christians in the University than they had imagined. Numbers so much increased that they promptly changed from a weekly to a daily prayer meeting. They then began a weekly Bible study, interspaced with expositions by one of the ministers of the city. Soon open evangelistic meetings were attempted with considerable success. The latter were addressed by the more prominent of the evangelistic clergy of the Church of Ireland, and Presbyterian ministers. These open meetings developed into a regular and very successful form of witness. Towards the end of 1922 two Unions, the Queen's University Bible Union and the QUBU (women's section), had become effectively established. They were later merged to become one of the most spiritually effective of the Christian Unions in the British Isles.

Following demobilization, the ex-servicemen in the University of Edinburgh took a little longer to adapt to their new academic environment and the evangelical Christian students at first failed to find each other. At length, chiefly through the medical students living together in the George Square hostel of the Edinburgh Medical Missionary Society, and through several ordinands for the Church of Scotland ministry, a small circle of Christian students began to coalesce. The first steps towards a public student witness were taken after a particularly inspiring conference organized by the China Inland Mission. Several members of this student group were present and heard reports about what had been happening in other universities. After an increasingly encouraging exchange of views during February 1922, sixteen men and six women unanimously founded the Edinburgh University Evangelistic Association. From the outset its membership was marked by determination and courage in making plans to reach the main body of students. By 1925 the Union felt strong enough to launch a full-scale mission to the University. Led by one of their own number, Eric Liddle (the Olympic runner) and with addresses by the Rev. J. R. S. Wilson, the Church of Scotland Minister of Leith parish church, an effective bid was made for the ear of the University. From the start of the Union a lively missionary interest, which had also characterized the late 19th-century Edinburgh students, was strongly in evidence.

Of those Unions which were founded during this period, Cardiff was unique for its courageous method of announcing its presence. In 1922 a single Christian student, anxious to ascertain if there were any others likeminded, placed notices on all the student notice boards of the University buildings with the caption, 'Will all those who know that their sins are forgiven and have thus accepted the Lord Jesus Christ as their own personal Saviour, kindly communicate with David John Thomas, New College.'(!) It is not known how many did so, but (to quote from *Christ and the Colleges*) 'At the beginning of the Lent Term 1923 seven students turned up to a meeting. In the meantime Dr. Rendle Short (of Bristol) had been communicated with, and on January 31st, the seven students were privileged with a visit from him. He informed them of the CICCU and similar movements in other Universities. "A feature of these societies", the speaker said, "is the spontaneity of their formation."' One of the Welsh students had come into possession of a copy of the London (women's) IFCU constitution and this was used extensively in the drafting of the first constitution of the Cardiff Students Evangelical Union.

At the beginning of October 1923 there were twenty members and a president had been installed. In March 1925, having grown further, the Union received full recognition by the Senate, with Dr. Morgan Watkin, Professor of French, as its representative spokesman on the Senate. The Cardiff Union in the following years proved attractively adventurous in its efforts to spread the gospel, and in 1926 we find the leaders putting on a meeting in the largest lecture theatre, which was filled. The Principal of the University was in the chair and Dr. Rendle Short from Bristol spoke on 'The Christian Message to the Modern Student'.

Whilst the Glasgow University Christian Students Fellowship did not become fully organized, with a constitution and recognition from the Senate, until 1923, there had been the beginnings of evangelical activity over the previous two years. In the spring of 1921 three evangelical students had resigned from the Student Christian Movement because of their reluctance to support its increasingly broad theological outlook and policies. They were joined by several others and, by Easter 1922, there were seven who met weekly for prayer and discussion. Their evangelistic activity was at first directed, however, outside the student world in witnessing to the villages during the vacations, using a caravan and tent.

In late 1922 two 'mass' meetings were attempted at the University. On the first occasion Dr. Rendle Short addressed a well attended 'open meeting' in the Union Debating Hall. The small, but energetic, group was very satisfied with the results. For one thing they discovered a number of committed Christians in the student body and there were many more enquiries concerning their beliefs. A repetition of the experiment of holding an open meeting was attempted on a date which, too late, was found to be in the week of the election for the Rector of the University. This is usually the occasion for student high spirits. The Debating Hall was filled to overflowing. At first the noise was deafening. It proved impossible to open in prayer. The speaker, Mr. Arthur Taylor (of the China Inland Mission), however, rose to the occasion. He told humorous stories until he could get the students quiet and eventually managed to come to the real point of holding the meeting. Having said what he wanted to say he closed with prayer during a profound silence. A deep impression had been made and many enquired about the Union's message. Membership increased. In subsequent years repeated attempts were made to reach the main body of students by such mass methods, mostly, but not always, successfully.

A further Union came into being during this period, at Magee College, Londonderry. At that time Magee was a large Presbyterian theological and training college which sent its students for their final year of studies, and to take their degree, either to Trinity College, Dublin, or Queen's University, Belfast. During the spring of 1922 the Irish evangelist, W. P. Nicholson, held a number of successful missions in County Londonderry. Many young men, including Magee students, became Christians. Some of them subsequently dedicated their lives to missionary service. One of these, Austin Fulton, who was later Moderator of the Irish Presbyterian Church, with the help of Hugh Jack, later a minister in Canada, determined to bring together the more evangelistic of the students for action. They started with six, and soon became ten. On 19 January 1925 they became the first members of the Londonderry Students Evangelical Union. From the start several unusual traits characterized this energetic group. Before the end of their first year they had carried through during a long vacation a mission of nearly four weeks duration at Culmore, near Derry. They had also conducted evangelistic open air meetings in the Diamond (at Derry) during the Hiring Fair days and also in connection with the camps at Portstewart Convention. Looking back to their student days some of the original members have constantly reiterated that, from all the Union's activities, they derived most help from the Friday night prayer meetings held in rotation in the rooms of different members.

By 1925 there were the beginnings of interest and activity in several other university cities, but no further unions were born.

The importance of doctrine

In view of the later careers of some of the LIFCU's founders, it is interesting to note the early promise when they faced the daunting

109

task of overcoming the geographical handicaps posed by the distances separating the many affiliated colleges of London University. The college furthest east is distant from the furthest west by some thirty miles, whilst the north to south axis is well over ten miles. Additional difficulties for the unity of the LIFCU arose from the repeated pleas for reunion from the SCM secretaries calling on its branches from their nearby HQ in Golders Green. These distractions, however, were to a large extent offset by the future medical missionaries training in the medical schools, the large group of evangelical ordinands in St. John's Hall (the London College of Divinity) and the enthusiasm of the leaders in some of the women's colleges. In addition, there was a number of senior friends and advisers amongst prominent preachers in the London pulpits. These factors tended to work towards a growing awareness in the London leaders of the importance of clarity and definiteness about the theological issues at stake.

Initially the men's LIFCU had taken over the membership declaration of the London Inter-Hospitals CU. This in turn had been adopted from the CICCU's, 'In joining this Union I declare my faith in Jesus Christ as my Saviour, my Lord and my God'. The rest of the constitution, so far as doctrine is concerned, simply referred to the motto, 'That God in all things may be glorified through Jesus Christ' (1 Pet. 4 : 11). The aims were '(i) to unite men in the University of London who desire to witness for Christ; (ii) to bring men in the University to a saving knowledge of Jesus Christ; and (iii) to deepen the spiritual life of all members of the Union; and (iv) to uphold the truths of Christianity.'

From the first, however, the women of the LWIFCU had urged that the times called for the doctrinal position to be made much more explicit. They were supported in this by the theological students of St. John's Hall and the senior advisers. The Women's Union's motto was, 'Hold fast till I come' (Rev. 2 : 25) and their aims, '(i) to unite women upholding the truths of Christianity, who are earnestly desiring to extend Christ's Kingdom in the University; (ii) to witness for Jesus Christ among the London Colleges, Hospitals and Medical Schools; and (iii) to deepen the spiritual lives of all members, especially by means of prayer and

Bible Study.' There were further pressures for a stronger declaration of membership and the adopting of a summary of 'the irreducible minimum of Christian doctrine'. The Women's Union finally agreed on a membership declaration as follows: 'In becoming a Member of this Union, I declare my belief:–(i) In God the Father, God the Son and God the Holy Spirit; (ii) In Jesus Christ as my Saviour, my Lord and my God, Whose atoning sacrifice is the only and all sufficient ground of my salvation, and in the power of Whose resurrection I desire to live; (iii) That the whole Bible is the inspired Word of God.' After its adoption this declaration was subscribed by 127 of the women students.

At the time of the merger of the men's and women's unions, the London women were preparing a more detailed statement of Christian doctrine to be signed by the members of their Executive Committee each year on taking office. The wisdom of this gradually impressed itself on the men's leaders and those who were in the pioneer stages of Christian Unions in other universities. The advocates of this course argued that in the pre-1914 years the Christian Unions could rely upon the influence of a stronger church background and knowledge of Christian doctrine in the majority of their members. The Christians entering the universities would mostly be well taught doctrinally and would at least be aware of the steps taken by most Churches to safeguard their official teaching. But with the increasingly wide divergences of outlook in official theological circles and the marked weakening of Christian education in the schools there was an increasing danger that both officers and members would not be clear about the essence of the Christian faith for which the Unions were organized. The women leaders had, therefore, been seeking advice from members of theological college staffs and well known preachers about how to safeguard the theological orthodoxy of their leadership.

The women leaders found ready allies not only in the theological students of St. John's Hall, but also some of the ex-servicemen, who had become fervent Evangelicals in the trenches and who were now members of the theological faculty of King's College. As soon as it was put to them, there was scarcely less interest and enthusiasm on the part of the medical students in the

111

hospital Christian Unions. Many of these were training to serve as missionaries in the overseas hospitals of the chief missionary societies. Indeed, the future medical missionaries in most of the universities were always in the vanguard of evangelistic activity and advocacy of a crystal clear basis of belief and principle for Christian action. Those in other faculties, who had not thought much on the matter, eventually conceded that an alarming number of their contemporaries seemed to be biblically and theologically illiterate. Whilst there were a residual few who could not see the need, or confused their disapproval of definiteness with the principle of 'religious liberty', the vast majority were in favour of 'a crystal clear basis'. The position was highlighted by one very well-meaning college CU president who, in going into detail when pleading for 'freedom' from all such safeguards, gave voice, as one theological student put it, 'to almost every ancient heresy known in the Early Church up to the year 461!' In uniting the two constitutions, therefore, it was agreed by a large majority to incorporate the drafted Doctrinal Basis and to provide for its annual signature by all officers on their election. The original form of the Basis will be found in the Inter-Varsity Conference Constitution (Appendix p. 359).

In view of the influence which this eight-point Basis was later to have in the LIFCU and on the Inter-Varsity Fellowship, and (in revised form) on the International Fellowship of Evangelical Students, tribute must be paid to the enthusiasm and the trouble to which the London students went in their anxiety to enshrine the essentials of Christian doctrine – biblical theology – in their official documents. We learn from one of the theological graduates, who at the time assisted in the search for 'essentials' that the theological students of St. John's Hall (the London College of Divinity), and even more their senior members of staff and some of the leading clergy and ministers of London, were repeatedly put on the spot by deputations of LIFCU students who were suspicious of any ambiguity when reference was being made to the authority of the Bible or the central facts of the gospel. They wanted no stone left unturned in order to find what was *essential*. When the work was finished and the last deputation had departed, the Principal of St. John's Hall is said to have remarked that *now* he really appreciated the true genius of those 'masters of short statement' who had compiled the Thirty-Nine Articles and the Westminster Confession of Faith!

The reference to 'masters of short statement' is relevant and important. Two documents chiefly influenced the student leaders and their theological advisers. These were the official doctrinal statements of the 'established' churches – the Thirty-nine Articles (1562) of the Church of England and the Westminster Confession (1647) 'the subordinate standard' (i.e. subordinate to Scripture) of the Church of Scotland. The choice fell on these because, amongst documents of their kind, they have exercised most direction on the English-speaking churches during the past three hundred years. Also, the combined number of members in the evangelical unions at that time, which were drawn from these two churches, greatly exceeded the rest. Other doctrinal statements taken into consideration were those of the Evangelical Alliance (1846) and the larger missionary societies to which ex-members were offering as missionary candidates.

It needs to be emphasized that the primary aim was not to summarize all Christian doctrine! It was intended that the basis of the movement should be *'the fundamental truths of Christianity'*, and the addition of the words, *'including . . . .'* (followed by eight points) was simply to call attention to certain doctrines which, during the vicissitudes of so-called 'progress' and through changes in theological fashion, were apt to become overlooked, harmfully modified or rejected. The emphasis then must be put on 'fundamental truths'. Also, in each successive age of the church, the well-informed and faithful Christian will look for these truths in the teaching of our Lord and His apostles as this is recorded in the Bible. Hence the student leaders and their advisers sought to be consciously controlled by the documents of Scripture, which are the only *primary* source. It was because they were so definite about this that their SCM critics were apt to taunt that 'they worship the Book'. But they never came measurably near to doing so. Theirs was rather the outlook of members of a family, who have heard that they have been bequeathed a fortune, and they cannot be too interested in the validity and accuracy of 'the title deeds' to their inheritance.

113

In their search, some students came upon the gem in Article 6 of the Church of England, 'Holy Scripture containeth all things necessary to salvation: so that whatsoever is not read therein, nor may be proved thereby, is not to be required of any man, that it should be believed as an article of the Faith, or be thought requisite or necessary to salvation'. The Presbyterians also warmed to their task as they recalled their childhood answers to question 2 of the Shorter Catechism, 'What rule hath God given to direct us how we may glorify and enjoy Him?' ... 'The word of God, which is contained in the Scriptures of the Old and New Testaments, is the *only* rule to direct us how we may glorify and enjoy Him'. On Scripture they all found chapter I of the Westminster Confession the most satisfactory statement, with its, 'The authority of the Holy Scripture, for which it ought to be believed and obeyed, dependeth not upon the testimony of any man or Church, but wholly on God (who is truth itself), the author thereof; and therefore it is to be received, because it is the word of God ... our full persuasion and assurance of the infallible truth, and divine authority thereof, is from the inward work of the Holy Spirit, bearing witness by and with the word in our hearts'.

One of the Church of England students who had read the Westminster Confession for the first time, wondered if it ought not to be adopted, in Church of Scotland style, as 'our subordinate standard'. For, as he commented, 'These fellows really seem to know what they are talking about!' There was an admirable concern about the great importance of Christian Doctrine and its value to posterity. As Archdeacon T. C. Hammond was constantly to remind evangelical students in later years, many loyal Christian leaders down the centuries have been cruelly persecuted, and sometimes martyred, for their care and faithfulness in passing on 'the words of eternal life', and 'some of the Oecumenical Creeds and Confessions of Faith are stained with blood'.

Chapter 7

The inter-university conferences (1919–1927)

As mentioned above, the first (post-war) inter-university Conference had taken place in the small hall of the headquarters of the Egypt General Mission at Drayton Park, London from 8–11 December 1919. It had been brought together by the initiative of the Cambridge Inter-Collegiate Christian Union after Norman P. Grubb had shared with the committee the vision which had come to him in his room in Trinity College early in October of the Michaelmas Term.[1] A minute records a meeting of the CICCU Executive Committee in the rooms of B. Godfrey Buxton (President) in Bridge Street on the 21 November.

'N. P. Grubb then placed before the committee the proposal to hold meetings in London for prayer for all Universities. It was suggested that the meetings should extend over three or four days at the beginning of the first week after full term as this would enable members of Oxford, London, St. John's (Highbury) and others to attend on their way home. ... Some of the meetings would be on convention lines and others solely for prayer. Also agreed that notices should be sent to the Life of Faith and the SCM, partly to arrange for accommodation of students in private houses. ... A committee consisting of N. P. Grubb, H. L. Sutton and the President was appointed to carry on.' Norman Grubb subsequently wrote 'We had to work quickly and met almost each evening in Leslie Sutton's room (after 8) in Queen's College.'

The decision coming so late in term made extensive advertisement impossible and did not leave much time for more than a series of personal letters to be sent to the leaders in the other cities. It says a good deal for the co-operation of some of the latter that a conference could be held at all. In later years Noel Palmer (Oxford) wrote 'I can remember jellygraphing some crude notices announcing the Conference to all concerned that the Gospel should be preached in their Universities, and telling them to contact me!' Later estimates by those who were present at this conference differed about the final number of those who took part. This is given as 'twenty-five', 'well over 30' and 'about 60' and 'over 100' (!). Circumstantive evidence, however, such as the arrangements for hospitality, suggests that there were 30–35 present *full-time*, but that more students attended at the evening sessions, when the London clinical medical students could arrive from their hospitals. The majority were from Cambridge, with four from Oxford (led by the redoubtable Noel Palmer) and a few London medical and theological students. One or two also are mentioned as from Durham, probably being theological students from St. John's Hall, London (who were up at St. John's, Durham for their last year in order to take the Durham degrees, under the arrangement which then existed between the two colleges).

A faded copy has survived of the unobtrusive conference programme, bearing all the signs of hasty printing at some small local printing press. Indeed, the early leaders were certainly more marked by their devotion to prayer than for any attempts to impress by attractive advertisement. It is doubtful whether many of those attending could have seen the programme before their actual arrival at Drayton Park. In archaic black print on poor quality card, about the size of a sporting fixture list, come the unembellished statements:–

An Inter-Varsity Convention for all University Men

will be held (D.V.) from
Monday, December 8th to Thursday, December 11th, 1919
in the Hall, 10 Drayton Park, N.5.

Programme:

Monday, Dec. 8th. Chairman, M. H. Webb-Peploe (Treas.
C.I.C.C.U.)

2.30–4.0   Prayer
5.30–7.0   Convention meeting. Rev. Barclay F. Buxton

Tuesday, Dec. 9th. Chairman, K. S. Maurice-Smith (Sec.
L.I.H.C.U.)

11.0–12.30 Bible Reading. Mr. G. H. Lang
5.30–7.0   Convention Meeting. Rev. G. C. Grubb

Wednesday, Dec. 10th. Chairman, B. G. Buxton (Pres.
C.I.C.C.U.)

11.0–12.30 Bible Reading. Mr. G. H. Lang
5.30–7.0   Convention Meeting. Rev. G. C. Grubb

Thursday, Dec. 11th. Chairman, F. N. Palmer (Oxford)

11.0–12.30 Prayer
2.30–4.0   Convention Meeting. Rev. E. L. Langston
5.30–7.30 MISSIONARY MEETING. Chairman,

Rev. B. F. Buxton
Asia – Arthur Moore, C.I.M.
Africa – Mr. A. B. Buxton
Mohammedan Lands – Mr. J. G. Logan
South America – Mr. A. S. McNairn

No report on this conference has been found and no minutes
were kept. This, and the following year's conference, were called
by the CICCU executive and regarded as its responsibility. The
chairman was Godfrey Buxton as CICCU President, and it is
thought that Leslie Sutton, or, possibly Clarence Foster, was the
secretary. The original resolution in the Cambridge records gave
'prayer for the universities' as its primary purpose. That this aim
was certainly achieved is shown by personal letters from those
who were present, and the unanimity with which they all mention
earnest prayer as their outstanding impression. One who had
come up from school that term has written, 'Both then, and
throughout those early years, the greatest blessing and inspiration
to me was to be able to join in prayer with these men who had been
through the worst years of the war. (Many of them had been
decorated for bravery and a number had only just recovered from

severe wounds.) I remember especially Norman Grubb, Godfrey Buxton, 'Tiny' Palmer, Murray Webb-Peploe, Clifford Martin, Jack Warren and Clarence Foster.'

Fourteen days before the opening of the conference *The Christian* for 20 November 1919 had published a review of the latest SCM Press publication (*God and the Struggle for Existence:* G. G. D'Arcy, Lily Dougall, B. H. Streeter) under the heading 'Whither Are We Tending?' This was accompanied by a long editorial, entitled 'Toward What? – The Student Christian Movement'. The review of the book was outspokenly critical, particularly of Dr. Dougall's contribution to it on the grounds of its full acceptance of an evolutionary philosophy, without apparently seeing the implications for the theological sections. The two theologians were criticized for their acceptance of the hypotheses of modernism. The editorial took this review as its starting point for a brief history of the outlook of the SCM and its departure from its evangelical origins. The editor especially focused attention on its moving away from the CICCU's original Membership Declaration (adopted by the SCM in 1901). This read as follows; 'I desire, in joining this Union, to declare my faith in Jesus Christ as my Saviour, my Lord, and my God.' Revisions in 1913 had moved into a vaguer expression of the Declaration and then to a much weakened and longer form in 1919. It had just been published in full, with explanations, in the October issue of *The Student Movement*. This 1919 revised SCM Constitution reads as follows:–

'*Aim and Basis:* The Student Christian Movement of Great Britain and Ireland is a fellowship of students who desire to understand the Christian faith and to live the Christian life.

The Movement seeks to set forth Jesus Christ as the supreme revelation of God and of the true nature of man.

It sees in Him the one sure guide for all mankind in every sphere of thought and conduct, in art and industry, in politics and the professions, in science and education; the course of power for the overthrow of evil and the renewal of all human life.

The Movement challenges students to recognise the urgent need of the whole world for Christ, without limit of race or nation, and to respond by dedicating their lives to His service as

He may guide them.

It calls them to explore His teaching and to follow the guidance of His Spirit in the pursuit of truth, beauty, and righteousness; to prepare themselves by study, discipline, and prayer for the tasks of the future; joyfully to accept God's gift of deliverance and life for themselves; and to enter the fellowship of worship, thought, and service which is the heritage of the Christian Church.

Membership Clause: The membership of affiliated Christian Unions and of the Student Volunteer Missionary Union, shall be open to students who, having considered the Aim and Basis, desire to enter the fellowship of the Student Christian Movement. Those Theological Colleges may be associated which are recognised colleges of denominations whose principles are in harmony with its Aim and Basis.'

The editor's comment on this is 'To us it appears that the joyous note of personal faith in and relationship to Jesus Christ, as seen in the earlier Bases, has gone entirely; and has been replaced by a cold and passionless statement. ... There is also no reference to Christ as Saviour, nor any statement to declare His Deity. There is, indeed, nothing to which a Unitarian would object.'

In the 4 December issue of *The Christian* there were three letters referring to both the review and the editorial. They were from Robert Stevenson of Stirling (an eirenicon), Colin C. Kerr of Norwood and from the chairman of the SCM. The latter, E. S. Woods, who was at that time Vicar of Holy Trinity, Cambridge and, later, Bishop of Lichfield, wrote in defence of the SCM and explaining that the omission from the Basis of words such as 'faith', 'sin', 'regeneration' and 'salvation' did not mean that the SCM had ceased to believe in the gospel, but 'we have sought for more living and less technical language in which to try to set forth absolute supremacy of the Christ Who was and is nothing less than God Incarnate'. He explains that the book, which had been reviewed so adversely, was 'addressed, not to convinced believers, but to doubters'. He pleads for a greater understanding on the part of *The Christian* and the Evangelicals generally about what the SCM was trying to do. The editor's comment on this is that whilst he recognizes 'the characteristically courteous tone of his communication, it is, however, true to say that his letter begs the question at issue, and does nothing to relieve the anxiety at recent departures felt by friends – not hostile critics – of the Student Christian Movement.'

The student evangelical leaders were meeting for the first Inter-Varsity conference. Their attention had been called to the correspondence and a good deal of time between the sessions was taken up in drafting a letter to *The Christian*. This duly appeared in the 18 December 1919 issue. The opening two paragraphs refer to the review of the book and the occasion which had brought them together in conference. It continues, 'The writers of this letter claim to represent those who do not accept as true either Higher Criticism or Evolution, where they conflict with the facts revealed by the Spirit of God in Genesis and the rest of the Bible.

With reference to the statement that the vast majority of students accept the principles of Higher Criticism, we venture to say, that a considerable and increasing number are finding that in accepting the whole of the Scriptures by faith as the Word of God, they derive food and strength from every book in daily life.

We are witnessing term by term in the Universities, through the preaching of Christ crucified and risen, such radical changes in the lives of men of various temperaments, abilities, and types of thought, as are evidence that this Gospel is still "the power of God unto salvation", and that the blood of the Lord Jesus Christ is still the only remedy for the sin and evil in the human heart. We believe that the only acceptance of man by God, for forgiveness (the first essential), for sanctification and service, is by belief in the Lord Jesus Christ. We must be born again into a new life, in which the Holy Spirit first directs the will and heart to desire to do His service, and secondly, gives the power to do it. We can see nothing in Scripture or in history to lead us to believe that social work on any other foundation lasts to eternity, or is to the glory of God; or that in this dispensation the whole world will turn to God.

We write this in view of our confident expectation of our Lord's Return for His people, and desiring thereby "to give a reason of the hope that is in us with meekness and fear", fully realizing our own short experience in His service. – Yours,

B. GODFREY BUXTON   M. H. WEBB-PEPLOE
(CICCU, Cambridge)   (CICCU, Cambridge)

F. N. PALMER (Oxford) F. A. C. MILLARD (Oxford)
K. S. MAURICE SMITH I. H. C. BALFOUR
(LIHCU, London) (LIHCU, London).'

There was further correspondence by others, then the matter was allowed to rest. But it was now clear both to the student leaders and to their senior advisers, most of whom had earlier been officers in the SCM in its heyday as an Evangelical movement, that its wider policy had now been determined. It could be expected to continue in the broad stream of Liberal Ecumenical churchmanship. The distinctive doctrines of Evangelicalism (whilst they would no doubt be tolerated as 'one point of view') would no longer be really welcome.

Further conferences

In 1920 a second conference was called by the CICCU Executive and carried through on similar lines to its predecessor in the period 6–9 December. The sessions were held in Sion College (the clergy library near Blackfriars Bridge, London) with a daily service, and a closing communion service in nearby St. Bride's church. There was no conference in the year 1921, because of a change of date from the December dates to 9–12 January 1922. The meetings were held at the Eccleston Hall, near Victoria Station. Very few traces or descriptions of these conferences have survived beyond programmes. It is known, however, that soon there was a marked increase in representation from new Christian Unions from distant universities and Oxford began to play a fuller part in the leadership. A. W. Habershon, the Oxford President, chaired most of the sessions of this 1922 conference. A minute book, in the form of a cheap exercise book, at last made its appearance and from this academic year (1922–23) inadequate and very brief minutes of 'the Committee' for the conference began to be kept. They are just notes and for some time do not even record who was present at the meetings!

After considerable search and checking from other sources the sequence of the first Inter-Varsity Conferences is now clear and can be listed as follows:

I. *Conferences in London*

(Members were given hospitality in Christian homes)

1919 8–11 December   Egypt General Mission, Drayton Park.

1920 6–9 December   Sion College and St. Bride's Church.

(No conference in 1921 because of change to a January date.)

1922 9–12 January   Eccleston Hall.

1923 16–19 April   Church Army headquarters
and (originally planned for 9–12 January 1924) –

1923 11–13 December   Church Army.

1924 8–12 December   Church Army.

(No conference in 1925 because of change to an April date
and to the residential conference centre, High Leigh.)

II. *Residential Conferences*

1926 26 March–1 April   High Leigh, Hoddesdon, Herts.

1927–1934   Spring conferences were held at High Leigh until
they became too large.

1935–1973   Spring conferences were held at The Hayes,
Swanwick, Derbyshire (except during the war-years
1940–1946)

1974   There was an experimental division of the conference
into north and south.

Two further references to the Inter-Varsity Conference appear in the minutes of the CICCU Executive. On 28 May 1920, at a meeting held in Murray Webb-Peploe's rooms, it is recorded, 'Finally, dates were discussed for a meeting in town to talk over the proposed "Inter-Varsity Christian Union".' It would, therefore, appear that there were already early discussions of the desirability of closer links between the CUs, and the formation of a national organization, which did not come to fuller discussion until 1924, and finally took place in 1927. A doleful note is struck by the entry for a meeting on 14 January 1921, 'It was reported that £6.15.0 was still required to meet the expenses of the Conference in London in December, and the Hon. Treasurer was authorized to pay one-third of this (£2.5.0) to the Conference Treasurer.'

The foreshadowings of some rational organizational links first appear in minutes of a meeting of university representatives held on 10 January 1922 during the Conference at the Eccleston Hall. There is a resolution by the Rev. Stather Hunt (Cambridge) who proposed 'that the Inter-Varsity Conference in future shall be held in each year and shall be opened to members of all universities and their associated colleges'. Whilst the minutes are difficult to decipher, there is sufficient to show (i) that this meeting may be considered the first recognizable general committee of delegates from the Unions, (ii) that something like a recognizable first executive committee was at that time elected by the delegates. The first steps were also taken towards the drafting of a constitution for the conference.

A representative general committee

The conference had clearly now become annual. More Christian Unions were about to apply for a link with the conference. There was also a need to provide for the future leadership and policy making. Until 1922 the initiative and responsibility had been taken by the executive committee of the CICCU. At the 1923 conference general committee the future responsibility was clearly transferred by the CICCU to this representative body of delegates, consisting of two appointed representatives from each Christian Union in sympathy with the aims and basis.

The organizational arrangements provided that the general committee should meet annually at the conference. At this meeting it would elect an executive committee to undertake the detailed planning and preparation for the next conference the following year. These two committees were written in to the Fellowship's constitution in 1928 and the representative general committee of student delegates from the Christian Unions, and the student executive, have remained the basic committee structure for the students' work down to the present.

A draft constitution, embodying the aims and providing for the committees and procedure, was adopted at a special meeting of the general committee in the Reeve Hall on 1 April 1922. It was reported that 'Four more universities have accepted the invitation in future to send representatives to the General Committee. Mr. Clarence Foster proposed that provision be made to welcome

123

representatives from the *separate* Women's Evangelical Unions, which existed in Belfast, Cambridge, Dublin and London.' (At previous meetings a representative from the Student Christian Movement seems to have been invited and to have been present. This is suggested by a resolution from the London committee that, in future, a SCM representative should not be invited.) Additions to the constitution were proposed, which needed to be confirmed at the next general committee for which full provision was to be made at the 1923 conference.

The 1923 and 1924 conference general committees had as one of their major topics steps necessitated by the increasing load of work for the Secretary. There were two proposals (i) the appointment of a full-time (paid) general conference secretary; and (ii) plans to organize an Inter-Varsity Christian Union, which it would be the main duty of this new secretary to develop. The Oxford and London delegates were both somewhat reluctant to proceed with these proposals because of their apprehension about the financial implications (for there was already each year a deficit on the conference expenses, which had to be made up). They were also afraid, (in the light of the SCM's recent history) that the autonomy of the infant Christian Unions might be impaired by such a full-time central secretariat. Oxford and London, therefore, proposed that 'It first be made clear that the General Conference Secretary has no control over local Unions and that no direct financial liabilities are to fall on the individual unions'. Most of the unions, especially London, were in difficulties with their own budgets. Some of the other delegates were also uncertain concerning the views of their own committees and supporters. These proposals were, therefore, temporarily left in abeyance.

During 1923 and 1924, with indications that there was to be a considerable increase in the number of Christian Unions, and in view of the potential for expansion, a series of more ambitious proposals was made. Some delegates advocated a 'federation' of the Unions, with a full-time general secretary. Others, who were anxious about maintaining the autonomy of the Unions, proposed that any appointment should rather be that of a travelling secretary, and possibly also of a women's travelling secretary. These would act as advisers and visitors to the weaker Unions, particularly those unable to secure the services of the more prominent speakers and missioners, who seemed willing only to serve the older and bigger Unions. At length it was agreed to call a full meeting of delegates from all the existing Unions, together with several senior advisers, including the Rev. G. T. Manley, who was to be in the chair. It met on 2 July 1924 in the church room of St. Paul's, Portman Square.

Special consultations

An efficient plan was submitted to the meeting for 'a central bureau with a permanent secretariat', and the appointment of a man (and, possibly, a woman) travelling secretary, with arrangements for the production of evangelical literature particularly designed for students. The majority in the meeting were in favour, but the London delegates (supported by the delegates from the informal group in Trinity College, Dublin, and by those from Oxford, who made it clear that they were rather lukewarm in support of the proposals) again expressed their anxiety. Their main point was that the financial burden would become too great and that the autonomy and initiative of the Unions would be impaired by over-centralization. The truth was that there was more behind the reluctance of the LIFCU Committee than its delegates wished to state. They had no confidence in either of the two graduates, whom (they had heard) were to be nominated for the new posts. One was an advocate of the viewpoint and methods of the Oxford Groups (now known as 'Moral Rearmament') and the evangelical churchmanship of the other was uncertain as understood by the student delegates. Subsequent biography would suggest that the London leaders were probably wholly justified in their hesitations, and that the delay may ultimately have been in the best interests of the movement, though the effect was to postpone the birth date of the Fellowship.

It became clear in the meeting that London which, by that time, was the strongest Union numerically, would withdraw if the project were passed as presented. With Dublin and Oxford also both very uncertain, it was agreed to leave the proposals 'on the table' for later re-consideration. The rest of the meeting was devoted to discussing how the movement generally could be strengthened and the witness carried as soon as possible into all the universities. It was agreed that, whilst it was by then too late to alter the site of the 1924 conference, the next conference in 1925 should be residential and that search should be made for a suitable conference centre in the Midlands or north of England. It was further agreed that a part-time travelling secretary should be appointed to visit the new and smaller Chritian Unions. He would also seek to promote the formation of new Unions in those universities which were at present unrepresented. It was noted that an additional advantage of employing such a 'traveller' would be the publicizing of the next annual conference and the issuing of pressing personal invitations to attend.

There was a possibility that Harold Earnshaw Smith might consider giving part-time help for a year, or two years, in such an appointment. He had recently returned from serving as Chaplain at Trinity College, Lagos and had filled in waiting-time as Acting-Warden of the Cambridge University Missionary Settlement in Bermondsey. His apparent willingness to consider this invitation was specially important at this juncture because the London students had full confidence in him. He had already given considerable help to the hospital CUs. They were ready to support his appointment, provided that the finance could be obtained by subscription from graduates, avoiding too heavy a load on the student unions. These promising possibilities, however, were cut short by his accepting an appointment as Chaplain of Caius College, Cambridge. This was a post which he held with distinction until returning to London as Vicar of Christ Church, Brixton and became once more locally available to the LIFCU.

The delegates to the special meeting dispersed with less accomplished than they had hoped. There were, however, several gains. A growing momentum and unity of aim was developing between the various new evangelical Unions. Something in the nature of a loose inter-university affiliation, short of federation, could not long be delayed. It was recognized by all that since the secretarial work of pioneering and co-ordinating Christian

Unions was clearly beyond the amount of free-time which any student could, or ought, to devote to it, there was need of at least a travelling secretary. More important still, there was a growing consciousness amongst the potential leaders that, with the SCM now plainly determined to maintain its considerably broader policy and basis, the need to develop a distinctive Evangelical witness was now put beyond doubt.

The Cambridge and, especially, the London leaders were becoming more concerned about the doctrinal standards of the movement. One indication of this was the wording of resolutions which the LIFCU sent at this time to the executive committee of the Inter-Varsity Conference. At a meeting of the London General Committee held on 17 October 1924, it was resolved:

'That this General Committee of the London Inter-Faculty Christian Union wishes to point out to the Executive of the Inter-Varsity Conference of Evangelical Unions that the present doctrinal basis (i.e. for the Conference) does not emphasize such important truths as–

a. The universal sinfulness and guilt of the human race.
b. The *necessity* of the atoning sacrifice of Christ to each individual.
c. The resurrection of the Lord Jesus.
d. The indwelling and work of the Holy Spirit.
e. The personal return of the Lord Jesus Christ.

After the fullest consideration, therefore, we are prepared to consider sympathetically the proposals of the Executive Committee of the Inter-Varsity Conference, provided that our doctrinal basis, which includes these points, should be incorporated in the Inter-Varsity Conference Constitution, together with Clause 13 of the Constitution of the LIFCU, and that all officials (paid or unpaid) connected with the Conference should sign it on election. We feel these measures to be necessary in view of the general extension of the Conference, which will follow the appointment of a Travelling Secretary.'

In the covering letter, the London Committee also made it clear that their further co-operation depended upon more definiteness about essential Evangelical doctrine and no further wavering about co-operation with other movements, which were not really on the same doctrinal platform or working for the same ends.

Secretaryship

One need had still not been met. The question of organizational personnel for this important conference, with all its growing correspondence with an increasing number of new Unions, had been still left open. The 1923–24 Conference Secretary, Julian Thornton-Duesberry (Balliol College, Oxford),[2] a Triple First, whose high academic standards did not take kindly to being distracted by constant pressures of organizational correspondence, had repeatedly emphasized to the Committee the need for a full-time secretary, if the work was to be able rapidly to grow. When the General Committee of delegates met on 12 December in the vestry of Holy Trinity Church, Marylebone, at the close of the 1924 conference, one of the most important items on the agenda was the election of the next Executive Committee. There was, however, no nominee for the secretaryship. All who had been approached to allow themselves to be nominated as secretary had declined nomination because of the anticipated deleterious effects that this work would have on their academic careers.

This matter was postponed whilst the rest of the agenda was completed. Then Clarence Foster (treasurer) proposed that since the London students had been the chief opponents of the original plans which earlier had proposed a full-time secretariat, it was up to them to be responsible for organizing the next conference. He suggested that the experience would soon demonstrate to the LIFCU committee the need for a full-time worker. It was therefore proposed, seconded and agreed that the London representative should be responsible for finding a secretary, with the London Secretary's[3] name put in to complete the Executive Committee list. With visible relief on the faces of all the rest of those present, the meeting rapidly broke up and the university representatives hurried off to their destinations. The hapless nominee, who had only that summer graduated in the Faculty of Arts and was just completing the first term of the medical course, was left in a somewhat confused state with a relieved Julian Thornton-Duesberry, the retiring secretary, getting ready to hand over. The latter kindly endeavoured to improve the occasion by suggesting how best the pressures of secretaryship could be tailored to fit in with academic requirements!

A further complication arose at the following meeting of the LIFCU Executive Committee. Whilst some of its members took the view that the situation now gave London the opportunity to begin to take the conference in the direction in which they thought it ought to go, others were somewhat alarmed at the Committee's shouldering these undefined larger responsibilities. It was finally agreed to accept the situation for one year, to instruct the secretary to concentrate on planning the best possible next Inter-Varsity Conference, and to think again after that. For the new secretary, however, this was not the end of his troubles. The LIFCU itself was growing, and there were by then well over twenty 'branches'. It was already in itself a microcosm of the Inter-Varsity movement. All his efforts to transfer as soon as possible the LIFCU secretaryship, so as to be able to take the new load, dismally failed. Potential volunteers after due thought, or consultation with parents, declined to consider it on the grounds that it would ruin their futures! The double load, therefore, had to be carried for some time until the LIFCU could arrange for several assistant secretaries to share its secretaryship as far as it could be conveniently co-ordinated.

Eventually, to the great credit of the members of the 1924-5 LIFCU Executive Committee, several further firm decisions were taken. They agreed to plan enthusiastically for the next Inter-Varsity Conference and to make it residential. Also, they agreed to back the secretary's efforts to the extent of their resources. The secretary himself was living in the same medical students' hostel as the retiring president of the St. Bartholomew's Hospital Christian Union (Howard W. Guiness). The latter's 'vision' and 'drive' was just what both the LIFCU and the wider Inter-Varsity conference movement needed. Howard Guiness, although himself beginning to approach medical finals, was persuaded to become President of the LIFCU and Vice-Chairman on the Executive Committee of the Inter-Varsity Conference. The London students agreed to do their best to work for the national movement as a whole and to take a fresh look at the situation at the close of the 1926 conference.

Pressures from the SCM

Before the next conference met, however, there were two results of the continuing pressures exerted by the SCM on the new evangelical Unions encouraging them to reconsider their separate activities. After an impressive start under such leaders as Noel Palmer, Willoughby Habershon, Talbot Mohan and others, the Oxford University Bible Union was invited to co-operate more closely with the SCM in Oxford. After two uncertain terms, one of the new leaders (whose later marked commitment to mysticism and religious syncretism were already being foreshadowed) persuaded the OUBU committee to give up its separate existence and to become a 'devotional unit' in the SCM. In addition, the new Oxford leadership began to write to the Christian press and to other universities advocating that their policy should be adopted by the other evangelical Unions. They clearly were no longer loyally in support of the general policy of the committees of Inter-Varsity Conference. After several vain efforts to persuade the Oxford leaders to reverse their decision, and whilst individual members were, of course, always welcomed at the conferences, the Conference Executive had to make it clear that Oxford's DU delegates would no longer be welcome at subsequent General Committees. To the regret of all, Oxford was unrepresented in both the 1926 and 1927 General Committee, and not represented again until 1928. On that occasion the delegates of the reorganized Oxford Inter-Collegiate Christian Union (under that name instead of OUBU) were welcomed with all the more enthusiasm because of the outstanding example of prayer and evangelism which the new union from the start had already given in their University.

London's policy difficulties

Since the Student Christian Movement's office was at Golders Green, North London, its headquarters staff were constantly in close contact with the London colleges. The newly formed

130

branches of the London Inter-Faculty Christian Union, some of them small and led by very inexperienced students, were from time to time pressed to follow the 'example' of Oxford. After one rather glaring case of what the LIFCU Committee regarded as an unfair 'takeover' bid by the SCM, the London leaders invited the SCM General Secretary, Tissington Tatlow, to meet them at the Student Movement House. Their intention was simply to complain of the distractions and constant muddles which these approaches were causing to inexperienced young leaders who were doing their best as Christian witnesses. They began to explain the resentment they felt and to make it clear that these pressures only increased their desire to maintain their independent activities. It is possible that the SCM secretary had initially thought, or hoped, that the meeting would enable him to canvass successfully his viewpoint and the SCM's policy. Soon after the start (and clearly disappointed), Tissington Tatlow's attitude changed. He courteously, but firmly, made it clear that, though 'the contribution of Evangelicals was, as always, welcome in the SCM', yet the latter was no longer what it was in the pre-1900 period, that is, it was no longer an Evangelical movement. It now welcomed 'all schools of thought' on equal terms. It was committed to an ecumenical policy and wished to draw in all Christians. In describing the wide comprehension of the SCM the General Secretary reverted to some of his favourite, but unfortunate, expressions about the finality of the 'outmoded' nature of Evangelicalism. He reiterated his dictum that 'the doctrine of the verbal inspiration of the Bible is as dead as Queen Anne' and 'no theologian worth the name accepts the penal view of the Atonement'. The interview, therefore, ended rather abruptly when the LIFCU president said 'Well, Sir, it seems that the gulf between us is so wide, that there is no point in going further. We hope, however, that those Evangelicals, who so wish, can be left free to give their witness in college in their own way'.

The result, on the side of the LIFCU, was that its leaders drew up a memorandum more definitely clarifying and explaining their resistance to further talk of co-operation. Christian Unions in other universities did the same. Into the Inter-Varsity Conference Constitution, and into those of some of the new Unions coming

131

into being, went two clauses concerning policy. These were that 'Only those speakers whose religious beliefs are known to be in accordance with the Doctrinal Basis shall be asked to take part in the Annual Conference', and 'In connection with the Conference, no joint activities shall be arranged with any religious body which does not substantially uphold the truths stated in the Doctrinal Basis'.

The advice of experienced senior graduates was sought on the future development of the movement and its general policy. One of the best of the memoranda setting out the essentials, came from the pen of the Rev. G. T. Manley. He had remained closely in touch with the history and the progress of the two movements.[4] He very definitely stated that, in his view, Evangelicals now had no choice but to go forward independently on a frankly Evangelical platform.

Further progress

Meanwhile more Unions were coming into being. Three new ones emerged in 1927, at Manchester, Reading and St. Andrews. In Manchester two students had prayed and waited for other Evangelical Christians to join them until the Inter-Varsity Conference's 1927 summer term prayer leaflet happened to come into their hands. From this they learnt that Hugh R. Gough, a recent ex-CICCU president, would be available to visit Christians in any of the universities who liked to invite him.[5] During the summer term they discovered a few other students and together they formed the Manchester Inter-Faculty Christian Union in early October. Hugh Gough spoke to their first open meeting in the University a little later in the autumn term.

At Reading several students had discussed together for some months how they as Christians could influence their student body and, in the autumn of 1927, ten students, one man and nine women, formed a society under the name 'the Association of Christians'. On becoming aware that the SCM branch, and others, might possibly regard their title as indicating an exclusive use of the word 'Christian', it was quickly changed to 'Reading University Evangelical Union'. What at first had witnessed as a comparatively small group, became an influence to be reckoned with after the Rev. Bryan Green (a university missioner on the Oxford 'Pastorate') had in 1931 brought with him a 'team' of twenty university undergraduates for a new type of mission to the University. At this time, there were several such university missions in which large parties of Christian students visited other universities.

St. Andrews is the oldest university in Scotland. The birth of its small Christian Union proved something of an inspiration and a model. Eight men, mostly theological students and all very convinced Christians, had been discussing how they could start a witness which would have some resemblance 'to the glowing spirituality of the Reformers'. They had heard about the Inter-Varsity Conference and agreed together to make the long journey to High Leigh for the 1927 conference. On arrival they found that there were two women students from St. Andrews also present and J. Rollo, a recent graduate, who was at that time training for his teachers' certificate at Dundee. At the close of the Reports Session, Rollo made a fervent plea for prayer for his University of St. Andrew's, telling the meeting with great effect of the direct persecution which he himself had experienced when he had tried to witness alone as a 'fresher'. This fired the eight 'reformers' and they immediately resolved to found the St. Andrews University Christian Students' Fellowship. Their first plans and their constitution, (including a quite uncompromising Doctrinal Basis, which at the time alienated some) set the Union off steadily on what has proved a long and fruitful course of service to God's Kingdom in their University.

The beginning of residential conferences

The 1924–25 Executive Committee had been commissioned by the 1924 General Committee to search for a residential conference centre in central or northern England. Efforts to find a convenient place *at student prices*, however, had proved difficult. Swanwick, with preferential student rates, was in those days regarded as the SCM's preserve. Eventually, though it meant missing a year (because this centre was not free for the 1925 Easter vacation) High

Leigh, Hoddesdon, Herts. was finally booked for the late March of 1926. This country house had earlier been the seat of Robert Barclay, the banker, and it had recently been adapted for conferences, including the addition of a large hostel having many single rooms. It was ideal for a student conference's purposes. The annual gatherings were subsequently held here for the next eight years, until in 1934 greatly increasing numbers, and the desire to hold the conference in a more central area, brought about a move to Swanwick in Derbyshire, which by then was being more generally used by a number of Christian societies.

It was with great enthusiasm and high expectations that delegates from the Unions, and other members, eighty-two in all, assembled at High Leigh, 26 March–1 April 1926. At that time, when ecumenical co-operation between the different churches was not as familiar as it is now, many quips were exchanged between those who were members of very widely divergent ecclesiastical traditions. The composition of the team of speakers set the fashion. It included amongst others Major and Mrs. Mainwaring Burton (as host and hostess), who were virtually interdenominational, the Rt. Rev. Bishop Taylor Smith (recently retired Chaplain General of the Forces), and Mr. George Goodman of the Plymouth Brethren[6]. The addresses of Bishop Taylor Smith were admirably supplemented by those of George Goodman, to whom the Bishop consistently referred because of his church affiliation, as 'our excellent *Devonshire* Friend' (!) Attempts by the more mischievous undergraduates to create diversions at discussion times by questions designed to raise denominational differences between the speakers only produced greater harmony. The speakers, by adhering to scriptural phrasing, united in a wholly salutary emphasis upon love for the church of God and due observance of the means of grace appointed by its Head. As the spirit of unity in the faith, zeal for the gospel and the needs of overseas missions became more real in the conference there were many challenging moments. A number of students subsequently dated their call to the Christian ministry, or to the mission field, from that conference.

Travelling secretaries and missionary activities
At a meeting of the Executive Committee held in January 1925, in spite of the fact that some were still a little apprehensive about the potential costs of a travelling secretary, steps in this direction were taken. Harold Earnshaw Smith had already served as stimulus to the London CUs and had visited as many other universities as he could from Cambridge. Having completed the term of his appointment as a college chaplain, he had been asked to stay on in Cambridge as a personal counsellor in association with the CICCU (a form of extra 'Pastorate'). It was a role for which he was ideally fitted. He was also asked by the Conference Executive Committee to continue to make as many visits from Cambridge to other universities as possible. His visits proved popular. He was by then, however, beginning to feel that he should return to the parochial ministry and he came in the following year to Christ Church, Brixton. Hence, in June 1925, the Committee invited Hugh R. Gough,[7] the retiring CICCU President who was approaching his final examinations, if he would postpone entry to the theological college for a year, and complete a full tour of the British universities. He agreed to do so, as long as he could also combine his visits with contacts for the Children's Special Service Mission for which he had promised to recruit students for its seaside missions. Hence the first *full-time* travelling secretary was H. R. Gough. He brought a timely impetus to the existing Unions and was able to help in the initial stages of some, such as the Union at Manchester.

A proposal that the 'Prayer Circular', a leaflet which was circulated each term to provide news from the Unions, should be expanded into an inter-university magazine was not at that time taken up by the Committee on the grounds of costs. This desirable development had to wait until 1929. But one pioneer step was taken at this time which continued to exert considerable influence for a number of years thereafter. In 1927 the enthusiastic CICCU Missionary Secretary, L. F. E. Wilkinson[8] (Queen's College, Cambridge), brought together for a 'missionary conference' at Old Jordans, Bucks. the existing missionary secretaries on the Union Committees (with a suitable 'committee representative' from

135

those Unions which had not yet appointed one). This occasion proved to be the precursor of the annual missionary conferences. It also provided the seed-bed of the Inter-Varsity Missionary Fellowship, which in its time must be regarded as the successor of the pre-1900 Student Missionary Volunteer Union.

NOTES

1   See pages 13 and 15.
2   Later, Master of St. Peter's Hall, Oxford.
3   Douglas Johnson, at that time the LIFCU's Secretary.
4   See also pages 93f.
5   See page 135.
6   He would have preferred the name 'Christian Brethren'.
7   Later Bishop of Barking and then Archbishop of Sydney.
8   Later, Principal of Oak Hill Theological College.

Chapter 8

The watershed
(1928)

The year 1928 was to prove the turning point in the history of the second phase of the Evangelical movement. It brought five major developments. First was a growing pressure from the Unions that the effective spiritual links which existed between them should now be recognized. Behind the annual conferences there had grown up a close fellowship and interchange, which called for fuller expression and a name. Second, Oxford's delegates were again welcomed back to the General Committee, representing the new Oxford Inter-Collegiate Christian Union. Third, the Executive Committee was challenged at the 1928 annual conference to send one of its leaders as a pioneer emissary to Canada. The response was to lead on to wider overseas ventures. Fourth, though it took several years before success was attained, a start was made to plan special literature for the use of Evangelical students. Finally, encouraged by a substantial gift to bring down the costs per head, L. F. E. Wilkinson organized the first residential conference for the missionary 'volunteers'. It was a sequel to that for missionary secretaries in the previous year.

The recognition of the Fellowship

The General Committee of 3 April 1928 brought together a greater number of delegates from the universities than had so far been seen. Definite proposals for organizing a loose affiliation to be known as a 'fellowship', and its draft construction, were before the meeting. The proposal was that the Unions should be linked under the name of the Inter-Varsity Fellowship of Evangelical Christian Unions. Support was very much greater than had earlier seemed likely. But by now it was clear that the Student Christian Movement was still taking additional steps away from its Evangelical origins and was in process of a further official widening of its basis and a greater liberalizing of its policies. The Evangelical Unions had, therefore, come definitely to stay. It had also become accepted by the Christian Unions that the members of the successive conference executive committees were as anxious as they ever were to preserve the autonomy of the Unions and the distinctively Evangelical character of the movement.

The proposals for affiliation into an organization had first arisen simply in the form of the suggestion of a change of name. The need for this had been voiced by senior graduates visiting the Cambridge camp at Keswick in July 1927. Hugh Gough had also reported from his travels that a considerable number of friends and subscribers had repeatedly asked why the Unions were not united under some title such as an 'Inter-Varsity Christian Union'. Even more important was the fact that in the 1927 and 1928 General Committees some of the delegates from new Unions had made a strong case that their difficulties in obtaining recognition from their university authorities might be lessened if they were able to claim that they were affiliated to a university movement of national status.

As soon as the meeting looked more closely at the draft constitution it was at once recognized that the changes simply and essentially involved little more than substituting 'Fellowship' for 'Conference' in the existing Constitution except where a reference to the annual conference was, in fact, still meant. A few additional necessary organizational procedures needed to be recognized, and the anxieties of some of the smaller unions about their liability for any financial obligations duly met. It was agreed that there should be no fixed membership subscriptions or 'levy' on the Unions and that the Executive Committee would have no power to commit the Unions to financial expenditure. The principle of support was to be voluntary, and any contribution to central funds would be as the result of a free vote of a Union's own committee. At that stage the name preferred was 'Inter-Varsity Fellowship of Evangelical Christian Unions'. In a later year this was shortened to 'Inter-Varsity Fellowship of Evangelical Unions', with general use of the initials 'IVF'. On being put to the vote the draft constitution, as amended, was enthusiastically adopted. It has subsequently received modifications and several additions as the activities, responsibilities and influence of the Fellowship have steadily grown.

Oxford

The representatives of the reconstituted Oxford Inter-Collegiate Christian Union, led by Louis Gaussen the first President, made a particularly valuable contribution to the 1928 conference. It was of special encouragement to the committee of the smaller Unions to learn how such a small new group had been prepared at once to attempt to speak to the whole of their University. The story of their new start and first public meeting was infectious. The following account is as described by one who was present.[1]

'In Oxford from 1924–1927 the main "evangelical witness" was represented by the 'Devotional Union' inside the SCM. The liberal theological outlook and broad comprehension of the "parent" movement, however, was not at all conducive to Evangelism as we understood it. There was soon a good deal of discontent amongst those who had come up from active Evangelical churches. In 1927 a freshman entered Oriel who had been a leader in a very active school Christian Union. He already knew several members on the Devotional Union committee. This had no representative in Oriel and, although it was still in the vacation and he was only a freshman, the executive pressed him into agreeing to be the Oriel rep. His name was duly printed on the card for the beginning of term.'

'Just before term started, the Fresher had to come up to college to take a preliminary exam. In the evenings he had time to think and pray. Wherever he read in the Bible, and however hard he tried, he could not expel the thought that he ought not to join the DU,

139

which he increasingly came to regard as an unhappy compromise. After a week of inner turmoil he went round to see one of his friends in Corpus. This DU committee member had also come up early before term. After mentioning it to others on committee, it was agreed to remove the new rep's name. The card, however, had already been printed. So it was overprinted, though the name was still easily decipherable and an embarrassing situation developed. For it led to questions about the attempted erasure, and widespread discussion of the reasons. Others began to voice their reservations.'

'In the next term, at the Annual General Meeting to elect the new committee, there was a frank discussion, and a somewhat stormy meeting. It was clear that quite a number of the members took the Fresher's view. Eventually it was resolved to sever the link with the SCM and to recover freedom of action. Eighteen convinced Evangelicals joined the new union, which adopted a strong doctrinal basis and applied for affiliation with the IVF. The SCM, on this second occasion when application was made, courteously permitted the new organization at last to take over the original name of "Oxford Inter-Collegiate Christian Union".[2] The most striking feature in the new Union was its spirit of prayer. Every Saturday after tea a group of undergraduates varying from a few to 15 members met in the President's digs in Divinity Road to pray. Their chief concern was "God's honour in the University".'

'From one of these prayer meetings came the plans for what, subsequently, the Bishop of Rochester (C. M. Chavasse) described as the most remarkable meeting he had ever attended in Oxford, so conscious was he of the presence of God's Spirit. The OICCU leaders boldly booked the Town Hall and invited three members of the CICCU to come over from Cambridge to speak on "What Christ means to me". Large six feet by three feet posters in dark and light blue were put all over Oxford. Hymn sheets were printed, a piano hired and *much prayer was made*!'

'On the day three Cambridge men – Kenneth Hooker (CICCU President), "Ted" Yorke a recent convert of the "Willie" Nicholson Mission in Cambridge and "Jim" Walkey, a running blue – came over for a picnic lunch on Boar's Hill and to pray with the OICCU Executive. Before the meeting was due to start, several OICCU men went into the Council Room behind the platform to pray. They were beginning to pray that many more undergraduates would come to the meeting, when one of the number (who had crept to the door and opened it a crack to look into the hall) returned and gave thanks that the hall was packed to the doors! So all three remained to pray for the three speakers and the impact of the meeting. The interruptions which had been feared were absent and the audience heard the speakers in a hushed silence. The three Cambridge men left no doubt about what they thought was missing in Oxford. Much interest was aroused. A number of undergraduates were converted to Christ in the weeks following.'

'The biggest lesson learnt by the OICCU was the importance and power of prayer. For example, they had prayed for the expenses of hiring the Town Hall to be covered. Members were at that time few. They had ventured to take up a retiring collection at the meeting. When the stewards had finished counting it, there was ten shillings above the expenditure to which they were committed. They had just commented on the fact of this surplus when the treasurer came in and said that he had given one of the Town Hall staff a ten shilling tip! No one present could believe that this exact figure in the collection was "just a coincidence",'

'The daily prayer meetings (held in what is now the Northgate Hall in St. Michael's Street) became crowded. On average 80% of the increased membership of the OICCU were regularly present. "If you were not there you were missed!" More conversions were constantly reported as a result of personal conversations and especially following the OICCU Sermon each week-end. Without doubt it was a small, but deep, and lasting revival of religion in Oxford.'

'Towards the end of the year, however, there was a further marked increased of membership not accounted for by recent conversions. Who were all these new members? It soon became suspected by the Committee that they were SCM members quietly infiltrating into the Union. These new people had joined, but did not come to the weekly activities. They seemed only to be concerned to advocate to other individual members a reunion

141

with the SCM. At the next (1929) Annual General Meeting there was a record attendance. Soon after the start (as had been feared by the Committee) the proposal was advanced by a new member that the OICCU should once again merge with the SCM. Speaker after speaker rapidly rose in support of the motion. The newly elected President, however, was not to be stampeded. Each speaker was pointedly asked if he had ever attended an OICCU meeting? Few had. The President then calmly ruled that the Constitution provided that there must be a two-thirds majority for any "*change*" in the Constitution, but that the proposal then before the meeting was not a "change", it was an "abolition". He, therefore, ruled the motion out of order, and directed that the meeting should proceed to the next business! The infiltrators stamped out in an uproar and the OICCU's faithful "rump" remained.'

'The SCM, however, did not give up. Much time was consumed in seemingly endless discussions with their representatives. Eventually, during a particularly pressing, and depressing phase, the OICCU President found that his daily Scripture Union readings were taken from Nehemiah and described the latter's attempts to rebuild the new walls of Zion. Tobiah and Sanballat persisted in interrupting and urging him to stop and come down to discuss things in the plains of Ono. Nehemiah, however, had declined on the grounds that he wanted to get on quickly with the job. Dr. Graham Scroggie who had written the SU Notes had headed the section – "'Oh No!' on the plains of Ono". The OICCU President – with typically student directness – simply posted as his answer to the SCM's negotiator these Notes of Dr. Scroggie with the heading underlined! The resulting reactions of the recipient – a future Bishop – are unknown. At least there was a temporary cessation of pressures on the OICCU.'

An invitation from Canada

During the months preceding the 1928 conference, Norman Grubb had been travelling in Canada on deputation for his missionary society. He arrived back in Britain on the day on which the Inter-Varsity conference had started. He came on to

High Leigh the next day and immediately asked if he could address the Executive Committee. Although the schedule was very full, a special meeting was arranged in which he graphically described to the Committee the needs of the Canadian universities. He had been told by the retiring Principal of McGill University, Montreal, who was an active churchman, that in the days before World War I there had been excellent camps run by the SCM of Canada. These were now largely social, rather disorganized and lacked even the shadow of their former effectiveness. He (the Principal) offered that, if a suitable representative from the British Inter-Varsity movement, of which he had heard good reports, could be sent over he would arrange for him to be given a base and financial support in visits to the Canadian universities.

Norman Grubb reported that at that time in North America there was only one small evangelical Christian Union in Vancouver, and in the USA only a comparatively small 'League of Evangelical Students', consisting mainly of theological students in Philadelphia. But he was sure that if a leader experienced in the work being carried on in the British universities could go over for a three months' tour in Canadian and United States universities, evangelical groups could be formed in almost every one of them. He urged that the Committee should consider prayerfully the appointment of a deputation to the Canadian universities during the coming Michaelmas term. After brief discussion, it is recorded that 'the Committee was unanimous in feeling this to be a definite challenge from God and resolved to seek the support of the General Committee in praying, and arranging, for a deputation to be sent to Canada in the coming October'. At the next day's General Committee, the delegates from the Unions enthusiastically endorsed the decision of the Executive.

But the vital question remained, *who* should be sent? The Chairman of the Executive at the time was Hugh Gough, who had completed nearly two years as President of the CICCU. He had already postponed his entry to a theological college in order to serve as travelling secretary in the universities (page 135). The Committee unanimously invited him to postpone his theological course for another year, and to leave for Canada in September! Gough tentatively accepted the invitation, making it clear, however, that this was dependent on the consent of the respective ecclesiastical and theological authorities to whom he was now responsible. At this point the Committee had reckoned without the experience and shrewdness of (i) Dr. Winnington Ingram, the Bishop of London and (ii) Dr. Gilbert, the Principal of St. John's Hall (the London College of Divinity). To the great disappointment of the youthful Executive Committee, who were tempted to doubt his 'Christianity'(!), the Bishop declined to give his permission. He had noted that there had already been one year's postponement and, in his experience, further deferments for such exciting reasons would make it difficult for the ordinand to settle back again into study and parish work. In view of Hugh Gough's subsequent career (see page 136 note) the members of that year's student Executive have been compelled grudgingly to concede that, perhaps, after all the Bishop was right.

At first somewhat crestfallen, the members of the Executive remembered Howard Guinness their Vice-Chairman, who had recently taken the London Union (LIFCU) from strength to strength, and that he had qualities of leadership and the unquenchable optimism of a pioneer. His final medical examination, however, was not far ahead, coming at the close of October. Without thought of the consequences for him, the question was put whether, if he qualified, he would postpone the usual two six-months 'house appointments' and leave immediately in early November for a six months tour in Canada. Howard Guinness thought silently for a moment and then said 'Yes. If I get through the exam, I will'! The then IVF Secretary still remembers very vividly his secret forebodings when the only (and gentle) protest came from Howard's saintly widowed mother. She quietly and correctly prophesied, 'Well, if he *does* go, knowing Howard, I fear he will never return to Medicine!'

Howard Guinness duly qualified in the following October and early in November 1928 left for Canada. This time most or all of the 'faith' had to be shown on the part of the new ambassador. For the youthful and inexperienced IVF committee only awakened at the very last minute to appreciate some of their duties and responsibilities, if they were going to act as an embryo missionary society. Apart from any personal finance which he may have had, Howard Guinness left bearing a single ticket to Canada (provided by Mr. A. Rendle Short), an immense fur-lined coat purchased and given by Norman Grubb, and £14 (the results of a last-minute 'bring and buy stall') as 'pocket money' from the students on the committee. It was fortunate that there was a Canadian skilled man of business at the journey's end! What followed Guinness' arrival in Canada will be recorded in a later chapter (page 174).

Publications

For several years there had been suggestions urging that the small leaflet, which was circulated once in each term to give news from the Unions so that members could support each other by prayer, should now be expanded into a termly magazine. Because of the Fellowship's weak financial position, however, and the absence of capital to launch either a magazine or other publications, the Executive Committee had been dragging its feet. But in the 1928 General Committee there was an increased demand for an 'inter-university magazine' and for suitable publications which would be geared specially to the student world. It had been already found that the average general publisher did not welcome such MSS because of his view that the market for them would be comparatively limited. The General Committee therefore resolved that, as soon as a suitable author could be found and sufficient capital became available, a beginning should be made with a journal and a series of booklets for Evangelical students.

Shortly after that decision had been made a Glasgow business man, Mr. Hugh Brown, was in London. He had heard from a Christian friend about the growing number of university Christian Unions, and through his family he had already been in touch with some of the leaders of the Glasgow University Students Christian Fellowship. His own son was about to go to Cambridge. He therefore arranged to meet the Secretary, and offered to subscribe £50 (a substantial sum in those days) and said that he was sure that numerous senior Christian friends would be willing to buy a short account of what was an important new

145

development in evangelical circles. The outcome was *Inter-Varsity Booklet* No. 1 – *A Brief History of the Inter-Varsity Fellowship of Evangelical Christian Unions*. It provided a short account of IVF's antecedents and early history, together with a series of introductory accounts of those Unions which had so far come into being. As the Fellowship had no address, other than the student residence of the Secretary, this and several of the later booklets were published from the CSSM Bookroom in Wigmore Street, London, W.1.

In keeping with the General Committee's resolution on publications, other 'Inter-Varsity booklets' followed at intervals; No. 2. *The Foundations of the Christian Faith*, by Sir Ambrose Fleming; No. 3. *The New Birth*, by Prof. Albert Carless; No. 4. *The Christian Faith in Relation to Modern Thought*, by Sir Ambrose Fleming; No. 5. *The Veracity of Holy Scripture*, by Sir Ambrose Fleming; No. 6. *Miracles*, by Prof. Albert Carless; No. 7. *Old Paths in Perilous Times*, a reprinted account (1913) of the Cambridge Inter-Collegiate Christian Union; No. 8. *The Body & Its Lessons*, by Prof. Albert Carless. Except for No. 8, the covers of all of these booklets were of dull brown paper, which was made more sombre by the black type. Art, advertisement and publicity were certainly not the strongest points in the early IVF leaders.

With the appearance of booklets and the magazine the development of the Inter-Varsity Press may be said to have begun. Several years, however, were to elapse before there was anything which could fittingly be called a publications department. For one thing, at the time it was the view of the senior advisers that it was appropriate for the Fellowship only to publish under its own name such booklets, Bible study aids and other literature which had particular interest for the student world and could not be marketed through the regular publishing channels. It was not until 1936 that a number of factors converged to bring about the appointment of a Publications Secretary and a bolder approach to this aspect of the work (see page 314).

The first issue of the '*Terminal Magazine of IVFEU*', later to be called '*The Inter-Varsity Magazine*', appeared in the Lent term of 1929. Again, it was printed unimaginatively in black on dull brown-grey paper. Its comparatively good circulation depended wholly on the loyalty of its constituency and the members' interest in news of the Fellowship and of the various Unions. Soon its pages were to be enlivened by racy extracts from Howard Guinness's journals and, after a long interval, some signs of interest in the magazine's format and cover-design at last made their appearance.

Increasing interest in overseas missions

The Old Jordans (1927) conference, which was limited to bringing together the existing missionary secretaries of the Unions, had been a sufficient success to encourage the missionary secretary, L. F. E. Wilkinson, to attempt bigger things. Just as he was wondering how to attract a wider number of students, he was offered £200 to lower the conference fees to a sum that would enable far more students to be present. As a result he was able in September 1928 to assemble at High Leigh over 160 students – some had to sleep in the village, others in tents. All were interested in Christian missions overseas. Amidst mounting enthusiasm plans were laid at this conference for carrying the missionary call to *every member* of the Fellowship. The project included a strong plea for a missionary secretary to be appointed to the committee of every Union, however small it might be. It was agreed to print a classified list of graduate ex-members of the Unions who were already serving overseas in order to stimulate prayer both for them and the countries they served. This was issued under the title *Witnesses Unto Me*. Several pages of the new magazine were also 'commandeered' in order to convey regular news of the mission fields. Plans were further made to organize tours of the universities by graduates on furlough from their overseas churches, hospitals and schools.

In this and subsequent conferences the seeds of active interest were carefully sown which in 1933 blossomed into 'the Inter-Varsity Missionary Fellowship'. It was founded to unite and encourage all those students intending to apply to various missionary societies for service overseas. The Fellowship was able to benefit from a succession of enthusiastic and energetic former missionary secretaries of the CICCU who were already skilled in their task. L. F. E. Wilkinson (Queens' College) was followed successively by J. G. Billington (Trinity and St. Thomas' Hospital, London), D. H. Adeney (Queen's College) and F. D. Maddox (Trinity College and St. Bartholomew's Hospital).

This rising tide of missionary interest in the developing countries overseas was happily being matched by a parallel evangelistic zeal in the home universities. Stimulating and strengthening both of these trends during this period were Howard Guinness's electrifying dispatches from 'the front line'. Having crossed Canada, founding university Christian Unions as he went, he had gone on from Vancouver to Australia and New Zealand where he met with similar results. In all three spheres, evangelism at home, offers for overseas service in the developing countries, and new initiatives in the English-speaking countries of the Commonwealth, the IVF moved a long way forward at the beginning of the 1930s.

NOTES

[1] The description was given by the late 'Freddy' Crittenden not long before his homecall. He had asked for it to be anonymous during his lifetime. He was the freshman at Oriel.
[2] See page 130.

Chapter 9

Growth in the universities (1929–1939)

With the gradual recognition of the new national scale to which the movement had grown came increased practical steps for interchanges and mutual support between the universities. Small deputations of students were sent to neighbouring universities and exchanged. In some cases the visits resulted in the beginning of a new Christian Union. This was especially the case in a related educational sphere where groups of two or three undergraduates from a university would visit a neighbouring teachers' training, or technical college. In a later chapter (page 251) reference will be made to the growth of parallel Evangelical movements in these other fields of higher education. Frequently there would be a welcome surprise. As soon as some of the small groups, which had been slowly and nervously feeling their way, were encouraged to come out into the open and make their presence felt by organizing and properly advertising an 'open meeting', they would discover that there were more committed Christians and those interested in 'religion' in their college than they had earlier dared to hope.

A good example was provided by Glasgow. As already described (page 108), a small group, mostly medical students, was bold enough in 1922 to hire the Union Debating Hall and to hold what proved to be something in the nature of 'mass' meetings. The membership of the resulting Glasgow University Christian Student Fellowship grew steadily until, during the presidencies of

John M. Laird (1926–28) and Cyril W. Nye (1928–29), it was well over 200, a significant proportion of the student body at that time. A reliable index to the health of any Christian Union is its attendance at properly led meetings for prayer. Numbers at the short midday daily prayer meeting grew steadily from twenty, to thirty and then to fifty. A larger room had to be found and (out of several possibilities) the students opted for a large basement room in an old building on the opposite side of the road from the University gate and where the library now stands. It was well used for a number of years.

Soon the Glasgow Union's growth in membership became matched by its increasing university influence. In 1928 Bishop Taylor Smith, the ex-Chaplain General of the Forces, was invited by the committee to spend a week in Glasgow. He was put on to speak in the big Union Debating Hall for five successive nights. Attendances were never less than 200–250, and on the Tuesday evening about 500 students sat spell-bound for nearly fifty minutes. The University was clearly deeply impressed and challenged. There were many private interviews between students and the Bishop, or one of the supporting ministers from some of the city churches, who came to assist. During the 1930s Glasgow boldly and frequently repeated such a series of evening meetings with well known evangelistic speakers.

New Christian Unions

During this period the Fellowship was continuing to grow both in the membership of its constituent Unions and also in the number of universities in which Christian students were taking action to found new Unions. In date order, beginnings were reported from Aberystwyth and Dundee (1928); Birmingham and Leeds (1929); Swansea (1930); Durham, Hull and Southampton (1931); Sheffield and Exeter (1933); and Nottingham (1934). Space precludes separate accounts of all of these new circles. Two will serve to illustrate the enterprise which was shown by those who took the initial steps.

Three Birmingham students happened to hear of the Inter-Varsity Conferences and felt sure that they shared the ideals of the students from other universities who had informed them of them. They saved up for the cost of the conference and travelled cheaply by road to the 1929 gathering at High Leigh. Here they met and talked at length with Prof. Rendle Short. He encouraged them to begin to think of starting a similar witness in their own university. They had several talks with him about how to make the start. Eventually they agreed on the wording of a notice which they went back to put up on all the student notice boards. It invited any 'who know Jesus Christ as their personal Saviour and hold the more conservative views of the Christian faith' to meet them on a Saturday afternoon in the reception room of a nearby well known restaurant. They had invited from London the IVF Secretary to be present and briefly indicated the purpose of the meeting. He was instructed to introduce an account of the activities of the Inter-Varsity Fellowship and to ask why an Evangelical Union had not been formed in Birmingham!

About a dozen students arrived. In addition were several graduate sympathizers, including the Senior science mistress of a well known girls school. Some of the students, however, were Birmingham SCM members who had come to protest that there was no need for a new Union, and that anyone interested in the IVF's outlook should form a 'devotional unit' inside their own organization. Being but a visitor, the IVF Secretary found himself in the embarrassing position of being put in the chair and having to induce the seven or eight keen, but inexperienced, students to overcome their shyness and to take some appropriate action for *themselves*. The move had to come from members of their own University. Eventually they took heart and moved that a Union be founded, adopted a provisional draft constitution (to be later revised) and elected for an initial period two officers, a president (N. Sargent, later a CMS missionary) and a secretary (J. de Carteret, later a medical practitioner in the West Indies). With somewhat faulty procedure, to the plaudits of the graduates in the 'gallery' and the questionings and murmurings of the SCM students, all that was necessary was finally completed. Going back in the train to London the question in Ezekiel came into the Secretary's mind, 'Can these dry bones live?' and the reply 'Ah, Lord, Thou knowest'! However, as has happened so often before

151

and since, that 'grain of mustard seed' began vigorously to grow and became quite a large bush. Through the good offices of an affable SCM president it was soon able to gain official recognition by the University. In a year or two it was repeatedly holding impressive open meetings attended by an encouraging number of interested non-members.

In Durham there had been several informal, but short-lived, groups since 1922. It was not until 1931 that a freshman of Bede College, who had attended the Inter-Varsity Conference at High Leigh in that year, returned to Durham to form a men's group in his college. This as usual was moving forward rather uncertainly, when there occurred what can only be called a small 'revival' of religion in one of the women's halls of residence. It happened one Saturday evening during a social 'buffet supper', which had ended in a discussion started by two or three of the Christian women. Soon after the choice of a subject for conversation had been chosen and one of them had suggested 'religion' the whole room became very interested about how one could have spiritual certainty. That evening, and in the following days, altogether about twenty of the women students became committed Christians and their new zeal immediately began to make itself felt. The men's group got to hear of it, the two groups combined and soon a definite Evangelical Union took shape. From then on it was repeatedly able in various ways to bring its witness to bear on the main body of students.

In the subsequent summer some of the Durham men set a fashion for Christian work in the vacations, which was taken up by some of the other Northern England Unions. Beginning in 1932, and continuing up to the outbreak of the 1939 War, they organized vacation 'treks', the object of which was to evangelize some of the villages in the northern counties. The student leaders did not keep lists of 'results', but the leader of the 1932 trek reported that they had to divide up amongst the members of the 'team' the addresses of over 200 correspondents to whom they continued to send letters, Christian literature and Bible reading aids. To some who complained that this work was not witnessing in the University, the leaders always replied that the 'trek' members regularly returned at the beginning of each academic year all the keener and better equipped to influence their fellow-students.

Increased senior support

In the earliest days of the Evangelical Unions there had been comparatively little active support from prominent senior graduates, especially from those who were in more important positions on the university staffs. This had also been largely true in 19th century Cambridge and Oxford. Few of the prominent 'dons' had been prepared to be identified with the Evangelical cause. Also, most of the Christian members of the university staffs tended only to be identified with the college chapel, or with the local branch of the Student Christian Movement. Over the years the student leaders had to learn not to expect too much from their seniors, who mostly followed the contemporary intellectual or ecclesiastical fashions. It was therefore with some surprise that, at the beginning of the 1930s, the leaders of the IVF began to receive letters of encouragement from some of the more distinguished seniors, who even let it be known that they were willing to take the chair at a meeting or to speak. The majority of them were medical consultants and scientists. At first, the youthful pioneers were a little suspicious of such 'patronage'. They failed to make as much use of it as they might have done.

It remained something of an enigma to the SCM leaders, that some of the distinguished seniors were sympathetic to the Evangelicals. They , however, would pass it off with the comment that scientists and medicals, however well trained, would not know any better theologically. For SCM's approach to the Evangelical student leaders when it was pressing for co-operation was often the suggestion (more politely worded) that 'You have a lot of enthusiasm and zeal and we have most of the brains and the money. How much better it would be for us all to work together?' Yet several of those ready to support the Evangelicals were amongst the leading members in their faculties and specialities. When the Cambridge Inter-Collegiate Christian Union came to celebrate in 1927 its fiftieth anniversary, the 'jubilee breakfast' was chaired by the Master of Trinity College, J. J. Thomson, the well-known physicist. It is recorded in his biography that when he had finished working long into the early hours in the Master's library, and before he mounted the iron stairs (which went straight up to his bedroom) it was his habit to pause to read a short passage from a Bible which lay on a small table at the foot of the stairs. He had learnt the habit as an undergraduate from the influence of a friend in the CICCU.

Similarly, at the same anniversary celebrations, the banquet in Caius College was addressed by T. R. Glover, the classical scholar, and Public Orator of the University. He was really a long-standing supporter of the SCM, but he would always defend the basic *message* of the CICCU. A former member of one of the committees of the Senate reported that on one occasion when one of the professors had sneered at some aspect of the CICCU, T. R. Glover commented, 'That may well be, X. But I tell you that those CICCU boys are the only people left in this University who have the courage to tell you that, if ever you are to enter into the Kingdom of God, then Christ said "You must be born anew"!'

In other universities several other respected senior members of staff gave unobtrusive, or sometimes more active, support. From time to time they would speak or write quite strongly urging the student leaders to retain their theologically conservative views of the Bible and to keep alive in their generation all the essential elements of 'the religion of our Lord and the Apostles.' In Edinburgh, Sir William Ramsay, the archaeologist, was especially strong in his support. So, also, in London was the redoubtable Sir Ambrose Fleming (Professor of Electrical Engineering in University College). The latter worked with Marconi when he sent the first message across the Atlantic and his work contributed to the stages in research which helped to make broadcasting possible. A number of the judges and distinguished lawyers were warm in support. These included Sir Thomas Inskip (later, Lord Chancellor and Lord Chief Justice). He remained for many years identified as a Vice-President of the CICCU. Perhaps, however, the faculty from which most senior graduates gave the maximum support was the medical faculty. Only a few names can be mentioned here. The immense service given by A. Rendle Short (later Professor of Surgery in the University of

Bristol) has already been mentioned and was of the greatest importance to the IVF from its beginning.

He was closely followed in the extent of active participation by Duncan McCallum Blair (first Professor of Anatomy in King's College, London and later Regius Professor of Anatomy in Glasgow). There were also Albert Carless (Professor of Surgery in King's College Hospital and joint author of the well-known text-book, Rose and Carless' *Surgery*) and Frederick W. Price (cardiologist and editor of the well-known Price's *Text-Book of Medicine*).

The theological critics of the movement, however, would comment that the IVF's senior supporters counted for little in the world of theology and apologetics, with which the IVF's activities were chiefly concerned. Similarly, the staffs of the Evangelical theological colleges (who were virtually unanimous in support of the IVF) were usually politely discounted as not really being in the front academic ranks. So it was with appropriate gratitude that the IVF leaders received support and encouragement from a few of the more prominent theological teachers. One such was the Very Rev. Professor Lamont (a former Moderator of the Church of Scotland and Professor of Practical Theology in New College, Edinburgh). 'Danny Lamont' was popular with the Edinburgh theological students and he became equally so whenever he spoke at an IVF conference or a CU open meeting. He gave to the IVF publications department one of its early books, *The Anchorage of Life*. His approach to the students was marked by great clarity and he was of direct help with the problems of the interested science and medical students. Before his call to the ministry, Professor Lamont had begun to specialize as a physicist and had worked in the laboratory of Lord Kelvin at Glasgow University.

A President and Vice-Presidents

At length the student leaders awakened to the value which support from the more senior graduates on University staffs could have for their witness.[1] They also lost their fear that the result of senior patronage might be an increasing 'respectability', which would lead to compromise. In 1930 the General Committee

155

made provision for a president (changing annually), to be elected from a list of vice-presidents. The latter were to be elected from, and be representative of, the different faculties. It was also provided that the president should be invited to give a presidential address during his year of office, preferably to be delivered during the main annual Inter-Varsity Conference.

So anxious were the student committees that the graduates, who might have 'become at ease in Zion and less keen in maintaining the faith', should not be an influence for future compromise that a clause was inserted into the Constitution that the vice-presidents should sign the Doctrinal Basis annually. Far from resenting this, the majority of the seniors, and especially some of the most respected of them, have 'gladly and humbly' subscribed to the Doctrinal Basis. Sometimes they have congratulated the committees on 'taking such matters seriously', for the act of signing 'challengingly reminded' them of their 'allegiance to Christ and His Gospel'. Professor Duncan Blair, who dated his conversion from war-time naval days, when a medical officer of a mine sweeper escort off Northern Ireland, used to sign with great enthusiasm and would say, 'I regard it as running up my ensign to the masthead in order to show where my allegiance belongs'.

Other graduate supporters

Assistance from senior graduates or business men was becoming urgently necessary in other ways. The mounting expenditure had become the student treasurer's nightmare. In later years Mrs. Cecil Bewes (née Sylvia Berry) used to comment that, when she was at Cambridge serving as the student treasurer, she used 'to keep all the IVF's financial resources in a biscuit tin in my room in Newnham College'. Her successors had also handled comparatively small sums, which needed to be spent almost as soon as they were received. Professor Rendle Short's annual gift, known as 'the Rendelian cheque', for £20 to pay for the speakers' fares and hospitality at the conference would regularly come on its opening day and be spent soon after its close. Meanwhile the student secretary (with only a small margin available from each term's personal finances) was often contriving out of his own pocket to meet postages, printing bills and the costs of roneo circulars. On top of this the Executive Committee had added what was becoming a minor magazine circulation. At last he was reluctantly forced to admit to the Committee that, at least, *his own* faith and finances were beginning to give out. He suggested that more practical financial arrangements were necessary or else the budding George Müllers and Hudson Taylors would have to take over the treasureship and secretaryship themselves. For everybody, though admirably 'full of faith' when they met in committee, were not all that much good when the next lot of bills came in.

The Committee began to discuss whether Heaven had ever intended an organization of this type to be run and financed by what at the time were known as 'faith methods', that is, without any public 'appeal' and mentioning financial need only in prayer as in the story of the China Inland Mission (Overseas Missionary Fellowship) or George Müller's orphan homes in Bristol. Following a rather emotional and confused discussion of a principle which the student delegates did not really understand, the 1928 General Committee agreed to seek senior graduate aid and to ask Professor A. Rendle Short and Mr. Clarence Foster to become the honorary co-treasurers. The latter, being resident in London, was yoked to Professor Rendle Short so that he would deal with the minor day-to-day details. The change not only lifted the rapidly increasing burden from student shoulders, but also gave greater confidence to any potential subscribers who might think of donating more substantially. The two senior treasurers rose nobly to the occasion. 'The Rendelian cheque' regularly arrived almost up to the year of the donor's death. To it were apt to be added further 'Rendelian' cheques such as the one for the Cunard fares in the 'emergency' of Howard Guinness's first journey to Canada. The treasurers also began to interest graduates and business men some of whom had members of their own families up at the universities and so had a direct reason for being interested in the work of the IVF.

The advice of business men

It was only a matter of a year before new initiatives, all involving expenditure and a moral obligation towards any graduate willing to offer voluntary service between the time of graduation and the beginning of his professional career, called for experienced planning and further attention to finance. The necessity came to be recognized in two stages. First, it was already obvious that more adequate office and secretarial arrangements were needed. Second, there was an increasingly urgent call for the early appointment of a graduate travelling representative, or representatives.

In the June of 1931 a joint meeting was called to bring together representatives of the student Executive Committee and some of the graduate supporters. The students present were Kenneth Hooker (Chairman), J. G. Billington (Missionary Secretary), Geoffrey Lehman (Vice-Chairman) and Miss Jean Strain (Representative for Women Students), who acted as minutes secretary in the absence in the West Country of the secretary, Douglas Johnson, who was at the time completing 'house appointments' at the Bristol General Hospital. The graduates and business men present were Mr. Lindsay Glegg (in the chair), Mr. F. D. Bacon, Mr. F. Kidner, the Rev. G. T. Manley, Dr. W. Loudon Strain, Commander Ronald G. Studd, Mr. J. Tetley (representing Dr. Thomas Cochrane) and the Rev. C. H. Harding Wood. Reports were given by the students of Howard Guinness's journeys in the overseas universities and evidence of the promising situation in many of the home universities. To the graduates and business men it seemed obvious that it was only finance which was holding up many potentially successful developments in an area of Christian witness of great potential importance. Commander Studd, members of whose family, C. T. Studd and Kynaston Studd, had made such great personal contributions to the Christian movements in the universities at the end of the 19th century urged, 'Let us press forward. I believe that spiritual revival is coming, and coming through the Universities. If this is the Lord's wish, surely the money will be forthcoming.' This summarized the general mood of the meeting.

It was unanimously agreed to recommend to the Executive Committee an immediate budget of £1,250 for the forthcoming year.[2] This included provision for (1) the renting of a one-roomed office, (which, with rates and other costs, would require £250); (ii) the appointment of a part-time graduate secretary (with an honorarium of £150 p.a.), and (iii) an invitation to Dr. Howard Guinness to become for three years travelling secretary with a roving commission at home or overseas (with an honorarium of £300 p.a. and £400 for travelling expenses). As it was said that he had 'a gift for writing letters', it was recommended that Douglas Johnson should be strongly urged to postpone offering for overseas missionary service and to give three years to IVF as part-time secretary in order to lay the foundations for a really national organization supporting the university Christian Unions.

At a later stage, during the chairmanship of the Executive Committee of Geoffrey Lehmann (an engineering graduate from Oxford, who had transferred to medicine and was at University College Hospital) the Executive Committee agreed to invite a few interested business men to form a business advisory committee. In 1932, with Mr. Lindsay Glegg in the chair, six business men who were representative of several types of financial and industrial experience, began the many years of service which has been given by the Business Advisory Committee in supervising the financial and business side of the IVF's work.

Theological problems and general policy

Advice from senior graduate friends of the movement had long been gained in another form. From the year 1922/3 during the early development of the Inter-Varsity conference, a small advisory body had been appointed composed of those experienced in university Christian activities, amongst whom Dr. Stuart Holden (Vicar of St. Paul's, Portman Square) Mr. (later Professor) Rendle Short of Bristol and the Rev. H. Earnshaw Smith had been the most prominent and active. When the Fellowship's constitution was drawn up in 1928 provision for such an Advisory Committee was enshrined in the document. It was designed to provide for the benefit of wisdom and experience

159

in matters of theological difficulty and general policy. The first members were Clarence H. M. Foster, MA, J. Stuart Holden, MA, DD, J. Russell Howden, BD, W. Graham Scroggie, BD, A. Rendle Short, MD, FRCS, and H. Earnshaw Smith, MA. Added later were Professor Duncan Blair MD, (Glasgow), Archdeacon T. C. Hammond, MA, BD (Dublin) and the Rev. D. Martyn Lloyd-Jones, MD, MRCP (Minister of Westminster Chapel).

It would be impossible to over-emphasize the part which was played by members of this committee in the years when the student committees were sailing in uncharted waters. It also says a great deal for the wisdom and the forbearance of these seniors that, throughout, they cautiously offered advice when it was sought and then left it to the student and other committees freely to make up their own minds. At times successive generations of student leaders have accepted only some of the advice given. They have usually discovered, however, that, in the event, it might have been better to have followed suggestions from experienced advisers more closely.

The office and secretaryship

With growing correspondence, an increasing amount of it from abroad, it became clearer than ever that the Fellowship needed to have a fixed address, other than the Hon. Secretary's lodgings. For example, the number of published booklets was expanding and the Committee wished to increase this publishing side. By the summer of 1932 the Hon. Secretary had come to the end of his second hospital appointment and could no longer postpone a decision concerning the next step. The recommendations of the joint meeting in June described above (page 158), between representatives of the student Executive and senior supporters brought matters to a head.

The Secretary, on receiving the communication which suggested that he should postpone offering to a missionary society, consulted Professor Rendle Short. At other times the latter's well known zeal in recruiting junior doctors for overseas medical missions would have come into full play. On this occasion he seemed unusually reserved. Perhaps he perceived correctly that the would-be candidate's medical value to a developing country was negligible! In the end his attitude seemed to be, 'Perhaps you should think in terms of staying at home, building up the IVF and sending as many as you can to fill the vacancies in the field. Does this not constitute a sufficient "call"?' The Secretary said as he left, 'Well, what shall I say at the Judgment Seat at the end of the day if I am asked why I did not after all go to the Mission Field?' To which Professor Rendle Short, shutting one eye, as he often did for such pleasantries, replied, 'Oh, you just leave that to me'.

Back in London the Secretary found that, as there was little money in the treasurer's keeping, the student Executive Committee had been compelled to adopt (in rather a modified form) the recommendations of the business meeting. It resolved that 'a part-time General Secretary be paid at the rate of £150 p.a., *subject to the money's being in hand*, and that the appointment be considered to have commenced on September 1st.'[2] It was also clear that the London Co-treasurer, in view of the realities of an empty exchequer, was in no mood for steps to lease even a one-roomed office at that stage. One of the student Unions' representatives in General Committee had earlier in the year objected that '*paid* secretarial help would be injurious to the work and detract from its spirituality.' At that time, also, even part-time typing help was virtually out of the question.

The Secretary, to make some use of his medical training, had meanwhile taken steps (in co-operation with a local committee of interested people) to open the Landsdowne Place Medical Mission in a former 'Ragged School' to serve an underprivileged and under-doctored area in 'the Borough' near Tower Bridge.

Then came what was, at least personally for the Secretary, the turning point. He had been discussing with the editor of the Inter-Varsity Magazine (F. Donald Coggan),[3] the vicious circle in which on the one hand there were no funds to stimulate action, whilst on the other those who had promised to be interested were not subscribing because there seemed no action to indicate the need. They later walked down Southampton Row and were discussing the lack of a good fixed address. The editor had just asked 'How much would one room cost, for the sake of the address?' when they found themselves at Russell Square and were looking at the open door of an estate agent's office. They decided to go in to ask. Behind the counter was someone they knew, Paul Broomhall, later a chartered surveyor, who was in his first 'trainee' appointment. On explaining their quest he replied, 'Oh, I have just the job for you, a large room on the 2nd Floor along in the corner of the Square. All you need to do is to pay £50 annual rent *in advance* and put down a deposit of £50 (which is really another year's rent in advance, in case you default next year!)'. The room was at once inspected. The editor suggested, 'It is a good address. Let's book the room and then tell the Committee we've done it! I'll put down £50, if you can do the other fifty.'

The room was booked and 43 Russell Square, W1, became the first address of the IVF. Suitable apologies and a defence were prepared to mollify the Co-treasurers and Committee. But, as usual, they were not needed, for once it was done, the Committee congratulated itself on both the welcome event and its own foresight. When some members of the Committee met on 12 October 1932 to dedicate the use of the room to God's service, it was the chief member of the section of the Committee who had objected to immediate action who brought a visitors' book for use at the office. On the first page he had had typed an inscription which recorded the committee's thanksgiving at God's provision of the first office for the Fellowship!

Members of the Committee now began to contribute an assortment of chairs, filing cabinets and other necessary articles. One bought a large roll-top desk (£4) and an old-fashioned adjustable dining-table for committees (£2), acquired from a junk-shop in the Old Kent Road. A beginning of something like office work at last began to look possible.

Clerical help at the office

It was, however, far from clear how the office could be manned. For, as had been vaguely feared, the Medical Mission in the Borough soon attracted hundreds of patients from the (at that time) under-doctored area and these soon invaded most of the Secretary's day, except when he could escape into central London in the mid-afternoon for the IVF work. The situation, however, was met through the generosity of Dr. Loudon Strain of Wimbledon, who encouraged his daughter, Jean,[4] who had just completed her training at Bedford College, London, to occupy the office in the mornings and to give as much (honorary) clerical assistance as was possible. The months of work which she was able to offer at that transitional period proved crucial to the Fellowship's development into a growing national organization with appropriate staffing.

It was not long, however, before this valuable honorary worker began to show her value as a speaker in the women's colleges and for the leadership of women students' study groups. The number of pressing invitations from the women's colleges increased. The need for these visits was obvious to all, and the Executive Committee was soon compelled to face the fact that Jean Strain's gifts could be more suitably and profitably employed in these directions. It was, therefore, unanimously agreed to appoint her as the first (honorary) women's travelling secretary and to release her from the office to give as much time as she could to this more important field work.

The Secretary struggled on for some time longer, torn between the ever more insistent calls of both of the worlds he was trying to serve. At last, in 1934, it was possible to appoint a doctor, just returned from the mission field, to be full-time medical superintendent at the Medical Mission. The IVF committees were also able to authorize the appointment at the office of a full-time clerical secretary. Miss Mary Milton-Thomson,[5] daughter of the Vicar of Emmanuel Church, Croydon, who had just completed her secretarial training, offered and was appointed. Subsequently, she was able to give outstanding and conscientious service to the Fellowship for a period of over fifteen years, including the difficult years of the War.

Travelling secretaries

The number of Unions was still growing and their greater evangelistic activity led to increased requests for visits from graduate speakers. The smaller Unions could not command the list of well-known speakers who were prepared to give week-ends to the larger Unions. As mentioned above, the Rev. H. Earnshaw Smith (part-time 1923–26), Hugh R. Gough (1927) and Norman Grubb (1929) and Kenneth Hooker (1929–30) had already demonstrated the value of travelling secretaries' visits. They had established that it was in the best interests of the Fellowship to maintain a succession of travelling secretaries, both men and women.

When, in 1930, Howard Guinness at last turned for home and arrived back in January 1931 after two years' absence as the IVF's emissary in Canada and Australasia, the committees had virtually come to regard him as their permanent travelling secretary, sometimes at home, but often 'at large'. He continued to serve the Fellowship in this way for the next seven years and to visit the home universities when not on international journeys. This arrangement continued until he resigned in April 1938 to begin to prepare for ordination. Owing to lack of experience, however, the committees at first were to meet a big disappointment. Unaware of how tiring such overseas travel can be, they had arranged a tour in the home universities beginning far too soon after his arrival in the Lent Term of 1931, leading up, as they thought, to the April conference. Guinness's nervous reserves had by now been exhausted, however, and his over-taxed voice began to give out. This home tour had to be cancelled. Later, however, after several months rest and light work he was to bring much inspiration and challenge to the university Christian Unions and at the conferences. He was working full-time in the British universities mainly in 1932, 1935 and 1937 and altogether he was working at home in this way for the equivalent of some three and a half years.

Just as the committees were faced with the loss of Howard Guinness, who seemed irreplaceable, it became possible in 1937 to invite Rev. Hugh Evan Hopkins (a former CICCU President), on his return from Dohnavur, India, to devote two years to the universities before he too went into the parochial ministry in 1939. Similarly, on the women's side, when marriage claimed Jean Strain from the Fellowship, Norah Nixon (a graduate of Westfield College), who had had experience in deputation work in the Zenana Bible and Medical Mission, became available. It is scarcely possible to do justice to the thorough and unobtrusive work which Norah Nixon subsequently gave to the Fellowship in a number of capacities. In turn she was women's travelling secretary, Graduates' Fellowship women's secretary and study secretary and, during the war, virtually editorial secretary working on the proofs of such new publications as paper rationing permitted during the war years. She will be most remembered for her friendship and assistance to many overseas women students through the IVF's Overseas Students Department.

The first travelling secretary in Scotland was Alistair Rennie, appointed in 1937.

Greater outreach

The whole of this period under review was one of rapid growth. The very small central 'team' was never quite able to match the opportunity. The majority of the Unions steadily grew in membership, and the scope of their activities constantly widened through bolder initiatives and more imaginative experiments. At first there had been a tendency to take it for granted in the smaller civic universities that full-scale missions were only possible in those cities where all, or most, of the students were resident in the colleges, as at Oxford and Cambridge. But, as the news of successful experiments in publicity spread through reports in the magazine or conversation at conferences, more of the Unions began to attempt to speak to the whole student public. Some Unions boldly advertised open meetings which were addressed by some well-known speaker of repute, whilst others, who had in their membership those with the necessary skills, attempted various forms of discussion and debate. Perhaps the most successful in their own way were the informal 'squashes', which were held over tea or coffee at suitable times in student rooms in the halls of residence.

Some Unions, which could not manage a mission or campaign, had marked success with two or three short meetings on consecutive nights addressed by an appropriate speaker. The Christian Unions in the following universities were at this period successful with such a series; Belfast, Birmingham, Bristol, Dublin, Durham, Edinburgh, Glasgow, Leeds and Newcastle. A

165

welcome comment in many of the reports on student activities during these years was that this or that Union had been compelled 'to find bigger rooms' for their members' meetings and 'bigger halls for their Open Meetings'. A few examples of such initiatives can be given.

Several Christian Unions, Oxford, Cambridge, Cardiff, Durham and King's College, London, were enterprising enough to run open air meetings for some years on a Saturday or Sunday, or in a week-day lunch hour. Some of these took place in the neighbourhood of their colleges. One lunch hour in 1929 the editor of the former daily paper *The Morning Post*, which in those days was much read by many of the Church of England clergy, happened to see from his window a crowd gathering in the street below. It was due to the King's College medical students' conducting an open air meeting in the disused half of Aldwych. He went down to see what it was all about. He addressed the next day's leading article to any of the clergy who were discouraged by empty pews. They were advised to imitate the Christian students from King's College, who came out on to the streets 'earnestly pleading with the crowd' to come to Christ.

At first the Bible Union in the Queen's University of Belfast did not receive recognition from the authorities and so were unable to meet in Queen's buildings. They were not long daunted. First they ran a very successful mission, led by Captain Wallis of Dublin, in the nearby YMCA building. On the crest of a wave of enthusiasm and with the borrowed leadership of Mr. Tom Scott, they started an open air meeting each Sunday evening of term at the main gate of the University. Later on, having been recognized as a university society, they were able to hold their freshers' meeting annually in the Great Hall. Up to 150–200 new students were addressed in successive years by speakers such as Dr. Howard Guinness, Capt. J. W. McCormack, Mr. Montagu Goodman and Dr. J. H. Gillespie.

London University, with its 40 or more colleges scattered over many square miles, constituted a permanent geographical problem for the LIFCU leaders. Therefore central meetings remained comparatively few. The emphasis needed to fall on the local strength of the Christian Union in each college. Yet in each academic year a number of successful united meetings were attempted. In the Autumn of 1935 a particularly well planned bid was made to reach the whole University. That year's committee, led by James Broomhall,[6] organized a full-scale University mission under the title 'Out of World Chaos'. An assistant missioner was attached to each of over 30 LIFCU branches for the week for mid-day meetings and personal consultations. In the evenings united central meetings took place in two of the best placed great halls of the colleges. Throughout that week 'religion' was certainly the chief talking point in most of the colleges and hospitals and by the end of the week there had been an impressive total of enquiries concerning the Christian faith. Each of the missioners knew of a number of definite decisions for Christ. As a result of requests after the mission for a short book which would make clear the teaching of Christianity, the LIFCU committee urged on the IVF the need for the early production of a book on Christian doctrine addressed to a sincere student enquirer. The result was what would become one of the Inter-Varsity Press's best sellers – the study book on Christian doctrine entitled *In Understanding be Men* by Archdeacon T. C. Hammond.

The mention of the publication of this cloth-bound book of 248 pages, which sold widely for the princely sum of half a crown(!), calls for a further reference to the growing number of publications bearing the IVF imprint. Compared with the position a few years earlier (page 146) when eight booklets represented the total output, there had been several further successful publishing ventures which had attracted considerable attention. Whilst the Business Advisory Committee still adhered to its view that it was only right and necessary for the IVF to publish under its own imprint the manuscripts of special relevance to the student world, there was a growing number of supporters who pointed out the great lack at the time of suitable Christian books for educated young people generally. It was emphasized that this offered a wider market, which would assist in keeping the prices low for students as well as creating more capital for future titles if a 'profit' were made. Besides the popularity of *In Understanding be Men* there had been wide sales of such earlier publishing ventures as *The Quiet Time* (1933), *The Bible and Modern Research* by Professor A. Rendle Short (1933), *Effective Witness*,

167

edited by F. Houghton (1933) and *Christ and the Colleges*, a history of the IVF edited by F. D. Coggan (1934).

The interest and suggestions, elicited by such quickly selling titles, led to further discussions in committee and consultations with Mr. A. W. Churchill, the Managing Director of J. & A. Churchill, the Medical Publishers, who became a member of the Business Advisory Committee. Eventually these business advisers came to the view that a Publications Secretary should be appointed and capital set aside for the careful development of an IVF literature, which could also sell to interested young people in the churches generally. Eventually in the Autumn of 1936, Ronald Inchley, a graduate who had been one of the early leaders in the Birmingham University Evangelical Christian Union, was appointed as the first Publications Secretary. He was given the task of developing the IVF's publications department which eventually became the Inter-Varsity Press. He himself has outlined its history in Chapter 18 (page 314).

Larger conferences

Pressure on space at the annual conference continued to grow. Students booking late had often to be disappointed. Some (not realizing the difficulty for the catering staff and pressure on dining-room space when extras to the number of residents expected meals) would come at the last minute in vans[7] adapted for use as dormobiles. Some also came ready to sleep in tents, forgetting that early April is rarely suitable camping weather. High Leigh was plainly too small, even after allowing for a drop in attendances from Scotland with the growth in popularity of their own conference at Bonskeid near Pitlochry. Larger numbers were now customary. From 1935 it was, therefore, unanimously decided to book the whole of the very much larger centre at the Hayes, Swanwick, Derbyshire. The IVF never had reason to regret that decision and, except for the War years, when the Hayes was a prisoner of war camp, the annual conference has remained there. It has seldom failed to approach the full use of the capacity.

In addition to their general conferences few Christian organizations are without their study conferences. It was during the 1930s that the IVF came to have an array of supplementary special conferences in addition to those at Swanwick and Bonskeid. First in order came the conferences for missionary study, then the theological students' conference. Meanwhile, a parallel student movement was arising in the teacher-training colleges and there was soon an annual Training Colleges Christian Union conference. Various regions, too, because of the travelling and other costs, found that they could attract a greater number of students to local week-end conferences. The first Northern England conference was held over a week-end in 1933 at Heightside, Rossendale, Lancs. with the CMS missionaries Mr. and Mrs. George Ingram as host and hostess.

The most important of all the additional conferences was to be the Leaders' Conference. The main conferences needed to give basic Christian teaching for the sake of many students who were attending for the first time and who had perhaps been converted recently through a mission. As a result the needs of committee members and the planning of the work of the Unions received too little attention. The suggestion, therefore, arose that a conference should be arranged for leaders in early September, in time to put the leaders into gear for the commencement of the new academic year. Membership of this conference was confined to those on the committees of their Unions. The first of these conferences took place in 1934 at Carey Hall, Birmingham. In subsequent years (except in wartime) the Leaders' Conference took place at Swanwick.

City missions

For many years the 'recognized' summer vacation activities for Evangelical students were the three weeks of seaside services in August run by the Children's Special Service Missions or Scripture Union; but with the growth of the Christian Unions there was a considerable excess in the numbers of students available. Also students in more recent times were unable to afford the cost of the traditional-style house-parties. Numerous new plans, therefore, emerged concerning the best use of 'unemployed Christians' during the long vacation.

One of the most popular activities in the 1930s was to take part in parish missions. The first was organized in Birmingham in September 1934 and led by the Rev. Hugh R. Gough. The five teams were based on one centre, Bishop Ryder's Church, but their activities spread out into the areas of four of the surrounding parishes and a Free Church. The deputy leader was the Rev. L. F. E. Wilkinson. As Hugh Gough was not free for 1935, L. F. E. Wilkinson, assisted by Miss Edris Ellis,[8] became the leader of this and subsequent annual missions. Sometimes these were large, taking in as many as twelve parishes and Free Churches, as at Nottingham. Before the Second World War student parish missions took place in Birmingham (1934), Sheffield (1935), Leeds (1936), Nottingham (1937), Derby (1938). The Liverpool mission (1939), about to begin, was cancelled on the outbreak of war.

In the post-war years Welsh and Scottish students began to organize similar campaigns in a number of their cities and towns, from which the ministers had united to send joint invitations. Many students learnt on these missions how to spread the gospel and to counsel young Christians. They returned to the universities to carry forward more effectively their witness to fellow students.

New offices

The progress of the 1930s had not been without its severe pressures on the small office and very small full-time staff at 43 Russell Square. After a year, however, it had been possible to add to the room two others in the building which became free. The beginning of a new policy of expansion of the publications department meant that a larger stock had to be ready for use at the office. The committees reached another of the seeming impasses with which their history has been strewn. Then, as so often in the long story, the man for the occasion appeared.

Mr. J. W. Laing (later Sir John Laing), chairman of the company of building contractors, John Laing & Son, was introduced to the IVF by a member of the Business Advisory Committee and consented to join it. His interest in IVF had been deeply aroused by having put into his hands by Mr. F. D. Bacon, of the Crusaders Union, the recently published IVF book *Christ and the Colleges,* edited by F. D. Coggan (see page 168). With his usual skill in spotting possible developments he decided that this movement had great potential and deserved support. He became one of its best and most reliable friends.

Paul Broomhall, who had been successful in the discovery of the original room, was immediately despatched to the University area of Bloomsbury with plans to house the next phase of office growth. He advised taking a lease from the Bedford Estate of a part of 39 Bedford Square, which later was exchanged for the headlease. This building served as the office of the Fellowship from 1936 until 1976.

The further effect of the Business Advisory Committee's new vigilance was that it was discovered that the few pounds of the 'salary' of the secretary, and sometimes of the rest of the workers, was in arrears, and often near to being unpaid. This was particularly so in the months of June to September, because immediately the universities broke up for long vacation everyone forgot the IVF until the freshers arrived for the new academic year in October! Three business men proceeded to give guarantees to the bank manager to ensure that the rent could be always promptly paid and the salaries, especially in the Long Vacation, were not to be in arrears. This aspect of support became vital shortly afterwards with evacuation of offices from London and the temporary reduction in subscriptions to Christian societies during the strains of the war years.

NOTES

[1] The British students at the time did not realize the full significance of letters received from Professor Karl Heim of Tübingen. He sent messages and wrote before, and twice after, the 1939–45 war years encouraging the IVF not to weaken in its grasp on the authority of the Bible and the central place which the death of Christ should occupy in its message.

[2] In those days this seemed a very large sum to the student committee.

[3] Later Bishop of Bradford, Archbishop of York and Archbishop of Canterbury.

[4] Later Mrs. Donald Coggan.

5 Later Mrs. Baring-Young of Canberra.
6 Later Dr. James Broomhall of the China Inland Mission.
7 One year at a later Conference a student party from a northern university arrived with a hearse which had been converted into a dormobile!
8 Later Mrs. Howard Rose.

Chapter 10

International relations (1929–1939)

From 1929 the international influence of the IVF steadily grew. As described above (p. 164) Howard Guinness's overseas visits became extended, and what had been intended to be a single journey to Canada developed into his becoming the Fellowship's travelling secretary at home and overseas. During the ten years from the end of 1928 until 1938 he spent much of his time abroad. The influence of the movement is best illustrated by tracing some of the more important of Guinness's journeys and the beginning of the IVF's links with continental Europe.

Before Guinness had arrived in the English-speaking countries of the Commonwealth there were already the beginnings of Evangelical witness in the universities of Canada, Australia and New Zealand. In 1926 a small evangelical Christian Union had come into being in Vancouver and, shortly afterwards, a similar start had been made in the University of Western Ontario. In Sydney a number of committed Christians amongst the medical and theological students had begun each mid-day to climb the many steps leading to the room under the bells of the University for what became known as 'the Tower Room Meeting'. It was for united prayer. The timing of these brief meetings needed to be controlled with some care otherwise the War Memorial Carillon effectively drowned the rest of the proceedings. By 1927 this group became more active, adopting the name 'the Sydney

University Bible Union' (a name which was later changed to 'the Sydney University Evangelical Union' on Howard Guinness's advice). One of the chief effects of the arrival of the British visitor in these and other universities was to encourage the Christians to venture more boldly into the planning of activities to reach the main body of students.

Howard Guinness's evangelistic tours

After leaving Britain for Canada in November 1928 (see above p. 144), Guinness spent the next 14 months crossing and recrossing the Dominion, with several weeks spent in the more difficult and less hospitable maritime provinces. He also initiated the 'Pioneer Camp' for senior schoolboys, which steadily grew year by year under Canadian student and graduate leadership. In more recent years it has become one of the best run camps of its kind in Canada. On reaching Vancouver for the second time in late 1929 he received a pressing invitation from Mr. J. B. Nicholson of Sydney to continue his journey from Vancouver on across the Pacific to Australia. Mr. Nicholson offered his own home as base for making university visits. Guiness, therefore, went on to Sydney and in 1930 spent a further nine months travelling in the universities and schools chiefly of New South Wales, Victoria and Queensland. During this period three more of the Australian universities, in addition to that at Sydney, came to have Evangelical Unions.

From Australia Guinness crossed to New Zealand for two months. It was not the right time for the visit as the universities were in the long vacation. Activities were necessarily very restricted. However, a medical practitioner in Auckland, Dr. W. H. Pettit, who had earlier prompted some Christian students to start a small group calling itself the Student Bible League, meeting in a room of the YMCA, was not willing to let the opportunity pass. He encouraged a few students who were still around to organize a not-soon-forgotten meeting in the Town Hall. A large audience was addressed by Guinness, who graphically described what was happening in other parts of the student world. Interest and enthusiasm rose to a high pitch. The student leaders changed the name of their group to the Auckland Evangelical Students' Fellowship, and began to make it live up to its name. Among the results were a series of open evangelistic meetings addressed by prominent speakers, and special occasions such as a lunch addressed by Bishop Howard Mowll of West China and later Archbishop of Sydney. An Auckland graduate, reporting on this, comments that Bishop Mowll gave 'a clear-ringing testimony that was a great stimulus to us'. It was the zeal of the Auckland students which spread the movement to the universities of the South Island.

Guinness returned to Britain via Vancouver, endeavouring to strengthen the Canadian Unions on his way home. He finally arrived at Southampton in early January 1931, after a little more than two years' absence. After a year at home, he was again on the move. In 1933, for ten days, he revisited the main centres in Canada and crossed the Pacific (during one day ashore holding a rousing meeting in Auckland) to Australia. On his second tour of Australia, Christian Unions were founded in Adelaide and Perth, so that representatives of all six Australian universities joined later in the founding of the Inter-Varsity Fellowship of Australia in 1936. In spite of the great distances between the university cities effective links were forged and have been maintained. On the way home from Australia, at the invitation of some evangelical leaders in the SCM of India (which at that time was still theologically conservative), he travelled for six months of 1934 in India addressing university audiences. In 1936–7 he returned to India for a further seven months and on this occasion was also asked to speak at several of the great Evangelical conventions in South India.

The South African leaders, on hearing of the success of the India tour in 1935, sent a request that a similar tour should be made for the Student Christian Association of South Africa. Dr. Frank Liebenberg, the General Secretary of the SCA, explained that the SCA had been affiliated from its earliest days to the World Student Christian Federation. It was therefore indirectly linked to the British SCM. But it was emphasized that its original basis was unchanged and that it regarded itself as being in the same evangelical tradition as the IVF. This was amply confirmed

175

by graduate ex-members of the IVF, such as Frank Millard, who was an Oxford graduate serving in South Africa as General Secretary of the Scripture Union. They urged that it was the 'message', not any new organization, that was needed and would be welcomed everywhere. Arrangements were made, therefore, for Guinness to be loaned to the SCA. He gave seven months to this tour and his visits both to colleges and schools proved extremely fruitful. The sound doctrinal teaching of the South Africa churches only needed Guinness's typically clear and direct message to bring many students and schoolboys to decision for Christ. A number of the undergraduates and senior schoolboys, who at that time professed conversion, later became prominent in the Christian life of the Republic.

All the while the IVF's contacts with student movements in the universities of continental Europe were increasing. Here again, between his world journeys, Guinness's ambassadorial powers were put to good use. He was an ideal leader for the student parties which the IVF began to dispatch to the European universities and student camps. A list of the more important of the journeys during Howard Guinness's fruitful ten years of service indicates the growing international influence of the IVF:

The Commonwealth	*Europe*
1928–29 Canada	1933 Spain
1930 Australia and New Zealand	1934 Norway (1st International Conference)
1933 Australia and New Zealand	1935 Sweden (2nd International Conference)
1934 India	1937 Finland
1936 South Africa and India	Hungary (3rd International Conference)
	Switzerland and Belgium

Spiritual gains from the tours

The benefit of such visits from evangelistic student and graduate leaders to students are well illustrated in Howard Guinness's diaries. In the first place introspective cosy groups of Christians, which could so easily be content with attractive Bible studies and prayer for their own spiritual development, are stimulated to venture into various types of experiment to reach the main student body. Then, beginning with the local situation and later on a more national scale, the indigenous leaders are discovered and drawn into the activities which will give full rein to their gifts and future usefulness. In countries where the Christian groups are small, and they are surrounded by those of other faiths, the leaders are given great encouragement. For they are made to feel that they belong to a worldwide movement of Christians in their age group. Publications, too, may play their part. Several illustrations will be given.

Late in 1933 an Australian clinical medical student, whose parents were missionaries on the mainland of Asia, began to find himself succumbing to the scientific materialism of the hospital environment. He was gradually drifting from his Christian moorings. He was aware of how much he had owed to the faith of his parents but the question arose whether their old-fashioned faith had now been outmoded by advances in modern knowledge. Then one day he happened to go into the common room and found a new British journal lying on the table, the *Inter-Varsity Magazine*. Later he found that Guinness had sent it to one of the more active Christians in the medical school. On looking at the list of academic supporters of the IVF, to his great surprise, he saw the names of the Editors of the two text books he was using, Professor Albert Carless and Dr. Frederick W. Price. A few days later Howard Guinness arrived with his contagious advocacy of the faith of this student's upbringing. Guinness also told of many students all round the world who were sharing in new enthusiasm for Christ. This student promptly halted the drift and later became one of the leaders of the Australian Fellowship.

Until Guinness's first visit the small Union in Vancouver had not attempted to influence any beyond its own membership. He soon showed the members how they could reach out and described what other students were doing elsewhere. They were encouraged in an attempt to bring their friends to a well organized public meeting and were surprised by the results. For they discovered many more sympathetic Christians in the University

177

and these were only too glad to join in as soon as there were worthwhile activities. They also had several conversions at their first meeting and this occurrence continued to be a feature of later meetings. The Vancouver Union did not look back, but became one of the strongest of the Canadian Unions in active evangelism.

Then Guinness seemed to have a penchant for meeting people on trains, buses and other forms of transport, who were to prove key persons for his projects. Returning to the east of Canada from Vancouver on a Canadian Pacific train, he had planned to stop off at Winnipeg in order to see if any interest could be aroused in the University. He wrote 'On the train was the senior student of the Anglican theological college in the city. He related to me how during the summer of 1928, whilst on a vacation charge of a prairie church, he had an experience amounting to a new conversion. . . . He came to a new peace of heart and the power of the Spirit had filled his life since. In college there was a spirit of seeking and he had become the centre of a group of students. . . . Before we parted at the station he took the name, address and telephone number of where I was staying. I was just beginning to get to know my new host and hostess and their family when the phone went – "Dr. Guinness, the men want you to come over right away tonight. They are tremendously eager . . ." After the meal, I apologized to the family and explained why, and where, I was going. . . . When I reached the senior student's room I found it crowded with over a dozen men. . . . I spoke for an hour and then they began to ask questions . . . up to 11 pm. By midnight at least five were rejoicing in the liberty and grace of Christ.' The hostess was telephoned to say that they were retaining their guest for the night. The senior student slept on the floor and gave the visitor his bed. Guinness adds, 'From that beginning a movement of God's Spirit spread right through the University and resulted in the years that followed in a strong Winnipeg Varsity Christian Union.'

There were similar occasions in Australia. On his first visit to Brisbane, Guinness had been given the names of only two students in Emmanuel College as likely to be in sympathy. These, however, managed to persuade one of the professors to put his name to an invitation to a meeting on Sunday evening and to promise to chair it. The diary records, 'I have just had an amazing meeting. Ninety people turned up at the YMCA – professors, university students and graduates, for example, school-teachers. The power of God was clearly present. I spoke for some eighty-five minutes (!) on the "new birth". About sixty remained for an after meeting ... and several of the students stood up to say that they wished to accept Christ that very night. They were also at an early morning prayer meeting the next day.'

'This Brisbane group then went ahead, on its own, to arrange a welcome for Freshers in the Canberra hotel. About sixty of them came. The leaders had not invited a special speaker for the occasion and the student leaders ran the whole thing themselves, speaking from their own personal experience of Christ. This, of course, cut much more ice than any outside speaker would have done. It put the members, especially those who had done the speaking, in a strong position to get alongside the freshers at a deeper level.'

On the second tour in Australia (1933) Guinness was accompanied by three, sometimes four, Australian graduates. These were Lindsay Grant, Stafford Young, Robert Haines and Paul White, when the latter's medical duties permitted. This was important. For it soon became clear that Australia had plenty of leadership. It was only a case of deciding where to encourage them to put their 'drive'.

Guinness later wrote, 'At Sydney, two things stand out vividly in one's memory – a hotel reception and a later house party. The host at the Sunday evening reception in a hotel was a leading surgeon of the city. The response to his invitation was overwhelming. After the address in the packed ballroom, many surrendered to Christ especially after personal conversations with the speaker and other Christian graduates and students. No one seemed to want to go home that night! Exactly the same sort of thing happened at a house party at Thirroul where at least twenty-five per cent of those who came were not known to be Christians. On the first evening we started by giving everyone a chance to say why they had come. This produced statements so deep and challenging that we found ourselves commencing the week-end at the place where often in the past we had sometimes finished. The

179

spirit of prayer was tremendous.'

In Melbourne, Lindsay Grant and Guinness were received in the colleges so enthusiastically that time seemed to cease to matter. 'Night after night we would be discussing basic Christianity until the early hours of the morning, and once we had to get a taxi home at 3.30 am. Also, the hotel receptions for school boys and girls were packed to the doors. These younger listeners were electric in their interest and deep concern.' A number of those who made their commitment to Christ during those unforgettable evenings went on later to prove themselves strong leaders in their university Christian Unions.

The outcome in the commonwealth

So far as the English-speaking countries are concerned there can be no doubt that Howard Guinness's visits provided the needed stimulus which encouraged a number of the university groups to adopt measures and practical methods which have enabled them to develop into strong national movements. By the Autumn of 1929 the Inter-Varsity Christian Fellowship of Canada had been organized, with Arthur Hill (President of the Evangelical Union of Western Ontario University) as President of the committee and Arnold Hart-Davies (President of the Toronto Inter-Collegiate Church Union) as Vice-President. At first, Kenneth Hooker (former CICCU President and Chairman of the IVF Executive) followed up Guinness's work by giving six months as travelling secretary. He paved the way for the Rev. Noel ('Tiny') Palmer (the founder of the post-1919 Oxford University Bible Union) to take three years' leave from the Anglican ministry to engage in many arduous cross-Canada journeys as travelling secretary. A little later, after he had completed his postgraduate medical appointments, Dr. Arthur Hill became General Secretary. When the latter could no longer delay his entry into medical practice, the name of C. Stacey Woods entered the North American international scene. He, an Australian by birth, had graduated in the United States. He was first a travelling secretary in Canada and, then, succeeded Arthur Hill as General Secretary of the Canadian Fellowship. Later he was to pioneer the Inter-

Varsity Fellowship of USA and in 1947 became General Secretary of the newly formed International Fellowship of Evangelical Students.

In Australia the leaders of the widely separated university Christian Unions overcame with much determination the great distances involved and held two Inter-Varsity conferences in 1931 and 1934. By 1935 the Australians had gone ahead and had founded the Inter-Varsity Fellowship of Evangelical Unions (Australia). The New Zealand leaders organized their IVFEU (NZ) in 1936.

Links with Continental Europe

The earliest contact made by the IVF with the Continent was when British language students going to the University of Grenoble and Montpelier discovered the activities of a group of Protestant students known as 'La Brigade Missionaire.' These were concerned to awaken the churches, especially L'Église Réformée, to their evangelistic and missionary responsibilities. However, apart from the exchange of students and the exchanges of literature, there was no further or more permanent link. About 1928 a more deliberate effort by the IVF leaders to find other Evangelical students took the form of assisting a German-language student from Bristol, H. Bromiley, to travel in the universities of West Germany to search for any German Christian student groups. At the time he found a very few individual students who seemed interested and first alerted the IVF leaders to the fact that 'Evangelical' in Germany simply meant 'Lutheran', and membership of one of the Protestant state churches. However, it was found a little later that the organization in Germany which corresponded to the SCM, Deutsche Christliche Studenten Vereinigung had remained 'positive' (*i.e.* theologically conservative). It had been led by 'orthodox' leaders such as Dr. Gerhard Niedermeyer and Professor Karl Heim. No formal link was made, but several visits, letters and publications were exchanged.

It was not until 1930 that one evening, as he returned from hospital, the IVF Secretary came upon what the committees had been seeking. A fair-haired overseas visitor enquired the way to a Christian guest house in the vicinity of his own student hostel. He was intrigued to know the visitor's nationality and found it was Norwegian. The visitor said that he was studying English before going overseas as a missionary. He was invited to a meal the following evening, and brought magazines and photos of the united conferences of the Scandinavian student movements. He described the great influence of Professor O. Hallesby in Norway in the early 1920s. It became clear that there was a movement in the universities and schools of Scandinavia which corresponded in outlook and aims with the British IVF. Both movements actually had arisen at almost the same time, following World War I. The missionary, however, forgot his promise to report to his friends on getting back to Norway and at that time no closer contact was made with the evangelical student movements in northern lands.

But in 1934, when Dr. Robert Wilder came from Oslo to speak at the High Leigh Conference he brought with him two recent Norwegian graduates. They made it quite clear, with further explanations from Dr. Wilder, that the two movements were very close in outlook and spiritual tradition. There was clearly every reason for closer links. On the way back to London, after the IVF Secretary had been showing the Norwegian visitors parts of Oxford, one of them, Carl Frederick Wislöff[1] suggested that there should be a meeting of delegates from the two movements to discuss international co-operation. On his return to Norway, and after consultation with the leaders of the Norwegian Studentlag, Carl Wislöff sent an invitation for the IVF to send a small group of leaders to meet them and Professor Hallesby in the early autumn.

The International Conferences 1934–1939

The IVF deputation met the Norwegians in September 1934 at Lofthus, the China Inland Mission's centre in Oslo. It consisted of Howard Guinness (leader), Arnold S. Aldis (Chairman of the IVF's Student Executive), two women representatives, Dorothy M. James[2] and Jean B. Strain, and Douglas Johnson (Secretary).

182

Present in this conference were Professor O. Hallesby, Dr. Robert Wilder (acting as interpreter, with the Rev. Ernst Hallen) and representatives of the student organizations in Norway, Sweden, Finland and Denmark. It resulted in a firm alliance between the British and Norwegian movements. A constitution was drafted for the International Conference of Evangelical Students. Also an agreement was reached that each co-operating movement should do its best to inspire evangelistic activities in all the neighbouring countries in which they had influence. It was finally agreed to hold a second conference in Sweden in the following year at which the draft constitution could be amended and, it was hoped, would be adopted.

The second conference took place in Johannelund, Stockholm, in the Autumn of 1935. Before the outbreak of the Second World War in 1939, four international conferences had been held. There had also been three regional conferences coinciding with the visits of student teams sent by the IVF. They were:-

International	*Regional Conferences*
1934 Oslo, Norway	1936 Beatenburg, Switzerland
1935 Stockholm, Sweden	and Helsinki, Finland
1937 Budapest, Hungary	1938 Copenhagen, Denmark
1939 Cambridge, England	

During the period 1934 to 1938 the IVF was invited to send small representative deputations to several of the other countries where the movements were sufficiently strong. The purpose varied and sometimes it was to help a new movement to gain confidence. In other cases it was to inspire a stronger movement to come more into the open with evangelistic public meetings. It was for this last purpose that, in response to an invitation from the Evangeliska Fosterlands Stiftelsen, Howard Guinness took to Sweden in September 1935 what the Swedish papers labelled 'the English Seven'. Actually there were eight in the party, which was drawn from Cambridge (G. Harman, C. G. Scorer and J. Taylor), London (A. S. Aldis, A. J. Broomhall and J. Lockett) and Oxford (D. Bentley Taylor and A. T. de B. Wilmot). They received a warm welcome not only in the universities, but at several of the larger 'gymnasia' (senior high schools). A great final meeting was

183

held in the vast Blasieholm Kerk in central Stockholm at which Professor Ole Hallesby gave the closing address which was widely reported in the Swedish national press.

A further deputation in 1936, led by Captain and Mrs. B. Godfrey Buxton, responded to a similar invitation from Finland. Again there was a great final meeting in the largest public hall in Helsinki at which Professor Hallesby gave a memorable closing address. A smaller party, again led by Captain and Mrs. Buxton, went in 1936 to Beatenburg to meet Swiss students and graduates. This informal conference resulted in the start of the Groupes Bibliques Universitaires in French-speaking Switzerland.

The outlook in 1938

When Howard Guinness let it be known to the Executive Committee that he had become convinced that he should now offer for ordination to the ministry of the Church of England, the IVF's international situation was very different from what it had been at the time of Guinness's first journey to Canada ten years before. It was already in active correspondence and was exchanging representatives with eleven comparable national movements, Australia, Canada, Denmark, Netheralnds, Finland, Hungary, Iceland, New Zealand, Norway, Sweden and Switzerland. There were also encouraging reports of the beginnings of evangelical witness in China, France and USA. In addition to these hopeful signs, the leaders of several strong movements, which were affiliated to the World Student Christian Federation, particularly those in Germany, India and South Africa, had indicated that they would like to keep closely in touch and to receive communications.

It was with increasing optimism, therefore, that the British leaders gave their minds to preparation for the next in the series of the international conferences at Cambridge.

The Cambridge Conference 1939

Though the war clouds were gathering it still seemed inconceivable to the average undergraduate that responsible statesmen would allow Europe to plunge into another devastating world conflict. The IVF leaders consulted several government officials who were well-informed in international affairs to ask if it would be wise to bring together a large number of students across Europe for the period 27 June to 2 July 1939. They advised that, in their view, these dates were reasonably safe, but that the visitors should be back in their own countries early in July!

Accommodation was reserved in six of the Cambridge colleges and, on the opening evening, there were over 800 overseas students in residence. They had come from thirty-three different countries. With the addition of British students (many of them living in their own colleges or lodgings, or coming in for the day) the attendance in the Examination Hall at most of the main sessions approached 1,000. There was a great spirit of expectancy and enthusiasm ran high. There were many useful exchanges of view and a great deal of purposeful planning was done between the sessions. Perhaps the most encouraging sign of progress was the way in which even small national movements were planning to send deputations of students to the universities in their neighbouring countries. Several of the larger movements were discussing exchanges of deputations on the model set by the recent British parties.

The conference host and hostess, Lord and Lady Kinnaird, were assisted by Major and Mrs. W. Mainwaring Burton, Captain and Mrs. B. Godfrey Buxton, Mr. A. W. and Miss Beatrice Churchill, Professor and Mrs. A. Rendle Short and the Rev. and Mrs. H. Earnshaw Smith. The conference theme was 'Christ our freedom' and the list of speakers was designed to bring in the typical viewpoints of the various nations and chief ecclesiastical traditions represented. Amongst the contributors were, Denmark: The Rev. C. Nygaard Andersen (Copenhagen); England: The Rev. W. H. Aldis, the Rev. H. Earnshaw Smith, the Rev. Howard W. Guinness, Mr. J. H. Parker; Finland: The Rev. U. Muroma (Helsinki); Holland: Professor F. W. Grosheide (Amsterdam); Hungary: Professor F. Kiss and Professor E. Sebestyen (Budapest); Norway: Professor O. Hallesby, Rektor H. Höeg and the Rev. Ludvig Schübeler (Oslo); Russia: Dr. V. Ph. Martzinkovski (former secretary of the Russian SCM);

185

Scotland: Professor Daniel Lamont (Edinburgh); Sweden: the Rev. Nils Dahlberg and the Rev. Knut Landgren (Stockholm); USA: Professor Clarence Bouma (Grand Rapids); Wales: Dr. D. Martyn Lloyd-Jones.

Amongst the highlights of the conference was the service broadcast from the University Church, Great St. Mary's on Sunday morning at 9.30 am. During the following week letters poured in from former members of the CICCU who wrote to say what a thrill it was to hear 'the well-loved hymns from Great St. Mary's and the familiar tones of Harold Earnshaw Smith still busy proclaiming the Gospel of the love of God for all mankind'.

The conference members dispersed with a great surge of hope for the future of international co-operation. But they had not long been back in their homes before a second world conflict cut them off from one another. Some were to experience the invasion and occupation of their countries, whilst not a few were to lose their lives in the armed services of their respective countries. Yet from time to time, even during the darkest hours and through letters posted in neutral countries, the IVF leaders received such messages as 'We still think of Cambridge and often look at the programme. Yes! Christ is now our *only* freedom – but that is enough'.

NOTES

[1] Professor Carl Frederick Wislöff became Chairman of the International Fellowship of Evangelical Students and later its President.
[2] Later, Mrs. Douglas Johnson.

Chapter 11

The missionary volunteers (1929–1939)

During the years leading to the outbreak of war in 1939 there was a remarkable resemblance to the history of the earlier Student Missionary Volunteer Movement of 1892 and its influence before 1914 (page 65). Some of the founder-members of the Inter-Varsity Conference in 1919, such as Norman Grubb and Murray Webb-Peploe, had gone straight from their colleges and hospitals to missionary service in Africa or Asia. Such a trend was still strong in several universities, especially Cambridge, Dublin, Edinburgh, London and Oxford. In several of these, 'missionary bands' had been organized. Members of these were mostly friends of the same academic years. They agreed to pray for, and support financially, those of their number who volunteered for missionary service. No full student conference programme, even that for a short week-end, was regarded as complete unless it contained a session where a missionary on furlough could bring a challenge. Missionary study groups, classified according to the area of the chief interest, existed in most Christian Unions.

Perhaps the most effectual way in which the missionary 'call' was kept before the larger Unions was by the missionary breakfasts. These were held in a centrally situated restaurant, having a large enough hall, at 7.45 or 8 am whichever time did not discourage attendance at 9 or 9.30 am, lectures for those students who had them. Many graduates have commented in after years

187

how vividly they remember these occasions and the stirring appeals of some of the 'great' missionaries. Perhaps it was having to make the extra effort to get up earlier and also to pay for one's breakfast when it was already provided by the college, which made for increased awareness. It also says much for the London students, some of whom had to cross the city in the early morning, that there were few mornings when there was anything but a worthy audience for the missionary speaker.

Many of the older pioneer missionaries, however, were not satisfied. They would constantly recall the days when Dr. Robert Wilder of Princeton had so effectively challenged the Student Volunteer Movement in the universities of North America and Europe that literally thousands of graduates, not only from English-speaking countries, but from Germany, Holland, Scandinavia and Switzerland, had poured out to all corners of the world. The movement's watchword, 'The Evangelization of the World in this Generation', had been no empty slogan. It was not, however, for the first generation of volunteers to know of the imminence of the tragedy of the 1914 War and the immense changes it would bring in world affairs and the church. When the 19th-century volunteers returned home on furlough they expected the same response from the student world as had been possible in their own day. There *was* a response in the 1930s, but it was inevitably different. Already there were signs that the indigenous churches would look for experienced advisers and colleagues, rather than greater numbers of new missionaries.

Apart from the spontaneous formation of year-group prayer fellowships and missionary bands, the first real initiative came, as so often in other areas, from Cambridge. The 1926–7 CICCU Missionary Secretary, L. F. E. Wilkinson of Queens', had shown himself an active and successful secretary with drive and infectious zeal. He had greatly increased the depth of interest in missions in the CICCU. Suggestions arose in the IVF Student Executive that there ought to be a new office of (Student) 'Missionary Secretary', whose duty would be to stimulate missionary interest during the conferences and throughout the Unions. The 1927 General Committee added such a secretaryship to the student officers and the choice inevitably fell on L. F. E.

Wilkinson who had just completed his term of office on the CICCU Executive and handed over to a successor at Cambridge.

He took up the task with alacrity and at once brought to bear his characteristic and jocular enthusiasm. As described above, he first called together the handful of missionary secretaries who had so far been appointed in the Unions, together with any other interested officers he could lay hands on. When they met at the conference centre of the Friends at Old Jordans, in Buckinghamshire, his first action was to press them to agree that they would agitate for every Union to appoint a capable energetic missionary secretary. The conference then went on to discuss the most effective methods of missionary study and, also, how to ensure that each member of every Union faced up to the missionary 'call'. They did not, of course, expect that everyone would go abroad. But they *did* expect that every member would become interested and be ready to pray and to support those members who later would go overseas through one of the missionary societies. The chief practical outcome of this conference was the organizing of the special missionary conference at High Leigh in September 1928 as reported on page 147.

L. F. E. Wilkinson was succeeded as IVF missionary secretary by the next ex-holder of the office in the CICCU, J. G. Billington of Trinity College. He contributed new methods for spreading information obtained direct from overseas. At the cost of a good deal of correspondence, he drew up a classified list of some 350 graduate ex-members who were already on the various mission fields. He published it in leaflet form under a heading, bearing the scriptural phrase *Witnesses Unto Me*. This was sent in quantity to all the Unions hoping it would get into the hands of every member. His next form of industry was to send every Union's missionary secretary a card index with the academic and other relevant details of each of the ex-members of that particular Union who had so far gone overseas. Affixed to each card, where he could obtain one, was the ex-member's photo. Billington became also an adept at selling large quantities of missionary biographies and other missionary literature at each of the conferences.

When J. G. Billington left to serve with the CMS in China, he was succeeded by another ex-CICCU missionary secretary, David Adeney (Queen's College). Adeney was already showing the transparent sincerity and almost ascetic devotion to the cause of Christ, which was shown to the full in his long spell of service to Asia, first in the China Inland Mission and, then, the IFES. As soon as he was appointed, he began to agitate for a more definite place in the central organization for missionary activities. On the eve of the 1933 Inter-Varsity Conference, he called together all the missionary secretaries (and most Unions now had them,) and they drew up a memorandum urging the formation of a special circle of all those intending to serve abroad, under the title 'The Inter-Varsity Missionary Fellowship'. They were, however, preaching to the converted. Possibly to the surprise of the missionary secretaries, who seem unnecessarily to have anticipated opposition, the whole proposal and the (slightly modified) draft constitution were readily and even enthusiastically accepted by the General Committee. Where there was any reserve on the part of any of the other leaders it was simply due to anxiety that (i) the appeal of the IVMF should not be merely emotional and (ii) that sufficient allowance should be made for the duty of the university authorities to ensure that the day to day academic work of any student was being properly done. Surprising as it may sound, the majority of the most energetic in the cause of overseas missions remained in good standing with their academic supervisers and examiners.

The Inter-Varsity Missionary Fellowship

Whilst the missionary volunteers hoped that all members of the IVF would be interested, it was intended that only those should join the IVMF who were seriously proposing to go abroad with a missionary society. The following is taken from the memorandum embodying the provisions agreed at the 1933 General Committee:–
    'The Aims of the Fellowship are:
1.   To present the claims of Foreign Missionary Service to each student generation.

190

2. To unite by prayer students who intend to go abroad in Missionary Service.
3. To provide help and advice during the time of preparation.
4. To link with their ultimate objective Members who have gone down from the University.
5. To maintain contact between Members who are already in the Field and those who are still in training.

Conditions of Membership

1. Definite Purpose to serve God in the Foreign Mission Field.
2. Full agreement with the doctrinal basis of the Inter-Varsity Fellowship of Evangelical Unions.
3. Membership of a University or a recognised Training College.

Declaration of Membership

Acknowledging Jesus Christ as my Saviour, my Lord, and my God, I purpose, if God permit, to serve Him in the Foreign Mission Field.

The Declaration is more than a mere expression of willingness or desire to become a Foreign Missionary. It is a statement of a definite life-purpose formed under the direction of God. The purpose of those who sign this declaration is by God's grace to spend their lives as Foreign Missionaries. Towards this end they will shape their plans; they will steadily set themselves to prepare for this great work; they will do all in their power to remove the obstacles which may stand in the way of their going; and in due time they will make the necessary arrangements to go out. Only the clear leading of God will prevent their going to the Foreign Field.

It is the duty of every Christian to face this question and to think to a conclusion, but let no one decide it without careful thought and earnest prayer.'

Increasing interest

When the time came for David Adeney to start his own period of missionary training, he nominated as his successor yet another Cambridge man, Christopher Maddox of Trinity College. As a

191

medical student he was due shortly to come down to St. Bartholomew's Hospital for the clinical part of the training. He was thus able to keep in closer touch with the IVF office and fellow members of the Executive Committee. He promptly sent to all the Unions specially printed cards with the IVMF membership declaration on them. The leaders of the Unions were asked to pray that each of their members would consider carefully where his ultimate future should lie in relation to the missionary needs of the Church. By July 1934 over 150 had joined the IVMF and the numbers continued to rise.

Perhaps the factor which made the biggest impact on the students at the time was the visit to the 1934 High Leigh Conference of Dr. Robert Wilder, the pioneer of the Student Volunteer Missionary Union. His arrival not only proved providential for the strengthening of the new IVMF, but, as described in the last chapter, he brought two leaders of the corresponding Evangelical student movement in Norway which led to the foundation of the international movement. Whilst serving the Near East Christian Council in Egypt, Robert Wilder had heard of the rise of the IVF and, through a fellow missionary, he had seen some of the early issues of the new *Inter-Varsity Magazine*. He also had known at first hand a good deal of the history of the CICCU from his years as SCM travelling secretary. He had written several years before from Egypt encouraging the Executive Committee to adhere to the basic essentials of the Evangelical faith and the missionary obligations of the Christian. On retiring from the Near East to Norway he had kept in touch through mutual friends in England. It was they who had suggested to the IVF leaders that he should be invited to speak at their Annual Conference.

With the uncanny capacity possessed by the average student for recognizing a man of real worth, Dr. Wilder was at once welcomed with deep respect. Every word of his brief, but very telling, addresses was heard in concentrated silence. In every free period he was surrounded by students and at the end of each day had to be dragged away at a reasonable hour for bed. Many present never forgot their brief conversations with him. In his talks to the conference the whole concept of the IVMF was put into the perspective of church history.

The Unions urged that Dr. Wilder be invited back and, if possible, to make a tour of the universities. Although not resident in Britain, he was elected a Vice-President 'honoris causa' and in order to 'put Missions *properly* into the Vice-Presidents' List'. He was also invited to return for a Lent term tour of the British universities and to be at the Scottish conference at Bonskeid. He nobly responded in spite of his advanced age. Unfortunately, the February and March of 1935 were unusually cold and damp and it soon became clear that too much had been included in the tour. The arrangements had to be curtailed, but not before the Scottish students had responded with a similar enthusiasm to those at Swanwick, especially in Edinburgh and that year's conference at Bonskeid. Each time he spoke it became easier to appreciate the force of Wilder's first impact on the British students of the year 1891.

The watch-word

At the time there had been a great deal of discussion concerning the watch-word of the original Student Missionary Volunteers, adopted in 1896. Robert Wilder himself had several times referred to it and explained it. Some of the student and graduate leaders now began to suggest that a similar rallying call was needed to crystallize the message of the IVMF. Whilst travelling with two others by car to the Keswick Convention in the summer of 1934, Howard Guinness' party was delayed in Ripon by an engine defect and had to stay over the week-end. Guinness wrote at a later date, 'A short distance from Ripon stood the ruins of Fountains Abbey and it was here that we went for quiet prayer and consultation. During the following 48 hours there slowly emerged the watch-word 'Evangelise to a finish to bring back the King'.[1]

The suggestion that this should be adopted was put to the Unions and leaders of the IVMF by post. They were asked to consider it carefully and be ready to vote on it at the next General Committee. A missionary conference organized by the Scottish IVMF members in January 1935 enthusiastically adopted the first phrase 'Evangelise to a Finish'. They felt, however, that this was in itself sufficient and they were not sure about the meaning of the second part. Eventually, at the Swanwick Conference of April 1935 the proposed watch-word was adopted in full, but with the option left open that the first phrase could stand by itself where it was so desired, as in Scotland.

The first publication of the IVMF, Inter-Varsity Missionary Paper No. 1 (1935), entitled *'Evangelise to a Finish'* – was written by Alfred B. Buxton and Howard W. Guinness. It is prefaced by a long extract from an address by Robert E. Speer, one of the 19th-century volunteers, explaining the value of such a watch-word. He was introducing the older watch-word, 'The Evangelization of the World in this Generation', at the Student Volunteer Movement convention in Cleveland, Ohio, 1898. The booklet goes on to explain how the 1935 watch-word arose and its relevance to that generation of students.

The war years

Membership of the Fellowship had steadily increased until the marked change in the country's mood in 1938, when it was realized that another world conflict was inevitable. Many young people of student age were already being recruited for the 'militia'. The leaders of the IVMF, therefore, became a little uncertain of policy when preparations for war were being pressed ahead. To speak of volunteering for missionary service just then seemed unrealistic. But it was not for long.

Many of the earliest members of the Fellowship had already reached their designated places of missionary service. Whilst in some areas of British influence the more experienced doctors, and other professional people, were asked to join the African and other regiments being raised (because of their familiarity with their needs and tribal customs), the newly trained arrivals were left to cope with the local need as best they could. In either case, when these junior over-worked missionaries had time to write at all, they left the people at home in no doubt what 'the front line' thought of the desperate missionary world need. Some of the letters almost scorched the paper on which they were written. None of Robert Wilder's earlier generation of missionary volunteers could have done better.

Two trends at home also fanned the zeal of the new members of the IVMF. Some of those entering the Forces were destined shortly afterwards to see for themselves the needs of the developing countries. Others earlier had had no thought of offering to missionary societies. When they were taken in the course of military duty into immediate contact with the developing countries, they began to join the IVMF. Some of them became the most successful of the post-war missionaries. Also, since there were very few senior missionaries at home on furlough at any time during the war years, those who had retired from their earlier fields of work had to make up for them. No one was more active in urging thought, prayer and preparation for 'the post-war opportunities' than Mr. Roland Hogben, the Candidates Secretary of the China Inland Mission. He was roped in for many of the student conferences and such university discussion groups as were considering these matters. He became their very active missionary adviser, until lost through an accident on the Burma Road.

Another factor in increasing the number of missionary workers overseas even during war emerged from the Government's enlightened use of conscientious objectors to military service in alternative employment. For example, members of the Society of Friends (Quakers) were allowed to join the Friends Ambulance Units, which went to war-fronts as stretcher bearers and also did valuable work in relief of refugees. Those qualified in medicine, agriculture and other skills were able to enter the colonial medical services, and similar government services in the most needy of the overseas countries, on condition that they signed on for three years. Those who were *bona fide* candidates, already accepted pre-war by a missionary society, were, again on certain conditions, permitted to go overseas in the society to take up medical, agricultural and similar much-needed work. The membership of the IVMF, therefore, may temporarily have remained stationary but did not fall. The stream of inspiring air letters from the Forces mailbag from all over the world must have been one of the most challenging missionary recruiting campaigns in history.

It was, therefore, not at all out of place for those interested in missionary service to sit down at the fewer conferences, or in crowded study-bedrooms, with Mr. Roland Hogben to plan a great post-war wave of new workers 'to complete the task of world evangelization'. That generation of students was not to know how changed the world would be. They bent their imaginations and wills to planning for the completion of the task which their Master had given His Church.

NOTES

[1] The phrase comes from a combination of Matthew 24:14 and 2 Samuel 19:10 in the AV, 'This gospel of the kingdom shall be preached in all the world for a witness unto all nations; then shall the end come', and 'Now, therefore, why speak ye not a word of bringing back the King?'.

Chapter 12

The Second World War (1939–1945)

The outbreak of war brought its quota of surprises to the universities. Most of the colleges did not immediately empty, as they had in the first phase of the 1914 war, although the students of the London colleges and medical schools were at once scattered by their evacuation from the Metropolis to other university cities. For this Second War the Government and academic authorities were considerably better prepared. From the start, provision was made to ensure a sufficient supply of replacements for the engineers, scientists, doctors and chaplains who would become casualties later in the war. With the arrival in their cities of the London students and a quota of cadet officers on technical training courses, some of the university Christian Unions had a larger membership than in pre-war days. A further surprise was the unexpectedly slow start to active hostilities on the Western Front. For seven months there was what became known as the 'phoney war'. It served to enable the Christian Unions and the committees of the IVF to make practical plans for the maintenance of the work as far as possible into the months ahead.

In the autumn of 1939 the leaders in the Christian Unions found that attendances at meetings, and at such conferences as could still be held, had encouragingly increased and continued to do so. There were considerably more non-members regularly coming to the open meetings. Whilst this could have been accounted for partly by the fact that in the evenings students had fewer counter-attractions (because the strictly enforced 'black-out' restricted movement between the colleges and halls of residence) that was not all. A new mood of seriousness became evident and a greater readiness to hear what the Christians had to say. The idealism of youth had certainly been rudely shocked when confronted by the ugly truth that supposedly civilized nations were once again locked in mortal conflict and attacking each other with increasingly lethal weapons. Another factor may have been that, on the eve of war, literary circles had been deeply interested and influenced by the writings of pro-Christian authors such as C. S. Lewis. Religion had once again become a respectable talking-point in polite circles. Again, whilst a large section of the student population despaired of any rational explanation of the folly of mankind and still tried to dismiss it all as being 'the law of the jungle', there was a growing number who began to wonder if the Bible might after all have been right in its explanation of what was wrong with human nature. Most of the Christian Unions were able to capitalize on this situation and, provided that they could gain the help of sufficiently able speakers, to secure an increased hearing. Numerous undergraduates who later became active as witnesses in the forces, were won for Christ during those first months of the War.

Wartime office and staff

From September 1939, most of the members of the small full-time staff who were working at 39 Bedford Square became scattered across the country to undertake various forms of work of national importance. In view of the imminence of air attack, the records and vital sections of the office were evacuated first to the third floor of Holy Trinity Vicarage, Redhill, where Hugh Evan Hopkins had not long previously become Vicar. As he had been so recently in contact with the Unions as travelling secretary, it had been agreed that he would endeavour to act as (part-time) honorary secretary for the duration of the war. Instead of falling off, the correspondence and work from the universities and colleges began to make greater demands on the office. The difficulty of the Unions in getting speakers, and the large number of names and addresses to be transferred to the cities receiving the colleges in evacuation, enlarged the correspondence. The Fellowship fortunately was able to retain a typist-secretary and a junior (under call-up age). Later, when additional help became available, for the convenience of staff travelling from their homes, the war-time office was moved first to Wimbledon and then to Epsom Downs, where it remained until the end of the War.

The General Secretary, whilst waiting for the expected transfer of qualified doctors to one of the respective armed services, began to combine IVF secretaryship with voluntary assistance to an over-worked medical officer of health, by doing such of his night duties as were transferable and helping to train some of the latter's street ambulance parties. His combination of medicine and an exacting secretaryship proved for a *second* time too much. A severe coronary occlusion brought a visit from a cardiologist and three months enforced unemployment. Later advice from the service doctors, 'to go home and take life quietly', proved a counsel of perfection since the IVF continued to grow in every direction. During the Secretary's absence, the Fellowship was well served by a student member of the Executive, Brian Aldis (Oxford), who 'covered off' whilst completing his theological course. The later period saw much hard work done by a devoted, but minimal, office team. Government regulations required that in all offices, which were not officially scheduled as of national importance, those members of clerical staff retained should work two hours longer than the length of what would have been its ordinary office day. The load, including dispatch of publications (growing all the time), was borne throughout the war by Norah Nixon (serving also as women's travelling secretary) and two secretaries, Mary Milton-Thomson and Lilian B. Baker. For the small office team these years were an organizational and spiritual marathon. At the end of it all, however, the Fellowship found itself in every way in a very much stronger position than it had been when the War started.

Meetings and war-time conferences

In spite of the 'black-out' open meetings in the universities were well attended and were even sometimes crowded. In the four years, however, there was no male travelling secretary, except in Scotland. Norah Nixon, the women's travelling secretary, found herself restricted from extensive travelling by certain home responsibilities and the need continually to reinforce the office staff. Few suitably experienced speakers were now available in the Unions. Most of the senior ministers were substituting for the younger and middle-aged ministers away on service as chaplains to the forces as well as bearing the burden of their own churches. The situation was saved in three ways. Some of the hard working older ministers, at considerable personal cost, gamely made themselves available for local student meetings in their cities. Sometimes graduates on university staffs were able to travel to speak in other universities, if at not too great distance. Best of all, some of the more gifted leading students led the public witness in their own student community. Sometimes they took a team to visit a neighbouring university. At the week-ends some of the abler preachers amongst the theological students were the means of starting small spiritual revivals in their colleges, and, as in the case of St. Andrews, in some of the village churches in their presbyteries.

The student committees of those years became especially indebted to several former members of the IVF on the staffs of their universities and to several representative leaders of their own denominations. For example, Dr. Martyn Lloyd-Jones was elected President for the three opening years of the War. In each of these years he gave an outstanding presidential address. His contributions to the main annual conferences and at the theological students conferences were invaluable.

The Annual Conference

The Hayes, Swanwick had been commandeered on the outbreak of War and made a prisoner-of-war camp, so the 1940 annual conference could no longer be held there. The postponed 1939 leaders' conference, normally held in September, took place, however, on 2–6 January at Westhill College, Selly Oak, Birmingham. As there was still a strong demand from the student Unions for the annual conference to be continued, it was moved to one of the university towns for the duration of the War. The twenty-first Inter-Varsity conference was, therefore, organized for 2–8 April 1940 in Westhill College and Carey Hall, Selly Oak. When the next Conference came to be planned, as numbers were clearly growing, the Chairman of the Committee, Oliver R. Barclay (who was in Trinity College, Cambridge, engaged on post-graduate research of national importance) approached the authorities to ask if the 1941 conference might be based at Trinity College. The conference was permitted to use the largest lecture room for its meetings and to house the largest section of the men in the college rooms. The rest of the men were placed in the college hostel and university lodgings, whilst the women students were accommodated in two of the women's colleges. This further war-time experiment proved a marked success. The Trinity College authorities, with the goodwill of the reduced quota of college servants, generously permitted the conference to meet in Cambridge for a second time in 1942. In both years the Master, Sir George Trevelyan, honoured the Fellowship by attending the Presidential addresses given by Dr. Martyn Lloyd-Jones.

Numbers of those applying to come to the conference were still tending to rise and the circumstances had also changed at Cambridge. For the 1943 conference a move was made to Oxford, where the next four conferences (for 1943–46) were each held in the hall of Regent' Park College. The overflow of men from available college rooms was accommodated in university lodgings in the environs of Wellington Square, with most of the women students residing in St. Peter's Hall. The Regent's Park College hall and gallery could only just take the crowd attending the meetings, especially when the graduates and undergraduates in uniform contrived to arrive in the evenings from the Royal Air Force and other units stationed near Oxford.

Throughout the War most of the other conferences of all types continued to make use of university accommodation. The Scottish conference (unable to use Bonskeid House, Pitlochry, to which a Glasgow girls' school had been evacuated) booked in at St. Salvator's, St. Andrews, with the use of some of the nearby halls of residence. Similarly, the leaders' conference held in the autumn and theological students' conferences in January took place in one of the university cities. Owing to the generous services of certain speakers, the standard of speaking at most of the war-time conferences remained high, and sometimes was even above average. For example, few present will easily forget the President's (Dr. Lloyd-Jones) brilliant dialogue with D. R. Davies in the senior common room of Trinity College, Cambridge during a theological students' conference. The latter, who had earlier been a Communist, had recently become a Christian and an influential advocate of Christianity. Dr. Lloyd-Jones was concerned to bring out vividly the points at which there could be no possible compromise in a truly Christian view of God and the world.

One of the chief lessons of war-time was how little the things of the Spirit depend upon material conditions. Both student and graduate evangelists showed to the full their great resourcefulness in overcoming all sorts of barriers to the spread of the gospel. Emergency conditions, by confining the students to their colleges, tended to promote the lively discussions which in the evenings filled much of their free time. Such occasions were used to the full by the Christians. Many of the college rooms and the common rooms in the halls of residence became the areas for passionate discussions on spiritual things.

Travelling secretaries

Apart from Scotland, where the Rev. Alistair Rennie was succeeded by the Rev. Kenneth MacKenzie in 1941, the absence of travelling secretaries soon began to be felt. It was at first more serious on the women's side. It became especially difficult for the women's colleges to get speakers and many of the women students hoped to have frank talks with someone who could be an experienced counsellor. There seemed little chance of rectifying the situation officially until the end of the War. Phyllis Z. Bennett, however, a graduate of Bristol and at the time on the staff of a girls' school, had proved particularly helpful in these situations at some of the smaller week-end conferences and at several of the women's meetings. She herself had wished at the time that she could have talked longer with several who had come up after meetings. The women student leaders wrote in to ask if there were any possibility of securing her services as a travelling secretary. In view of the national emergency there seemed small hope of this. It was agreed, however, to make an application to the authorities on the ground that the well-being of the student world was regarded officially as one of national importance. To the great relief of the committees permission was given for her to be seconded from the teaching profession for three years, and in 1941 she was able to begin what became an outstanding piece of teaching, evangelistic and advisory service amongst women students. To a number of the Unions, especially where women students were in the majority, her visits again and again brought fresh inspiration, strength and urgently needed personal counsel.

A year later, in a most unexpected manner, a similar gap on the men's side was also closed. The Rev. A. T. Houghton was on his way from England to be consecrated as Bishop of Rangoon, when his ship was torpedoed off Northern Ireland. He was compelled to return to England. Meanwhile the threat of Japanese invasion and other crises in Burma closed any further immediate possibilities of his reaching Burma. The Executive Committee boldly wrote to ask if he would become the men's travelling secretary 'for the duration of the war'. He would be left free to help in the services of the churches at week-ends and in the intervals between his travels. His acceptance made a crucial difference in several ways to the hard-pressed Unions. Not the least part of his contribution was that his seniority enabled him to give experienced counsel to the large number of post-graduate students and others engaged in work of national importance in all the university cities.

A. T. Houghton's first visit to one of the northern universities provided a cautionary illustration of what may confront any travelling secretary or speaker as a result of the constant changes in the student committees and secretaryships. At the outset the General Secretary had warned him that it was wise, when preparing to speak on a subject set by a student committee, to prepare three sets of notes, one for a purely Christian audience (*i.e.* composed of members), the second for a somewhat mixed audience (but composed mostly of those really interested), and a third for a more open situation, where there might be a considerable number of non-members present. The new travelling secretary smiled benignly and somewhat incredulously.

For his first visit to speak in a northern university he had been primarily asked to give a Bible exposition on a given subject at a members' meeting, and subsequently to be available for consultations with the committee. On arriving, as instructed, at the main entrance of the University about half an hour before the time of the meeting, he was duly met on the steps by the secretary and taken to tea in the refectory. Some ten minutes before the time due for the meeting he was conducted to the main entrance hall, where he noticed a number of students pouring into what seemed to be the Great Hall opening off the concourse. The secretary then happened to mention that the Principal had said that he would come to meet them there. It was now five minutes to the hour. At that moment the eye of the hapless visitor caught the message on a full length poster on a large notice board. The statement was devastatingly clear! In five minutes' time, it said, 'the Bishop of Rangoon' would be speaking on 'The Burma Road', with the Principal of the University in the chair! Very bravely, the visitor made a quick mental effort so as not to let his side down. Rapid extemporization did its best to outline the purpose of the strategic military road at that time being built over the mountains to link up with Western China. It was not so easy, however, quickly to determine how to introduce a Christian adaptation to this subject, except from a missionary point of view.

The explanation? As has sometimes happened before and since, a student secretary had retired with the former year's committee, shortly after sending the original invitation. The incoming committee had thought that it was rather a pity not to make a fuller use of the distinguished speaker's visit. But they had forgotten to inform the speaker!

Financial resources

With increased expenses and a rising salaries' bill, the financing of the growing Fellowship began to present its own problems. Students at that time were not in receipt of any substantial educational grants. Most of them were at the university on their parents' money or on slender scholarships of various kinds (mostly paid direct to college authorities in academic fees). Members of the Christian Unions usually had quite enough on their hands to balance the budgets of their own local activities without being able to contribute to central funds. Churches, missionary societies and charities of all types were beginning to feel the pinch of war conditions and rising costs. The IVF office staff began to wonder how long they could keep up the struggle. They certainly made it a matter for prayer. Once again, however, the indirect effects of War brought yet more surprises. Graduates and undergraduates who had been called up into the Forces, began to write from their military camps, aerodromes, naval garrisons and overseas expeditionary forces, enclosing generous gifts. These sums were often accompanied by such notes as 'Out here there is nothing much we can spend our money on! But, whatever else happens, do keep the IVF intact and make it go greater guns than ever throughout the War!' The staff, already working at full stretch all round the clock, were sometimes exhorted in no uncertain terms by such correspondents to press into service 'every fleeting moment' in order to maintain the cause of Christ! One of the most poignant of such letters received was from a graduate who was lost at Tobruk and who must have been amongst those who were last to leave the garrison at its fall. The letter graphically outlined the writer's view of the key importance of the university Christian Unions and of the witness of the IVF. His plane was shot down by enemy fighters as it attempted to rise from the encircled base.

The Business Advisory Committee also became more concerned about the IVF finances. Three steps were taken to meet the situation. First, Mr. Ivor Crouch, the Treasurer of the British and Foreign Bible Society, was appointed financial 'controller' of the IVF's affairs for the duration of the war. Mr. A. W. Churchill, of

J. & A. Churchill, medical publishers, was appointed to superintend such publication as might still be possible under the increasing limitations of paper rationing. Finally, the Committee elected to the chair Mr. J. W. Laing (later Sir John Laing, CBE). As Mr. Laing's familiarity with the work grew, he increasingly made the IVF one of his major Christian interests, in addition to his earlier deep attachment to societies such as the Crusaders Union.

No words are strong enough to convey an adequate impression of the importance of John Laing's contribution to the development of the organization at this time and subsequently during the years of his chairmanship from 1942–60. Throughout his service with the Fellowship he welcomed and supported the initiatives of the successive student Executive Committees, and never sought to intrude his own opinion as against theirs. Yet, in his own characteristically gentle manner, he brought great wisdom to bear on any crisis and helped to smooth each of the frequent growing pains of what was by now a sizeable national society. His primary interest was in the evangelistic work of the Fellowship and his basic approach concentrated on the selection and backing 'of good and able men and women to do the work. Given the right workers, the rest will take care of itself.' To his transparent faith and business experience there was added more than his fair share of common sense and native shrewdness. Whenever he had made up his mind to support some substantial new project he would seek to promote support in the form of an offer to contribute £1 for every £1 given by others, up to some stated figure. 'They mustn't be allowed to leave it all to me and I don't wish to deprive them of the pleasure of giving!'

When in post-war days the IVF was able to expand to keep pace with demand and then to maintain its drive, a great deal of the credit was due to the leadership of Sir John Laing. The skill and experience required in the chair of a giant industrial undertaking was freely and efficiently applied to the growth of the Fellowship. Few of its members have been more concerned to see that the IVF was what it was meant to be and should adhere strictly to its original aims and basis to the glory of God. His commonest question to the staff on arriving at the office was,

'And have *more* students been won to the Lord Jesus lately?'

The darker years

The later years of the war became considerably more difficult for all those contriving to maintain the Fellowship's activities, whether locally or centrally. The increasing call-up of the older age-groups was continually reducing the number of experienced speakers and others who had earlier been available to help. Food rationing complicated the difficulty of putting on meals for social activities or of offering the fullest hospitality. The reduction in railway connections and over-crowding of trains, which were sometimes packed down the corridors with servicemen going or coming on leave, made travel for students and travelling secretaries an increasingly formidable undertaking. Bombing of inland cities increased the hazards locally and served to tighten up the black-out and to discourage meetings in the late evenings. Paper rationing reduced to bare essentials what could be published, though four useful new books made their appearance in war-economy editions in 1940 to 1942.[2]

As early as 1941 had come the first blast damage to 39 Bedford Square. The thick glass dome over the well of the staircase was shattered and was not later replaced. Later bomb blasts in succeeding years made more inroads, especially when a furniture depository was hit in Morwell Street, at the rear of the office. Incendiary bombs later fell on the roof, but were speedily removed by the fire watchers and housekeeper, who was a veteran of the First World War. Tribute is here due to Mr. and Mrs. Davies, housekeepers, who chose to stay on in the basement of the building throughout the war. On one occasion at least Mr. Davies was solely responsible for shovelling incendiaries over the parapet from no. 39 and a neighbouring roof. In the event the damage to the building was comparatively slight and (after repair of windows and the roof) this permitted an early reoccupation of the building soon after the War.

A symbol of the quiet persistence which characterized the small clerical staff under war conditions occurred towards the end. A flying bomb fell one morning on Epsom Downs some yards from the war-time office. It fortunately dropped behind a high thick hedge, which reduced the effects of the blast. When the immediate commotion had died down, Norah Nixon was missing. A hasty search was made. But she had quickly swept up the broken glass and debris, blown the dust off the printer's urgently required page-proofs, which she had been in process of correcting, and was making sure that they would not miss the second post!

Losses

The distressing, sometimes really shattering, occasions during all stages of the war were the reports of casualties. Month by month the list steadily mounted of some of the promising young leaders and active members, who would never return. The lists on the war memorials in all the university and college chapels stand as silent witnesses to the real cost of man's inhumanity in modern war. Whilst it is true that those from World War II were, mercifully, rather shorter than those from the First World War, yet they were still calamitous. When the names of ex-members, who had recently fallen, came to be mentioned in the university prayer meetings, and the bereaved families were remembered, there would be a great hush as the real meaning of it all came home once more to those present. Then, as many have subsequently said, many of that generation rededicated their lives to Christ and vowed that, if they themselves were spared, they would give themselves more whole-heartedly to God's service. Later history has shown how fully a number of them have redeemed these vows.

Perhaps one of the most attractive of the war-time student initiatives in this context was in Aberdeen. Soon after the outbreak of war a theological student, William Still, later minister of the Church of Scotland in the city, asked the University authorities if there could be a short service of intercession in King's College chapel during the half-hour mid-morning break. Permission was readily given. The procedure each morning was that he (or his substitute) would play the organ whilst the student congregation was assembling. There was a hymn and then one of a rota of ministers from the city, or one of the members of University staff would read a Scripture and offer prayer for the students and graduates of the University who were away in the armed services.

New developments

In most universities a minimum of Christian Union activity was maintained. Several new developments in the Fellowship also became possible. Planning for a better world after the close of the conflict became a late-war occupation. In the early and middle stages of the war years interest was concentrated on better Bible study and on better application of the faith in all walks of life.

In 1934, in response to many student requests, a three years' course of Bible study was begun under the editorship of the Rev. G. T. Manley and Archdeacon H. E. Guillebaud. Experience showed, however, that it demanded, in the short space of twenty minutes, too much of the average student. Later it had to be somewhat modified. Yet it helped many of the students and graduates to get started on a life-time of serious study of the Bible. The effect also was to stimulate a greater interest in Biblical theology. It further helped in the promotion of a desire for up-to-date books on Christian doctrine and apologetics. The older standard evangelical treatises were mostly out-of-print and increasingly difficult to obtain second-hand. Much that had been written in the late 19th and early 20th centuries had become dated by the progress of modern discovery and in any case they had been addressed to the problems of earlier times. Strong pleas were made by the Theological Students Fellowship, led by its secretary John Wenham, that an *ad hoc* committee should review the total situation and take appropriate steps to secure for the current generation of students the up-to-date help and guidance which they needed.

One result was that in the autumn of 1938 and the spring of 1939, at the invitation of the Rev. G. T. Manley, several interested graduates met in the vicarage of St. Luke's, Hampstead to discuss what could be done. They were the Rev. G. T. Manley (chairman), F. F. Bruce, the Rev. Norval Geldenhuys (from Pretoria on post-graduate studies in Cambridge), the Rev. H. E. Guillebaud, John Wenham and D. Johnson (secretary). It was

209

unanimously decided to recommend to the Executive Committee that a small committee of graduates be appointed, to be known as 'the Biblical Research Committee'. Its first task would be to survey the position and then to plan appropriate action to meet the more urgent needs. This would be by the production of conservative commentaries on the books of the Bible and a scholarly re-examination of the linguistic and historical problems connected with the text of the Old and New Testaments. A major interest would also be the hope of encouraging post-graduate students with the necessary linguistic training to undertake research at the growing points from the point of view of conservative scholarship. H. E. Guillebaud became the first Secretary of the BRC, and he continued in this work until he was pressed to return to Rwanda-Burundi as Archdeacon and to complete the work of the translation of the Rwanda Bible.

The Biblical Research Committee took a further important step early in the war when, with the Rev. G. T. Manley as host, a number of Evangelical leaders were invited to an informal conference held from 7–10 July 1941 at Kingham Hill School, Oxford. At this school were the few remaining theological students of Oak Hill College, who had been evacuated there from London under the leadership of the Vice-Principal, the Rev. Alan Stibbs. The subject of the BRC's conference was 'The Revival of Biblical Theology'. Amongst the more senior graduates accepting the invitation were F. F. Bruce (at that time a lecturer in classics at Leeds University), Dr. Martyn Lloyd-Jones (Minister, Westminster Chapel), Professor Donald Maclean (Principal of Free Church College, Edinburgh), Dr. W. J. Martin (Rankin Lecturer in Semitic Languages, Liverpool University), the Rev. Alan Stibbs and the Rev. J. Stafford Wright (Principal, BCMS College, Bristol). There were also several younger graduates, including the indefatigable John Wenham. Following papers on 'The Evangelical Aim' (G. T. Manley), 'The Causes of Recent Weakness' (D. M. Lloyd-Jones) and 'A Long-Term Policy', there was a whole day of lively discussion. Unanimity was reached concerning three main needs, (i) The necessity of training a new generation of younger scholars to take up at *university* levels new projects of biblical research, (ii) Provision for the encouragement and financing of selected graduates to stay on at university in order to take the necessary post-graduate degrees so as later to specialize in the ancient languages and historical background of the books of the Bible, (iii) Intensive work to prepare new commentaries on the Hebrew and Greek texts, written by those linguistically and in other ways suitably equipped.

There was also agreement on several immediate practical steps, (i) To start an annual summer school for post-graduates and to explore Dr. W. J. Martin's proposal of the possibility of founding a residential library on similar lines to that of St. Deiniol's, Hawarden (the Gladstone Memorial Library), (ii) To make post-war provision for promising post-graduates to receive appropriate research grants ('Fellowships for Study') to enable them to stay on for two or more years at university to gain the necessary qualifications for the desired type of research, (iii) To produce a one volume Bible dictionary for which W. J. Martin and F. F. Bruce were asked to prepare a list of articles, and to propose names of available scholars to write them, (iv) To collect second-hand copies of the most useful older commentaries and books on Biblical theology for use by Evangelical students pending new productions, such as a one-volume Bible commentary, which had been earlier discussed by the Publications Committee.

It was realized, of course, that immediate progress would be slow. The war was beginning to enter its most serious phases. Many more in the higher age groups were being called up and the extra pressures on those who were left at their regular posts were becoming more acute. A beginning, however, was made with the implementing of the decisions. The first summer school was held at St. Deiniol's, Hawarden in the following July. The new series of Tyndale Lectures, one on the Old Testament and one on the New, was begun in 1942. A start was also made on the planning of the one volume commentary. In the event, it was this project, which had been vigorously advocated for several years by A. J. Vereker (General Secretary of the Crusaders' Union), which, in spite of the restricting conditions, was able to make most headway. A foundation was laid for this major work in 1943 by the Rev. G. T. Manley, the Rev. Alan Stibbs and Professor Davidson (Glasgow), with F. F. Bruce serving in an advisory capacity. None of the

211

desired projects, however, could proceed far because of the acute shortage of man-power. The publications programme had to await the post-war demobilization of the younger scholars and the return of Ronald Inchley, as Publications Secretary, to the IVF Publications department.

The reasons for the comparatively slow growth of the publishing department have been mentioned on page 181. A more detailed account will be given in chapter 18 (page 314).

In mid-war years during the campaign in North Africa the Secretary received an urgent letter from a Cambridge biblical scholar who was serving at the time as an army chaplain. It asked him to go to the British and Foreign Bible Society's depot and to buy as many of the pocket editions of Nestlé's Greek New Testament as the Society would allow him, and to post them all as soon as possible to the field address given. Whilst taking a mail bag full of Greek Testaments to the GPO the Secretary felt somewhat uneasy about the wisdom of burdening the Services' mail with extra cargo in the midst of the great national war effort. He had forgotten about the incident until sometime after the battle of El Alamein, after which the Eighth Army had moved across North Africa. He then received an airmail letter from a senior chaplain telling of the pleasure which the following incidents had recently given him. One evening he had joined an officer who was sitting on top of a tank reading a little book. He found that he was a classical scholar from Cambridge reading a little Greek New Testament which he said had been his cherished companion for some weeks. Not long after this, in a new forward base, the chaplain had come upon another officer lying in the shade of a rock reading another little Greek New Testament! Both said that they hoped to offer for ordination in their respective churches, after demobilization.

Tyndale House

One further major step in this sector of the work was taken before the end of the War. The Biblical Research Committee had continued its quest for a suitable property to house the projected residential library. In 1943, Oliver Barclay reported from

Cambridge that one of his relatives was about to put on the market, at a very reasonable price, a freehold property in Selwyn Gardens. It had an acre and a quarter of garden. After consultation between the members of the Business Advisory Committee and all other committees concerned, and the timely intervention of Mr. John Laing, the house was purchased. A non-profit making trust was set up to hold and develop the property. The name 'Tyndale House' was unanimously agreed and, due to the generosity of Mr. Laing, a start was immediately made in beginning to collect the basis of a library. Several weeks later a well known biblical scholar's library was put up for sale at Oxford and its contents were at once obtained to form the nucleus of the present collection.

Leo Stephens-Hodge was brought into residence at Tyndale House as the first librarian and began to further some aspects of the Biblical Research Committee's plans. At the close of the war, the first full-time Warden was appointed. It was J. N. D. Anderson (later Professor of Oriental Laws in the University of London) who was able to offer the committee two years of residence in a period of uncertainty after demobilization. During this time, whilst furthering the BRC's projects, he was able to increase preparations for his own later academic research. Reference to the later implementation of the plans of the Biblical Research Committee will be made in chapter 16 (page 298).

The Graduates Fellowship

In another department where tentative preliminary steps had been taken on the eve of war, considerable progress was also made. It had long ago been suggested that all the graduate ex-members still interested should be linked more effectively to the Fellowship and not just be on address lists to receive *Inter-Varsity Magazine* and the fixture card of their Union. There were two desirable aims. The first was to unite former members in prayer and financial support for their Christian Unions and the central IVF; and then to stimulate them to active Christian witness amongst their professional colleagues at their places of work and their neighbours. Since the latter activity would be pursued mainly through their churches, the accent was placed upon the first – the sphere of professional work. The underlying concept was of a series of active Christian Unions formed within the various professions, which would bear a similar witness in their more senior setting to that borne by a student CU in the universities and colleges. A beginning was made, but this second aim was only achieved in a few of the professions.

Tentative steps in such a direction had already been taken in the early 1930s, when the Schoolteachers' Prayer Fellowship was formed and held a number of informal conferences for schoolteachers. But it was not until late in 1938, and early in 1939, that definite proposals for the organization of the Graduates Fellowship came in a form on which definite action could be taken. In 1939 the Universities Staffs Circle had been founded (secretary, Dr. R. W. Brookfield of Liverpool) and the Inter-Varsity Overseas Fellowship for graduates serving in government or business overseas. Because in war-time many of the other national Christian societies were in abeyance, the Graduates Fellowship ('GF') tended to grow steadily from year to year. At the cessation of hostilities it was possible to capitalize on this and to make more ambitious plans.

In pre-war years there had been talk of the production of a journal designed for the needs of the graduates. As these were beginning to join the forces, the GF suggested in the summer of 1939 that a letter, entitled 'the Graduates Fellowship Newsletter', be circulated to all ex-members of the Unions whose names and addresses were known. It carried a message from the President 1939–40 (Dr. Martyn Lloyd-Jones) and up-to-date news of the Unions. The first of these letters was printed and circulated about two months before the war-time paper control ruled that no new periodicals, bulletins or newsletters could be started during the period of hostilities. Although the date of no. 1 of the GF Newsletters had been so close to the deadline, the authorities agreed to permit it to continue through the War. It was circulated with the *Inter-Varsity Magazine* to the ex-members of Unions receiving the latter. When peace came and the paper controls were lifted, it was soon increased in size and grew into the quarterly *Christian Graduate*.

214

The war-time SCM

Some brief reference might here be made to the war-time fortunes of the Student Christian Movement. Of course, it had to meet precisely the same conditions and difficulties as the IVF. It could, however, count on a great deal more official support from church leaders and senior members of the staffs of the universities and colleges. Yet, strangely, it seemed to lose a great deal of its vigour and appeared to emerge from the war years a very much weaker organization in several respects.

Several debilitating influences would seem to have been responsible and they to some extent reinforced each other. The local leadership of the branches was sometimes in the hands of those who were not definitely committed Christians. Some of the officers would frankly describe themselves as 'seekers'. One reason for this uncertainty in the leadership must be attributed partly to further weakening of the basis in 1926. In that year the membership qualification was altered to 'The SCM is a fellowship of students who desire to understand the Christian Faith and to live the Christian life. This desire is the only condition of Membership'.

A second factor, which seemed to have an enervating effect on the local branches, was the outworking of the policy, derived from the ecumenical movement, which tended to regard most corporate Christian activity as being the function of the church. This view interpreted 'church' in the narrower sense of the Christian ministry and allowed little place, for example, for a lay movement organized for the purposes of evangelism. The result for the SCM was that in the immediate post-war years the SCM branches in many cases became 'the chaplain's groups' or parts of the denominational societies. To some this might not have seemed a loss, but history and experience suggest that it is salutary for Christians of student age to have to take the initiative in college to share the gospel with fellow students and to work out for themselves the implications of the faith in daily life. A student group tends to suffer if it is 'over-officered'.

Today, in many of the universities and colleges, a majority of the student body fail to understand the vocabulary of those who are theologically trained. The thought-modes of 'religious' people are almost as far from their thinking and conversation as those of a different culture. The times call for more rather than fewer Christian students who can act on their own initiative as the 'bell-ringers' to make contact and awaken the interest of fellow students. It is then, as the latter become more deeply interested that, under the guidance of the Holy Spirit, they may be ready for the next steps into the Christian family and Christian worship. The typical student-led Christian unit, living and functioning within each student community, is more important than ever. On it may largely depend how far the Christian 'presence' can survive even in some of the colleges which were once 'church' colleges.

The basic outlook

Towards the end of the war, many students became even more seriously interested in the Christian message, when clearly and effectively put. Some of the larger universities reported strikingly increased attendances at such open meetings as they could get addressed by any of the best available evangelistic speakers. The interest of the outsiders was primarily in the truth of the Christian message and they wanted it without frills.

This was confirmed towards the end of the war by a conversation overheard in an Oxford senior common room. The writer, having been taken there by one of the fellows of the college, could not help overhearing the comments of one of the dons. He was declaiming, in a loud and emphatic manner, about the poor response to their invitation by graduates and students serving with the Forces stationed in and around Oxford. Some of the clergy, with the SCM, had laid on a reception, with a meal, which was to be closed by an address on post-war reconstruction by the Master of one of the colleges. Very few had come. 'Yet those ranting fundamentalists, those schoolboys in the OICCU, have only to offer tea and some buns and a Bible-punching evangelist and they get crowded out!' It had never dawned on him that those 'schoolboys' in uniform on the aerodromes were about to have to get into their planes and gliders to be dropped under enemy fire. Some were to be lost at Arnhem shortly after. They were really wanting to know whether the Christian religion was right when it said that Jesus Christ 'came into the world to save sinners' and that 'the gift of God is eternal life through Jesus Christ our Lord.'

The evidence seems to be clear that there was a striking number of conversions during the later war years of which the larger proportion was the result of the personal witness of students with an aptitude for sharing the gospel with their friends. Since the intake from the schools had to a great extent fallen off, many of those being influenced were cadet-officers and others on special service courses in engineering and mathematics at the universities. Some of those converted at this time came back after this period in the services to be on the committees of one or other of the Christian Unions.

The prelude to reorganization

When the tide of war began to turn in favour of the Western Allies and the end was in sight, the Fellowship committees began to plan for post-war expansion. It was expected that both with those being demobilized from the Forces and others coming up from the schools, the total available accommodation at the universities would be strained to its limits. The opportunities would be great. There were soon enough suggestions and draft plans to have diverted the leadership of the Fellowship into a hundred and one desirable channels and at a total expenditure greatly exceeding any hitherto envisaged total budget! The Publications Committee became inundated by many suggestions of the desirable books 'which *ought* to be published as soon as possible', but which would have speedily exhausted all the reserve capital. In addition, several friends of the Fellowship, who prided themselves on their foresight, called attention to the many stately homes and broad parks likely to come on the market at low prices and which would make an ideal conference centre for the IVF. (Some of the prompters would no doubt like to have been settled there as resident wardens.) But they over-looked that the larger the house, the greater the maintenance cost and that there were 365 days in the year when economics demanded that every room needed to be gainfully filled.

It was here, as at so many junctures in the history of the Fellowship, that the singleness of purpose of the student Executive's leadership and the balanced advice of the Business Advisory Committee combined to pursue relentlessly the original and essential aims of the Fellowship. With primary interest centred on the student Christian Unions everything was geared to serve the spiritual health, evangelistic outreach and best interests of these primary units in the *raison d'être* of the Movement.

NOTES

1 Canon A. T. Houghton later served as General Secretary of the Bible Churchmen's Missionary Society, and as Chairman of the Keswick Convention.
2 These were Andre Schlemmer, *The Crisis in the World of Thought*, Daniel Lamont, *The Anchorage of Life*, H. E. Guillebaud, *Some Moral Difficulties in the Bible*, and H. A. Evan Hopkins, *Henceforth*.

2 These were Andre Schlemmer *The Crisis in the World of Thought*, Daniel Lamont *The Anchorage of Life,âl H. E. Guillebaud Some Moral Difficulties in the Bible,* and H. A. Hopkins *Henceforth*.

Chapter 13

Challenge and response
(1946–1970)

For both nation and Fellowship the aftermath of the Second World War was different from that of the First. For example, compulsory National Service remained in operation for over ten years, being slowly relaxed in practice up to 1957, but not officially ending until 1962. This brought a much slower return to normal and a longer period of disruption in the lives of many in the student age groups. In all forms of higher education one effect was that throughout the period the average age of the students in the universities and colleges was some two to three years higher than in earlier years. For the Fellowship this circumstance brought several advantages and also some disadvantages. One of the gains was that for some twelve years the student leadership of the Christian Unions was more mature and more thorough in pursuit of its aims. The ex-servicemen (and ex-servicewomen) had the courage and tenacity to attempt more thoroughly organized missions and other effective means of presenting their Union's message to the student body than younger ones might have done.

It meant also that the leaders of the Unions could be less easily deterred by opposition. There were several early incidents similar to one (in a later year) when, on being forbidden to hold an evangelical prayer and Bible study meeting in their college, the ordinands of a Free Church theological college simply went out to a church in the town during their legitimately free periods. As those interested constituted up to half of the college's membership, the authorities began to think again.

A prominent minister of one of the largest denominations tells of an occasion during his year in the highest representative office in his church. After a lecture in their largest theological college, he was in the study of the rather austere and impersonal principal. The latter began to tell him of the strange things which some of the new ex-servicemen ordinands wished to promote. One group wished to organize a weekly meeting in which they would read the Bible *devotionally*, of all things! and pray for each other's future ministry. He adds: 'To his discomfiture, I had to confess that when I myself was in college I had initiated just such a meeting. It had been of the utmost help to us all and we have continued to pray for each other's ministry ever since!'

There was one possible disadvantage, however, in the increased age of the students. During their time in the services many of the other men and women in the college had made up their minds about their future attitudes to 'religion'. They had seen more of human nature and the world than was true of most of the earlier type of undergraduate leader. Any approach to them needed to be well-grounded and of convincing quality. Fortunately, with the steady return of the war-time chaplains and of many good speakers from amongst the earlier called-up graduates, the means of matching the new need was not lacking for long.

Perhaps the most pervasive change was the steady increase in the total numbers of students in the universities and all forms of college education. This enlarged intake was destined to continue until the student world became almost eight times as large as when the Fellowship was founded (1928). There was also a steady rise in the number of universities, beginning in the form of charters granted to the civic 'university colleges' enabling them to give their own degrees, Nottingham (1948), Southampton (1952), Hull (1954), Exeter (1955) and Leicester (1957).

Other new conditions

The increase in size of each university and the widespread increase in availability of educational grants, gradually brought about a major social change, and it came to stay. Even in Oxford and Cambridge, where some of the well-known ancient schools have their own scholarship endowments, the earlier dominance of undergraduates from the public schools was much reduced. The student world now included more students from all types of educational and social background, as it should long ago have done. From the point of view of the church and the Christian organizations, however, there was a price to be paid. Social unification was accompanied by further stages in the secularization of all the universities and colleges. Many of the new undergraduates came from schools and families where there had been little or no effective religious influence. It increased the difficulty and the task of the Christian Unions. But it also constituted a new challenge to those busy rebuilding them. Sir Walter Moberley, Fellow of Lincoln College, Oxford, wrote at that time in his *The Crisis in the University* that a culture, which had hitherto been based upon, and sustained by, the Christian religion, now in eclipse, was attempting to go straight ahead as if nothing had happened. The 'crunch' might somehow be postponed, but ultimately was inevitable.

The spiritual outlook

At the outset the spiritual promise in the universities was quite encouraging. Interest in religion was generally high. The college chapels in many cities, especially at Cambridge and Oxford, notably the former, were relatively well attended. Several general theological lectures put on by both the academic and ecclesiastical authorities drew large undergraduate audiences. The size of the response surprised everyone including those in several of the non-residential universities. Good attendances greeted any well-organized activity of the Christian Unions. The CICCU Sunday sermons and Saturday night Bible readings in Holy Trinity Church and the Union's Debating Hall respectively, were crowded, as were also the corresponding OICCU sermons and Bible readings in St. Ebbe's Church and the Northgate Hall. Similar undergraduate attendances were reported at some of the city churches, for example, St. Ebbe's and St. Aldate's, Oxford. To some it seemed that a quiet revival of religion must be taking place. Whilst attendances in the college chapels later began to fall off, interest in Evangelical sermons (of all types) was, on the whole, well sustained.

This prevailing interest encouraged the Christian leaders (including, also, some of the university chaplaincies) to put on full scale university missions. For example, the CICCU invited as missioner in 1947 and again in 1949, Dr. Donald Grey Barnhouse, Minister of Tenth Presbyterian Church, Philadelphia. There were large attendances and an encouraging response in both years. Opinions differ concerning the permanent effects of Dr. Billy Graham's visit to Cambridge in 1954 and mission (sponsored by CICCU) in 1955. In 1954 the Cambridge Students Union had voted by a majority of 50 to welcome him back. There were immense queues night after night to get into Great St. Mary's (the University Church), and nearly 200 are said to have professed decision for Christ.

Triennial missions

During these years of favourable conditions at Oxford and Cambridge, it became the custom to arrange a full university mission once every three years. This same practice also spread to other universities where something of the same pattern was adopted with much local success. This was surprising in places where fewer students were resident in colleges. In the two older English universities, missions were held at the following intervals (and subsequently):-

Cambridge	Oxford
1947 Donald G. Barnhouse	1947 Thomas C. Hammond
1949 Donald G. Barnhouse	1951 Hugh R. Gough and
1952 John R. W. Stott	D. Martyn Lloyd-Jones
1955 Dr. Billy Graham	1954 John R. W. Stott
1958 John R. W. Stott	1957 John R. W. Stott
1961 Kenneth F. W. Prior	1960 Richard C. Lucas

It was during this period that the special gifts for university missions of John Stott became more and more apparent. He had succeeded Harold Earnshaw Smith as Rector of All Souls Church, London, W1. In spite of his comparative youth and early days in the ministry of a large church, his training, personality and aptitudes just fitted the need. As God's blessing seemed to be increasingly evident on this aspect of his ministry, the officers at All Souls over the years have put the student world more and more into their debt. He was again and again spared for sermons, missions and Bible readings in the universities, not only in the British Isles, but in most of the English-speaking countries overseas.

It was not all plain sailing, however, during some of the missions. There were often veiled attacks from some of the ecclesiastical authorities and criticism from some of the college fellows. Professors of psychology seemed to feel that their rôle should be to enjoy field days, studying the psychology of conversion. Judged by their reports their genius mostly fell rather short of that of Henry James in his *Varieties of Religious Experience*! At Oxford, a Humanist Society was founded and conceived its chief function to be antagonism to such missions. It did its best to hinder the one in 1960, but in 1964 'launched a vehement advertising campaign against the OICCU during the Mission led by John Stott'. It picketed the meetings and handed out anti-mission leaflets. The phenomenon seems to have been typical of the changes in the mood of the younger age groups which were beginning to come over the nation at that time.

Whilst there were necessary modifications, depending on the local geography and the relative proportion of residential accommodation available for students, a similar challenge to their student communities was undertaken by many of the Scottish and 'redbrick' universities. As also between the World Wars, Edinburgh and Glasgow were both soon to the fore in organizing missions. During this time a new evangelist was discovered, who revealed particular talents for the conduct of missions in non-residential (or partially residential) universities. Leith Samuel, who was a Liverpool graduate, and had been trained in an environment similar to those met in the other great

223

cities, revealed his aptitude for these conditions. He could make quick contact from the start and gain the confidence of a typical student audience in a few minutes. This was of special importance for a number of other types of evangelistic initiative which later took place in universities especially in northern England. Since he came free from another commitment at that time, Leith Samuel was asked to join the staff as a 'roving' evangelist. He was soon reinforced by A. W. ('Bertie') Rainsbury in Scotland and, a little later, by Roland Lamb in England.

Further experiments in evangelism

There was no doubt of the value of a full-scale university mission. But the method demanded certain favourable local conditions, a considerable personnel and appropriate expenditure. Whilst the latter could be rapidly subscribed by the graduate former members of the Union, not all university buildings, environments, transport and other communications lent themselves equally to central meetings. There were few Christian Unions or situations where, as at 'Oxbridge', the main missioner could be supported by some 25 to 30 assistant missioners, each billeted in the guest room of a college. Similarly in few places did the crowded academic curricula of the various faculties provide times when all the student body would be free at the same time. On the other hand, there was no doubt that in most of the full-scale missions the 'message' could be got over to some 40%–50% of the entire student membership of the university. As a result the memberships of the Christian Unions steadily rose. For example, in the best of the post-war periods the CICCU's membership rose into the four hundreds and more.

The chief difficulty was in the universities which are only partially supplied with student residences and which have most of their students scattered widely over the environs of a great conurbation. They needed to find some effective substitute for a full-scale mission. The Bristol CU led the way. It pioneered a method which was speedily taken up by those in the midlands and northern England. Happily, it was also one for which Leith Samuel, and several of the travelling secretaries at the time, were ideally fitted. It might be called a 'week-end' mission, except that the name 'mission' was not used. It was a series of special meetings which was given an attractive title. The series began with a well-advertised open meeting in the Great Hall on the Friday evening and ended with an equally well-advertised final meeting on the Sunday evening. According to the university, there were different choices of open discussions, faculty groups, a buffet tea, or supper, on the Saturday. The Saturday evening was, however, mostly utilized informally for a free-for-all discussion ('bull-ring' style) or for another open meeting. This shorter period could be more easily sustained by the Union's membership and in most cases proved equally attractive to the potential public.

The Union in Manchester hit on another successful form of regular influence. Finding that attendances at large central meetings were hard to maintain, a series of 'evangelistic Bible studies' were put on in the halls of residence. They were also organized in the main university buildings for those coming in daily from their homes. This was in the form of 'faculty groups'. Non-members were invited and responded in a most encouraging manner. Some of the hall groups had to be divided and sub-divided several times to enable all the would-be participants to take part. When they were really introduced to it, many of the non-members openly expressed their great surprise about what the Bible really had to say and how 'incredibly relevant to life' it really was. A number eventually became definite Christians and continued as regular readers of the Bible. This approach was tried in other universities and residential colleges mostly with similar results. Success to a large extent depended upon the skilled touch of sympathetic leadership, which knew its material and what a group discussion should really be.

Another successful experiment in Northern England, though with a different purpose, might be mentioned here. Liverpool, finding its membership very scattered during the week was depressed about the lack of cohesion and fellowship in the Union. Premises were hired in the university area of central Liverpool for a Saturday evening buffet meal, and a united meeting. Several other 'civic' universities in the north attempted something similar and with comparable welcome results. A healthy balance between a united fellowship for the membership and an effective outreach is difficult to achieve, and even harder to maintain. During these years the student leaders often did well in spite of very unpromising circumstances.

The colleges of education and technology

Another trend in this period of the history of the Movement was the rapidly increasing importance of the work of the colleges' Christian Unions. The colleges were steadily being up-graded under a plan, applied from 1961 onwards, where training colleges had a year added to their courses and became colleges of education. Similarly, some of the technical colleges, became colleges of advanced technology (and, later, universities). The student Executive Committee and Advisory Committees of the Fellowship were soon aware that this vast area, which was much larger than the total university field, needed to be given special attention. There was here potentially a huge need for expansion. With the outcome of the training in the colleges of education the future quality of the teaching of the nation's children was at stake. In another area, rapid advances in technology were giving a new prestige to science and its applications in the engineering world.

In the midst of their planning the committees were sometimes considerably shaken to see the reports coming from some training colleges showing what the departments of religious education were teaching. They were goaded into action when specimens of lecture notes were received. For example, from one college, at that time still controlled by the Church of England, came a copy of one of the lecturer's duplicated notes, given out at the end of the first lecture on the Pentateuch. It began, 'When Moses set out to lead the rabble, that was Israel, out of serfdom in Egypt and across the waterless desert of Sinai, he soon felt the need for a set of regulations to reinforce his command and to achieve some order. He and his brother, the religious leader, therefore, compiled a Code of Laws and gave it to the people under the name of their tribal God, Jahveh'. After that there was virtual unanimity that *something* ought to be done, and that it should be done as soon as possible! (See chapter 14, page 251.)

226

The Annual Conference

With the considerable increase in the membership of the Unions from 1947 onwards the numbers attending the annual spring conferences at the Hayes, Swanwick, and the one in Scotland, steadily built up. Soon there was great pressure on space. Similarly numbers increased for the leaders' conference in September, and for that of the theological students in January. Eventually at Swanwick the crowds were only got in by the use of camp beds in the larger rooms of the house and stretcher beds in corners under the eaves of the Quadrangle. Those willing to take the more spartan accommodation were offered reduced fees, but this produced a flood of applications for these billets! At the conference there would then be remarks about the 'House of Lords', such as, 'What about those gentlemen who like travelling first class?' and the reply, 'Yes, but do you *really* give what you've saved to the missionary societies?'

It was this kind of cheerful outlook in the average student conference member which enabled the organizers to surmount emergencies such as one at the outset of the first post-war conference at Swanwick in 1946. The Conference Estate had not long before been released from being used as a German prisoner-of-war camp. The IVF was the first conference to return to it. The former managing director had died during the war and the new management was quite inexperienced in handling a place of that size. As soon as the central heating was put on, water poured from a series of burst pipes and flooded some floors. It had not been tested until the morning of the IVF party's arrival. When the IVF advance party arrived at midday, ready for over 300 arrivals in the late afternoon and onwards, some parts of the buildings had bedroom furniture still stacked up as it had been left by the government's retreating 'army of occupation'!

To anything but a student party it would have been a disaster. A quick plan had to be made. Working like a colony of beavers, the advance party conscripted every new arrival into one of the busy teams. Just in time all comers had some kind of sleeping quarters by the end of the day. The indifferently cooked food was then greeted by, 'Anyway it is much better than we had after we

227

had landed at Salerno!' or, 'It is nectar compared with what we had for two days in the open boats after we had been torpedoed'! The members of the conference cheerfully and gallantly made do. And the spiritual results? In several ways it was one of the best conferences for years. Perhaps the sheer determination to overcome the creature discomforts bred a unity and resolution on the spiritual side that was infectious. Three non-Christian students who had come with friends, not really knowing the nature of the conference, had become Christians before the end of it. One of them subsequently went overseas as a missionary.

The 1947 conference needed to have an overflow of sleeping quarters in a small conference centre several miles away from Swanwick. For the next twenty-five years the annual conference, together with the Scottish annual conference, remained the vital centre of the year's work. Scotland, too, had its problems with accommodation. After the War, Bonskeid House, Pitlochry (where the conference had begun in 1925) was far too small. So was Netherhall, Largs, and several other centres. Until university accommodation became too expensive, St. Andrew's (with the conference based on St. Salvator's and using the other halls of residence) remained the most popular. Later, youth hostels, such as that at Auchendennan on Lomondside, were pressed into service.

The needs of the greater number who would not travel or could not be accommodated at the two larger conferences were met by a series of regional and 'specialist' conferences. In the case of the latter, the theological students, medical students and missionary volunteers all developed their own annual conferences. Also, in Wales, Northern England and Ireland, annual conferences brought together many who for various reasons, particularly financial, would never be able to get to one of the central larger ones. As at so many points over the years, Dr. Martyn Lloyd-Jones proved of key importance in the growth from year to year of the conferences in Wales. Having the confidence of both areas he could give maximum help to the students from north and south Wales. He was also the leader from whom the Welsh theological students and graduates gathered inspiration.

Organizational expansion

The reader interested in organizational backgrounds may have wondered how the demands of the greatly increased membership and the multiplied specialized functions of the Fellowship could have been met and extended. At this point therefore, some reference must be made to the way in which reinforcement was brought to the minimal 'team' of workers which had seen the Fellowship through the War years. For the sake of clarity it will be better to sacrifice chronology in order to review the steps by which the functional needs of the organization were gradually provided.

In 1945 the first necessity was to find a new and enlarged central team to take advantage of the unparalleled challenge and opportunities. The second need was to reinforce this office-based team by another consisting of the younger graduates in key professional positions who could visit Christian Unions at the week-ends or in the evenings. There needed to be senior speakers to supplement the work of the travelling secretaries. The third need was to produce more up-to-date publications to fill the gaps in Christian literature and to arm the incoming generation of students. All this, however, demanded more income, better business organization and larger office space. Here, especially now that it is possible to look back and to trace the subsequent careers of some in the *dramatis personae* of that time, there can be no doubt that just the right men became available for that juncture of the Fellowship's history.

Finding a new team

The chairman of the Business Advisory Committee, J. W. Laing, thoroughly understood and believed in the IVF's principle that the essential initiative must come from the students who were in the front line of the academic fields. The IVF staff were simply a servicing corps which stood in where more experience was needed or organizational chores could be taken off the students' academic time-schedules. The chairman's approach to the future of the IVF was often expressed—'The first essential is to find the

229

right men and women, then we can soon think about how to pay them and put roofs over their heads.'

The first choice of personnel was obvious to all. Dr. Oliver Barclay has just completed his assignment in biological research at Cambridge and was thinking about his next step. He was an ex-president of the CICCU, a former chairman of the IVF's student Executive Committee and had been able to keep in close touch with the student leaders through his residence in Trinity College and attendance at war-time conferences. He agreed, temporarily, to postpone an intended offer to teach biology in one of the Chinese new universities in order to assist the IVF at this time. In the event the Fellowship not only gained an ideal Universities Secretary, but, later, an Assistant Secretary and General Secretary.

Following this in quick succession came three other vital appointments. Ronald Inchley, on being released from war-time work in Northern England, was encouraged to return as Publications Secretary and start more fully to develop the Inter-Varsity Press. Freddy Crittenden, of the OICCU's 1927 rebirth (page 139), one day walked into the office in the uniform of an East African regiment to say that he was about to be demobilized and was not sure what to do next. The IVF knew (!) and he agreed to act as one of the new travelling secretaries on a temporary basis. Finally he stayed to develop the Graduates Fellowship as its secretary and, then, to complete his unique piece of service for Overseas Students.

Things happened rather rapidly. Shortly after this the General Secretary had commented to the Chairman of the Business Advisory Committee that he and the second clerical secretary (Miss Lilian Baker, who had combined war-time secretaryship with the IVF's accountancy and cashier duties) were both getting rather out of their depth and overwhelmed on the financial side. With this the Chairman commented, 'Well, perhaps in the end, we shall have to get a qualified accountant!' In a matter of days a letter came from an Oxford aerodrome from George White (FCA!) reporting that his unit was being demobilized and he had been thinking about full-time service for Christ. He wondered if the Secretary had any suggestions? This, just in time, brought a very important addition to the team. For, in a matter of a few months, the turnover of the Publications Department began to rise steeply, general financial business grew in several directions and some six mainstreams of activity were burgeoning. It meant that the rest of the staff were able to give their undivided attention to their primary tasks, whilst a reliable and devoted Financial Secretary and Accountant took the strain.

On the women's side, the personnel also virtually chose itself. Phyllis Bennett was doing so well and was so much appreciated throughout the women students' side of the work, that everyone wished to leave well alone. A search was begun for additional women's travelling secretaries. Norah Nixon's experience at vital points was too valuable to lose. She was made Women's Secretary in the now growing Graduates Fellowship, and became the active and ever-ready 'base' for the welcoming of incoming overseas students.

Re-shaping the central organization

With continual growth in every department it was soon found that the original structure of the student-type organization called for some degree of rearrangement and buttressing, particularly in relation to all of its more senior activities, to the increased number of graduate staff and to what was becoming a sizeable publishing house. In all this the senior graduates were anxious, as much as student leaders, to preserve to the full the student initiative in the local Christian Unions, in the student conferences and in all the central activities which directly bear on the life and work of the students. Such considerations applied not only to the original field of service, that is, in the universities, but in the spheres of the teachers' training colleges (now called colleges of education) and the technical colleges. So in each successive revision of the Constitution care has been taken that the original provisions in each of these three fields remains as before, that is, that student work is planned by a representative (student) general committee, electing annually its (student) executive committee.

Careful steps were, therefore, repeatedly taken to adjust to the necessities of growth. These included adequate financial supervision, co-ordinating the increasing graduate activities and the control of the growing publications department. Most of these requirements were met in the form of a series of advisory committees and the Graduates Fellowship Committee. To ensure unity of policy and action in these senior committees there was set up in the spring of 1948 a Chairmen's Co-ordinating Committee, to meet regularly three times a year, and at other times if there was sufficiently urgent business. The meetings of this committee were supplemented by the calling once in every three years a 'Committees Conference', which was open to all members of the senior committees and some of the graduate staff.

At length, in 1960, whilst retaining the same basic structure (and guarding the initiative of the student committees), the name of the 'C.C.C.' was changed to that of Council. Also, in the background and solely for the purpose of holding the lease of the office, any property and investment held on behalf of the Fellowship, was the Inter-Varsity Fellowship Trust Ltd., which was originally called into being in order to hold the property of Tyndale House, Cambridge.

The non-professional teams

In any enterprise of this kind and of 'missionary work' in general, it is all too easy for the limelight to fall upon 'the professionals', that is, those who plain duty it is to get the day to day work done. The aura which may eventually come to surround them is often out of proportion to the measure of the work being done by others in the total enterprise of the Christian church. It is a point, however, on which the student world at its best has an unerring instinct. On two occasions it was illustrated in the writer's experience by a perceptive student who, with a sly grin, offered (in terms of cricket) a list of the IVF's 'first eleven'! He was nearly right, as was a later medical student's offering (in terms of Rugby Football) a list of the Christian Medical Fellowship's 'first fifteen'!

From the point of view of the student leaders of the Christian Unions, (thinking of their next open meeting, mission or conference) the important names were those of the most helpful speakers and wisest advisers. At this point the Fellowship was comparatively rich and becoming richer. It was still feeling acutely the loss in Scotland during the war years of such key figures as Professor Duncan Blair (Glasgow), the Very Rev. Professor Daniel Lamont (Edinburgh) and Principal Donald Maclean (Edinburgh). Each had made a distinctive contribution to the work of the Scottish Unions, especially for the theological students. Their loss threw an additional burden on to the three chief theological speakers and advisers, Dr. Martyn Lloyd-Jones (Minister of Westminster Chapel), Alan M. Stibbs (Vice-Principal of Oak Hill Theological College) and G. T. Manley (Chairman of the Publications Committee). It would be impossible in the space available to chronicle the varied ways in which each had given invaluable service. Over many years Dr. Lloyd-Jones gave an astonishing amount of time in speaking at university missions, open meetings, conferences, leading discussions and advising. Both in the pulpit and conference hall he provided a powerful example of fidelity in the truth and concentration on what matters most, which he advocated in personal counsel.

Alan Stibbs was primarily a careful exegete and interpreter of the New Testament in the best traditions of the Cambridge Exegetical School. He was equally at home whether lecturing on the New Testament to theological students or expounding it to those with only elementary knowledge. He spent most of his free time in the service of the student world. For from his university days, when he was prominent in the Missionary Volunteer Movement, and, later, when on the staff of the Church Missionary Society, G. T. Manley had remained in close touch with the Fellowship. For many years his wise counsels were available to the worried presidents or secretaries of the Cambridge and London Unions. He also gave outstanding service to the Fellowship as a whole, first as chairman of the *ad hoc* committee, which planned the 3-years' Bible study course *Search the Scriptures*, then of the Biblical Research Committee and finally of the Publications Committee (1934-1959). G. T. Manley's demanding standards, persistent pursuit of clarity and sheer common sense, were quite crucial in the early days of the

IVF's venture into publishing.

Although not so active after his retirement from the Chair of Surgery at Bristol, another of the senior speakers and advisers, Professor Rendle Short, was still a force to be reckoned with in the West Country. Until his sudden passing in 1953 he was as ready as ever to speak, produce literature or write letters of advice for the student world. Harold Earnshaw Smith (Rector of All Souls Church, Langham Place, London) was also continually active in advising and speaking to student groups.

A name to be joined with that of Rendle Short and Earnshaw Smith and one who also supported the Fellowship from its earliest days in the 1920s, was that of B. F. C. Atkinson (Under Librarian, Cambridge University Library). Whilst the members of the CICCU were the chief beneficiaries of 'Basil At's' Bible readings and inimitable exhortations, between the Wars he had travelled to other universities. He maintained a wide correspondence with students and graduates until the '60s.

But the new generation of graduates emerging from the same traditions were by now beginning to take up their positions. They included some with special training and experience which were later to prove of particular value to the new generation of students. They covered a wide range of specialization. The spirit in which they have volunteered their services was well illustrated by two graduates who have later devoted many hours to the Fellowship. On demobilization Brian M. Harris (a pre-war CICCU secretary) and John T. Aitken (a Glasgow graduate, already a senior lecturer, subsequently Professor in Anatomy at University College, London) mentioned to the the secretariat, 'We intend to have only one worthwhile Christian interest likely to demand much time outside of the duties of our church membership; would you like it to be the IVF?' The IVF did not hesitate, and both the volunteers have proved of outstanding value to the Fellowship; Brian Harris as Treasurer and, later, as Chairman of the Business Advisory Committee; and Professor Aitken as Chairman and the 'anchor-man' on several of the central committees. The latter has also served as Treasurer and Chairman of the Christian Medical Fellowship.

To enumerate all (even of the more prominent) of the active

graduates is impossible here. Yet any record of the past thirty years would be much the poorer for the omission of reference to the hours of travel, speaking and writing for the student world donated by Arnold S. Aldis (surgeon and latterly Postgraduate Dean in the Welsh National School of Medicine, Cardiff); C. D. Anderson (Physician, the Western Infirmary, Glasgow); J. N. D. Anderson (Sir Norman Anderson, formerly Professor of Oriental Laws, University of London); F. F. Bruce (formerly Rylands Professor of Biblical Criticism, Manchester); W. Melville Capper (late surgeon, Royal Infirmary, Bristol); V. Edmunds (Physician, Mount Vernon Hospital); W. J. Martin (formerly Rankin Lecturer in Hebrew, University of Liverpool); J. I. Packer (Vice-Principal, Trinity College, Bristol); J. E. Richardson (Sir Eric Richardson, formerly Principal of the Regent Street Poly-technic); C. G. Scorer (surgeon, Hillingdon Hospital); J. R. W. Stott (Rector Emeritus of All Souls Church, London W1) and D. J. Wiseman (Professor of Assyriology, University of London). The IVF has also been greatly indebted on the women's side to Muriel Crouch (surgeon, Elizabeth Garrett Anderson Hospital).

Increased financial support

The period of the 1950s and 1960s was one of almost uninterrupted expansion. The question is sometimes asked why there was such a marked growth at that particular time. First, of course, there were everywhere far greater numbers of students involved in the field of higher education. Evangelical Christians in the country generally also were increasing in numbers and influence. In fact, those of other outlook in the churches regarded the Evangelicals as enjoying a quiet, but very real, revival of religion. So far as the IVF as an organization was concerned the effects were seen in more demands on the central services.

The chief pressures came from three sources. In general there was an insistent call for much more frequent visits from a travelling secretary, especially from some of the weaker Unions, who found it hard to get speakers. Such requests were reinforced by those who wanted a certain degree of zoning of the colleges with similar needs, so that each member of staff visiting them would be as far as possible familiar with their local difficulties. Then, second, there were calls for higher standards in meeting the special needs of theological students, science students, medical students, overseas students and other sections of the constituency. Third, there was a great growth of interest and activity in the colleges of education and the technical colleges. This called for a definite task force of its own. For example, the more the secretary to the Technical Colleges Christian Fellowship, Raymond Turner, and his successor Arthur Pont, applied their energies to this vast field, the more insistent became the call for a bigger staff allocated entirely to it. It was hard to resist the appeal of those colleges and student groups who were only being contacted for one afternoon in the year, or only by letter.

Following the principle that the first essential was to ensure that the *right* men and women were the chief resources in a spiritual movement, the Business Advisory and various specialist committees moved to secure a minimum staff to respond to the most urgent calls. This involved a larger budget than had ever been contemplated in the pre-war years. It also meant a much closer study of the conditions, needs and suggestions which were coming from an increasingly diverse constituency. Money had never been plentiful. In one way its scarcity served as a useful discipline. This meant a tighter control on all new initiatives involving new expenditure, so that all the resources should be channelled in the most productive directions. Here the Fellowship was, again, well served by its Business Advisory Committee.

Little has so far been said about finance, because the constant aim from the beginning of the Fellowship was to divert as little as possible from the Lord's treasury in view of all the worldwide needs. It was only when the ultimate results of the Fellowship's work became clearer and the size of its own contribution to the world missionary enterprise more evident, that the justification for a commensurate access to sufficient funds was seen. The problem, however, was to whom should the IVF chiefly look for the support of its continued work? There was a general consensus that it must be to its own former members, who had a sufficient knowledge of what the Fellowship was all about. It is therefore of

236

interest that an analysis of income in a recent year gave the source of the Fellowship's funds as follows:-

Former members of the Unions	60%
Evangelical charitable trusts	12%
Publications department	10%
Rents, interest and such sources	8%
Churches	7%
Students (not including the Unions' payment of travelling secretaries' expenses)	3%
	100%

More office space

The loyal support of former members was available again when the Business Advisory Committee addressed itself to the task of providing more space, which was urgently needed by the Publications department alone. In 1949 a lease was taken and planning permission gained to place two temporary buildings on a bombed site at 16 Morwell Street, adjoining the rear of the main office in 39 Bedford Square. Whilst there was one large gift from a business source, it was mostly the former members who subscribed what was needed. The same was true in 1958 when the two (superior) huts were no longer adequate. A long lease was taken from the Bedford Estate and a new three-storey building erected on the site, having a large basement to serve as warehouse for the day-to-day stocks of literature. Whilst £10,000 of the total of £32,000 came from the business sources, much of the rest was donated by ex-members of the Unions.

Other financial considerations

As far as possible, all specialist ventures by the graduates' committees have been financed separately so as not to divert resources from the general funds from its primary aim of supporting the student work. One example was the Biblical Research Committee's venture at the Tyndale House and its Library in 1941 (page 298). When in 1954 much more room in the library was needed, and more residential accommodation, £18,000 was donated. Whilst one large gift helped to 'prime the pump', the rest again was largely the result of the loyal support of the former members. Similarly, a high proportion of the backing for the overseas students Alliance Club (with half of the capital from the Evangelical Alliance) was donated by the same sources.

The Graduates Fellowship

During the 'fifties, with Freddy Crittenden acting as Secretary, the Graduates' Fellowship developed in two main directions. First, there came growth in the number of specialist sections, of which the Schoolteachers Fellowship was the largest. It was followed in size by the Christian Medical Fellowship. There was also the Tyndale Fellowship, consisting mostly of ordained ministers who were interested in the work of the Biblical Research Committee and other forms of theological research. Shortly after the war, Oliver Barclay, impressed by the isolation, and often loneliness, of the backroom research graduates and their need to be kept in touch with other Christian minds working in similar fields, started the Research Scientists' Christian Fellowship. Comment on this and similar developments has been further made in chapter 16, pages 290–292.

On the initiative of the Graduates Fellowship Secretary, a second area of development was in evangelism amongst the members' own colleagues both at the place of work and also in the area of their residence. In neither sphere was it easy to gain the appropriate interest from busy professional workers. F. H. Crittenden hoped that the whole Graduates' Fellowship could be fully transformed into an evangelistic instrument, but such aims were not to be realized overnight. Degrees of success varied in the different professional contexts and according to the nature of the residential environments. Success ultimately depended upon ability to make contacts, skill in giving hospitality and the actual evangelistic gifts of the members concerned. But progress was made in some areas and in some professions.

The GF Secretary himself also pioneered several successful evening meetings gathered by personal invitation (with members

238

taking their guests for an evening meal beforehand in clubs, restaurants or hotels) in the hall of the Royal Commonwealth Society, London. Similar meetings, by personal invitation, were arranged in several other cities such as Bristol and Glasgow. On a smaller scale, where some members were equipped with houses which had sufficiently large dining rooms, dinners were arranged in much more informal circumstances. Whereas the larger gatherings would have an invited speaker, the smaller party would have an informal after-dinner discussion. Amongst the different professions, greatest progress was made where regular official social gatherings were the usual practice of that profession.

Regional growth

Expansion was taking place at so many points, especially in the number of new Christian Unions in the colleges of education and technology, that those responsible had repeatedly to adjust the work-loads of the few available travelling secretaries. Rising costs of transport and the time factor called for more rationalizing of the locations, the bases, from which they would work. There were also special needs in particular areas which called for consideration. The immediate result was that Scotland, northern England, Wales and Ireland came to have their own travellers.

Scotland had already led the way in days preceding World War II. Alistair Rennie, a Glasgow graduate who had just finished his theological studies, had been appointed and had served from 1937-1940. He was succeeded by Kenneth Mackenzie (1941-45) and A. W. Rainsbury (1946-51), and the succession has been ably maintained. A generous gift from the Scottish subscribers of a house for the travelling secretaries paved the way for the appointment of married graduates, whereas most of the earlier appointments in the south had been of those who, at the time, were single and coming straight from their student years.

In Wales the students had asked that any such graduate support would come from those who were Welsh-speaking, and so able to understand the outlook and needs of those whose devotional language was Welsh. The first appointment was of Gwyn Walters (1950-51). He was succeeded by Gwilym Roberts

239

(1953–55) and Elwyn Davies (1955–62). The latter's earlier experience in a spiritual revival which took place in college during his student days in Bangor, gave him a natural position of leadership amongst the students and graduates who later became some of the leaders in the Evangelical Movement of Wales. South Wales also asked for a women's travelling secretary, because of their special needs at that time. The first of these was Rhoda T. Bassett (1954–57), followed by Mary D. Clee (1957–60).

A Dublin graduate, Herbert H. Carson, found himself free from other work, just as Northern Ireland was needing similar reinforcement, and he served from 1948 to 1951. At a later date, a worker for Northern England, the Rev. Michael J. Cole (1961–64) was based on Leeds. These regional placings were, however, not made too rigidly and 'exchanges of pulpits' were welcomed and fruitful. The work-loads of the travelling secretaries have had increasingly to be adjusted in the light of the student populations being served.

Theological students

Each generation of Christian students has been troubled by the spiritual and intellectual outlook in many of the theological colleges, which have their own occupational hazards. Almost irrespective of denomination (although some in this respect have been better than others) there has been what might be called a process of attrition, reducing Evangelical fervour. Many a student officer of a Christian Union, a travelling secretary or senior graduate adviser could echo what follows from their own experience. An earnest young Christian, full of zeal for Christ, believing that he has had a call from God to enter the Christian ministry, offers to his denomination. During his days in the faculty of arts he may remain fresh in his personal devotional life, an enthusiastic reader of the Bible and full of evangelistic zeal in leading others to Christ. Having graduated, however, he must pass over into a theological hall for the theological and pastoral part of his training. A subtle change soon comes over him and he is not so much at ease with colleagues in ordinary life as he used to be. There is not the same warmth at the chance meetings with the old friends of the other faculties. More could be said of his second year in theological hall. The point is that by the time of ordination the freshness, the enthusiasm and the zeal has so often gone. Perhaps one of IVF's mistakes in the earlier years was that more direct help was not given to the theological students battling to keep their devotional freshness and their intellectual poise in spite of the conditioning process of the liberal theology.

During his period of universities' secretaryship, Robert Horn became more and more concerned about the needs of the Theological Students Fellowship. It needed more help from the centre. Since its inception in 1933 its secretaryship, in student hands, could do little more than organize an annual theological students' conference. In 1962 Robert Horn became secretary of the TSF (with responsibility also for the missionary programme). Considerably more could then be done to assist in a variety of ways, particularly in helping with intellectual difficulties and problems of conscience. Able senior ministers in the denominations of those finding the way hard have frequently been able to give much wise counsel from their own experience in college. Tribute should also be paid to the great help given both to individuals and TSF conferences by Andrew Walls when serving as Librarian at Tyndale House, Cambridge.

A second part of Robert Horn's work concerned a similar shortage of help for the missionary volunteers' side of the work. Whereas, when the IVMF was founded, many countries were still open to the older style evangelistic missionary, few countries remained so freely open. At first, however, there were some countries which had earlier been regarded as 'closed lands' which were at the time opening to western missionaries. Certain of the 'colonial' territories were also welcoming a greater number of western graduates in the pioneer stages of staffing their new universities, new schools and new hospitals. For the first ten post-war years or more, except, all too soon, in China, there were still open doors and too few to enter them. By 1960, however, a change was beginning clearly to show. Independence in formerly colonial territories bred new nationalisms (and the removal of strong central government let loose former tribal conflicts). A new era in missions was opening.

241

One aspect of this has been that the Western graduate must now be the equal colleague of the members of the indigenous churches, sharing his expertise as he would in his own church at home. The world in which the old Student Missionary Volunteer Movement of the 1880s and the Inter-Varsity Missionary Fellowship of the 1930s made their stirring appeals was no more. In the late 1960s and '70s things moved further in the direction of increased nationalism, political instability and wars, and more closed lands. There may still be room in the many tribal areas for something like the older medical missionary, but in many lands the welcome that remains is chiefly for an expert in a skill which is at present unavailable amongst indigenous personnel. The value of the non-professional missionary has certainly increased. It is a sphere in which the IVF is better placed than most other Christian organizations to make a larger contribution.

Theological tensions and debates

The '50s and '60s saw revived, in different forms, some of the tensions of the 18th and 19th century revivals. These gave rise to much discussion, sometimes rather heated, and brought some of the Unions near to division. On the whole, however, the result was mostly confined to healthy debate over what the Bible actually does teach on certain matters. Where eventually the debaters truly discovered what the Bible actually *did* say the outcome was entirely beneficial.

The process, however, threw into relief the importance of determining the purpose of a Christian Union and seeing its limitations. It is but a temporary association in university or college of those who are themselves members of a variety of churches. They are associated with each other for the restricted purpose of the period of their residence in a university. The Christian Union is not a church and is not therefore competent to dispense the sacraments or determine difficult points of doctrine. It is united on the basis of common allegiance to Christ, acceptance of the Christian faith as recorded in the Bible (emphasizing the major doctrines on which Evangelicals are united), and it has the primary practical aim of bringing the gospel

242

to fellow students. The spirit of sectarianism, and sometimes heresy, easily intrudes as soon as expression of opinion dogmatically goes beyond what can be *plainly* proved from Holy Scripture.

Some of the Unions, especially those which had large memberships from rather varied ecclesiastical backgrounds, were troubled by members who had embraced certain extremes and others who over-reacted to them. Such differences of opinion chiefly arose on such matters as the doctrine of the Divine sovereignty in relation to the free offer of the gospel, the doctrine of the Holy Spirit as emphasized by the Pentecostal (or later 'charismatic') movement, and attacks by liberal theologians on 'fundamentalism'.

During the years following the war there was for a time an acute shortage of publications competent to clarify the theological issues which had become more and more blurred by the hypothetical and subjective scholarship that was fashionable. Some of the Evangelicals went back to the writings of the Presbyterian tradition in the Princeton Theological Seminary of C. H. Hodge, A. A. Hodge and B. B. Warfield, and the later Westminster Seminary teaching of J. Gresham Machen. Many excellent volumes of reformed theology were reproduced by the Banner of Truth Trust. A much needed re-emphasis was restored on the fact of God's sovereignty, apart from which all other Christian doctrine is left without valid foundations and all prophecy becomes uncertain of fulfilment. But, as so often has happened at various times in church history, some students tended to overlook the fact that God's servants have not been given detailed knowledge of how His providence works from day to day, and of how He superintends the lives of individual persons. They have to work on general principles. The ultimate results of evangelistic preaching, apart from any evidence in altered lives, are known only to God. The teaching of our Lord and of St. Paul encourage the preacher to scatter the seed of the Word of God as widely and thoroughly as he can. He does not 'know which shall prosper, this or that'.

By wise counsel and even more by his own example in the pulpit, Dr. Martyn Lloyd-Jones helped many to retain the

Biblical emphasis and balance. Much guidance was also given to the members of the London Inter-Faculty Christian Union by Dr. James Packer in a brief series of lectures. They were subsequently published as a paperback, *Evangelism and the Sovereignty of God* (IVP, 1961).

In the late '60s there were several other sources of potential disharmony coming from movements which were influencing the churches. The chief was a widespread interest in what earlier had been known as 'Pentecostalism', but now the 'Charismatic Movement'. In so far as this challenged the cold formalism into which worship so easily can fall, revived due attention to the status of the Holy Spirit in the church and recovered the confidence and notable joy of the early Christians, it was to be welcomed. But in the hands of over-zealous extremists, as has so often happened in church history, something good in itself became a near-heresy, and produced reaction and, in some cases, over-reaction.

Those advocating the extreme views, in excess of what can be justified from Scripture, were claiming moral and emotional states which were more appropriate to angelic spirits than human beings. The doctrine of the Holy Spirit was so over-emphasized in theory and practice that the centre of Christian worship was virtually moved from its approach to the triune God through the High Priest and Mediator to the Third Person of the Trinity. Our Lord Himself had cautioned that when 'He, the Spirit of Truth has come ... He will bear witness to Me' ... 'He will not speak of Himself' (or on His own authority). In other words the Holy Spirit, working through all the other witnesses, prophets, apostles and Christians today, primarily points to Christ. Another rather surprising trend was that competent and clear exposition of Holy Scripture was replaced in the pulpits by autobiography or a catalogue of the Christian experience of others.

Although there were considerable tensions in some of the Christian Unions, patience and tolerance eventually prevailed. Here again the Fellowship was indebted to the counsels, teaching and examples in the pulpit of a number of ministers, such as Dr. Martyn Lloyd-Jones, John Stott, Leith Samuel and many others, who were concerned for the spiritual health of the students.

The student churches

At this point some reference must be made to the value and assistance given to members of the Christian Unions in the university cities by a number of hospitable churches. Many others also in the neighbourhood of residential colleges in smaller towns have been no less supporting. In the period under review the number of such 'spiritual homes' grew. Some deserve special mention; Gilmonston Church, Aberdeen; Christ Church, Clifton, Bristol; 'the Round' and St. Paul's Churches, Cambridge; Heath Church, Cardiff; Holyrood Abbey Church, Edinburgh; Sandeford Henderson Memorial Church, Glasgow; All Souls and St. Helen's Churches and Westminster Chapel, London; Holy Trinity, Platt, Manchester; St. Ebbe's and St. Aldate's Churches, Oxford; and Above Bar Church, Southampton.

Sometimes, and it is an understandable temptation, a church has simply welcomed students as extra sermon-hearers and sometimes it has made too big a demand on the time of its student members, forgetting the academic and other pressures on the members of an academic community. The most welcome situation is when the minister, being aware of their potential later influence, concentrates on giving students a clear presentation of biblical truth, which can be applied during the subsequent week in common rooms and all places of social contact in college. It gives real backbone to the Christian Union.

In general, during this period there was a growth in the provision of university chaplaincies. These were mostly in bishops' appointments of chaplains to Church of England students. There are few university (official) chaplaincies. The Free Churches have also appointed chaplains for their students, who usually are the ministers of churches nearest to the university buildings. The policy of the appointing authorities, however, has so often seemed to be to select clever, 'with-it', politically orientated young men who are more at home in topical discussions than in showing their students how to live as Christians and to witness. Where there has been a chaplain with marked pastoral and preaching gifts, and with a gift of evangelism, his work has been fruitful and rewarding.

'Fundamentalism'

Early in this period came another of the periodic attacks, which the Evangelical Movement has learnt to expect when things are going well. During the long war against 'fundamentalism' it has been interesting to note with more than a touch of irony the personal backgrounds of those who have been the most prominent antagonists. The criticism of the views they dislike so often come from leading figures in churches, in which the ordained ministers are officially committed in essence to propagating the very views they ridicule and virtually brand as heresy!

It is worth observing the actual position in the Church of England. Whatever may be the exact position at the present time, when those concerned in the critiques took their ordination vows they accepted, presumably *ex animo,* certain obligations. A deacon was asked, 'Do you unfeignedly believe all the canonical Scriptures of the Old and New Testaments' and answered – 'I do believe them'. At ordination as priest he was asked, 'Are you persuaded that the Holy Scriptures contain sufficiently all doctrine required of necessity for eternal salvation through faith in Jesus Christ' and he replied, 'I am so persuaded and have so determined by God's grace'. Those who became bishops, however, went further. After a repetition of the question and answer above, comes, 'Will you faithfully exercise yourself in the same Holy Scripture, and call upon God by prayer, for the true understanding of the same' and also, 'Be you ready, with all faithful diligence to banish and drive away all erroneous and strange doctrine contrary to God's Word: and both privately and openly to call upon and encourage others to the same?' The reply was 'I am ready, the Lord being my helper'. Nothing could be more in keeping with the Old and New Testaments' instructions.

But as a plain fact of history the result has been somewhat unexpected, to say the least. Prominent ecclesiastics and official teachers in the church have been permitted publicly to explain away some of the cardinal doctrines of the Christian faith, such as incarnation, the divinity of Christ, the resurrection and the second advent. Sometimes episcopal and professorial zeal for the truth has been mostly evident in attacking those who wish to retain the doctrines summarized in the Apostles Creed.

In a letter to *The Times* in 1955 Canon H. K. Luce of Durham complained that 'the proposal that Dr. Graham should conduct a mission to Cambridge University raises an issue which does not seem to have been squarely faced by Christians in this country. Universities exist for the advancement of learning: on what basis, therefore, can fundamentalism claim a hearing at Cambridge?' This gave rise to a considerable correspondence. Several bishops, including the Bishop of Durham, wrote against Dr. Graham, though one suffragan bishop wrote in his favour. A layman, however, put in the embarrassing question, 'Have your Right Reverend and Reverend Correspondents who are opposed to Fundamentalism forgotten that at their ordination they solemnly and publicly declared that they "unfeignedly believe all the canonical Scriptures of the Old and New Testament"?' That was a 'good shot', particularly as the attacks are usually made on the grounds of intellectual integrity!

Other papers took up the controversy in their own ways and several bishops wrote in their diocesan papers and periodicals. The Bishop of Durham (A. M. Ramsey) did so under the title *The Menace of Fundamentalism*. (We must note that the former orthodoxy of the Church of England has now become a 'menace'!) The Bishop was quite explicit about his attitude to Billy Graham and what he was thought to represent. 'He has gone, our English fundamentalism remains. It is *heretical* . . . It is *sectarian* . . . The Church must pray that men will be raised up with power so to preach, that the stream of conversions will not be followed by a backwash of moral casualties and disillusioned sceptics' (!). The irony is all the greater because earlier when he was a don at Cambridge he had been popular with the members of the CICCU and they were sorry to see him go to Durham! For, coming from a conservative High Churchman, his excellent lectures on the history of Christian doctrine in the first four centuries were amongst the more helpful offerings of a theological faculty which at that time was liberal and arid. His former students have always taken the view that he had been persistently misinformed and wrote from second-hand biased reporting on

247

the Billy Graham and fundamentalist issue.

A more constrained and comprehensive attack was made in 1957 by an Anglo-Catholic writer, Gabriel Hebert, in his *Fundamentalism and the Church of God* (SCM Press). This volume was concerned not only with views of the Bible, but the gospel and style of churchmanship. Hebert's book is largely based on a 'catholic' view of the church and the primacy of the church in determining Christian doctrine. A trenchant reply, which has been of outstanding help to many students in clarifying this issue, was produced by James I. Packer in his *Fundamentalism and the Word of God* (IVP, 1958).

A more varied membership

In the '60s it was found that the academic backgrounds in the membership had become much more varied in several ways, especially in the number of faculties and subjects of study then represented. In the '30s there had been a marked predominance of students from the faculties of theology, science, medicine and sometimes engineering. The faculty of arts was poorly represented, as were also the more philosophical aspects of Western culture. This frequently was explained by SCM leaders on the grounds that the IVF's supporters were mostly drawn from what were really the applied sciences in which the student was never compelled to think at the deeper levels of the true intellectual. There may have been some truth in that. However, whenever they were challenged, the SCM supporters (having jettisoned the reliability of the Bible) always came up with vaguest of intellectual grounds for continuing in the Christian faith. But now the IVF had a number of those whom even the SCM might recognize as intellectuals and who had experienced an Evangelical conversion. They wished to go forward in the Christian faith, applying it to all aspects of their thinking and lives. Some of them were obviously leaders.

The IVF had to meet yet another challenge. Amongst the most interesting of the new spheres, into which student initiatives were channelled, were the colleges of art. There seemed at that time few Christians on the college staffs or seniors to whom the leading students could go to discuss their problems. Eventually the students in these colleges, much as the research science students earlier had done, had to borrow from Christian circles in the Netherlands. Professor R. Hoykaas, formerly of the Free University of Amsterdam and later, Professor of the History of Science in the University of Utrecht, had brought many welcome new insights to the Research Scientists Christian Fellowship, both in their discussions and conferences. He introduced to the art students a former colleague, Professor Rookmaaker, Professor of the History of Art at the Free University of Amsterdam. The latter was invited to a conference of students of art, and all interested from the related specialized fields. It took place on 25 September 1967, was very well attended and much interest was aroused.

Professor Rookmaaker made a number of subsequent visits, speaking and discussing with college groups and reading papers at conferences. In order to help further, he contributed a book *Modern Art and the Death of a Culture* (IVP, 1970) and, at the time of his death, had nearly completed the MS for *Art needs no Justification* (IVP, 1978).

There were also other new departments of the universities and colleges from which members were drawn. In the late '60s the departments of sociology were everywhere growing fast. Amongst those in the ranks of the sociologists were some who began to come to Christian meetings in order to study 'religion' and 'religious people'. In not a few cases, however, they found that the Christian religion had more to it than they had thought. They were captivated by it and became zealous to spread 'the new truth' in their difficult field and amongst their critical colleagues. The latter could appreciate Christianity as one amongst many contributory studies, but it was a different matter to be confronted with its claims. Fortunately, in the social studies departments, there were a number of senior graduates on staffs of colleges and universities who were able to give timely help.

Other spheres

Whilst their fuller development came at a later stage in the '60s there were several successful initiatives in new areas. For example, the Therapy Students Christian Fellowship, which had started in 1952, made considerable progress in places where there was appropriate leadership. In certain of the hospitals where the location of the buildings and time schedules favoured meetings, there were good attendances and a number were brought to the Christian faith. In view of their size and sometimes the environmental difficulties to be overcome, the therapists have proved a vigorous and lively group.

With the great expansion of the work of the Technical Colleges Christian Fellowship there came a new interest amongst the many agricultural colleges. By this time there was one in almost every county, and in some of the large agricultural counties there were two. In pre-war days there had been a small Christian Union in Wye Agricultural College, Kent, which had had a rather fitful existence. At times there was no one left who was interested and it would lapse for a year or two. But the college travelling secretaries found a good deal of response in agricultural colleges. It depended on the quality and resolution of the leadership and the degree of welcome they could elicit from the student body in what were comparatively small communities. In quite a number of them fair-sized groups were brought into being and meetings in some of them proved most rewarding. It was much regretted that the available 'team' of travellers was so small and some of the colleges so remote, that visits could be paid only at wide intervals.

As the '60s drew to a close the Fellowship found itself, as at the beginning, still too small in proportion to the need and opportunity. With large numbers of non-members willing to hear the message of the movement all the travelling secretaries and other staff were fully extended. There was one more promising feature in the situation. There were now many former members of the Christian Unions at all levels on the various universities and colleges staffs. Others were also occupying many of the city pulpits or were scattered throughout the various professions. It meant that most of the student committees had access to senior aid if and when it was required.

250

Chapter 14

Colleges of education and technical colleges[1] (1935–1978)

As the preceding chapters have shown, the Inter-Varsity Fellowship originated in the universities and in its early years was entirely a university movement. Very early in its history, however, the leaders became aware of the importance of the student population in the various non-university colleges. This had been scarcely touched. The complete list of the teachers' training colleges (now known as colleges of education) and the various types of technical colleges ran into several hundreds whilst the total number of students involved, if those on part-time courses were included, comprised several hundreds of thousands. They greatly exceeded the number of matriculated students at the universities. From time to time in the IVF committees and conferences there was discussion of what ought or could be done for the spiritual needs of these colleges. In retrospect it can now be seen how slow and inadequate was both the recognition of duty and the accompanying action. There were, however, several mitigating reasons, quite apart from the fact that for a number of years the IVF had no full-time workers and then for a long time only a small team with which to cope with the calls from an increasing number of university Christian Unions.

First among the deterrents was the fact that, unlike the university degree courses of not less than three years' duration (with the courses in some faculties, such as medicine and engineering, extending to five or six years) the training colleges at this time offered only two year certificate courses. In the case of the technical colleges (except for those taking external degrees from London University) the position was even more difficult. For many technical college students were in full-time or part-time employment with day-release or part-time courses. The effect of these different conditions of work meant that in all of the colleges, except for a few favoured residential training colleges, there was not much opportunity for student corporate life and student-run cultural activities. The curriculum was almost wholly geared to a tread-mill of work, academic tasks (filling up what had promised to be free time) whilst the general college discipline did not greatly differ from that of senior school. In addition, in most colleges the pressures on room space often left few or no quiet corners where a Christian group could easily meet. The total environment was not at all promising for the delicate seeds of pioneer Christian Union activity.

On top of all these external discouragements were the even more formidable internal impediments of intellectual and spiritual opposition. The attitudes of the teaching staff in some of the departments of religious knowledge were almost wholly unsympathetic. Some not only showed undisguised hostility to Evangelicalism but sometimes actively persecuted those who persisted in the conservative viewpoints in which they had been trained by their parents or home churches. It was made abundantly clear that those who in due course failed to shed such hangovers from childhood could expect little sympathy. The religion of childhood may have served its purpose for that stage, but now it was time spiritually and intellectually to grow up into the offered blessings of the philosophy of materialistic and atheistic evolution and acceptance of the 'assured results' of the 'higher criticism' of the Bible!

The extent of the blanket intellectual rigidities of the teaching had to be seen in students' notes and the lecturers' hand-outs to be believed. Quite apart from spiritual considerations the whole process was educationally questionable as a form of training for the future teachers of the nation. When reported to distinguished senior members of the universities they were astonished at the

252

evidence about which the lecturers' own notes left no doubt. Even greater astonishment greeted several well authenticated reports of incidents in the women's colleges where students, who asked to retain the faith and attitudes in which they had been brought up, were invited to interviews with visiting psychiatrists (or sometimes psychologists) in order to help them 'to adjust to the demands of modern and progressive education'.

Commenting on this period in the training colleges one well-informed observer has written, 'In more than one college at the first lecture of the year all "fundamentalists" were asked to hold up their hands and then faced ridicule and sustained criticism'. CUs were not infrequently banned from meeting on college premises. This was one of the toughest battles and only gradually were the authorities brought to change their attitude. In one college, evacuated during the war, while no Christian meetings of more than three people were allowed in college rooms, between twenty and thirty students professed conversion in one year.

At a later stage, when CUs were being more freely formed, one principal, trying to dissuade a student from starting a CU, told her that she would be tightly controlled from IVF 'headquarters', to which the girl, wide-eyed with genuine astonishment, replied, 'Why, there is only Ros, isn't there?' ('Ros'[2] was at that time the total staff of the Training Colleges Christian Union!). Uniformity was presumed to be due to outside pressure, not to biblical truth. The living strength of a biblical Christianity became clearer only with time.

Beginnings in the teachers' colleges

Originally, especially after 1928 and with the greater growth of the Inter-Varsity Fellowship, there were increasing signs of more numerous and permanent initiatives in some of the larger colleges of education. From time to time those who had proved acceptable speakers in the universities would be asked to speak to a group in one of the colleges. Some of those situated in, or near, university cities invited the president, or one of the other officers of the university CU to come to help them run discussions and Bible studies. The colleges began to be a subject for prayer and

253

discussion at university committees and conferences. Effective tangible help, however, was not easy to give for, as noted earlier, until the late 1930s the IVF itself had only a general secretary, one travelling secretary (Dr. Howard Guinness), who was mostly overseas founding or encouraging new university Christian Unions, and a part-time women's travelling secretary (Jean Strain). Loans of suitable speakers were made from a 'pool' of graduates on the university and college staffs. The various IVF committees were becoming dissatisfied with the little they were doing and could do to help, when in 1935 the first significant step was taken.

In the colleges of education in the environs of London several Christian Unions had begun work. Members then started to apply to come to the Inter-Varsity Conference, which, however, were already overflowing. Feeling a real responsibility to help the colleges in some adequate manner the (student) Executive Committee of the IVF and the Executive Committee of the London Inter-Faculty Christian Union jointly invited delegates from all the known college CUs or groups to a meeting. The object was to discuss the formation of a Training Colleges Christian Union and to enable the Colleges' delegates to indicate what they thought should be the most effective way ahead. They met on 15 June 1935 at 18 Woburn Square, London, WC1 in the hall of the pioneer (and appropriately named) Regions Beyond Missionary Union. Those who were present will not easily forget the oppressively hot midsummer's afternoon through which the meeting battled with the business. As one of them later wrote, 'The sun that afternoon beat down mercilessly – so that the TCCU was almost red hot from the start!'

The chair was taken by Arnold Aldis, who was at that time a medical student at University College Hospital, and the current Chairman of the Executive Committee of the IVF. Delegates were present from the following training colleges: Chelsea College of Physical Education, Clapham High School TC, the Froebel Educational Institute, Gipsy Hill TC, the National TC in Domestic Subjects, the Royal School of Art, the Royal School of Needlework, St. Mary's College, and Shoreditch TC. There were also present, for purposes of encouragement and possible future

254

assistance, several of the appropriate officers of the IVF and
LIFCU. A draft constitution had been previously circulated to
the colleges and amendments agreed. It was finally adopted and
the Training Colleges Christian Union (later the Colleges of
Education Christian Union) was launched with the following
objects:

'(i) To co-ordinate the work, and to unite the members of the
Christian Unions in the Training Colleges.

(ii) Generally to seek to stimulate personal faith in the Lord
Jesus Christ and to further evangelistic work amongst
Training Colleges' students throughout the British Isles
consistently with the Doctrinal Basis of the Union.'

The Doctrinal Basis adopted was that of the IVF (which was also
that of the LIFCU).

The rest of the meeting was devoted to a discussion of plans for
contacting the small Christian Unions known to exist in other
parts of the country and how to make progress towards a national
conference, for the colleges. It was finally agreed to elect a
'Provisional Committee' for the TCCU and to call the first annual
conference. At this it was hoped to attract a greater number of
delegates, and to hold the first general committee, which could
elect the first TCCU executive committee. It was decided to call
the conference in the following September, towards the end of the
long vacation. The provisional committee included James
Broomhall[3] (acting chairman, who was the current President of
the LIFCU), Miss S. Canning (acting secretary, Froebel Institute)
J. J. A. Powell (Shoreditch Training College), and Miss M.
Wiseman (National TC). Miss Jean Strain (women's travelling
secretary of IVF) was present in a supporting role.

The first annual conference took place over the last week-end
of 27–30 September, at Oakenrough, Haslemere. The provisional
committee met for its final meeting on Saturday 28 September
and a representative executive committee of training college
students gradually took command. The work grew rapidly, and it
was a welcome surprise to find that the third training college
conference in the Easter vacation of 1937 was already taking place
in the greater accommodation at Swanwick. By now there was a
fully functioning General Committee, as well as an Executive

255

Committee, and the first (senior) president had been elected, Mr. Rowland Hogben, head of the training home of the China Inland Mission. Two more successful conferences were held in 1938 and 1939, before the outbreak of World War II curtailed activities. No conferences were held in 1940 and 1941.

Occasional hints in the records reveal that all had not always been plain sailing for the officers, especially for the treasurer. At the 1939 General Committee the latter included in his report a complaint which has been common to student organizations before and since. He said that 'subscriptions had increased on last year's amount, chiefly because of a few fairly large donations. Members were still often slack about financial support. There was a balance of only 1/11d. He stressed the need for a greater income if the Union was to spend more on printed promotional literature next year'. The war, by scattering many of the colleges during evacuation to distant parts, may have relieved temporarily the treasurer's anxieties, but not for long. Activities were much reduced and the General Committee minutes of 1 April 1939 were not confirmed until the next delayed General Committee on 9 April 1942. Strenuous efforts, however, were made by students throughout the War to keep in touch with each other. An Executive minute states that 'General information was given about the evacuated Colleges. As these were now scattered all over the country, a 'Round Robin' of letters had been started to link the colleges, and to keep members and committees posted with news.'

During the war-years there was a steady consolidation of the TCCU as an organization. A growing unity was promoted by the 'Round Robin' and it developed into the *TCCU Newsletter*. Whilst this brochure, owing to wartime paper rationing, could not exceed a single fold of four quarto-size pages, much was crowded into successive issues until the end of hostilities permitted enlargement. Letter no. 1, July 1941 carried (i) a short leading article on 'The Challenge of Education', (ii) a letter from the President, (iii) a brief article on 'the Place of the TCCU', (iv) notes, (v) news and (vi) (for mutual correspondence) the addresses of the colleges in evacuation and of the six TCCU officers. In addition a prayer card was circulated, listing all the training colleges, for united and personal prayer. Conferences, including several regional conferences, were held, but mostly in university accommodation in the university cities during a vacation.

It was a matter of surprise to the hard-worked early honorary officers of the TCCU, that they were able to get so far as they did before the end of the War. There were no full-time workers in the TCCU itself and only occasional help from the very small circle of the IVF travelling secretaries. It became obvious to all, however, that this state of things could not last if there was to be any marked progress. During the days of post-war reconstruction a search began for an ex-member of one of the Christian Unions who would be willing to give a period of at least three years as a TCCU general secretary. This would not be an office job but would necessitate visiting the Unions, especially those which were new, or most needing help. It was also hoped that it would soon be possible also to add one or more travelling secretaries.

The technical colleges

Except for a few isolated instances, promising developments in the larger educational sphere of the technical colleges came considerably later. There were a number of reasons for this as noted on page 251. All other types of corporate activity were rare. It called for uncommon courage and determination to propose the beginning of a CU when no other student society existed! It says a great deal for those who successfully pioneered independent Christian Unions in a few of the colleges such as Battersea Polytechnic (now Brunel University), Glasgow Royal Technical College (now Strathclyde University) and Loughborough Engineering College (now Loughborough University of Technology).

From time to time there were enough striking indications of the need and the possibilities to cause the IVF leaders to discuss what might or could be done. Already serving on a number of the staffs of these colleges were graduate ex-members of the university Christian Unions. In several of the more important colleges they had become the principals or senior lecturers. They would readily have encouraged students, if they had taken the initiative to enquire if they could meet for Christian purposes. The staff members, however, were also acutely aware of the academic pressures and the shortage of time under which their students had satisfactorily to complete their various courses. There could be no easy imitation of the times and methods of the university students. The Christian members of staff were clear that any move must come from the students themselves and in a form which took full account of the daily time tables of the student body as a whole.

It was midway through World War II during a Training Colleges Conference at Cambridge that several prominent members of the staffs of technical colleges informally discussed some isolated cases where students had enquired about the feasibility of starting a Christian Union. The prime mover was Dr. J. E. Richardson,[4] who was aware of the plans for the post-war upgrading of a number of the larger and most important of the colleges to the status of colleges of advanced technology and, in some cases, of universities. It was also thought probable that the proportion of full-time students would be greatly increased, bringing with it a commensurate spreading of the academic loads and revision of the time-tables to permit more student leisure. Dr. Richardson proposed that they should make tentative arrangements for linking an expected increase in the number of CUs in this field and should draft a tentative constitution which would be ready for any students who later might take the initiative. It was also suggested that the leaders of the few existing CUs should be informed of these tentative plans, in addition to the few technical college students, who were present as invited guests at this Training Colleges Conference.

No further action is known to have taken place until 14 October 1944, when, according to the minutes of a meeting held on that date, it was called 'to consider the establishment of a Christian witness in Technical Colleges, to be known as the Technical Colleges Christian Fellowship'. The meeting took place at 33 Roundhill Road, Leicester, with Dr. J. E. Richardson in the chair, and present were several technical college students and members of college staffs. The meeting went straight to work and appointed a provisional 'acting committee' whose task was to take appropriate steps to call a more fully representative meeting of the existing Christian Unions. It consisted of Dr. J. E. Richardson (chairman), Mr. J. R. Adams (secretary) and Mr. R. W. MacAdam[5] (treasurer). Those responsible wanted no hole-in-the-corner half-measures, for the second resolution was 'To inform Principals of Technical Colleges of the formation of the TCCF and to invite them to report any activities such as a Christian Union in their college'(!) The committee was asked to prepare a draft constitution for the Fellowship.

The next formal step took place on 6 January 1945 in the Upper Hall of All Souls Church, Langham Place, London, when the draft constitution was amended and adopted. Invitations were also sent to all existing CUs or groups asking for delegates to be present at the first full General Committee, which was held during a Training Colleges conference at Westhill Training College, Selly Oak, Birmingham. Here the first representative Executive Committee, and the first TCCF President, Dr. F. J. Harlow (Principal of Chelsea Polytechnic), were elected. It was also reported that the new Fellowship had been recognized as an integral section by the committees of the Inter-Varsity Fellowship, and that the IVF had offered to loan its travelling secretaries, whenever they were able to give assistance between their other duties.

One difficulty presented itself almost at once. The few active CUs in colleges in the London area had already formed friendly links with the nearest branches of the LIFCU in London University. The university students had been doing their best to give their personal aid and encouragement. Several groups in other parts of the country, for example the Glasgow 'Tech.', had also similar links with their local university CU. The TCCF committee, however, hastened to reassure the leaders that there was no intention of weakening, but rather strengthening such links. In London the problem was resolved by a *double* affiliation of the technical colleges CUs with both the LIFCU (for local exchanges) and the TCCF (for conferences). Even so, at first, a few of the pioneer CUs, such as that at Loughborough Engineering College, which had battled themselves into existence and had acquired a certain rugged independence, were reluctant to accept the TCCF's proferred help. It was not until the IVF travelling secretaries were compelled to concentrate on the increasing work in the universities (and the TCCF began to have its own travelling secretaries and speakers' lists) that the value of the link with the TCCF became more obvious. Also, the stronger units came to realize that through the TCCF they could help the weaker CUs in their areas. Above all, it was recognized that those trying to start new CUs were assisted in obtaining recognition by their authorities when it was seen that they were linked to corresponding groups in a number of well-known colleges.

By 1945–46 reports are found in the current literature, such as that from Battersea Polytechnic CU, 'This session started well with a Freshers' Squash and there were about 60 present. The number attending later meetings, however, somewhat rapidly fell off. Undaunted, the Union persisted with its regular Bible Studies and prayer meetings which had an average of 8 to 10 present, with peaks of 18–20.' A new group at Merchant Venturers College at Bristol could write that 'We are now able to report a very good term as far as attendances at weekly meetings are concerned. The number of definite members stood at sixteen, but there were between twenty and thirty at most meetings.' Belfast Technical Colleges Bible Union describe their difficulties in holding a weekly prayer meeting with some fourteen or more present. 'There were many difficulties, including the opposition of the authorities who would not grant permission for meetings of a religious nature. We tried to carry on for some weeks inside College. But one worry was the scant sympathy of a somewhat antagonistic janitor who seemed to derive great delight from sweeping all round us as we continued to go on praying!' They eventually gave up and went down the road to a church schoolroom, inviting ministers and Christian graduate laymen to address them. By the end of the session they reported that 'twenty-three students have signed the membership declaration affirming their belief in the Lord Jesus Christ as their personal Saviour and God, and in the Bible as the Word of God'.

By September 1946, the Chairman at an Executive Committee meeting is found remarking on the encouraging way in which the Fellowship had grown since its first meeting in Leicester in 1944.

The Training Colleges CU provided timely aid by offering a welcome at joint spring conferences at Westhill College, Selly Oak and joint leaders' conferences at Oak Hill College, Southgate, London. These joint conferences were the beginning of the close association and working partnership between the movements, which were later on to have an increasing unity of purpose. The two movements shared their conferences from 1946 to 1950, after which the considerable increases in numbers from both movements made separate conferences desirable.

Full-time staffs for the college CUs

As soon as the universities filled again after the war the IVF travelling secretaries had found themselves overwhelmed. They could not give much help to the colleges. Other graduate ex-members of the Christian Unions who had been helping also found themselves far busier in a number of ways. By this time it was suggested that both the training colleges and the technical colleges movements should have full-time workers to undertake routine organizing, for which students ought not to be responsible, and to be visiting speakers. Whilst the students were learning and able to take the initiative in all the local committees and the national planning committees, the two general secretary-ships were beyond what was academically feasible or right. The first step came from the training colleges.

In April 1946 the TCCU Executive Committee decided that, on the completion of her college course, their Hon. Secretary for the previous year, Miss Rosalyn Carrick, should be invited to become their first full-time Secretary, in a salaried post to begin on 1 September 1946. Almost immediately after appointment in October (with the eager backing of the TCCU Executive) the new Secretary is found writing to the IVF leaders asking if the training colleges could also now have a travelling secretary! The TCCU leaders were ready with the appropriate nominee, Miss Margaret Lea, who, they had ascertained, was prepared to start work in the coming January. Although the IVF was itself under pressure from other constituencies for an increase in the number of graduate workers, the crucial stage which had been reached in the

261

training colleges was fully understood. The members of the Business Advisory Committee proved ready to vote grants for these new ventures as far as resources allowed. This move was just in time to catch the tide and the TCCU itself quickly began to develop into an influential movement.

The technical colleges were not far behind in appreciating the requirements and opportunities of the TCCF. Student leadership, and fuller student representation on central committees, began to grow. The student honorary secretaryship began to find itself stretched to its limit in relation to nation-wide calls and growth. Another important factor now emerged. The London University Christian leaders had done their valiant best to help the numerous technical college groups in the environs of London. They were now themselves in difficulties. Owing to the very large number of colleges in London, they had found themselves with over 40 branches of the LIFCU scattered over quite a wide geographical area. It was impossible for a student executive to lead and administer such a large constituency. One solution was to ask the IVF to make other provision for the CUs in technical colleges, which were not constituent members of the University. Senior advisers and other members of the TCCF (mostly members of college staffs) counselled that the London technical colleges should now be content with a *single* affiliation with the TCCF, allowing the LIFCU Executive to concentrate on its proper sphere of the colleges of the university. Also, they suggested that the time had come to request the IVF to assist the technical colleges committee to have its own full-time general secretary and, in due course, its own travelling secretary. A happy solution was found when Raymond W. G. Turner, who had just graduated from the Sir John Cass Institute, was appointed in 1948 to serve as TCCF Secretary. Half of his time was to be allocated to the technical colleges generally and the other half to those outlying London colleges, to which the LIFCU Student Executive could no longer do justice. In due course, Raymond Turner became full-time secretary for the TCCF and served in that capacity until 1956, when he was succeeded by Arthur Pont.

Growing spheres of influence

With the rise of the Welfare State at the close of World War II there was a rapid extension throughout the country of many newer forms of education. The requirements for those seeking qualifications for entry to the professional-type services were continually being upgraded. Also the numbers entering for training were steadily increasing. This was specially true of the disciplines ancillary to medicine. A number of those accepted for training for physiotherapy, occupational therapy and similar therapies were the sisters and cousins of those who were so active in the university Christian Unions. It was not therefore surprising that soon there were a number of groups modelled on their university prototypes in the physiotherapy departments. They mostly met at times different from those of the medical students or the nurses' Christian Unions because the therapists found themselves free at different times from these others. Being in some cases well led, it was not long before several of these groups became relatively strong numerically.

After tentative efforts to find the most appropriate links, the leaders in these new spheres organized the Therapy Students' Christian Fellowship and applied to the IVF for affiliation in 1955. From the point of view of organizational structure it was not as easy as it might seem to arrange for the appropriate form.

At first it was thought best for the TSCF to affiliate to the Training Colleges CU. The latter, through its conferences and travelling secretaries, did its best to serve the therapists. After a time, however, it became clear that, with the growing unification of the IVF as an organization, a better link was with the Technical Colleges CF. A TSCF travelling secretary was appointed who had completed therapy training and so would know the field.

The Colleges of Education Christian Union

In more recent years, the world of teachers' training has been transformed by the lengthening of the courses to three years instead of two and by the upgrading of the institutions into Colleges of Education. Up to 10% of the students in these colleges are selected for a four year course to work for the Bachelor of Education degree. Certain of the colleges have a high proportion of their students engaged on the degree course. In keeping with the new nomenclature (in the General Committee held on 14 April 1966) the name of the TCCU was changed to the Colleges of Education Christian Union.

The field which the CECU served had increased considerably in importance. Christian Unions were found in about half of these colleges. There were also a number of contacts with individual students in others. A few of the Christian Unions were large, but probably the average attendance at weekly meetings was between 20 and 25. It is a sobering reflection that these figures only represent some 3% of the total student body in these colleges. Before long however this rose quite frequently to 10% in the residential colleges and some of the CUs reached a very high percentage of the student body. It was only later, when the colleges became far larger and often merged with polytechnics, that the figure fell again. It has been proved in experience that non-members are not greatly attracted to 'open meetings' at which there are directly evangelistic talks. The common experience in most colleges is that outsiders are more ready to join in well-led Bible studies or to take part in frank discussion of biblically-based themes, which are relevant to student life.

Later developments in technical colleges

As in the departments of education, sweeping changes have also taken place in the technical colleges. Many of these were upgraded in status to polytechnics, others to colleges of advanced technology, and then in some cases they became universities and now grant their own degrees. This deprived the TCCF of some of its best leadership as large CUs moved over to the universities' department of IVF. As the work expanded into art, agricultural, therapy and other non-technical colleges the name was changed in 1963 to Inter-College Christian Fellowship.

At the time of writing, in the non-university colleges of the British Isles were some 450,000 full-time students, working in 750 colleges. The Fellowship was in touch with in the region of 550 of the colleges, in which 200 CUs were affiliated to IVF. In the rest were individuals, who were anxious to be kept in touch by correspondence, literature and personal visits when the travelling secretaries were able to make contact. There were about 7,000 CU members and regular attenders at meetings. In an average year some 200 would be present at the annual conference (once up to 450) and over 400 more at regional conferences of shorter length. Another feature of the seventies has been the proliferation of day conferences, providing training to leaders and teaching for CU members. These are of great value where time-table problems preclude consecutive teaching programmes.

Spiritual conditions in the Unions

One unwelcome aspect of the present spiritual outlook in the country today makes its influence specially felt in the colleges. During the early years of the IVF movement the leaders could count on a high proportion of the 'freshmen' entering the Christian Unions having an adequate knowledge of Holy Scripture and a working grasp of the important doctrines of the faith. They could even confidently count on a certain elementary, though mostly very superficial, knowledge of Christian teaching amongst non-members who were attracted to their open meetings. This, however, has long ceased to be true. A much smaller proportion of the members now come from well-instructed churches, and many of those who can claim to be definite Christians have a somewhat shallow grasp of the gospel. Hence most of those who become Christians through the witness of the Unions have to begin almost from the beginning to acquire sufficient Christian knowledge. It is possible that one factor (which otherwise in itself may be favourable to the spread of the faith today), is the widespread availability of various modern versions of the Bible, may be having an adverse effect on Christian instruction. The variety of phrasing prevents the memorizing of Scripture because the concepts are not repeatedly heard in the same form. One of the major tasks of the student leaders and the travelling secretaries is to increase the true understanding of the Holy Scriptures, to offer a balanced

265

presentation of Christian doctrine. No efforts can be too great to achieve this.

It is impossible fully to assess the results of the constant sowing of the seed of God's Word into the promising soil of each student year. A northern college secretary is found writing, 'In this one-day-a-week college, with a different group of students coming in daily, we have Bible study each day with a rota of different students leading it. A member of staff was converted three weeks ago.' A London member wrote, 'One girl started the CU in this college during her first term. Ten students now come regularly to the meetings, but most of them are not yet clearly Christians. About 85 came to a special debate during which an evangelist was one of the contributors.'

A midland report informs the reader that 'Members of College staff come to our meeting as well as students. At our last meeting we had 12–15 students and 9 or 10 staff.' It is instructive to see from a report from northern England the outcome of the informal contacts amongst students, 'We had 35 students at our first open meeting. One of these was the Chairman of the Students Union of the college. I asked him to propose the vote of thanks to the Speaker. Afterwards he talked to us for quite a time. He has now certainly become – if he was not before – a definitely committed Christian.' The records left by officers of the Unions show constant signs of the uncertainties in the ebb and flow of their influence. Owing to the changing moods of a student body, an all too easily achieved clash of dates with some other function, and similar factors, the best laid plans may fail. One student leader wrote, 'At the time that the film was due to start there were only a few of us CU regulars present. Yet we felt that we had done all we could to advertise it and if God intended the film to be of any use and wanted the people to come, they *would*. During the next five minutes nearly 100 students poured into the lecture theatre!'

The merger of the CECU and the ICCF

As the work expanded and the travelling secretaries had to cover enormous areas and as the colleges of education began to be absorbed into polytechnics, the distinction between the CECU and the ICCF became less valuable. It had been of great value at the start in developing a distinctive style of work, but this was no longer meaningful. The two fellowships shared travelling secretaries for a while and then came a complete merger of the two organizations. Hence, from 1975 there has been the one united movement under the title of the Colleges Christian Fellowship. This itself is now an integral part of the Universities and Colleges Christian Fellowship of Evangelical Unions. The wording of the title is intended to convey that the Christian Unions in the whole field of tertiary education are collaborating in one Evangelical movement.

NOTES

[1] The author wishes to thank Derek Williams (formerly ICCF secretary) for his help with this chapter.

[2] Miss Rosalind Carrick, later Mrs. John Talbot.

[3] A. J. Broomhall was a student at the London Hospital (later Dr. A. J. Broomhall of the China Inland Mission).

[4] Later, Sir Eric Richardson, Principal of Regent Street Polytechnic.

[5] Principal of Acton Technical College.

Chapter 15

The International Fellowship
(1946–1978)

As earlier described,[1] it was possible throughout World War II to maintain communication with most of the movements, which had been associated with the international conferences, through neutral countries. During the 1944 and 1945 meetings of the IVF general committees in Oxford the post-war possibilities were discussed. It was agreed that the British movement should do all in its power to assist in the rebuilding of the Christian movements in enemy-occupied lands and also to send emissaries to those countries where new student initiatives were possible. Meanwhile a powerful ally had arisen in the growing IVCF of North America. It was clear that interest and aid in post-war reconstruction would be available from this new source.

In 1938 the Inter-Varsity Fellowship of Canada had sent its General Secretary over the border to the USA where, at the invitation of a group of students in the University of Michigan, he was able to help them to start the Michigan Christian Fellowship. This group was destined to serve as a prototype for other groups. The movement spread into some of the surrounding States. Officially beginning in 1940, the Inter-Varsity Christian Fellowship of the USA soon became fully organized. It continued to expand during the war years into what was to be the largest of the existing Evangelical student movements. For some twelve years C. Stacey Woods, an Australian who had graduated in the USA, combined the two General Secretaryships of Canada and the United States. Not until 1952 was he finally freed to concentrate more fully on the needs of the USA by the appointment of a Toronto graduate to undertake the work in Canada. Meanwhile Stacey Woods had been keeping in close contact with the British committee, and let it be known that he had been given by his senior advisers to think that North America would be interested in supporting any moves towards an International Fellowship.

Oxford 1946

As soon as the war had ceased, letters began to pour in from the European movements. It became clear that they had all deeply felt 'the isolation from our international friends' and wished to renew the pre-war exchanges of delegates. It was also apparent that all, even those who earlier had been reluctant to have more than the occasional international conference, were now in favour of uniting in some form of international organization. In late 1945, therefore, the British Executive invited the members of the Executive Committee of the International Conference (who had been elected in 1939 at the close of the fourth International Conference in Cambridge) to come as guests to the IVF's annual conference in Regents Park College, Oxford in the spring of 1946. They were also invited to stay on in college accommodation to hold a meeting of the International Executive in order to make plans for the future of international relations. Two-thirds of the members of that International Executive were able to accept the invitation, including the chairman, the Rev. Nils Dahlberg of Sweden.

The reports on the existing situation at the opening session brought many encouragements. Apart from the links with Germany there had been few casualties. On the contrary, in some countries wartime restrictions on student travel and most general social activities had increased spiritual growth in the student Christian societies. Then, as well as the new 'giant' in North America, another potential 'giant' was reported to be showing signs of vigour. Several years before Japan had occupied Eastern China, some of the missionaries of the China Inland Mission (the

269

Overseas Missionary Fellowship) had initiated student groups in the Chinese universities. Invasion from the east had sent many graduates and students as refugees into Western China with Chungking as centre. The concentration of Christians in Chungking led to the birth of a strong Inter-Varsity Christian Fellowship of China. As soon as peace came, the return of the refugee students resulted in the setting up of active Christian Unions in Peking, Nanking and Shanghai. Several other reports during this first post-war Committee brought justified optimism about the future.

The members of the International Conference Executive had no reason for doubting where their duty lay. The determination of the delegates from all the countries concerned was for the earliest possible aid to be given to those most in need and then for steps to be taken to forge more permanent links between the Evangelical national student movements. On most points the members of the Committee were agreed in principle. It was only in small matters where differences in national outlook and procedure raised a few difficulties which needed to be resolved.

After several discussions, which were relatively brief, except where clarification of terminology and procedure were concerned, it was enthusiastically and unanimously agreed: (i) that the Committee should accept an invitation from the joint IVCFs of Canada and the USA, that the next Conference General Committee should be held in August 1947 at Boston, Massachusetts; (ii) that a recommendation should be sent to all the co-operating movements proposing that, as an extension of the pre-war successful co-operation in the Conferences, there should now be formed the International Fellowship of Evangelical Students; and (iii) that a draft Constitution (which had been drawn up at Oxford) should be circulated to the national movements for consideration and, if welcomed, should – after being amended in the light of additional proposals from the national Fellowship – be adopted at Boston in 1947.

A further important step forward was taken. It was foreseen that heavy financial liabilities would arise in the near future, if all the decisions and proposed developments were to be fully implemented. The British and Scandinavian movements had hitherto borne the main brunt of the international activities. They now found themselves in the post-war years with smaller resources and some difficulties in strengthening their own available personnel. Stacey Woods had brought with him to the Conference Executive, Mr. John Bolton, one of the chief business advisers to the IVCF of USA. Since his own university years in Germany, he had been very interested in student Christian Unions. Mr. Bolton promised the Committee at Oxford that (provided that, from the start, the aim would be to work steadily towards self-support) the senior supporters in the USA would substantially assist in the founding and initial steps of the IFES.

The first international committee, Boston 1947

The Executive Committee's communication from Oxford was unanimously welcomed by all the original contributors to the pre-war conferences. In addition, several potential new members gave notice that they wished to send delegates to Boston and that they would like their applications to be considered, and if possible accepted at the outset, so that they could then take full part in the deliberations.

The International General Committee met towards the end of August 1947 in Phillips Brooks House, Harvard University, with the delegates resident in 'the Yard'. There was a certain fitness in this, for the latter is built on the site of the original theological college founded in 1642 by John Harvard, a graduate from the Puritan foundation of Emmanuel College, Cambridge. Another link with the Evangelical tradition in Cambridge was the presence (as one of the three Australian delegates) of Dr. Howard W. K. Mowll, the Archbishop of Sydney, who happened to be in the USA as one of the leaders in a world conference of missionary societies. He had been the 1911 CICCU President, following the CICCU's disaffiliation from the SCM (see page 78). A further fitting circumstance was the presence in the chair of Dr. Martyn Lloyd-Jones, Minister of Westminster Chapel, who represented the Presbyterian and Congregational traditions. His conference addresses in the evenings were the perfect embodiments of

271

Evangelical Reformed theology.

After a considerable number of amendments, the draft Constitution was finally adopted and the IFES launched on its way. The two North American movements, Canada and USA, generously agreed to allow their General Secretary to become the first General Secretary of the IFES and to release him at important times for international journeys. No small admiration must be accorded to the working-capacity and stamina of Stacey Woods, who was able until 1952 to carry the main burden of the two growing national movements in North America, together with that of the new international one. The first office of the IFES was set up in a suburb of Philadelphia. Plans were also completed for international developments on a regional basis. One of these was the appointment of David Adeney, a Cambridge graduate seconded from the China Inland Mission for work as Associate Secretary in the Far East. This was to prove a very productive step in the development of student Christian Unions in the Far East. Starting in China and later, based on Hong Kong (and then Singapore), Adeney gave a lifetime of service to Asia.

In support of international activities

For later developments in the work of the IFES the reader is referred to its own history.[2] What follows must be confined to ways in which the IVF has been able to make its particular contribution to international activities. This has been offered chiefly in four ways. First, the earlier experiences of the British Christian Unions have been shared with other delegates in the conferences and committees, and also through correspondence and hospitality. Then, British graduates going overseas to work in government, trade or missionary services have served to stimulate indigenous students and graduates to begin and develop Evangelical Christian Unions. Third, when invited, the IVF has sent deputations of students and graduates overseas to exchange information, to help in various evangelistic initiatives or to bring a particular contribution to the students in some specialized field where the national movement was feeling its way. Fourth, the Inter-Varsity Press publications, some of which have been translated and adapted into overseas languages and circumstances, have been welcomed in those countries where economic factors did not permit the local production of suitable literature for students.

Incidents from these interchanges could be described, but in most cases the personal nature of such meetings do not, for obvious reasons, lend themselves to publicity. It is never easy to assess the true value of such initiatives and how far one person has been responsible for a result. The spiritual experiences of an individual or a group are seldom isolated and other faithful workers for God may have played their parts in the total outcome. One circumstance, however, an encouraging one, has been consistently present. In very few places has there been just an imitation of a Western 'model', but in most countries intelligent adaptations and successful improvements have resulted in indigenous movements which are closely geared to local needs.

Spade-work by Christian graduates

Some examples may serve to illustrate the influence of graduate expatriates during their work, and service overseas. Soon after the war David C. C. Watson, a Cambridge graduate, went to India to teach at a Christian school near Madras. It was not long before he had several close contacts with Indian Christian students in the nearest university. Most of these students came from the areas where the theologically conservative Mar Thoma church in South India has always been strong. By 1949 he was already actively encouraging a number of students to meet for prayer and Bible study. Then he met a Christian member of staff, Professor H. Enoch, who was head of the Department of Biology in Presidency College, Madras. Their joint advice and stimulus to the students (in collaboration with Dr. Norton Sterrett, an American graduate who kept similarly in close touch with students in North India) led to the establishment of the Union of Evangelical Students of India in 1953–4.

In somewhat similar circumstances, Leon Dale, a London graduate and a former President of the London Inter-Faculty Christian Union, was appointed to the staff of the Department of

273

Geography in the University of Malaya, Singapore. He early came into contact with a small group of Christian students in the medical faculty who had begun to meet for Bible study and prayer. They had soon grown from their original four or five members to twelve. He then encouraged them to think of opening their meetings to Christians in other faculties and to think of the possibility of a Christian Union for the whole university. At their request, he put them into touch with the IVF so that they could receive the journal *Inter-Varsity* and any other publications which would be most suitable for their purposes. Finally, there came the establishment of a strong Christian Union in the University. Its further growth exceeded expectations for, in July 1959, the Union was strong enough to organize a full-scale University mission and invited Dr. Howard Guinness to come from Australia as their missioner. It has been no surprise to those familiar with the ability and zeal of the original founders of this Union, that they have become influential members of their university and city.

It has been chiefly in Africa that the former members of the British Christian Unions have made their biggest direct contributions. One successful development arose from the interest of an Oxford graduate in the senior schoolboys and students of his immediate area. His initiatives synchronized with those of another Oxford graduate in the IVF office and procured appropriate immediate action. A. T. de B. Wilmot, in a large West African trade organization based on Nigeria, wrote to Freddy Crittenden, at that time Secretary of the Graduates Fellowship, describing the number of colleges and schools in West Africa which were being upgraded, some of them into new universities. A short time before this some West African students in London had been talking of the new situation with the GF Secretary. Also one of the missionary societies had enquired how they could staff one of their new high schools. The Department for Overseas Technical Aid had also begun to advertise for applications to many posts in these institutions in the 'New Africa'.

Tony Wilmot used most of his leave periods in making explanatory journeys to neighbouring states. He got to know a number of Christian Africans in their first year at the new university and others in the high schools. He began a camp for Christian students and senior schoolboys, which proved a great success and became an annual event. What is more, he discovered several really promising leaders amongst the African students and began at once to devolve responsibility on to the leading Africans. They rose to the occasion and several CUs were formed in Nigeria and neighbouring countries. A Pan-African Fellowship of Evangelical Students was proposed and adopted. For student members to be able to do much in the way of meeting each other was, in view of the great distances and costs, a counsel of perfection. But, with the help of American and British students and graduates, a travelling secretary was appointed for PAFES. The first was Dr. A. Fairbanks, an American graduate of African origin. He was succeeded, before long, by an African who had graduated in Britain, the Rev. Gottfried Osei-Mensah. In spite of difficulties, including the dislocation of the movement during the war in Nigeria, PAFES made considerable progress.

The Far East also provided an illustrative example of the importance of a graduates' interest in a neighbourhood university. As described above (pages 269 f.), members of the China Inland Mission, who were former officers of Christian Unions, were responsible for the beginning of Christian Unions in the Chinese universities. After the Second World War there was something like a spiritual revival wherever Christians were gathered. At the beginning of this phase, David Adeney (a former CICCU secretary) arrived back from Boston as virtually the IFES Associate General Secretary for Asia (a title not given until 1956). Bishop Frank Houghton (Field Director of the CIM, who had always been interested in student work) and Leslie Lyall (a Cambridge graduate and former member of the CICCU Executive) conferred with David Adeney. The members of the Mission who were in contact with students were given full freedom to give their time to them. At that time Adeney was seconded to the IFES from the Mission.

The graduate advisers to the students adopted the IVF's traditional methods. They had not far to look for student initiative. Two very strong Chinese leaders emerged, and soon the groups, led by their own student officers, made immense progress

275

in every way. The number of Christians became large in what
were now very large student communities. Hundreds of outsiders
came to some of the meetings, addressed by the Chinese leaders
and evangelists. The IVCF of China looked like becoming the
largest of the Fellowships affiliated to the IFES. The annual
summer conference – (modelled on the USA's 'Campus in the
Woods' and called 'The Campus among the Bamboos') was
drawing hundreds of students, until the Communist invasion
brought down the curtain over the future of the Christian church
in China.

In the earlier years of the IVF, Latin America had received
rather little attention, because the orientation of the missionary
societies (and the topics for missionary study groups) were
towards the developing lands of Africa and Asia. In any case
South America was regarded as the sphere of interest of the USA,
though British missionaries in Argentina and Peru had had some
contact with students. When, however, the IFES was looking for
a worker to survey South America and to pioneer work there it
was a British graduate who was chosen. Dr. John White, a former
president of the Manchester CU, was appointed in 1960 with a
roaming brief for South America. He travelled vast distances and
put in much work whilst looking for the mature leaders and
initiating student groups wherever there was any welcome. The
value of his work became more evident at a later stage in the
growth of the work, especially in some of the countries such as
Argentina. But most important was his discovery of the obviously
right indigenous leadership. John White's own period of service,
1960–1965, gave place to the widespread influence of Dr. Rene
Padilla, Samuel Escobar and Pedro Arana.

Many other individual graduates have given valuable service at
important junctures. Perhaps one of the best illustrations of this
was the response of the IVF to a request from the IVCF (USA).
The latter had some excellent women leaders but certain new
problems were affecting its women members and it wanted to
compare notes with the experience of others. In response to this
invitation from North America, Phyllis Bennett (the senior IVF
women's travelling secretary) was loaned to the IVCF for the
summer and autumn of 1949 in order to take part in the IVCF's

Summer Vacation Camps and the opening activities of the next academic year. The visit appears to have been very useful to all concerned and the senior USA women's travelling secretary, Jane Hollingsworth, returned the visit in the following year. The importance of this exchange was that it set the fashion for other similar exchanges, which later became a feature of the international work when the various movements became much larger and met with the stresses and strains of the great post-war changes in all aspects of their work. The gains were not always on the one side, that is, in receiving what a larger movement could give. The emissaries of the IVF derived much from the challenge of being forced to go back to the elemental 'grass-root' problems all over again. Sometimes the new Christians in the small struggling groups had contrived to solve them better.

It is impossible to include the names of all those who made distinctive individual contributions to the fast developing work. But the first secretary for French-speaking Africa, covering an area of considerable difficulty, was a British graduate, Alistair Kennedy. Another crucial piece of work, again in a different cultural setting, was that by Michael Griffiths when serving the Japanese IVCF. Then, after the British missionaries had left China, David Bentley-Taylor (a former OICCU President) went to Indonesia, where part of his missionary work was related to the college population and circles of higher education. Subsequent to his leaving Indonesia (because of his wife's health) he was able to give a further spell of service to the student world in co-ordinating the work of the IFES in Muslim lands. He was succeeded in this task by another British graduate, Colin Chapman.

From 1966 to 1976 the General Secretary of the movement in South Africa was a former IVF travelling secretary, Jim Johnson.

Team work

In the early post-war years a number of international student teams were organized by Hans Burki of Zurich, the leader of the Swiss GBU, during his remarkable pioneer work. This was the means of the founding of the Studentenmission in Deutschland. During his 1947 missions in Germany and in subsequent years,

Hans Burki had brought together large meetings in Wuppertal, Bonn and Nuremberg and other parts of western Germany. Some 500 German Christian students had met in the neighbourhood of Wuppertal. It was found that, with financial help from the IFES, it was possible to get more new Christians, and those who were seeking faith, to training courses over the border in Switzerland. In 1949 the first of three well attended training courses for German students (each a month long) was held at Ballaigues, Switzerland. The courses were repeated in 1950 and 1951 and had even bigger attendances. After 1951 there were international summer schools based on Switzerland and these continued. In most of these, teams of British students gave a great deal of support to Hans Burki and his German-speaking helpers.

Perhaps that which was most in keeping with the IVF's earlier traditions and the late 19th century's comings and goings of Evangelical British graduates across the Atlantic, was an invitation from the IVCF (USA) to send a British deputation to New England universities. Whilst the IVCF had made strides in the rest of the States, the older universities of the east seemed immune or disdainful of the Evangelical Movement. Places such as Harvard and Yale, in sporting terms at least, belonged to the 'Ivy League' and the 'Big-Ten' and might consider themselves above other people in religious matters as well. It was hoped that with Harvard's earlier friendliness towards Cambridge (see page 271) and Yale's earlier partiality for Oxford, they might at least give half an ear to a team of 'Oxbridge' graduates. So in the academic year 1951–52 four graduates, Peter Haile and John Weston (from Oxford) and John Holmes and Dave Gordon (from Cambridge) travelled to the USA for six months work in the New England universities. Their brief was to look for Evangelical students and to encourage them to begin one of the more useful corporate activities, such as united prayer and Bible study and witness.

At first it was hard going for the visitors. In the end a few interested Christian students were found and the beginnings of Christian circles achieved. These steadily grew, but not to any large number at one time. When, however, there were some thirty or forty convinced Evangelical Christians in the groups there was interest in a more public witness. During the following year John R. W. Stott (another Cambridge graduate) was invited for a series of evangelistic meetings (it was a university mission with a small 'm'). Some headway was made with a few clear-cut decisions for Christ. Whilst never large in numbers, the student groups in both universities continued.

Another service, especially to the European movements, which the IVF has regularly performed has been its annual invitation to representative deputations from sister societies on the Continent to come to the Swanwick conference. From subsequent correspondence and comment there can be no doubt that it has served as a valuable stimulus to the guests. In some cases the 'lone' visitors, coming from no established group, have returned to start one in their country. There has also been a great gain to the IVF's own students in giving this hospitality. This overseas section has proved virtually a small international conference within the larger one and many of the visiting delegates have brought important Christian insights and much new challenge. It has been through such first-hand contacts with these international leaders that a closer interest has been aroused in those responsible for work in difficult environments, for example the small group in Italy. Through the continual contacts sent by Jean Elliot, the Colleges of Education Christian Union (and the LIFCU) took up the support of the work of the GBU of Italy.

Expansion of the IFES

During the '60s and early '70s the International Fellowship grew to impressive size as more national organizations came into being and sought application. There are now 40 affiliated national movements. It publishes a students paper, *In Touch*, which reports news, contributes ideas and stimulates action. However, the basic work is that of the students on the spot in every land, and the staff members who advise them. It is still in the small group Bible study, the discussion group or a one-to-one conversation that the deepest work will be done. It is still in the quiet college room, a hall of residence or an odd corner, however small, that 'the still small voice' of the Holy Spirit is most likely to

279

be heard and obeyed.

Through the generosity of American subscribers the European members of the IFES have had the use for some years of the international conference centre known as Schloss Mittersill in the Austrian Alps. It is ideal for international student committees, conferences, courses and summer schools. It can also be used at appropriate times for ski-ing and other parties. The latest experiment has been an international graduates' (as distinct from students') conference.

In 1976, after thirty years of devoted and strenuous service, Stacey C. Woods retired from the general secretaryship. From the Fellowship's foundation at Boston in 1947, he had been the architect of its steady growth, in the course of which he encircled the globe and visited almost every country with a university in the world, in pursuit of the best interests of the student Christian Unions. He could not help leaving a big gap, but he had built well and the work has gone steadily forward.

He was succeeded as General Secretary, by Chua Wee Hian from Singapore, a London graduate, who was, at the time of appointment, serving as the regional secretary in South-East Asia. It is interesting that his wife, a Hong Kong graduate, became a Christian whilst on post-graduate work in London. Chua Wee Hian has taken up the work with enthusiasm and already has almost encompassed the globe in the footsteps of Stacey Woods. Coming to the Fellowship from an Asiatic background Chua Wee Hian has already been able to add his particular contribution to the *international* nature of the work and to come close to the leaders in some of the countries where the cultural backgrounds most resemble those of South-East Asia and neighbouring lands. The student committees, graduate supporters and full-time staff have become welded into an increasingly internationally representative and united team.

The IVF has been able to add its contribution to this team by lending Dr. Oliver Barclay, its General Secretary, to be the chairman of the Executive Committee. He has brought a unique combination of knowledge of the student world, experience of student-led Christian Unions and the practical administrative know-how of the leadership of the British Fellowship. Britain has also welcomed the international office now settled at 10 College Road, Harrow.

Publications

In chapter 18 some account has been given of the history of the IVF's publication department. In the course of its service no doubt many of the productions have proved useful to many a student in distant lands. Whilst they were produced with the British student primarily in mind, account has increasingly to be taken of the much wider circulation which has proved welcome. But perhaps the services of literature which are of the most importance from the international point of view are those where the planning know-how and the production experience has been passed on to those concerned to develop their own student literature. In this Ronald Inchley and his colleagues of the publications department have given much thought, time and trouble to help some of the developing countries.

One of the most striking examples was West Africa. Based on Nigeria, a journal was published for the students of the PAFES groups, with an outreach to any other interested students. The name adopted was *Span*. Later there developed the 'Africa Christian Press'. With considerable help from London, a great deal of literature was adapted for the use of West African students and new writing and titles produced by Africans themselves. It is the type of development which the early leaders of the IVF wanted to see. It is hoped that the story of the Inter-Varsity Press's own growth from a few obscure booklets to a busy publishing house will prove an inspiration and incentive to many potential starters in other parts of the world.

NOTES

1   Page 186.
2   D. Johnson ed. *A brief history of the International Fellowship of Evangelical Students* (IFES, 1964).

Chapter 16

The specialized departments

Early in its life the Fellowship became aware that the intellectual problems met by Christian students in certain academic fields were more pressing than in those of others. Some had greater need of specialized experience and advice. A theological student early in his training has to come to terms with the contemporary outlook in critical studies which bear upon the foundation documents of the church. Some of his professors and lecturers may also be wedded to doctrinal and ecclesiastical views which differ considerably from those of his home church and earlier education. If he is an Evangelical and is to continue to hold the Evangelical views with which he has entered on the course for ordination, it is highly desirable that he should do so on clearly valid spiritual, theological and intellectual grounds. He may be much helped by the counsel of scholarly seniors who are experienced in both the theoretical and practical problems involved. It was to meet such a need that the Theological Students Fellowship was formed.

Support for theological students was soon matched by similar attention to other fields in which direct challenges to faith were being met, for example, in science and medicine. In these faculties the pressures also continued more pervasively into the post-graduate years. For the medicals the challenge to a daily practical faith comes at three points in the course. It comes at the beginning, when the basic sciences make their impact and then again on entering the more clinical parts of the course where the tragedies in life are seen in the raw. It recurs even more strongly when the new graduate is physically and nervously under strain during the first hospital 'house jobs'. Those in the science faculty similarly need to surmount the initial challenge from dominant hypotheses and atheistic attitudes taken for granted in the all-embracing scientific determinism of their faculty. Such pressures become even greater when a new graduate becomes more closely involved with colleagues in the research departments. Here again, as for the theological students, it is desirable that where scientists and medicals differ from colleagues it shall be on valid grounds. The shared experience of seniors at such times is quite invaluable. Between the World Wars, and especially following World War II, scientific and medical advances have moved at unprecedented speeds and have tended to accelerate. Consultation with, and advice from, workers in the same circumstances is of great value. For their generous assistance, involving much time and trouble, the Fellowship has incurred a heavy debt to the many senior members of the science faculties and the medical consultants, who have enabled the Fellowship to attempt to keep pace with the need and to preserve a measure of competence through the constantly changing situation.

Theological students

Originally assistance to the theological students took the form of special sessions held for them during conferences, and personal advice and correspondence from theological graduates. In the late 1920s several informal theological 'reading parties' were begun in the long vacations. These were organized by the more active student leaders, who brought their college friends and invited the help of a scholarly senior graduate to conduct the seminars. In some cases he was a member of one of the theological college staffs. It was in this way, at one of these reading parties, that the Rev. Alan Stibbs (who had recently returned from China) began his many years of valuable service to theological students and graduates.

It was not until June 1932 that there was more comprehensive initiative. Several college groups asked that a theological students' representative to ensure adequate attention to their special interests should be added to the Executive Committee by the General Committee. The first representative (1932) was T. Christie Innes, an Aberdeen graduate who was at that time engaged in post-graduate work at Cambridge. Soon after his appointment he made two proposals to the Executive Committee. First that he should be supported in his desire to organize 'The Theological Colleges Prayer Union'. Its primary object would be to encourage theological students regularly to pray for each other during their training. His second proposal was that he should have the Committee's approval in visiting (from Cambridge and, later, from his church in North London) as many of the theological colleges as he was able. At a later stage he asked to be able to use the title 'Theological Colleges Travelling Secretary' in order to make clear to those contacted the reason for his proposed visits.

At first there was considerable hesitation in the Executive Committee. Some members wondered how in some places a visitor would be received who had come 'to bring more Christianity' to the colleges which were training for the Christian ministry! Innes, however, was equal to the occasion. He demonstrated to the surprised members that, in his experience, the weakest part of many theological college communities was their devotional and prayer life. He went on vividly to describe how that the compulsory daily chapel service, then the whole of the day spent in lectures on, or else in reading in, theological subjects had the effect of producing a form of intellectual stasis, a mental 'stale-mate'. Essentially the burden of his plea was that what the students in these colleges most needed was a regular effective prayer meeting and also to pray for each other that their faith would be kept fresh.

Eventually, in the 1933 General Committee, approval was given to the founding of the Theological Colleges Prayer Fellowship and, following further discussion, to the appointment of a travelling secretary to the theological colleges. These first tentative steps, however, did not become really effective until the following year (1934-35) when headed note-paper bore the names of the new theological students' representative on the Executive (G. F. H. Wynne of Assembly's College, Belfast), who was also the Hon. Secretary of the TCPF, and of the Rev. T. Christie Innes as 'Hon. Travelling Secretary'. The latter made a number of successful visits to the colleges in the following months.

A clue to what may have been the feelings of isolated Evangelicals in some of the colleges at this time is provided by the format of the first TCPF prayer leaflet as it was initially circulated. The front carries a line block of the familiar painting of the prophet Daniel, with a scroll before him, kneeling with his face towards Jerusalem. Beneath is the reference, Daniel 6 : 10. Inside, the first page is headed *Omnes Unum Sint* and, then, all the theological colleges in the British Isles from Aberdeen to Wells are listed alphabetically under one of the days of the week. The list closes with the phrase *Soli Deo Gloria*. An accompanying letter asks theological students to join in united prayer for the preservation of their individual faith, loyalty and zeal in Christ's cause. The aims of the TCPF are expressed in one sentence, 'To unite theological colleges in intelligent and earnest prayer, for their teachers, their work and each other.' The motto proposed is 2 Tim. 1 : 7, 'Love ... power ... and a sound mind'.

At that time, as Christie Innes claimed, there was no other interdenominational link between the theological students of varying denominations, except for the official membership of each college (as a corporate institution) in the SCM Theological Colleges Department. But critics in some of the colleges complained that the 'colleges' in the title TCPF might be taken to suggest that the colleges themselves had *officially* agreed to be included in this listing. So, in 1937, the name was changed to Theological Students' Prayer Union. Again, in 1946, to bring it into line with other specialized sections in the IVF, the name was changed to Theological Students' Fellowship.

Successive theological college representatives continued to develop the services and spread of the influence of the TSPU. It was J. W. Wenham, however, who, during the period 1937-39, took the most positive steps towards organizing the TSPU and, later, its graduate ex-members, into a more constructive force. He persistently advocated that more prayer and effort should be put into well-planned projects for training specially equipped scholars and producing more suitable literature to challenge the modernists' control of the theological colleges and to reinforce main-line 'orthodoxy' in the Protestant churches. As a result, conferences were started for theological students, the Biblical Research Committee was brought into being (with G. T. Manley in the chair) and, as a result of a special conference called by the BRC in the early war years (see pages 210 and 212), Tyndale House and Library were founded at Cambridge.

The first theological colleges conference took place at Digswell Park in 1937. From the time of its earliest development the TSPU owed much to a number of preachers and scholars who gave prodigally of their time to make these occasions a success. The following deserve special mention: Professor F. F. Bruce, Dr. Martyn Lloyd-Jones, Dr. W. J. Martin, the Rev. Alan Stibbs and the Rev. J. Stafford Wright. A post-war development which caused some surprise at the time was 'A Conference for Women Theological Students' at Tyndale House in 1947 and several subsequent years. This brought together women teachers taking MAs in theological subjects or BDs, in order to become Scripture specialists in the schools.

Since 1946 the Theological Students Fellowship has continued to exercise its original function of uniting in prayer members of the various colleges and also in making a positive contribution to maintaining and propagating the Evangelical faith. With an increase in its influence it grew to need fuller administrative and office facilities. A major contribution was made to the TSF by Andrew F. Walls, an Oxford graduate, who was Librarian of Tyndale House, Cambridge, 1952–1957. The improved quality of the contributions to the conferences of theological students, and increasing relevance of the literature circulated owed much to this source. Another of his valuable contributions was the 160 page suitably classified bibliography, *A Guide to Christian Reading* (IVF). At last, in 1962 the TSF gained a part-time secretary. The first was Robert M. Horn.

Medical students and graduates

Before 1946 the needs of medical students had been met mainly by
a few special meetings held from time to time amidst the general
activities of the local Christian Unions or at a general conference.
In Edinburgh, Glasgow, London, and many of the universities at
home and overseas, it has often proved to be the medicals who
have taken the first steps to found an Evangelical Union and were
subsequently amongst its main leaders. The earliest known
meetings of students in the university medical faculties and
London medical schools were chiefly for missionary or evangelistic purposes. For example, a breakfast for London medical
students was organized by the Medical Prayer Union (founded in
1874) in the Cannon Street Hotel on 19 July 1894. 106 medical
students were present and the occasion was intended to be
missionary and evangelistic. Three years before, in 1891, the
MPU had organized a breakfast during the week of the annual
meeting of the British Medical Association. It was attended by
former members of the hospital Christian Unions and addressed
by two distinguished medical missionaries who were on furlough.
This occasion has continued annually, except for the late years of
the two World Wars, down to the present time.

In those earlier years the greater proportion of the doctors and
students attending were members of the Christian church and
so were influenced by Christian standards. Only a few of the acute
problems in medical ethics which now confront the profession
were then a matter for comment, whilst even these would come up
almost incidentally. Senior chiefs might sometimes share their
ethical views and experiences with their 'housemen' or the
students on their medical 'firm'. Occasionally there might be
references in lectures to a relevant ethical theme.

At the close of the Second World War, however, was found a
very different state of affairs. There had been throughout the
country a steady decline in church attendance and an increase in
permissiveness in the sphere of public morality. Great advances in
medical technology had brought many new possibilities of
medical intervention, some which affected ethical principle. It
soon became clear that there would be many new problems ahead

for Christians in medicine. A first informal conference for medical students and junior doctors was called at Old Jordans, Seer Green, in June 1946. The host was Professor John Kirk of the Middlesex Hospital. The chief stimulators of discussion were several junior doctors recently demobilized from the units in Germany, and two who were on leave from the Army of Occupation. (To the delight of the rest, one of these, in his bright new Royal Air Force uniform, was challenged by an elderly lady at the door of the Friends' Meeting House after the Sunday morning service, with 'Friend, hast thou not heard of our witness against War?'). It was unanimously agreed that ethical problems were destined to grow greater for Christians working in medicine and that they would need to be much better prepared for the difficult ethical choices which would be required in future practice.

Shortly after this conference, Major W. M. Capper, on being demobilized from the RAMC, returned as Consultant Surgeon to the Bristol General Hospital. Whilst in Italy he had been thinking about the increasing problems in medicine. He began to advocate that the medical members of the Graduates Fellowship should be organized into a 'medical section', which would actively give its mind to the practical and ethical needs of medical students and of junior doctors entering practice. So in 1947 a definite medical section was formed in the GF. This was a development in the GF, which was paralleled by the organization of several other specialist sections.

A further step came when the leaders of the Medical Prayer Union (whose membership of 200 by then consisted mostly of senior consultants and general practitioners) proposed to merge its traditions with that of the medical section of the Graduates Fellowship. They recognized that, as they said, 'the future lies with this younger emerging movement. It is aiming to do at this time what our Union set out to do in 1874'. The only condition they made was that the new body should undertake to perpetuate the MPU's two 'historic' annual breakfasts, as described above.

As a result of this merger, the medical section of the Graduates Fellowship changed its name in 1949 to the Christian Medical Fellowship. At that time it also reorganized in the form which it was urged that other of the GF's professional sections should do. It became a Fellowship, affiliated to the GF as a constituent section, but under its own constitution. One object was to enable the CMF to serve as a Christian society within the medical profession, and be able to welcome doctors who had become Christians since leaving university or hospital, since at that time the GF consisted only of former members of the CUs. The range of its activities provided for a number of forms of Christian medical service. Whilst its journal *In the Service of Medicine* is a 'house journal' designed for its members, the CMF's other publications have provided information and discussions of Christian principle for a much wider public.

On his retirement from the General Secretaryship of the IVF in 1965 the author became full-time Secretary of the CMF. The needs of the CMF membership, the volume of other related work and the scope of its services outgrew the capacity of a retired secretary. In 1974 Dr. Keith Sanders, a medical missionary returning from India, became the first salaried General Secretary with fuller resources to match the need.

The CMF has international connections with other societies of Christian doctors through its membership of the International Conference of Christian Physicians. Britain was the host country for the Second International Congress in 1966, when approximately 700 doctors, with some of their wives, and medical students met in Oxford. The students held their associated conference, the International Conference of Christian Medical Students, with separate sessions (apart from the Bible studies). These triennial Congresses (and associated Medical Students' Conferences) have been held in Amsterdam 1963, Oxford 1966, Oslo 1969, Toronto 1972, Singapore 1975 and Davos, Switzerland, in 1978.

Science students

In the large university faculties of science it is more difficult to give specialized help to the many advanced students and research post-graduates. The membership of a science faculty is less homogeneous than those in the two faculties mentioned above. In addition there are few unifying factors such as the vocational aspects of theology and medicine. From its earliest days the IVF had organized the occasional meeting, or conference address, the subject of which was one of the problems resulting from scientific progress. But for most science students help was chiefly in the form of individual advice and a few publications. Some help in this form was at first given by Sir Ambrose Fleming, Professor of Electrical Engineering at University College, London. But the approach of the senior members of the college staffs mostly followed the lines of the older apologetics of the early part of the 20th century. Further rapid advances in science and technology were already demanding a new approach, new terminology and new thought-modes. There have not been wanting, however, those who have sought to provide these for the newer generations of students in both speaking and writing. Two of the most prominent have been Professor Donald MacKay of Keele University and Professor Malcolm Jeeves of St. Andrews.

In the late war-years and especially round about 1944, Oliver Barclay brought together at Cambridge a number of Christians engaged in scientific research. Two immediate needs were found. Some of the loneliest people in the world proved to be some of the new post-graduates. Before graduation they had enjoyed the comradeship of undergraduate life, only suddenly to find themselves as isolated back-room boys in a research department. There they struggled depressingly with the beginnings of a thesis and the task of setting up the appropriate apparatus. Their first need was for suitable Christian fellowship. Then the new graduate had an urgent need to arrive at a coherent 'world view'. It was here that senior Christian colleagues 'who had been that way before' could be of such crucial value in friendship and advice. So, first at Cambridge, a 'Scientist's Study Group' was formed. In 1944 and 1945 'Scientific Research Workers Conferences' were held. From these beginnings eventually grew the Research Scientists Christian Fellowship. It has held an annual conference each September at which papers have been read on the problems which face Christians working in science. Meetings in various university cities have been arranged.

One of the most generally helpful influences of the RSCF has been the production of a series of booklets and symposia, which have emerged from its discussions, and have later been published by the Inter-Varsity Press or Tyndale Press. In August 1965 the RSCF was responsible for an international conference in Oxford to which came thirty-six scientists from ten overseas countries. They debated in depth the contemporary relationships of science and Christian belief. The findings were presented under the editorship of Professor Malcolm Jeeves in the symposium published under the title of *The Scientific Enterprise and Christian Faith* (IVP, 1969).

Another valuable initiative was the foundation of residential courses for VI form schoolboys and girls. These were later developed for the arts subjects as well as sciences and were run, first in conjunction with, and later solely by, the Inter-School Christian Fellowship (Scripture Union).

Educationalists

The Educationalists were the first of the IVF's graduate groups to take action in relation to their special professional interests. As early as 1930 there had been informal get-togethers of small groups of teachers in the vacation and exchanges of correspondence on such subjects as discipline in the class room, religious instruction and problems arising from the wide differences of background represented in the average school. Some teachers, particularly those who were responsible for religious instruction, were meeting with considerable opposition from headmasters or headmistresses due to differences of theological outlook. Other class-room situations also gave rise to a desire for discussion with, and the support of, Christian colleagues in the sphere of education.

The General Committee of 5 April 1933 discussed a proposal from its graduate members in the schools that two of their number be authorized to investigate the current situation for Christians who wished still to give religious instruction in the secondary schools along theologically conservative lines. Approval was also sought for the setting up of a fellowship of teachers who were ex-members of the various Christian Unions in

291

the IVF. With the General Committee's support a headmaster
and an assistant master made a survey, and later, in the 1933-34
school year, the Schoolteachers Prayer Circle was set up with
joint secretaries Christopher Cook (Radley) and Dorothy M.
James (Burton-on-Trent High School). Immediately, there was
an excellent response from the teachers. The membership of the
Circle grew rapidly. At first several informal conferences were
held to precede or to follow the annual IVF Swanwick
Conferences. The object was to plan the best forms of mutual
prayer support and to arrange opportunities for interchange of
views within the membership. In 1937 the name was changed to
the Schoolmasters and Schoolmistresses Prayer Fellowship and,
later, to the Christian Education Fellowship.

A number of constructive projects were soon undertaken by the
leaders of the Fellowship. One was the preparation of a carefully
compiled memorandum of Christian education in schools which
was sent to Mr. R. A. Butler at the time of the debates on the new
Education Act 1944. The schoolmasters took good care to ensure
that the Minister should see their work, for it was delivered by
hand by a graduate to whom Mr. Butler had been tutor at
Cambridge, accompanied by another, who had earlier been his
vicar! The first publication by the CEF was *The Giving of the
Scripture Lesson,* written by a headmistress, Miss Mullins of
Wadhurst College.

In 1944 the Schoolmasters and Schoolmistresses Prayer
Fellowship started a series of annual summer schools for teachers
at which papers on various aspects of education were read and
discussed. In the leadership of these summer schools, and in the
development of the CEF generally, outstanding service was given
for a number of years by J. W. Harmer (Chairman) and H. M.
Cundy (Secretary). They were responsible for *The Scripture
Lesson* (IVP) a volume to accompany the agreed syllabuses of the
education authorities The theory and practice of Christian
education (as far as this was practicable under the national
education system) were thoroughly debated. One of the more
influential special meetings, to which a few representatives of
other Evangelical Youth Movements were personally invited,
took place during the war and was addressed by the then Master

of Balliol College, Oxford. The subject of the address was the likely bearing of the 1944 Education Act upon the work of all the various Christian societies engaged in work amongst the children of the primary and secondary Schools. Lord Lindsay was asked to comment on such changes of policy and adjustment of methods as might become necessary and desirable as the application of the Act came to bear on the work of the youth organizations.

The Association of Christian Teachers

Alongside the work being done for Christian teachers by the Graduates' Fellowship, two other organizations were active. Since before World War II the Teachers' Prayer Bond, later renamed Teachers' Prayer Fellowship, had united teachers in many areas of Britain and supported their members overseas financially and by prayer. The Inter-School Christian Fellowship, Schools' department of the Scripture Union, came into existence after the War. In the early days the training of pupil leaders was the main priority, but as more and more Christian graduates were called to education and as the CUs spread to the Secondary Modern, and later to Comprehensive schools, work among teachers increased. This involved co-ordinating the teachers in their work for the CUs and also providing teachers' meetings for fellowship and professional help.

At this point the ISCF and the CEF overlapped. In some areas, three evangelical teachers' organizations existed side by side, arranging meetings for the same overworked teachers, sometimes on the same date, if diaries had not been consulted, or sometimes in ignorance of the others' work. It became clear that co-ordination was necessary. A Committee, representing the three organizations was formed in the mid-60s to try to rationalize the situation. In 1968 *Spectrum* a magazine for teachers at all levels of education was launched and has enjoyed the steady support of Evangelical and other educationists for ten years. In several places, local groups amalgamated to form a teachers' fellowship across the three organizations. Bristol, and then Camberley, began this trend and, after several years of prayer and committee work, all three organizations, TPF, ISCF (teachers' branch) and CEF

293

abandoned their individual identity to form the Association of Christian Teachers in 1971.

The Association has continued to grow and now has its own office and field staff, based on the ISCF's office but closely linked with UCCF as one of the Associates' professional departments.

This has been a happy story of co-operation and unity, where no organization has felt itself too proud to shut out the others and Christian work in education has benefited greatly as a result.

The ACT has an increasing voice in educational policy-making via the Press and other media and is more and more listened to by the churches and government. ACT groups exist in dozens of towns and cities in Britain. Book review services and matters of professional interest are circulated in *Digest* and ACT has published several books on matters relating to Christians in education.

Post-War expansion of the Graduates Fellowship

By 1943 and early 1944, though the War was by no means over, there was already a great deal of discussion about reconstruction and fresh starts. Amongst these were 'opportunities for Christian expansion' and some wildly over-optimistic plans. The remnant of the membership of the GF Committee hoped that the return from war-service of some of the more vigorous graduates would open up many vistas of departmental progress.

The forward-looking and zealous war-time Chairman of the GF, Alan Cook, led the way in outlining a comprehensive future for what had become an extensive series of advisory and ecumenical services being rendered by the IVF, at the time. Although they were all hard-pressed, the few remaining full-time officers of the IVF were fulfilling a consultative and supportive role for several of the related youth movements and smaller missionary societies. The latter were severely handicapped by the absence of many of their ablest and most active leaders in the Forces. Similarly, some of the other lay Christian leaders, who were left coping also with additional secular professional work, were glad to refer some of their technical and academic problems to the IVF. It was usually able to channel such requests to ex-members who were trained in specialist fields. It therefore appeared that there might be an extensive future for the GF as (i) an advisory forum, (ii) a bureau of information and (iii) a task force which might advance Christian activity in some of the spheres which were less open to the churches. Another aspect of this forward planning was a vision of the GF's potential as the central co-ordinating body for a series of Christian Unions operating in the various professions.

In the event, for several reasons, some of these more ambitious plans were not realized. One of the most important of these was that, on demobilization, many of the graduates were able quickly to take up their former roles in the various other youth and missionary societies. Most of these were able effectively to expand their work. There was no need to duplicate such activities, which gained from the more concentrated attention that the appropriate societies were able to give them. Similarly, most of the IVF's temporary war-time (advisory) functions shrank almost overnight as the various youth and missionary societies were able to bring their committees to full strength. But perhaps the strongest reason was the individualism of the average professional workers, a number of whom were not conscious of any special need for consultation with, or witness to, the members of professional colleagues at their places of work. Hence it was only in some of the professions that a clear need was felt for Christian solidarity in relation to their specialized problems. Another reason for reshaping the work was the vigorous reorganization of such co-ordinating bodies as the Evangelical Alliance. Any need for the GF (as such) to extend its peacetime interests beyond the educational and professional fields was removed. In view of the continued shortages in men and money, it was just as well.

Originally planned in April 1939, and adopted on 5 April 1941, the GF constitution envisages (i) a fellowship of graduate ex-members of the university Christian Unions, who would be kept in touch with the activities of their Unions and the IVF, with a view to support by prayer and finance; (ii) a co-ordination and development of the existing circles of ex-members in the various professions or for particular purposes. After several amendments of the constitution these aims remain the general outlook of the

295

GF, except that in the case of some of the professional groups it has been possible to proceed some way towards their being organized as Christian Unions for their own professional spheres.

In the post-war years there was an increase of the GF membership from new sources. Very soon after the GF's inception, the rise of the Christian Unions in the colleges of education and technical colleges began to produce a growing number of ex-members, who though not technically university graduates, were entering comparable forms of professional work. Provision was, therefore, made to welcome these 'graduate equivalents' as 'associate members'. In later years they have been fully integrated and played their full part in the local GF meetings and most of the sections of the GF.

After 1945 the Graduates Fellowship began to develop new methods. Soon after the War the Christian Education Fellowship raised the question of central united gatherings on a national scale for the Graduates Fellowship members as a whole. Whilst their own annual summer school had met their more professional needs, a number of schoolmistresses drew attention to the unmet, important spiritual needs, particularly of their more isolated members. The dates for school terms prevented them from taking part in such gatherings as the Keswick Convention and other 'devotional' conferences. They made a strong plea that the Graduates Fellowship should organize an annual conference primarily for Bible study, but accompanied by discussion of certain general problems, including those of up-to-date apologetics. The only time in the year which proved relatively free for the majority was the early New Year. The first conference, which was largely attended by the schoolmistresses who had orignally requested it, grew into what has become a growing series of the Graduates Fellowship conferences.

At subsequent times, such as 1954, there have been amendments to the GF Constitution to keep pace with expansion and new developments. Then the *Graduates Fellowship Newsletter,* which, at the end of the paper rationing after the War years, had grown in size and had altered in format, was recognized in 1949 as the second main journal of the Fellowship under the title of *The Christian Graduate.* There came also an increase in the number of sections, with recognition of new circles such as the Christian Dental Fellowship, provision for the graduates engaged in government and trade organizations overseas and also for those in industry in this country. Whilst there are members who are graduates in law in the GF, the Lawyers' Prayer Union has had a separate tradition since 1854, and continues independently under a new name, the Lawyers' Christian Fellowship.

At the time of writing the UCCF Associates, as the Graduates Fellowship is now called, contains twelve specialized or professional groups; the Agricultural Christian Fellowship, the Association of Christian Teachers (see page 293), the Business Study Group, the Christian Dental Fellowship, the Christian Medical Fellowship, the College Lecturers Christian Fellowship, the Historians' Study Group, the Research Scientists' Christian Fellowship, the Social Workers' Christian Fellowship, the Tyndale Fellowship, the University Staffs Christian Fellowship and the Veterinary Christian Fellowship.

Tyndale House and Library

Following the purchase of the house in Cambridge during the final phase of the war (see page 212), the Biblical Research Committee gave much thought to the way in which the project could best be administered. The task of bringing up to date the specialist library required senior advice. Initially the purpose of the house was not sufficiently appreciated except by the few leaders who were in touch with the younger impecunious scholars who were being encouraged to train for higher post-graduate qualifications. After tentative experiments, the respective committees, the Biblical Research Committee and the Business Advisory Committee, settled for a basic staff consisting of a Warden and Librarian (both of whom were themselves engaged in some aspect of biblical research), assisted by a typist-secretary. All further available resources were applied (i) to the purchase of books technically concerned with the languages and background of the Bible, and (ii) to grants for suitably equipped post-graduates, who were working on a university thesis which would contribute to the aims of the house.

297

In the first post-war years it was found that there were few post-graduates who could consider postponing the start of their intended careers in order to give two to three years for this type of work. The increasingly substantial national grants for research were mostly for work in the science, medical and engineering faculties. Hence, applications to take up residence in the house were at first fewer than the plans had envisaged, though a good deal of work on major projects was done in the house from the start. For example, the general editor's work on the New Bible Dictionary was done by the Librarian of Tyndale House, Dr. J. D. Douglas.

By 1954-5 there was an increase in the number of applications and more money had become available for grants. Hence there was need for more room. Those responsible for the house and library were unanimous that a major extension was now called for. Their decision was confirmed by an offer from Mr. John Laing of a gift of one pound for every pound which would be contributed by others towards the estimated costs. In July 1955 work on the new building was begun. When finished, the extension provided a large library room on the ground floor, over which were built twelve study bedrooms. A covered way linked the new building with the house. With these additions it was possible to offer residence to over twenty post-graduates. When unoccupied by a graduate who was engaged on Biblical research, or its equivalent, unfilled rooms were let to undergraduates and post-graduates from other faculties engaged in other types of university work.

From what was a comparatively small collection, based on the initial purchase of the books of a well-known biblical scholar, the library at Tyndale House has been built up until it is today an efficient centre for work on primary sources and for reference by biblical scholars. It has also built up a subscription list covering the chief journals in its sphere of study. Much of the credit for this must go to Andrew F. Walls (currently head of the Department of Biblical Studies at Aberdeen University) during his residence as Librarian 1952-1957.

Over the years under the leadership of the successive Wardens, much valuable work has been done. The Wardens themselves,

Leon Morris (until he returned to Australia to become Principal of Ridley College, Melbourne) and then Derek Kidner, and all four successive Librarians, J. D. Douglas, Andrew Walls, A. R. Millard and R. T. France, have completed doctoral theses, research projects or their equivalents in scholarly commentaries. Several well-known biblical scholars had lived in the house and made use of its facilities, whilst writing their books. For example, over a year and a half before his sudden death, Professor William F. Arndt made the house his base and made extensive use of the library. He there completed his part in the revision of the fourth (and augmented) edition of W. Bauer's *A Greek-English Lexicon of the New Testament*, Arndt and Gingrich; 1955, (Chicago and Cambridge University Presses).

In the post-war years there was encouraging growth in attendance at the July summer schools organized by the Old Testament and the New Testament groups. The two Tyndale lectures (on the Old Testament and New Testament respectively) were joined by Biblical Archaeology and Biblical Theology lectures. Out of the summer schools arose the Tyndale Fellowship for Biblical Research, with its main aim to increase the type of research work for which the house was founded. It has since done much to increase the output from younger biblical scholars.

All these developments, which have made a major contribution to the extension of Evangelical Christian faith in the English-speaking world, would not have been possible without the consistent support and tireless industry of three of the foundation members in this project, Dr. W. J. Martin (Liverpool University), who originally proposed the concept of Tyndale House, Professor F. F. Bruce (Manchester University) and the Rev. A. M. Stibbs (Oak Hill Theological College, London). After 1946 they were ably and assiduously supported by Professor D. J. Wiseman (London University). Each of these has devoted hours of his time in the interests of the house and in advising the younger scholars who have worked there.

Wider services

The account of these aspects of the work done by senior graduates and staff of the IVF would not be complete without some reference to the services given to other independent Christian organizations. For example, IVF loaned two graduates at the inception of the Nurses Christian Fellowship to share experiences gained in related fields. Similarly, in the immediate post-war years it was two IVF graduates who pioneered the work of the Inter-School Christian Fellowship until the CSSM (Scripture Union) was able to take up responsibility and appoint secretaries. Again, it was an IVF graduate who saw in the USA the original film in the series of the Fact and Faith films produced by the Moody Institute and arranged for the transfer to this country of the first copy sent overseas from USA. The IVF invited a representative gathering to see it at the National Club and proposed the setting up of a committee to test the British public's reaction to this first film, 'The God of Creation', and, if it were well received, to arrange for the next in the series to be imported. The American producers primarily had in mind as their original audience the schoolchildren of America. It so happened that just as the film was about to be started on this occasion, the late Lord Hazlerigg, at that time Lord Lieutenant of Leicester, entered the room and enquired if he could join in. He was so enthusiastic about the potential value of the film that he persuaded the embryo committee to let him take it back with him to his county's Education Department. It was in this way that many of the Leicester schoolchildren were the first viewers of the Fact and Faith Films.

When A. J. Vereker (Secretary of the Crusaders' Union) agitated for the foundation of an interdenominational Bible college in London, he met with little support. He continued to urge. At length, it was the IVF Committee which called two representative meetings of Christian leaders in London in 1939 to launch the project and it was to the IVF nucleus of supporters that the offer of the original site in Marylebone Road was made by Mr. J. W. Laing. This was to be the home of the London Bible College, later to move to more spacious quarters in Northwood.

The War almost immediately intervened, but it had just been possible to bring together the group of Christian leaders who were later able to act decisively immediately peace returned.

The object of recording these aspects of the Fellowship's wider influence is to illustrate the importance of the total history and the total effect of the work of the Christian Unions. Some of those prominent in the leadership of churches, missionary societies and other Christian institutions of many varieties were first spiritually awakened and led to Christ in a university or college Christian Union. They learnt first to take responsibility in active service for Christ when serving on the committee of their student Christian Union.

Chapter 17

Overseas students[1]

Since the special needs of overseas students first became a matter of concern to the IVF the student scene in Britain has drastically changed. From the relatively small numbers of commonwealth post-graduate students who came in the early years, numbers have now risen to well over 100,000 overseas students, who are following a variety of academic courses at the universities and colleges. In addition, probably as many as ½ million language students are coming for short-term, intensive courses in private institutions. The more academic of the students now come from over 180 countries, whilst those doing the short-term language courses are mainly from the continent of Europe and Japan. Whenever these overseas students within the universities and colleges are mentioned, the word 'opportunity' is always very much in evidence. The type of need and the opportunity to show appropriate friendship has now become almost overwhelming. In some of the colleges well over half of the student population are coming from overseas. The rapid increase in numbers has tested to the full all the resources of the educational, philanthropic and other voluntary organizations which were interested and were ready to help. Amongst them the UCCF has been able to play an important role by offering welcome, friendship and advice to many thousands of overseas students.

Before 1939

As mentioned above, before World War II the majority of overseas students were coming from the countries of the Commonwealth. They were post-graduates bent upon obtaining higher degrees and the appropriate further training in their own fields of study. They were financially assisted by various forms of national and Commonwealth scholarships. Being already experienced in university life they were mostly able to take their place in the student body without much difficulty. During these years the help which was most welcomed by a new arrival was a warm initial greeting, and then personal introductions to some of the senior members of staff and some of the students in their year in the colleges in which they were to work. Hospitality in a home environment was also valued, especially over the bank holidays and during the long vacation. So far as corporate activities were concerned the IVF leaders contented themselves with a few well-spaced informal receptions. It was clear that the newcomers wished not to be objects of special concern but as soon as possible made to feel a real part of the local community. The London informal receptions at this time would be attended by an average of 200 from overseas. Similar gatherings took place in other university cities where there were sufficient concentrations of post-graduates.

After World War II

By the beginning of the second academic year after the War the stream of new arrivals from all over the world steeply increased, despite the fact that a number of African and other countries were being helped to develop their own universities by upgrading the most progressive of their own advanced colleges. The committees of the IVF became increasingly conscious of the future value to the developing countries of the graduates who later would be returning from Britain with specialist training. In 1947 an important step was taken by the setting up of a sub-committee of the Executive known as 'The Hospitality Committee'. Over the next five years the chief areas of need were identified. Some of the activities which later formed the main basis of the work began to function. Whilst the British Council and other organizations primarily responsible in this sphere aimed at meeting and advising the growing numbers from overseas, they were at first quite overwhelmed by the size of the task and the IVF sought to complement this by giving a personal welcome to new arrivals wherever suitable contacts could be made. From late 1946 onwards Miss Norah Nixon (then the Women's Secretary of the Graduates' Fellowship), Captain and Mrs. Godfrey Buxton, and Mrs. Clarence Foster and others gave much thought and time to organizing receptions. They also developed a project for offering hospitality at the weekends in the homes of graduates. A series of 'Eastern Lectures' were arranged in London, at which experts – who had worked in the countries concerned – spoke and led discussions. Overseas students who came from Christian churches in their own countries were invited by a member of All Souls Church to her home in Welbeck Street for Sunday teas. This was a beginning of what became a nationwide trend in the other university cities.

The discovery of a genius

It was Freddy Crittenden who caught a vision of the opportunity that overseas students in this country presented, and developed the work into a specialist department of the IVF. After his own graduation at Oxford he had gone to Kenya as the first member of staff of the Scripture Union in East Africa, and subsequently had become a member of the staff of the Alliance High School in Kenya. During the war years he had served with one of the East African regiments on the north-west frontier of India, and on returning to this country had joined the African Department of the School of Oriental and African Studies in London. He therefore had a working knowledge of how to serve the best interests of overseas students and particularly the Africans. In 1951 he moved from SOAS in order to take up the secretaryship of the Graduates' Fellowship and to serve the overseas students. He certainly had outstanding gifts of genuine friendship and much to give to those who sought his advice. His ability to communicate with many of the East Africans in their own language proved to be a specially valuable asset. The overseas students' work began to take more and more of his time, and in 1959 he transferred from the general work of the Graduates' Fellowship and became the full-time Overseas Students Secretary.

There was a variety of ways in which the activities owing their origin to Freddy Crittenden's fertile imagination have further developed in later years. The clearest way to explain some of those developments will be to group them.

Christian Union involvement

A concern to reach out to overseas students had already developed before and during the time that Freddy Crittenden was the Graduates' Fellowship Secretary. Whilst most student leaders have appreciated the need to welcome members of the student body from overseas, it was the keenness of many Graduates' Fellowship members to assist in the receptions and to offer hospitality in their homes which provided much of the impetus in the early days. It was 'the International Friendship Campaign' in London, which more recently came to be known as 'the International Welcome Campaign', that committed the Christian Union members to greater involvement in the work, and it still continues to prove the most effective way of passing on the vision to each new generation of students.

Each September brings an invasion of overseas students into London, a proportion of whom are due to go to other student centres after a short pause in the Capital. Following a small-scale trial in the first year, Freddy Crittenden offered to the British Council a team of British students who volunteered to contribute a week of their long vacation to act as 'guide escorts'. These student volunteers usually worked for a week and soon became efficient at their task. The responsible education authorities and the British Council were offered increasingly valued help. Most of the students from other universities who had helped on the London campaign went back to continue to operate local friendship campaigns in their own universities in the following year. A network of welcoming programmes was soon developed. As a result, thousands of overseas students have been glad of the friendly faces, practical assistance in moving their luggage, an escort on new and strange forms of transport, a demonstration of what to expect in change for their money and advice on the best shops to patronize.

In 1965 an overseas student travelling secretary was appointed. This appointment gave more opportunity for the Christian Unions to be reminded of the missionary field on our doorstep and to receive practical advice on the running of activities. Handbooks of advice were produced, based on the rapidly increasing experience that the Overseas Student Department staff had been collecting.

The main body of the membership, however, was not as much awake as it should have been. The very varied range of exciting activities which present themselves to Christian university students tends to mean that in many of the Christian Unions too few of the members give a quota of their time to building up friendships with overseas students. In the polytechnics and technical colleges, the limited available manpower in the CUs prevents many of the groups from doing as much for overseas students as the leaders would like. However, with the support and encouragement of UCCF staff and graduates, a number of united overseas student houseparties have operated with considerable success. A large proportion of the Graduates' Fellowship members who now support the work, first began to see the need whilst they themselves were students.

The hospitality scheme

In the early days it was soon discovered that many students with whom contact had been made in the September International Welcome Campaigns, were left very much at a loose end when the students' residential halls and hostels emptied for the vacations. In some of the now silent buildings there would be no-one except a group of lonely 'lost' souls from overseas, who had not been fortunate enough to be invited to stay in some suitable and hospitable household. Freddy Crittenden began to write to the whole of the Graduates' Fellowship, saying that he would be glad to hear of any homes which felt that they could offer to welcome overseas students in the vacations. Following a quiet start in the first year, in most of the years thereafter a vast amount of hospitality came to be offered in the London area and elsewhere in the country. However, it was not all plain sailing. On numerous occasions a perturbed potential host or hostess would ring up to report that, having done a great deal of preparation, no potential guest had arrived! It became necessary over the years to go to much trouble, on the one hand to eliminate feigned acceptances from students who had not intended to turn up (but thought it more polite to appear to accept) and, on the other, to persuade once or twice disappointed hosts and hostesses to offer again to welcome such uncertain guests the following year!

The hospitality scheme was designed to operate throughout the year. It soon became evident, however, that the Christmas period was clearly the most important time at which a student could be brought into a friendly household. It also provided the most natural opportunity to explain the outlook of Christians. Striking brochures were therefore produced for Christmas hospitality, and a special attempt made to build up a list of families who could not offer such hospitality at other times of the year.

In 1972, in anticipation of Freddy Crittenden's fairly imminent retirement, a GF Overseas Student Committee was formed to advise the department. There had been many organizers and informal committees for overseas student activities in various cities (or university and college localities) throughout the country from time to time, but this central committee decided to suggest the appointment of an 'Area Co-ordinator for Overseas Student Activities' in each student centre. Many of the graduates and students who then accepted this title were already deeply involved in the work, but the standardization of this approach to the need meant that it could be more widely and easily publicized. It was easier, for example, to let the Christian Union members know exactly what sort of help they could expect from their local Graduates' Fellowship group. The total result has been that an army of hosts, hostesses and other members of families, can now look back with pleasure to the encouragement they were able to give to, and receive from, many a lonely student. Numbers of their overseas visitors became warm friends of the families. They would return at intervals for week-ends and often longer periods. Many of the hundreds who were introduced in these ways have developed long-lasting friendships. Some of the overseas students who have married in this country have set out from these adopted homes as their own 'home' base.

Houseparties and special groups

For several years Freddy Crittenden had been adjutant at the IVF student camp at Keswick, and he soon started to contrive ways and means of introducing overseas students from Christian backgrounds to the Convention. With financial help he was able to increase the number of overseas students attending, and a large number of them can now look back with gratitude to their visits to Cumberland. Later the experiment was tried of holding a small, independent students' camp after the conclusion of the convention week. This proved a great success, chiefly because of the more intimate fellowship and exchanges of view which were possible in a smaller group. It was the beginning of a whole series of such camps and houseparties held at other dates in the year. These additional international houseparties came to use a large number of different venues and included sites in Wales, Scotland, Lake District, Peak District, New Forest, Bude, Oxford and Sussex. Christmas and Easter became increasingly the most popular houseparty periods, because more and more of the overseas students tended to go home, get a job, or travel to the Continent during the summer vacation. For some years there was also an annual excursion to the Continent for a houseparty at the student centre in Moscia, Switzerland. The students attending these houseparties who had come from Christian backgrounds (and also quite often it proved, from those of other faiths), opted for the Bible studies and discussions on various Christian subjects. Others chose more general discussions, but sometimes changed in order to study the prevailing religion of the country in which they now found themselves.

The most successful of the informal groups proved to be that which had begun for Christians at an international Scripture

Union houseparty. In some years there were over 300 who were using the *Daily Bread* SU readings. A proportion of the students in this group also joined an SU training school which met regularly in London. Those who were not resident in the London area were also able to follow this training course by post. The keenness and industry shown by some of the students taking part in it was most refreshing to the organizers. One African student who had been sent to Britain to complete his training as a parliamentary reporter for his government, became more and more enthusiastic about the Bible. On returning to his own country he made a journey each Sunday to villages near the capital city in order to conduct Bible studies and to teach Christian doctrine to youth groups. Later, in his spare time, he gained an external degree in theology. He is now considerably in demand as a lay-preacher in his denomination.

The Bible discussion groups in London came to be known as 'Investigations'. Two cousins, who were African post-graduates and came from a nominal Christian background, became progressively more interested in the spiritual aspects of the discussions and began regularly to read the Bible. They also joined enthusiastically in several of the houseparties. By the end of their three years in Britain they had both become active Christians. One was later promoted to an important position in his government, and the other was made manager in a firm that has considerable national influence. The latter made it clear from the beginning that he would not knowingly countenance any corruption or dishonesty. He gained considerable respect amongst his colleagues and the confidence of those dealing with his firm.

Most of the overseas students who in this country come to faith have been able to benefit from membership of local churches and from taking part in various forms of Christian activity which will be of use in their future service. For example a mature student from Indonesia, who has since had a strong Christian influence on his own people, began to appreciate what it really meant to be a Christian through 'Investigations' and the fellowship of one of the more outgoing of the London churches. Many of the overseas students on becoming Christians seem quickly to have developed

309

into zealous disciples of the Lord. Some of them have used their time in this country to collect a library of Christian books and to sit regularly under the systematic exposition of the Bible. There is no shadow of doubt that, both for overseas visitors and our own younger Christians, systematic expository preaching and Bible teaching is crucial.

The international clubs

As mentioned above, in pre-1939 academic years the various academic authorities were able to accommodate a due proportion of post-graduates from overseas in the official student residences and hostels. When numbers increased, to be swollen also by many under-graduates and shorter course students, far too many were compelled to undertake the difficult hunt for suitable lodgings. In some cities extortionate rents were asked for miserable and poorly furnished rooms. An overseas student has always found that it is when he is seeking accommodation that he becomes most conscious of colour prejudice within our society. Overseas students who have tried to bring wives and families to London, have found that many doors were slammed in their faces, and these situations soon became a heartbreak to the IVF staff who were in touch with them.

Whilst interested to help, the IVF, expanding in almost every department, had no reserve capital with which it could buy a freehold or obtain a lease on suitably spacious property.

After prayer and consultation, and with the goodwill of the IVF committees, Freddy Crittenden determined to found an international (residential) club in which there would be a sufficient quota of British students to help to create the desired team spirit and practical day-to-day co-operation. The council of the Evangelical Alliance was interested and eventually helped to find the money for the purchase of a lease in Bedford Place. This was ideally situated in central London, near the British Museum.

In October 1952 the Alliance Club in Bedford Place, was opened and was filled from the start. Besides its value for a residential community, the premises also afforded a central meeting place for international study groups and socials. Many

310

strong friendships sprang up between the overseas and British students. Much daytime hospitality and meals could also be offered to less fortunate overseas students who had only bare lodgings which did not provide food. The Club proved such a success that when, after 11 years, the lease ran out and the landlords were prepared to renew it only at a cripplingly higher rental, there was widespread dismay. However the former missionaries' residence of the China Inland Mission at Newington Green became available, and the Alliance Club was able to move into this more spacious accommodation.

Despite this, by 1965 there were pleas from a number of students for a residence back in central London, which would have a suitable meeting room attached and which could be used for small meetings. After a search lasting several months, a tall, terraced house in central London, 5 Doughty Street, was bought with the help of gifts and loans from Christian businessmen. It was vested in a charitable trust. Two large rooms on the first floor, with a partition-door enabling it to be made into one room, were rented by the IVF to serve as a venue for international discussion groups and small meetings. The SU training school was transferred to it (from a central London hostel lounge which did not offer the same atmosphere of homeliness) and the house constantly demonstrated its value by providing a meeting place for a variety of meetings and groups. The example of the usefulness of Doughty Street led to the purchase in 1967 of a house in Birmingham – 29 Portland Road – to be used in a similar way.

During the sixties there were very few clubs and organizations which provided social activities for overseas students, and the space available at Doughty Street was often used to its full capacity. By the end of the sixties a number of charitable organizations and educational authorities became more conscious of the needs of overseas students, and most universities began to develop their own overseas students' social societies. In London several overseas student clubs began to open, providing a very wide range of elaborate facilities. Rapid increases in London bus and tube fares have meant that students became increasingly less inclined to travel to central London, and, although Doughty

311

Street is still used regularly for meetings, other venues are being developed as well. In this respect the UCCF is greatly indebted to the Alliance Club which has recently taken over the whole of the OMF site at Newington Green and which has provided a very convenient operational centre for the London Welcome Campaign teams.

The needs change

The international centre at 5 Doughty Street has provided a very suitable venue for a great variety of meetings. Many of these were geared towards students from a particular continent or ethnic background and often Bible studies were conducted in a language other than English. The Africa Fellowship and the Ghanaian Fellowship here came into existence. Today there are about a dozen different student national fellowships, operating in different parts of London. Some of these groups are strong and well organized. Together with some good central London churches they provide fellowship and teaching for Christian overseas students.

In the last ten years, however, two changes have taken place which fundamentally altered the work for overseas students. First, a tremendous increase has taken place in the number of overseas students coming to do non-university, and largely vocational, courses. The rapid increase in numbers in polytechnics, technical colleges and further educational establishments has been so great that local education authorities have now been forced to reduce their intake of overseas students. This has had the effect of causing a large increase in the number of private colleges for English language training and other courses. There are no CUs in most of these colleges. Christian students, however, have been able to contact many of the overseas visitors through the summer witness teams that have operated, for example, in the language school centres on the south coast, and at Oxford and Cambridge. These short-term evangelistic summer campaigns, working closely with local churches, have seen quite a lot of fruit for their labours. They have also galvanized some CU members to take more interest in the overseas students in their own universities or colleges.

The second main change has been that the original pre-dominance of students from the Indian sub-continent and Africa has now given way to a much higher total proportion of Muslim students coming from the Middle East, together with Chinese students from Malaysia and Hong Kong. As a rule the Chinese keep themselves very much to themselves, and quickly form their own ethnic groups and societies. There are, however, Chinese Christians who are effectively presenting the gospel. Muslim students are showing much greater reluctance to become involved in any activity with a Christian label, and will very rarely come to a group Bible study.

The numbers of students coming from overseas change constantly, their backgrounds and their attitudes alter, their physical needs vary from place to place, but their spiritual needs do not change and the opportunity to reach them is still open. Many overseas students have become Christians, grown in the faith, and gone back to their own country to stand firmly as Christians. As the student work develops world-wide, through the International Fellowship of Evangelical Students, opportunities for overseas students to be involved in their own countries increase. The greatest continuing need is for much greater generosity and willingness to go the second mile on the part of Christian Union members in universities and colleges throughout the country.

NOTES

[1] The author wishes to acknowledge the help of Miss Dorothy Martin, Secretary of the International Friendship Campaign; and of Bryan Knell, UCCF Overseas Students' Secretary, for supplying information and structuring this section.

Chapter 18

The Inter-Varsity Press
Contributed by Ronald Inchley
(Publications Secretary 1936-77)

Author's Introduction: Since *Inter-Varsity Booklet* No. 1 went to press in 1928, the Publications Department can now be seen to have brought a major contribution to the Evangelical Movement inside and outside the student world. It is a story by itself. And, whilst the author himself has had some first-hand acquaintance with the developments especially in the early years, a more intimate picture can be presented by the member of staff who was the most responsible for the results. Ronald Inchley, coming straight from his graduation at Birmingham University in 1936, started work in the very small, under-manned and under-financed IVF office to produce the literature urgently needed by the rapidly-growing Christian Unions. The production annually of a few booklets and one or two small books eventually burgeoned into a sizeable publishing house. The qualities needed at the pioneer stages were vision, great patience, resolute perseverance and self-abnegating concentration on the one job. Ronald Inchley rose to the occasion. To assess his success the reader has only to obtain the latest edition of the IVP catalogue!

What follows is in 'RI's' own words.

The place of publications

Ever since the invention of printing Christians have grasped the

314

importance of using Christian literature in the service of God's kingdom. At first it was the production of Bibles which received priority. No longer was it necessary for every copy to be written laboriously by hand. But very quickly other Christian books were being produced and widely disseminated. Luther was so convinced of the importance of the printed, as well as the spoken, word that he described the printing press as 'God's supreme gift to Christendom to aid the spread of the gospel'. A slight exaggeration, maybe; but when we look at the figures for the German book trade around the time of the Reformation, we can understand what he meant. Prior to 1518 the number of new books published in that country each year was a little over forty. Five years later the figure had risen to nearly 500 of which 180 were credited to Luther himself, although they probably owed their existence to enthusiastic printers' stenographers sitting in the back of the church when he was preaching. Times haven't changed much except that nowadays publishers use cassette tape recorders!

Church history shows that, in a similar way, most of the great movements of the Spirit of God in the church were accompanied by a renewed interest in the printed word. Wesley, who was himself converted, or at least brought to assurance of salvation, by listening to a reading from the preface to one of Luther's commentaries, was also a prolific writer, deeply aware of the need to help his lay-preachers to educate themselves. And as the evangelical revival continued its influence into the early 19th century, the importance attached by Christian leaders to the production and distribution of the Bible and other Christian literature is seen, not only in the books they produced, but in the societies which they founded to promote such work and the great emphasis they placed upon teaching the largely illiterate industrial classes to read.

Early days

It is no surprise, therefore, to find that from its earliest days the Inter-Varsity Fellowship included the production of Christian books and pamphlets in its programme. *Christ and the Colleges*

(1934) reported that 'by 1926 the Executive Committee had reached the stage of discussing the publication of up-to-date Christian literature for students'. The key word there is probably 'up-to-date', for at that time very few Christian books suitable for use by students in the growing Christian Unions were available. Evangelical scholars were few. Christian publishers tended to be somewhat old fashioned in their approach and were apparently not really interested in the questions students were asking. The early leaders, as they looked for books which would help the CU members to live out their Christian faith in the academic world, began to see that they might well have to produce their own books if students were to be given what they needed. They wanted literature which would encourage Bible study, personal devotion and evangelistic outreach (which were the special emphases of the IVF at the time) and there was very little to be found.

By 1932 seven titles in a series of Inter-Varsity Papers had been published, the majority of them on 'Science and Faith' subjects, and all of them produced in the drabbest of grey covers. 1933 saw the beginnings of a more attractive series of 'Inter-Varsity Booklets' with a collection of articles taken from the *Inter-Varsity Magazine* and published under the title *The Quiet Time*. A year later the first volume in a six-part Bible study course *Search the Scriptures* appeared. It was designed to take the student through the whole of the Bible in three years. In a much revised form this is still being widely used over forty years later. A special department to handle the publishing work was set up in 1936 when a recently qualified graduate with no publishing experience was appointed as Literature Secretary at a salary of £180 pa. It was on the understanding that he would combine this work with responsibility for the office-end of the organization of the big city campaigns which were such an important feature of the IVF's pre-war work. That year saw also the publication of another key book, *In Understanding Be Men*, a handbook on Christian doctrine by T. C. Hammond which, in its third major revision, still sells widely each year.

Those early days were far from easy. Apart from one publisher member of the Business Advisory Committee (Mr. A. W. Churchill of J & A. Churchill, medical publishers), no one had any real publishing experience. Capital was very short. The publishing operation was running at a loss mainly because arrangements for distribution were so poor. In September 1938 the BAC very nearly negotiated an arrangement with Messrs Hodder and Stoughton whereby they would have become the official publishers for books sponsored by the IVF. At the last minute this action was postponed; the Literature Secretary was hurriedly recalled from Birkenhead where he was helping to run a city campaign and told to concentrate on selling existing stock in order to reduce the amount of capital employed to around £1,000. This must have had some effect since it was later reported that sales for those last four months of the year were up 40% on the same period in 1937!

Nevertheless, total turnover for the full twelve months did not amount to much over £2,000. Yet when the matter was reviewed in the new year, there was a marked change of heart on the part of the business advisers. Although the year's trading had resulted in what was described as a 'serious loss' of over £300, they agreed that this 'should not be allowed to affect the planning of the literature committee'. Maybe they were influenced by the student Executive Committee which told them that 'such a loss was justified by the value of the work done'. But it had been touch and go. The publishing department had very nearly been closed down.

As the IVF's senior advisers looked at the publishing operation prior to the outbreak of war, and saw how small and amateurishly run it was, they may be forgiven for doubting whether it would ever grow into anything much bigger. For example, it was thought highly unlikely that it could become sufficiently profitable in the foreseeable future to support the services of a married man. So at the beginning of 1939, since the Literature Secretary had recently taken the bold step of getting engaged, it was agreed that he would have to seek other employment. When war broke out the whole situation became much worse. The department as such was put into moth balls. Existing stocks were transferred to the CSSM and Scripture Union Bookroom which agreed to act as trade agent for the duration of the war. With paper likely to be severely rationed it was thought that little more than a holding operation could be attempted as far as production

317

of new titles was concerned.

It is surprising how quickly a new spirit seemed to prevail, however. By 1941 the suggestion was being made that the Literature Committee, which was still meeting from time to time under the energetic chairmanship of the Rev. G. T. Manley, should begin to make plans now with a view to 'flooding the market with Evangelical literature as soon as paper restrictions were removed'. A Biblical Research Committee had been brought into being and was actively encouraging such Evangelical scholars as there were to think seriously of writing. One project on which it was working in 1942 was a Bible Dictionary; another was an Introduction to the Old Testament which some hoped might be extended to cover the whole Bible. It is significant also that, when the Graduates Fellowship was being set up in 1941, it included in its aims the desire 'to lead the way in the production of more adequate and scholarly literature'.

About this time, also, a literature committee was set up jointly with the CSSM and the two Crusaders Unions to plan a series of books aimed in the first place at teenagers in school sixth forms. The idea generated a great deal of discussion and took a long time to bear any fruit. It was 1946 before the first title (the small book *Creation*, by R. E. D. Clarke) appeared. But all this activity showed that, even in the dark days of the war, those who had this side of the work at heart were confident that better days would come and that there was a very worth-while future for IVF publishing work.

Finance

One way of estimating the success of a publishing operation is by looking at the turnover figures. They do not tell the whole story, but they certainly provide some indication of what was happening. In 1944 sales totalled no more than £2,400. In 1945, the year in which the former Literature Secretary (now married!) was invited to return, the figure went up to £3,375. The following year with paper restrictions still in operation, sales increased by more than 40% to £5,575 and this was regarded, rather smugly perhaps, as a 'most satisfactory achievement'. But in 1949 the

Business Advisory Committee was again getting very worried. Profit amounted to only £200. They thought it ought to be more like £2,000 and made some suggestion designed to achieve that end. 1951 saw a 'record total' for sales of just under £14,000 which was increased by a further £1,000 in 1952. But the BAC was still very concerned at the amount of capital employed and demanded that stock should be reduced and limited the amount of spending on new work to £500 a month. If there was to be any further expansion, then it must be paid for out of profits.

1953 saw the publication of the *New Bible Commentary*,[1] the IVF's first major work. It was financed largely by advance payments from the American publishers and the IVF movements in Australia and New Zealand who were acting as distributors for it in those countries. Turnover for the year shot up to a little less than £32,000 with what was then a staggering profit of £11,000. As the book caught on it carried other IVP titles with it. By September 1955 the BAC was reporting to the Literature Committee that 'capital was available for all work in hand and the sooner new books are produced the better'!

This happy state of affairs continued through the 1960s with steadily increasing turnover as the list was enlarged. It was only when the severe inflation of the 1970s hit publishers in common with all other manufacturers that drastic steps had to taken once again to conserve capital and to limit the amount of new work undertaken. Fortunately, although the medicine prescribed was at times hard to take, it had the desired effect, and the Press can be very thankful to its financial advisers who diagnosed so accurately what was wrong and knew what the remedy had to be.

Policy-making and the search for authors

In the early days of the IVF, as we have seen, personal and group Bible study were important features of the work of the Christian Unions. It was natural, therefore, that the chief emphasis should be on the provision of various kinds of Bible study aid. But the list of titles published before the war shows that steps were also being taken to help those facing the call to missionary service overseas, and there was further an attempt to help students with their evangelistic outreach. At first this took the form of a series of small booklets which began in 1936 with Howard Guinness's *Modern Problems* and included eventually such very popular titles as John Stott's *Becoming a Christian,* of which over a million copies have been sold. The first evangelistic *book* was Professor Rendle Short's *Why Believe?* which appeared in 1938.

From the outset the aim was to publish what the student committees felt they needed, not necessarily what would produce the greatest profit. Very early on it was pointed out by the Literature Committee that small booklets were a financial liability; but they were still produced and at certain times were deliberately subsidized out of the small profits on the larger works. The one recurring problem was the shortage of qualified authors able to speak with authority to the student world and in language which it recognized as its own. In the spring of 1939 the Student Executive Committee recorded in a minute that not only was shortage of finance making expansion difficult, but they queried 'whether there were sufficient new authors of standing and sharing the IVF viewpoint to supply material'.

That, of course, is in total contrast to the position today, a change for which the Tyndale Fellowship for Biblical Research has been in no small way responsible. In the later 1940s, when Professor Francis Davidson and the Rev. H. W. Oldham (later assisted by the Rev. E. F. Kevan and the Rev. A. M. Stibbs) were editing the *New Bible Commentary*, they had the greatest difficulty in getting together a team of the quality and experience that was wanted. Only five out of forty-three British contributors held university appointments and of those two had retired! Nine years later, when the *New Bible Dictionary* was being put together, the situation was very different although, even then, some were still pessimistic about the ability of the Tyndale Fellowship to find sufficient scholars to write a completely new work. Nearly 140 contributors were required, all of whom were to be in complete sympathy with the IVF's known biblical position. In the majority of cases highly specialized academic knowledge was also required. But a first class team was recruited and this time over fifty of the contributors held teaching posts in universities or equivalent institutions. But increased skill

320

in communicating has not always been so marked. One of today's major concerns for IVP, therefore, is the need to discover qualified men and women who not only have something worthwhile to say, but can write in a language and style which will grip and hold the attention and respect of the modern student.

As the work expanded after the war there was always the temptation to move across into more general Christian publishing. Authors for such books would not be so difficult to find, and, with a wider market for the books, the financial return would be quicker and greater. But these temptations were resisted. In 1946 we find the Literature Committee re-stating that 'the distinctive policy of IVF publishing should be to produce books concerned primarily with what the Bible teaches on the great major doctrines of the faith'. Two years later we find a special minute recorded, 'It was agreed that the Literature Committee should make it an overriding rule never to be committed to the publication of a book which does not satisfy the main requirements of our market, viz, fidelity to the Scriptures, scholarly accuracy, good English style, and strict relevance to the constituency which we serve, it being understood that it is better both for our imprint and for our constituency not to issue a book on any given subject unless it is plainly up to the required standard.' That year, to make certain, no doubt, that these ideals were attained, the staff was doubled by the appointment of the first editorial assistant, Ruth Bolton, later followed by Mary Gladstone.

From time to time attempts were made to overcome the shortage of authors by importing suitable books from the USA, by translation, and by re-issuing older classics. In 1946 arrangements were made to import small editions of *The Infallible Word* by N. B. Stonehouse and *Christianity Rightly So-Called* by S. C. Craig. Negotiations were also begun for the purchase of the copyright in James Denney's *The Death of Christ* (later bought outright for £50), and for the right to publish British editions of a series of books by the well-known Norwegian Christian leader, Professor Ole Hallesby. Among these his book on *Prayer* was outstanding, and is still selling in considerable quantities.

It was a policy discussion on whether or not IVF should tackle

321

subjects on which Evangelicals were themselves divided which led to the suggestion during the war that an alternative neutral imprint might be adopted. A book on sex was being considered at the time and obviously some thought that a work on such a subject could easily prejudice support for IVF! In discussion it was pointed out that such an imprint would be useful for any books for older teenagers which the Youth Organisations' joint literature committee was sponsoring.[2] Many headmasters and headmistresses at that time were strongly pro-SCM and would have reacted strongly against anything bearing the name IVF. The idea received a general welcome and the name Tyndale Press was eventually chosen. The first titles to be published bearing this imprint were the inaugural Tyndale Lectures. The first major British work was Professor Bruce's *Commentary on the Greek Text of Acts* published in 1951. So concerned was the Press at the time about the prejudice shown by some college principals, and also many bookshops, towards the IVF, that for some years separate IVF and Tyndale Press letter headings and invoices were used. But that has all changed. Evangelical scholarship is now respectable! The neutral imprint has been dropped in order to simplify marketing and warehousing procedures. The name lives on only in such series as the Tyndale Commentaries.

Key books

Every publishing house looks back to certain key books as highlighting its history. IVP is no exception. Reference has already been made to several of the early publications, both casebound books and pamphlets, which were so much on target – as far as students and graduates were concerned – that they have gone on selling through reprint after reprint and revision after revision for thirty or forty years.

Post-war the book which did more than anything else to help IVF publishing come of age was *The New Bible Commentary*. The idea of such a work had been around for some time. The earliest reference is found ten years earlier in a minute dated January 1943 when the Secretary reported 'that there appeared to be an urgent need for a one volume commentary'. It was agreed to urge the recently constituted Biblical Research Committee to undertake this on the understanding that it would sell for not more than one guinea when it was produced. Over the next two years discussions seem to have proceeded at a gentle pace with the BRC suggesting that a two-volume work would be better and the Literature Committee sticking firmly to its original proposal. In September 1944 we find that Professor Francis Davidson of Glasgow was considering an invitation to plan and edit such a volume and Mr. H. W. Oldham, a retired Church of Scotland minister living in London who had recently joined the Literature Committee, had agreed to collaborate with him. It is sad that neither lived to see the finished work published.

The first printing was 30,000 copies, an unbelievably large quantity for the Press in those days. Of these, 22,000 had been ordered and partly paid for in advance by Eerdmans and the IVCF in the USA. Printing and paper bills amounted to a little over £11,000, an enormous sum when it is realized that the total IVF expenditure on these items for the whole of the previous year had been approximately half that. An order for a reprint had to be placed immediately. An American book-club edition of 5,000 copies was authorized. The book was undoubtedly a great success. Between 1953 and 1970 when a complete revision and re-setting was carried out, nearly 87,000 copies were sold, and sales of that revised edition are already matching these figures in almost half the time.

Three years after the launching of the NBC came the publication of the first two *Tyndale New Testament Commentaries* under the editorship of Professor R. V. G. Tasker. The suggestion for a series of exegetical commentaries appears first in the Literature Committee minutes of 27 January 1938 where the proposal was discussed that IVF should sponsor the production of a set of 'scholarly commentaries half-way between a highly technical and a purely devotional approach. But the only action taken then was to refer the matter to yet another committee! The idea appears next in the minutes of 26 September 1945 when Mr. Oldham reported strongly in favour of producing commentaries on various New Testament books, but spoke against what had apparently been an earlier suggestion that IVF should consider negotiating for permission to reprint H. C. G. Moule's commentaries in the 'Cambridge Bible' series. He felt strongly that something much more modern was required for the current student constituency. The matter was not taken up again, apparently, until after the NBC had appeared, possibly because, until then, the chronic shortage of capital prohibited any ambitious plans of this kind. In September 1954 the Publications Secretary was able to report that, following a thorough discussion with Professor Tasker, the Committee's first choice as editor, the latter had agreed to undertake the work. It was to be eighteen years before the final volume, that on Luke, appeared. Maybe, if the editor had realized that, he would have been more reluctant to take on the job! The series was based in the first place on the Authorized Version because at that time it was the most commonly used study Bible. As the years went on, pressure built up to switch over to the RSV and this was eventually done with the very last title to appear.

The Old Testament series was even more difficult to get launched. In the immediate post-war years Evangelical Old Testament scholars were still few and far between. Discussions took place with several leading American scholars in the late 1950s, but nothing came of them. Then Professor D. J. Wiseman, who in October 1961 had taken over as Chairman of the Literature Committee following the death of the Rev. G. T. Manley earlier that year, agreed to act as general editor. The first volume to appear was Derek Kidner's commentary on *Proverbs* which was published in 1964 followed three years later by the same author's *Genesis*. Since then ten other volumes have been published, and authors for all the books in the series have been commissioned so that completion is, at the time of writing, in sight.

The first reference to the production of a Bible Dictionary appears during the war years in the minutes of the Biblical Research Committee. Nothing came of it, however, the reason no doubt being the shortage of well-qualified Evangelical writers at the time. What eventually appeared was the *New Bible Handbook* (1947) based on ideas put forward by the Rev. Godfrey Robinson and edited by the Rev. G. T. Manley. Twenty-six contributors were brought together for the task and the book was a great success.

Nothing more is heard of the idea of a Bible Dictionary until 1953 when the Publications Secretary reported that Eerdmans, the American publishers of the NBC, had suggested the production of a 'New Bible Dictionary and/or Encyclopaedia as a joint British–USA venture using material already available in the International Standard Bible Encyclopaedia'. Eerdmans were the publishers of this latter work and were anxious to revise it. For some months various proposals were tossed backwards and forwards. The Biblical Research Committee, conscious still of the shortage of man-power, was not too anxious to get involved in a major revision of the very large American work and recommended, after some hesitation, that members of the Tyndale Fellowship should be invited to co-operate in producing a smaller dictionary which would be an entirely new work. Eerdmans approved of this proposal and also agreed to contribute financially to the cost of employing a full-time organizing editor for a period of three years or more. After some delay the Rev. Dr. J. D. Douglas was invited to take on this major task with Professor F. F. Bruce, Dr. J. I. Packer, Professor R. V. G. Tasker and Professor D. J. Wiseman acting as consulting editors. The result published in 1962 was again an outstanding success in both the British and the American markets. Over 130,000 copies of the British edition have been sold.

Paperback editions

One of the main differences between Christian publishing in the 1970s and forty years earlier is the use of the pocket book format in paper covers for original publications. At first many publishers resisted the change. They felt that a book was not really a book unless it had a hard cover on it. Editions in paper bindings were acceptable only as a kind of 'catch-crop' after the reward of the proper hard cover edition had been appropriately harvested. IVF had its pamphlets and small evangelistic booklets, but there was no thought, at first, of trying to compete with the mass market appeal of the Penguins and Pans, the pioneers in this field. Then one day in 1957 the Publications Secretary found himself looking at six titles, four of them new works with a varied but popular appeal and still only in MS form, two of them books which had already proved their worth and needed to be reprinted. Suddenly he realized that, if IVF was to enter the pocket book market, this was the chance to do so, since six titles making their appearance all at once would make a much bigger impact than one. So in March 1958 the IVP series of pocket books was launched with *Authority* (D. M. Lloyd-Jones), *Basic Christianity* (J. R. W. Stott), *'Fundamentalism' and the Word of God* (J. I. Packer), *The Story of the Church* (A. M. Renwick), *Towards Christian Marriage* (W. M. Capper and H. Williams) and, a little later, *Why Believe?* (A. Rendle Short). Since then many outstanding books have appeared in this format under the IVP imprint. Notable among them have been the evangelistic titles by Michael Green, books on the practical outworking of the Christian faith by Michael Griffiths, Walter Trobisch's *I Married You*, Francis Schaeffer's *Escape from Reason* and many others.

Helping the missionary cause

The IVF/UCCF has always had a strong interest in overseas missions. Some of the earliest books published were designed to challenge students to consider Christian service overseas and to help those who were already planning to embark on missionary training. It was natural, therefore, that ways and means should be sought of helping the spread of Christian literature in Third World countries. From the start, with our authors' whole-hearted co-operation, a very generous policy was adopted towards overseas publishers who wished to translate IVF books for use in the countries where they were operating. Often the rights were conveyed free of all charge or in return for a very small fee.

There are, as well, many developing countries where English is the language used in all higher education and where the only thing preventing Christian students from making greater use of the books published by the IVF, particularly the more expensive reference works, is their inability to afford them. This was the background to the introduction in January 1960 of cheap editions of several of the larger books and a considerable number of paper backs in what was known as the 'International Christian Handbook Series', marketing of which was limited to the Third World. It included specially produced paper bound editions of the Tyndale commentaries which were available only in hard covers elsewhere. The IVF agreed to forego all profit, authors generously accepted a smaller royalty and discounts to book-sellers were slightly reduced. In this way the selling price could be cut by as much as half. A modified version of this scheme is still in operation as far as the *New Bible Commentary* and the *New Bible Dictionary* are concerned; but the cheap paper-back editions of the commentaries and other titles eventually had to be with-drawn. This was because small print runs (in contrast with the more sophisticated methods adopted for the printing and binding of the standard editions) meant that what were supposed to be more cheaply produced books began to cost more than the copies produced for sale in Britain!

Another example of this overseas interest was the initiative taken in helping to set up the Africa Christian Press as an independent publishing house producing books specially written for English-speaking Africa. In the early days of this Press IVF handled all production, warehousing and marketing in return for a nominal charge and put up all the capital required in the first four years. At the end of that period ACP was able to repay the money invested and a little later was able to become completely independent of IVP help.

Selling and marketing

Between 1945 and the present day, the turnover of IVP has increased a hundredfold. Marketing has always been important, but the kind of distribution world-wide which is now being achieved demands professional expertise. One result is that the Press has had to become much more sophisticated in its warehousing and despatch techniques. During the war, as we have noted, warehousing of the small stock and the handling of orders was helpfully looked after by the CSSM Bookroom. After the war the IVF took back these responsibilities, using first of all a small

327

wine cellar in the basement of the 39 Bedford Square building as its 'warehouse'. As the work developed and more office and storage space became essential, two small temporary buildings were erected within the walls of an empty static emergency water supply tank which had been built on a bombed site at the back of the Bedford Square building. In the early 1960s, these were pulled down, a long lease on the site obtained, and a four-storey office block with a basement warehouse built in their place. Later still, when stocks outgrew this warehouse, under a co-operative warehousing and marketing arrangement with Scripture Union, Falcon Press and OMF, all IVF stock and despatching was handled by Scripture Union, first from London and then from their new warehouse at Bristol. This arrangement lasted until 1974 when IVP opened its own warehouse and Book Centre at Nottingham and at the same time installed its own small computer to handle invoicing and records.

This steady growth was also evident on the selling side. In the early 1950s a sales manager was appointed, but at first he had not much more than himself to manage! From time to time agreements were entered into with other publishers for their traveller (or travellers) to represent IVF books to the trade. Eventually in 1965 IVF took responsibility for setting up a joint selling organization in which Falcon Press, OMF and, for a time Scripture Union and Lion Publishing co-operated, and this has continued as the basic pattern up to the present. The big problem facing any sales manager is that the majority of Christian bookshops in the United Kingdom are really quite small and the size of the orders they are able to place rarely justifies the expense of a visit by a sales representative. Yet their buyers need to be kept in close touch, not only with the new books as they come out, but with the back-list as well.

Traditionally IVF has always encouraged every Christian Union to have its own bookstall and the press had relied heavily on the enthusiasm of the student literature secretaries in getting its publications known and bought by the students for whom they are primarily intended. In 1972 a Bookstall Service was established at Nottingham, and a literature travelling secretary was appointed to establish a close liaison with the CU bookstalls.

328

He did this by visiting the colleges to advise generally on literature promotion and by organizing well-run bookstalls at all conferences and other joint student activities. This service seems to have been much appreciated and the amount of literature distributed directly through the Christian Unions has considerably increased.

The post-war years have also seen an enormous growth in the number of church bookstalls which operate as officially recognized agents of supplying booksellers. IVF has done all it can to encourage this development. It realizes that many church members rarely, if ever, visit a Christian bookshop and the only answer to that is to bring the literature to them.

Overseas the decision was taken early on to work wherever possible through the student groups linked together in the International Fellowship of Evangelical Students. By agreement they have in most countries a prior claim on translation rights. They are also welcomed as partners in any local distribution scheme. In the USA the American Inter-Varsity Press is now very active and a two-way traffic of books across the Atlantic helps to strengthen their list and ours. In Australia, Canada, New Zealand and South Africa agency arrangements have been established, sometimes in close association with the students work. These overseas markets have been, and still are, very important to the British publisher.

Committee structure

No history of IVF publishing would be complete without a special reference to the Rev. G. T. Manley who chaired the Literature Committee from its earliest pre-war days until about a year before his death in 1961. Committees always seem to proliferate very easily within the IVF and the Publishing Department was certainly not without its full quota of them. They could have stifled initiative and hindered, rather than aided, progress. But G. T. Manley set an example of informed and energetic leadership, combined with a very clear vision, which later years never dimmed, of what IVF literature could contribute to a revival of evangelical scholarship and the strengthening of the church at home and overseas.

As the work developed, however, and staff became more 'professional', there was a danger that contact with student leadership and thinking might be lost. To prevent this, in 1964 a Student Literature Committee was set up to sound out student opinion and to examine and sift suggestions for new books received from the student executive committees before forwarding them to the Literature Committee for action. This student committee also did much through the organization of literature workshops to encourage students to think about writing, about magazine and broadsheet production for student use, and the setting up of evangelistic book weeks which were introduced first in the colleges of education and were taken up with enthusiasm in many universities. At the same time a graduate Literature Advisory Committee was also brought into being as a kind of 'think tank' in support of the main committee's work. This system worked well for ten or twelve years until the move away from London to Leicester and the changing publishing situation meant that the committee structure had to be thoroughly reviewed.

All the committees we have mentioned so far have been concerned with the editorial side of the work, not with its success as a business undertaking. Literature finance was originally the direct concern of the IVF Business Advisory Committee. But in 1950, as the work developed and economic problems increased, a special Literature Finance Committee was set up under the chairmanship of the IVF Treasurer, Mr. Brian Harris, as a sub-committee of the BAC, and given the job of 'considering all financial and economic matters governing the production and sale of IVF publications with a view to preparing recommendations to place before the Business Advisory Committee and advising the Literature Committee and the Publications Secretary.' After two meetings there was a gap of over a year. The committee was then recalled under the chairmanship of Mr. W. G. Norris and supervised the difficult years of expansion leading up to and following on the production of the New Bible Commentary. In recent years its work has once again been under the chairmanship of Brian Harris whose business experience and financial expertise had guided the Press in its later years of expansion and development, and helped to bring it safely through the stresses and strains of the inflation of the 1970s. Any surplus, after the capital needs of the growing work have been met, is transferred annually into the funds of the Fellowship.

During the past year these two sides of the work, business and editorial, have come together in the setting up of an IVP Board made up of outside advisers and senior staff, and responsible to the UCCF Council for all aspects of the Press. The overall planning and direction of the editorial side continues to be in the hands of the Publications Committee. Editors now attend the relevant discussions of the student executive committees, ensuring that the Publications Committee gives priority to the literature needs of the student work.

Looking forward

It is certainly good again to look back and to remind ourselves of how much we have to thank God for. But we have in IVP a publishing operation which is forward looking, and which is adapting continually to meet changing situations in the student world made up these days of men and women drawn from every kind of home background. Then in recent years Evangelicals have become much more aware of the world in which they live, the culture which influences their thinking, and the social implic-ations of decisions which they are continually having to make. Important books dealing with the debates going on in these areas have already been published and others are in preparation. They range from pocket books such as *Whose World, Unafraid to Be* and *Taking Sides*, to larger works such as *The Christian in Industrial Society, Modern Art and the Death of a Culture, The Dust of Death* and *Morality, Law and Grace*, to mention only a few.

For theological students, facing the challenge in their studies of a still vigorous and sometimes sceptical liberalism, a new series edited by Dr. Howard Marshall on 'Issues in Contemporary Theology' is being prepared, the first title being a book on *The Origins of New Testament Christology*. Then an important new set of expositions is being published under the general title of 'The Bible Speaks Today' edited by Alec Motyer and John Stott. Here the emphasis is on the practical application of biblical teaching to our 20th century situation.

NOTES

1 See pp. 211, 322.
2 See pp. 291, 292.

Chapter 19

New environments
(1970–78)

By 1970 the Fellowship found itself in a world very different from that of 1928. Throughout the country generally there were major changes in politics, economic outlook, social stability and international affairs. There could no longer be easy assumptions about indefinite industrial expansion or unlimited achievements in higher education. Inflation had already begun to put a brake on optimistic planning, new building schemes and generous staffing in the academic world. Whilst the universities and colleges were full to overflowing, it was already clear that some of the earlier hopes of expansion were due for disappointment. Then in the early 70s came one of those indefinable changes in the mood of the nation, which mark a change in moral and spiritual direction. The country was entering on a new phase of history. As usual, the student world proved the barometer recording the changes in climate amongst the youth in general.

The changing background

A new restlessness came over the student world, there was a new impatience with discipline of every kind. Whatever those responsible for academic progress wanted to encourage became an object of doubt and suspicion. Those 'in statu pupillari' no longer wanted instruction, but virtually to educate themselves by

333

trial and error, or assertion and counter-assertion. There was almost what one might call a 'student counter-culture'. In parts this was often good and amounted to learning by participation, which indeed is necessary in some subjects. But in its extreme forms it could result in rejection of authority in all its shapes, academic, moral and religious, and a determination 'to do one's own thing'. Amongst the authorities rejected were, of course, all forms of religion and 'authoritarian' morals.

But the changes which affected the Christian Unions most were those bearing upon the degree of knowledge and experience with which the leaders and members began in Christian matters as was described in chapter 14. It meant that it was harder to make up the committees and the leaders were often out of their depth. It was harder for them to know how to gain and hold the interest of the increasingly 'mixed multitude' around them. These difficulties were often greatly accentuated after a successful open meeting or mission. For a number might have become Christians but were starting in their new Christian life further back and needing more aid than was often true in earlier times. Sometimes the greater part of one of the smaller CUs would be composed of all very 'young' Christians.

A further difficulty was that the 'normal' outlook of the older church members, coming from conservative communities maintaining ethical standards which would have been all-pervasive in earlier times, was now quite foreign to the newcomers. For example, the older-style views on sexual morality seemed to these new Christians merely antiquated rules bequeathed by Victorian middle-class great-grandparents. The present moral freedom of association of the sexes in the academic communities was to them the 'normal'. A number of what were seen as 'middle-class fashions' had also lapsed. For truth, honesty and respect for other people's property were certainly not as universal as they once were. It seemed that many, even of the stricter Christians themselves, had not realized that these middle-class fashions were mostly the products of distinctively Christian ethics and were the remains of an earlier stronger and purer Christianity.

The Christian response

There will be no need to elaborate further on this theme as the accompanying factors are currently working themselves out in our society. But for the Christian Unions there were two main results.

First, the committees had to find the most knowledgeable and strongest Christians amongst the freshers and to bring them into an appreciation of what would shortly be required of them if the Unions were to go on. It meant that risks had to be taken and efforts made to step up the equipment of the younger leaders somewhat earlier than had been the usual practice. But, second, it meant that something like a 'crash course' in Christian doctrine, Christian ethics and Christian action had to be given to these in their first academic year, that is, almost before they had acclimatized to their university or college. In the nature of the case, a lot depended upon the quality of their leaders, the travelling secretaries and graduate supporters.

In so far as there has been time to assess the results, the picture on the whole is encouraging. It is in keeping with the traditional principle of the movement that, under the guidance of the Holy Spirit and promptings from those who have already been through the same experiences, the Christian students can and should, work out their faith and witness in the new spheres into which God has brought them.

One general feature in the situation greatly helped. Throughout this period of changing moods in the academic world, as a general rule, there was still a friendly and tolerant attitude towards those who were 'religious'. There was still a willingness to hear, if what was being offered was clearly relevant to the student situation.

Training programmes

The situation called for some hard thinking and planning from the central committees which came to the conclusion that the emphasis should be put on basic training to enable the local leaders to cope better with the situation. Since pre-war days there had been a leaders' conference, bringing together the committee members for mutual exchanges of information and stimulus. Something more concentrated and direct was needed in the form of a training course designed for a much more elementary type of 'starter'. In the outcome a series of training programmes was brought into being, specially directed to the needs of the first and second year committee members. Additional committee 'reserves' were also invited. There have also been trends away from the large annual conferences and greater emphasis upon a series of smaller conferences and houseparties. For one reason a much larger total number of local student memberships can be drawn into them than would be represented by the quotas which would travel far to an annual conference.

Another advantage of these measures has been that the more informal, discussion type of programme, on the lines of a seminar, fits in better with the prevailing methods of teaching in the universities and colleges and with the contemporary student outlook. This method has also called for an additional literature. Several paper-backs and booklets were written in pursuit of what might be called 'basic Bible study' or 'Bible seminars'. Great care needs to be taken with the degree to which the message of each section of the Bible is construed in keeping with the context and original purpose. Ultimate success depends on how far the Bible is allowed to speak for itself and on its own terms, rather than having imaginative 'improvements' foisted upon it as can so often happen today.

There is, however, an obverse side to the increase of the smaller conferences and the smaller training programmes. The two larger annual conferences at Swanwick and in Scotland used vividly to bring home to those who made the journeys that they were part of a much larger whole. The strength and role of the IVF/UCCF nationally and internationally were demonstrated to the successive leaders of the local Unions. In to-day's circumstances many will probably only be at one of the smaller conferences. They easily overlook the wider fellowship, the value and constant service of the Executive Committee and the supporting secretaries, and this is to their loss. Again and again letters in the earlier years telling of the inspiration that Swanwick or the Scottish Conference had been to them would come from students.

They would write saying 'Until I went to the Conference I often felt that I was almost alone, struggling with a feeble few to carry the banner of Christ in our place. When, on the first night in the crowded Conference Hall at Swanwick, the hymn was given out and everyone burst into song (as if to lift the roof) I almost cried for joy! I was no longer alone, for here were people from every place, filled with enthusiasm for the Lord.' Let us hope that this form of inspiration can be kept alive in the UCCF until all can join, as in St. John's vision in the book of the Revelation, in the Song with 'a multitude which no man can number of all nations, kindreds, people and tongues before the throne of the Lamb of God'.

The increased field

The size and scope of the mission field of the Fellowship were now formidable. It was stated in the early seventies that approaching 26% of all young people in the 18-year-old age group were engaged in some form of higher education. The number of universities had continued to rise in the 60s, especially as more colleges of advanced technology became universities. The majority of all academic institutions were stretched to capacity by the courses offered and all their residential accommodation was overflowing. The effect on the central team of the Fellowship was to exceed their capacity to maintain regular visits at the optimum times, especially as a number of the colleges were situated in places where transport was difficult.

To take the number of new universities alone, there had been twenty-one added to the list during the 1960s. These were: Sussex (Brighton, 1961), Keele (1962), East Anglia (1963), York (1963), Lancaster (1964), Essex (1964), Warwick (Coventry, 1965), Kent (Canterbury, 1965), Loughborough University of Technology (1965), Aston (Birmingham, 1966), City University (London, 1966), Brunel (Uxbridge, 1966), Bath (1966), Bradford (1966), Surrey (Guildford, 1966), and Salford (1967). In Scotland the following received university status: Strathclyde (Glasgow, 1964), Heriot-Watt (Edinburgh, 1966), Dundee (1967) and Stirling (1967). Also in Ireland came the New University of Ulster

337

Contending for the faith

(Coleraine, 1965).

The size of the challenge to the central committees of the Fellowship in their planning for more adequate services to their total outlying constituencies can best be put by a few figures.

The most useful way in which such growth can be shown is to give the totals in the year of the founding of the Fellowship (1928) and the comparable position at each tenth year subsequently.

	Full-time Students	University CUs	College CUs	Travelling Secs	Supporting Office Secs
1928	50,000	14	0	½	0
1938	65,000	27	10	3	1
1948	140,000	32	50	6	3
1958	215,000	40	150	10	4
1968	460,000	52	300	22	5
1978	665,000	54	500	41	6

(The figures for the office do not include literature staff and clerical secretaries, but only those directly serving the student fields).

Integration and name changes

The dictates of administrative economy had more and more forced the Government to increase measures for the co-ordination and unification of the whole area of tertiary education. Similar considerations, especially reducing the overlap in the geographical areas served by what were virtually three sets of travelling secretaries (that is one each for the universities, colleges of education and technical colleges respectively), began to impress those concerned with the best use of the Fellowship's resources. As described in chapter 14 the college's work was unified under the title 'The Inter-College Christian Fellowship' in 1970.

For some years there had also been questions concerning the continued suitability of the overall name of Inter-Varsity Fellowship. First, the use of the contraction 'inter-varsity' had gone out of fashion in the student world. Apart from the annual inter-varsity rugby football match in early December (which may have helped in the choice of the name of the first Inter-Varsity conference in December, in 1919) it has later had few other usages and for example, a Glasgow student no longer talks of going up

338

on to the hill 'to the varsity'. Second, there were by 1970 very many affiliated Christian Unions in the colleges which could not suitably use this overall name. Again, after much deliberation in 1975 the overall name was changed to the 'Universities and Colleges Christian Fellowship' functioning in two main parts, the universities section and the colleges section. In view of the large number of books carrying its imprint and its worldwide trade connections, it was unanimously agreed that the publications department should continue as 'The Inter-Varsity Press' (IVP).

Change of address

The 1932 one-roomed office at 43 Russell Square had soon had to give way to the larger accommodation at 39 Bedford Square, which also needed to be enlarged. In the late 60s, as the dates for renewal of the lease in Bedford Square began to approach, it became apparent to the business advisers that the cost of leases, rentals and rising rates in central London, as well as the increasing cost for staff who travelled in to the office made it wise to look elsewhere for an office in a cheaper area and smaller city.

After considerable search, it was decided to move to Leicester, leaving only the Overseas Students department in London. The move was accomplished in 1976.

This latest in the series of the Fellowship's growing pains was on a greater scale than it had hitherto known. It was with considerable relief to those responsible on the respective central committees that the move was carried through with so little dislocation of the main activities. There have since been a number of confirmatory indications of the wisdom of the steps taken.

Relations with the churches

Growth in some cases tempted student leaders, especially those who had become Christians after arriving at university or college, to overlook and underestimate church membership. From the earliest days of the Fellowship, again and again, the wisest speakers and ministers with the greatest pastoral gifts had

339

emphasized the importance of church membership and its privileges and duties. In most periods and most cases the leaders have fully understood that their Unions were only temporary associations of like-minded Christians for the limited purposes of encouraging one another in the Christian faith and witnessing to the new communities in which, for a time, they would be resident. Whenever travelling secretaries, graduate ex-members or others qualified, called attention to the fact that the limitations of a Union were being exceeded, there was usually prompt attention to the point made.

Two influences in the 60s and 70s made the lines of demarcation less obvious to inexperienced student leaders. First, the usually salutary and helpful parish missions have carried the Gospel and Bible study into many of the homes throughout the country. 'House-groups' have drawn in many neighbours who would not go into the church's buildings and undoubtedly led to a new influence of the Gospel message in the national community as a whole. It is a movement which is normally led by the ministry and elderships of the churches. A second informal spread of Christian interest and action has come through the Charismatic Movement. In this context arose what called themselves 'house churches', claiming the New Testament references to the early days of the church as 'models'. In some localities where there might have been no immediate 'true' Churches (that is, where 'the Word of God is preached and the sacraments are duly administered according to Christ's holy ordinance') there might have been some place for such. But the effect in some areas, especially where dominating personalities impressed their wills, was to cause unnecessary and harmful schism. Inexperienced student leaders were sometimes over-influenced in these directions and several Unions were confused.

After a particularly disappointing example, the committees of the IVF gave thought to this important matter. Eventually the Council issued a policy document entitled *Christian Students and the Churches*. The object was to set out the teaching of the New Testament concerning the importance of the church and the limitations within which students, temporarily away from their home churches, can stimulate each other as fellow-Christians and witness to their student communities.

Looking at the main Christian denominations in the contemporary context it is now possible to see some of the fruits of the work of the Christian Unions. There have not only been many examples of former members of the Christian Unions who have occupied some of the most important pulpits and held some of the highest offices in their churches, but many examples of loyal and industrious service on the part of churchwardens, elders and deacons who learnt to begin to take spiritual responsibility on their student committees. In fact, much the same could be said of some of the other walks of life. A surprising number amongst those who have been prominent in public life and in their varied professions began to wrestle with the problems of government, morals and social cohesion as former presidents and secretaries in their student Christian communities. Some have been so sure of it that they have publicly acknowledged the fact.

Adapting the publications

One of the more practical of the challenges arising from such backgrounds was that which prompted the IVF leaders to reconsider the relevance of its publication list. As soon as they did so, it became apparent that though some of the best sellers, with adaptations, might continue their run, many of the older books were couched in the vocabulary and thought modes of a past era in the university world. The students of the contemporary generation, with regrettably little biblical or theological knowledge, were thinking and speaking in quite other terms. It was not simply a superficial change of terminology or colloquial phrase, but a cultural change based on different foundations, or lack of them.

The Publications Committee set to work and within a comparatively short time, with the ready co-operation of many members of university and colleges staff and evangelical leaders, produced what was a new literature. A series of paperbacks on almost every worthwhile and important topic relevant to the contemporary Christian student made their appearance.

Strangely enough, however, in a university and college setting,

341

one of the chief difficulties to be overcome is the modern student's resistance to 'intellectualism'. Anything produced must not be too 'cerebral'. How any subject can be truly studied without due attention to its history or background, or proper attention to principle and theoretical accuracy, before passing on to practical applications will remain a mystery to those trained in earlier times. But those responsible for the literature of the Inter-Varsity Press continue to endeavour to meet the needs of the students in their own idiom. In the process they might claim to have produced a new school of younger Evangelical writers, who will help to meet the challenges to come in the rest of the twentieth century.

The new Liberalism

In the light of its past history, and in the experience of Christians everywhere, the biggest single danger to the Evangelical Movement at each stage comes not from its declared opponents, but from some of those who claim to be its friends. Many of those who have been nurtured and developed in evangelicalism would seem frequently unaware that they have ceased to act in its best interests when they relax their vigilance and maybe from good motives begin to advocate dangerous departures from the beaten pathway. The misleading suggestions are mostly made in the name of progress or the needs of the movement's 'camp followers' or the multitudes which might otherwise be reached, if only the platform of the movement were not quite so strict and there could now be concessions to human nature at certain points. In particular, the stricter applications of what the Bible actually says concerning some of the cardinal doctrines of the faith, it is said, need not be quite so definite. For some small compromises would attract many more of the hundreds of seekers who might otherwise not be reached.

It all sounds so very plausible, charitable and promising, that an inexperienced student leader, himself of not many months' age in faith, can be forgiven if he fails to spot the fallacy. Whole churches and Christian colleges have started on the wrong path at this point and to-day are standing warnings to their false steps as

342

seen demonstrated in the fully developed results! The point of departure from the true course, which the Divine Guide has plotted for him, comes for the hesitating disciple at the moment that Holy Scripture ceases to be for him the completely reliable record of the Divine Revelation. It is at this point that Liberal Evangelicalism is to an inexperienced leader a bigger menace than outright Modernism. For with the latter he knows where he is. But the Liberal Evangelical appears in general to retain much that is good, including most of the gospel. It is not easy to notice that fatal step from the firm ground of objective truth, once given by God, on to the quicksands of tentative hypothesis and subjective reconstruction from documents compiled by religious genius. After that step, it is only a matter of the degree and how far one plunges on into the quicksands.

From the very beginning it has been his art in seduction at this point which has brought the church's enemy his richest rewards. Once injected, a little of the virus goes a long way. The process in all ages is essentially the same. To Eve in the garden it was simply, 'Yes! But did God really say that?' and then, 'No! It is not certain that you will die'. (Gen. 3 : 1–4.) It makes all the difference to the nerve of obedience whether an order just received is valid and precise or whether it is doubtful and obscure. As the classical proverb says, 'Speculation on the justification of things evades the obligation'. After receiving the Law on Sinai it made a great deal of difference to a devout Israelite whether 'God spoke these things, and said . . .', or whether He didn't, and whether they were really only compiled by Moses.

Such matters cannot here be discussed at length. But from the historical point of view it is a fact that, at the end of the last century when the SCM moved from its original Evangelical position and began its progress to a developed modernist position, it was not the influence of the Modernists which first caused the deviation. It was a number of Liberal Evangelicals (as it was also in the case of one of the great Evangelical missionary societies) who made the first move and for apparently good plausible reasons. It is, as it were, the Archimedean point at which truth comes to a focus, with widely different results on each side of the choice.

343

In a recent book, *The Battle for the Bible,* (Zondervan, 1977), Harold Lindsell, editor of *Christianity Today,* has traced the history of a number of the Evangelical churches, theological colleges and other institutions of the United States. In a comparatively few years some have moved from a most orthodox Evangelical foundation to a widely different outlook, sometimes almost to the negation of their original principles. He would seem to have proved beyond doubt that the point of departure in every case has been where staff members have been appointed (or charitably overlooked) who have been unsure of the authority and reliability of Holy Scripture as guide. Lindsell goes on to show that, in a very short time, it is no longer a matter of defining the true place of Holy Scripture, but a question of holding some of the cardinal doctrines of the Christian faith. For it is only on the basis of the divine revelation, accurately recorded, that we can assert with confidence that Jesus was (and is) the Son of God, that he was born of a Virgin, that He made a full offering and atonement for sin, that He rose again from the dead and now sits at God's right hand and will come again. Quite apart from this, the Bible's own assertion is that the Lord and His apostles expected the Scriptures to be accepted by His disciples as 'inviolable' (our Lord's word), 'infallible' (St. Luke's word) and 'certain' (St. Peter's word).

This, however, does not please the present Professor of the Interpretation of Holy Scripture at Oxford. For in his book of 350 pages, *Fundamentalism* (SCM Press, 1977), James Barr sets out to undermine any such claim. The book is aimed primarily at the IVF. It is, however, disappointingly written and reads like a hurried compilation from a vast amount of material sent in by collaborators, some of them possibly students. The result is something of a 'rag-bag' into which the author puts everything which seems to suit his purpose. Making little allowance for errors during the transmission of the Sacred Text he seeks to list everything which can undermine any continuing concept of the inerrancy of the Bible. Perhaps the best comment on the result was by a medical student, 'Well! If they can't do better than that, then it looks as if the Bible has a considerable future!'

But this book was Professor Barr's negative approach to the

subject. Earlier he had sketched his positive approach in *The Bible in the Modern World* (SCM Press, 1973). This illustrates very well the developed intellectual position of those who build on earlier hypotheses with their own hypotheses. Modern scholarship builds on a wide scaffolding of reconstructions which are as secure, or as unsafe as those on which the first rest. It seems to be a canon in such scholarship that practically no named ancient writer can ever be regarded as having written the document which bears his name. By the close of the book it is hard to know what the author really thinks of the Bible, and, as a consequence, what he believes about the doctrines which the church holds on the Bible's authority.

What is clear amidst the present theological confusion in the official teaching centres of the church and the *avant-garde* opinions coming from some of its official teachers, especially at Oxford and Cambridge, is that the witness of IVF/UCCF is needed as much as ever it was. If, however, it is to remain true to its heritage, if, indeed, it is to be of any use as a vehicle for God to use in the future for the spiritual good of the student world, then it must remain quite uncompromising in its adherence to the infallibility, that is complete trustworthiness, of Holy Scripture. Only so can it be certain of its sense of direction and its message. Our Lord, according to the witness of the Gospels, expects complete confidence in Him and unhesitating obedience to His commands.

Former members

Now that many former members are in places of prominence in teaching, research and administration in the universities and colleges there ought to be ensured support for the student witness of the future. History, however, tends to show that it is all too easy for those 'who did run well' spiritually to allow their pace to slacken. Some may even give up running in the Christian race. Our Lord's words, alas, are all too true, 'The worries of this life, the deceitfulness of wealth and the desires for other things come in and choke the Word making it unfruitful'. But some seniors are running more purposefully than ever and gathering speed. This appeal is to them. The present stage in the history of the Evangelical Movement is a crucial one. The whole world itself is at a cross-roads. The situation calls for the utmost loyal support in every relevant way by all those who in their student days derived benefit from an Evangelical Christian Union. Only so can the movement be helped to remain true to its calling and give a better account of its service to Christ during the *next* fifty years.

There is one place at which new crucial steps could clearly be taken in the service of the gospel and where academic prowess could become the servant of the gospel. The time seems ripe to challenge the false philosophies of evolutionary agnosticism and atheism. After one hundred years of research very few things have gone as expected in modern science. The universe is more incredibly constructed than anyone in Darwin's time could have anticipated. To deny purposive thought and planning behind the natural phenomena is in sheer defiance of the facts and the teaching being given to many young minds on these matters to-day is a travesty of the true position.

In the 1978 Rendle Short Lecture 'Medical Missions – Regaining the Initiative', Dr. Stanley G. Browne, a leading leprologist and current President of the Royal Society of Tropical Medicine and Hygiene, appealed for Christians again to help man the frontiers in the war against the killing tropical diseases. In an aside he pointed to other areas where pioneers are equally needed and where the initiative should be regained, and he commented: 'It is most unscientific to credit 'blind chance' with the unbelievably complex and omniscient intelligence which fashions the intricate biochemistry of a living cell, or the beautiful development of the fertilized ovum – and deny the possibility that the Creator could reveal Himself to men. This is not obscurantist anthropomorphism – it is a reasonable conclusion from the scientific discoveries of human intelligence. Is not the time opportune to say so, boldly and publicly? The closed system of science, self-explanatory and self-sufficient, admits no possibility of any factor that cannot lend itself to objective investigation. The closed system is thus accompanied by a closed mind, impervious and impenetrable, and (be it said) by a closed shop in some quarters when academic staff appointments are concerned.'

'Should we not now redouble our efforts to regain the initiative in this sphere of scientific medicine? Should we not boldly assert that the god of blind chance, whom many ignorantly worship and virtually invest with the attributes of supreme intelligence and intelligibility, is the God we make known to them? Rather than abandon one by one the citadels of belief, in a spirit of craven fear and resignation, should we not now take the war into the enemy's camp and offer a bold and reasoned statement of the faith we hold? Some people call it nature – others, God. Let us call this supreme intelligence God, and unashamedly confess that He has revealed Himself in His Word and, best of all, in His Son.'

Student initiative

This unashamed confession of faith in the God of the present and the future was well demonstrated in July 1978 at the Vocation Conference staged in the Yorkshire spa town of Harrogate. Entitled 'Serving Christ in Tomorrow's World', this was a new venture on an unparalleled scale and promises to be a real watershed in the unfolding history of student Christian witness in our land.

The conference was the consummation of a long-standing vision in the hearts of some UCCF students and staff workers, and the culmination of over three years' detailed planning. The aim behind this biggest gathering of Christian students in Britain was to assemble as many students and young graduates as possible and together work out the implications of our faith with regard to areas of study, job prospects, vocation, life-style, industry, mission, and church life.

The packed timetable for the week-long conference included Bible readings on the Christ Whose world this is and Whom we serve, and conference addresses by leading Evangelicals in ministry and mission, establishing principles of service and communicating the biblical imperatives in today's terms. A host of other speakers (over 50 in all), all leaders in their own field, led the 1200 students through a variety of work sessions on specific areas; science, law, management, unemployment, ecology, the arts, education, politics, and helped put all these in context by a right understanding of man, sin, work, the family, society. An exhibition of opportunities for Christian service worldwide, from graphic arts to missionary aviation, and the chance to talk to those actively engaged in these fields, completed this full-orbed picture of purposeful Christian living in the future.

A serious, business-like determination permeated the sessions; an unwillingness to settle for anything less than the full implications of the Christian faith. Easy answers would not do. And if the students were eager and expectant, the speakers and representatives from so many Christian organizations were thrilled by what they saw of a significant and radical change in the attitude of these young people. The talk was of a 'new generation' with a fresh vision of their place and their purpose in God's world, a generation which the conference, by its very size, gave witness to. Many said that such an event could not have taken place even a few years ago.

With God's grace that conference will prove a seedbed, a consciousness nurtured in the hearts of the committed young people there and promoted by them in the churches they will go on to lead. The seed, a Christian presence in today's world; the fruit, a positive Christian alternative in tomorrow's world.

A Thanksgiving for fifty years of the IVF's service for God was held in Westminster Chapel on September 16th, 1978. Present student members and graduate-ex-members combined to give typical and challenging expressions to the Fellowship's outlook and activities. There was still the basic evangelistic witness to fellow-students, whether in a small or large Christian Union, which has characterized the IVF from the beginning. There were still the ambitious attempts to organize, with the help of senior graduates and experienced evangelists, open meetings and full-scale missions. Robust attempts were still being made to defend the faith. A stream of student missionary volunteers was still going overseas for Christian action, not always as members of one of the missionary societies, but often in various forms of non-professional Christian service.

The Rev. John Stott was able to describe striking signs of growth. As he compared the smaller and tentative university missions, in which he had first taken part in the forties and fifties,

348

with the large gatherings of students which he in recent years had led in almost all the English-speaking countries, the causes for devout thanksgiving were increasingly obvious. In the closing address, the Rev. Eric Alexander (of St. George's Church, Tron, Glasgow), having paid his own tribute to the value of the help received from the Theological Students' Fellowship in his early student days, went on to demonstrate the contemporary mounting need for that very message, that outlook and those qualities on which the movement had been founded. In the Sermon on the Mount the Lord called upon His followers to prove, in every community to which they came, 'salt' and 'light'. Whilst the IVF itself cannot pretend to have been all that it ought to have been in either of these forms, the message is clear. The contemporary universities, colleges and the world as a whole need more 'salt' and 'light'.

Envoi

By now the reader should be in no doubt why the leaders of the IVF have held so firmly to their distinctive witness, and especially to the Bible as the source of authority for their message. The American scholars who in 1910 wrote the series of books entitled *The Fundamentals* (which gave the name to 'Fundamentalists') were not so wide of the mark after all. The faith of Christ and the Apostles was then already being undermined. It is now under frontal attack. It may yet prove that the 'Fundamentalists' will have the honour of helping to carry *basic* apostolic Christianity into the 21st century.

The vital principle remains and it must always be tenaciously observed. It was stated with the greatest clarity by St. Paul to Timothy,

'You then, my son, be strong in the grace that is in Christ Jesus, and what you have heard from me before many witnesses entrust to faithful men who will be able to teach others also ... Evil men and imposters will go on from bad to worse, deceivers and deceived. But as for you, continue in what you have learned and have firmly believed, knowing from whom you

349

learned it and how from childhood you have been acquainted
with the sacred writings which are able to instruct you for
salvation through faith in Christ Jesus. All scripture is inspired
by God and profitable for teaching, for reproof, for correction,
and for training in righteousness, that the man of God may be
complete, equipped for every good work.'

2 Tim. 2; 1–2; 3: 13–17

Appendix 1

Officers and Secretaries of the Fellowship

Presidents

1930–31 Sir J. Ambrose Fleming, Kt, MA, DSc, FRS, Hon D Eng
1931–32 The Rt Rev. J. Taylor Smith, KCB, CVO, DD
1932–33 The Rt Hon. Sir Thomas Inskip, PC, KC, CBE, MA, MP
1933–34 Prof. Albert C. Carless, CBE, MB, MS, FRCS
1934–35 The Rev. T. W. Gilbert, MA, DD
1935–36 Prof. Duncan M. Blair, MB, ChB, DSc
1936–37 Prof. Duncan M. Blair, MB, ChB, DSc
1937–38 The Rev. Prof. Donald MacLean, DD
1938–39 Prof. A. Rendle Short, MD, BS, BSc, FRCS
1939–40 The Rev. D. Martyn Lloyd-Jones, MD, MRCP
1940–41 The Rev. D. Martyn Lloyd-Jones, MD, MRCP
1941–42 The Rev. D. Martyn Lloyd-Jones, MD, MRCP
1942–43 Prof. Duncan M. Blair, MB, ChB, DSc
1943–44 H. J. Orr-Ewing, MC, MD, FRCP
1944–45 Prof. G. C. Steward, MA, DSc
1945–46 The Very Rev. Prof. Daniel Lamont, DD
1946–47 A. S. Aldis, MA, BSc, FRCS
1947–48 The Rev. Canon T. C. Hammond, MA
1948–49 The Most Rev. Howard W. K. Mowll, MA, DD
1949–50 W. Melville Capper, MB, FRCS, MRCOG
1950–51 The Rt Rev. H. R. Gough, OBE, MA, TD
1951–52 The Rev. D. Martyn Lloyd-Jones, MD, MRCP
1952–53 The Rev. L.F.E.Wilkinson, MA
1953–54 J. N. D. Anderson, OBE, MA, LLB

1954–55 F. F. Bruce, MA, Dip.Heb
1955–56 A. S. Aldis, BSc, MB, BS, FRCS
1956–57 W. J. Martin, MA, BD, PhD
1957–58 Prof. N. C. Hunt, B.Com., PhD
1958–59 Malcolm Dixon, MA, ScD, FRS
1959–60 The Rt Rev. Frank Houghton, BA
1960–61 Prof. M. Guthrie, PhD, BSc
1961–62 The Rev. J. R. W. Stott, MA
1962–63 W. Melville Capper, MB, BS, FRCS, MRCOG
1963–64 The Rev. D. Martyn Lloyd-Jones, MD, MRCP
1964–65 Prof. D. J. E. Ingram, MA, DPhil, DSc, FInstP
1965–66 Prof. D. J. Wiseman, OBE, MA, FSA
1966–67 Prof. A. D. Hitchin, DDSc, MDS, FDSRCS
1967–68 Prof. J. N. D. Anderson, OBE, MA, LLD
1968–69 Prof. D. M. MacKay, BSc, PhD, FInstP
1969–70 H. F. R. Catherwood, MA
1970–71 A. S. Aldis, MB, BS, FRCS
1971–72 The Rev. J. R. W. Stott, MA
1972–73 Prof. M. A. Jeeves, MA, PhD
1973–74 Prof. D. J. Wiseman, OBE, MA, DLit, FSA, FBA
1974–75 The Rev. W. Still MA
1975–76 Prof. Sir Norman Anderson, OBE, QC, MA, LlD, DD, FBA
1976–77 The Rev. G. B. Duncan, MA
1977–78 The Rev. J. R. W. Stott, MA, QHC
1978–79 D. J. E. Ingram, MA, DPhil, DSc, FInstP

Chairmen of the Universities Executive Committee

1922–23 J. Stuart Holden (Cambridge)
1923–24 W. Habershon (Oxford)
1924–25 C. H. M. Foster (Cambridge)

351

1925-26 C. G. Thorne (Cambridge)
1926-29 H. R. Gough (Cambridge)
1929-30 K. H. Hooker (Cambridge)
1930-31 L. P. Ashton (Bristol)
1931-32 K. H. Hooker (Oxford)
1932-33 G. D. Lehmann (Oxford and University College Hospital London)
1933-35 T. B. L. Bryan (Cambridge and St. Mary's Hospital, London)
1935-36 A. S. Aldis (University College, London)
1936-37 C. G. Scorer (Cambridge and the London Hospital)
1937-39 J. W. Wenham (Cambridge)
1939 K. Moynagh (St. Bartholomew's Hospital, London)
1939-40 B. C. Aldis (Oxford)
1940-41 R. H. Turvey (Cambridge)
1941-42 R. Drown (Oxford)
1942-45 O. R. Barclay (Cambridge)
1945-47 Roland J. Hart (St. Mary's Hospital, London)
1947-48 Donald J. Wiseman (Oxford)
1948-49 C. L. Laurence Binder (Oxford)
1949-50 F. H. T. Rhodes (Birmingham)
1950-51 John White (Manchester)
1951-52 J. D. C. Anderson (Cambridge and Middlesex Hospital, London)
1952-53 J. T. Bendor-Samuel (Oxford)
1953-54 Michael C. Griffiths (Cambridge)
1954-55 Nigel Sylvester (Cambridge)
1955-56 John Skinner (Bristol)
1956-59 Robert M. Horn (Cambridge)
1959-60 David Innes (Edinburgh)
1960-61 Graham Harrison (Oxford)
1961-63 Richard France (Bristol)
1963-64 David Wright (Oxford)
1964-65 David R. J. Evans (Bristol)
1965-66 Donald Shell (London School of Economics)
1966-67 Howard Peskett (Cambridge)
1967-69 Ernest Lucas (Oxford)
1969-71 John Banger (East Anglia)
1971-73 Steve Russ (King's College, London)
1973-75 Alan Gillespie (Cambridge)
1975-76 Christopher Doig (Manchester)
1976-77 Graham Herbert (Birmingham)
1977-78 John Wyatt (St. Thomas's Hospital, London)
1978-79 John Chapman (Strathclyde)

Hon. Treasurers
1927-29 Miss L. M. O'Hanlon

1929-32 A. Rendle Short
1948-51 B. M. Harris
1951-53 J. T. Aitken
1953-65 B. M. Harris
1965-78 J. W. Haig-Ferguson
1978- S. Webley

Hon. Senior Co-Treasurers
1932-53 C. H. M. Foster and A. Rendle Short
1953-54 C. H. M. Foster
1954-58 Ivor Crouch and C. H. M. Foster
1959-61 Ivor Crouch

Editors of Journals
Inter-Varsity Magazine
1929-31 Hugh R. Gough
1931-35 F. D. Coggan
1935-37 R. J. Cobb
1937-40 J. V. Taylor
1940-55 H. Evan Hopkins
1944-48 Norman Baker
1948-49 D. J. Wiseman
1949-51 B. S. Mackay

Inter-Varsity
1951-54 B. S. Mackay
1954-57 J. C. King
1957-59 S. M. Houghton
1959-62 P. W. Dearnley
1962-63 Robert M. Horn
1963-66 Gordon C. Neal
1967-69 Donald Shell and Pamela White
1969-70 Ernest Lucas

Voice
1970-71 Graham Davies
1972-74 Roger Mitchell
1975-77 Pete Broadbent
1977- Tom Morton

Christian Graduate
1948-61 C. G. Scorer
1961-76 J. D. Marsh
1977- M. D. Elston

Publications Secretaries
1936-77 Ronald Inchley
1973- The Rev. Frank R. Entwistle

Editorial Staff
1948-51 Miss Ruth Bolton
1951- Miss Mary Gladstone

1957–58 Norman Richards
1958–67 Miss Pat Holmes
1961–62 Dudley Reeves
1962–71 David S. Alexander
1966–67 Miss Pamela Jackman
1968–74 Miss Clare G. Richards
1971–72 Michael Wenham
1973–   Miss Jo Bramwell
1974–77 Miss Caroline Thomas
1976–   Derek R. W. Wood
1977–   Miss Sue Mills

Production Managers
1966–70 Tony Wales
1970–76 Len Chart
1976–   Michael Sims

Production Assistants
1964–66 Miss Susan Thurlow
1969–71 Miss Brenda Eaton
1972–73 Peter Lloyd
1973–75 Philip Derbyshire
1975–76 Miss Laetitia Barclay
1977–   Miss Katy Zanker

Designers
1968–72 Miss Heather M. Williams
1972–76 Peter Wyart
1973–   Adrian Fewins
1976–78 Jonathan Roberts
1978–   Neil Stanton

Sales Managers
1949–64 Eddie Bradley-Feary
1964–74 Chris Mungeam
1975–77 Richard Barnes
1978–   Stephen Hey

Marketing Manager
1976–78 Clive Rawlins

This list does not include those employed on a short-term basis for special projects.

Travelling Secretaries
Adcock, Miss Margaret 1954–56 (TCCU)
Alexander, Miss Elizabeth 1974–77 (Literature)
Algeo, Miss Tricia 1971–74
Apter, Miss Elaine 1978–

Bagust, Adrian 1972–75 (Literature)
Balchin, John A. 1955–59 (Scotland)

Ballentine, Miss Ann M. 1968–71 (Scotland)
Barker, The Rev. J. H. J. 1946–48
Bassett, Miss Rhoda T. 1954–57 (Wales)
Bathgate, Andrew 1978– (Scotland)
Beckett, Miss Fran 1977–   (Colleges)
Bellingham, Miss Christine 1972–74 (Colleges)
Bennett, Miss P. Z. 1941–46
Berry, Miss Janet 1975–78
Berry, The Rev. John 1970–73
Blackmore, Vernon 1977–
Bowen, The Rev. John 1973–77
Breakspear, Miss Beryl 1971–75 (Colleges)
Britton, Miss Ann 1952–54 (TCCU)
Brockman, Miss Betty 1960–62 (TCCU)
Brown, Lindsay 1977–   (Wales)
Brown, Miss Susan 1970–73
Burbridge, Graham 1958–61 (TCCF)
Burns, Robbie 1967–71 (Ireland)
Butterworth, Miss Margaret 1951–52 (TCCU)

Cable, Miss Mildred 1937–39 (Hon. Missionary)
Caligari, Miss Sheila 1966–69 (CECU)
Carson, The Rev. H. M. 1948–51 (Ireland)
Charlton, Clive 1967–70
Churchill, Miss T. J. 1936
Clarke, Miss Rosemary 1959–61
Clee, Miss Mary 1957–60 (Wales)
Clements, Roy D. 1971–74
Clowney, Paul 1976–   (Art Colleges)
Cocking, Paul 1975–78 (Scotland, Colleges)
Cogan, Kevin 1976–77 (Literature)
Cole, The Rev. Michael J. 1961–64
Cole, Miss Nina T. 1945–46
Collier, Peter 1970–73
Collins, Miss Gill 1974–77 (Therapy students)
Collins, Miss Hazel D. 1969–72
Cottom, Miss Gwyneth 1978–   (Wales)
Coupar, Miss Mary-Jane 1975–78 (Colleges)
Crittenden, F. H. 1946–47
Currie, Miss Mary 1974–78
Cutler, The Rev. Robert 1970–74 (ICCF)

Dalton, Andrew 1977–   (Overseas students)
Dalzell, Gordon 1964–67 (Ireland)

353

Contending for the faith

Davies, Miss Christine 1973–77 (Colleges)
Davies, The Rev. J. Elwyn 1955–62 (Wales)
Dean, Tim 1973–76 (Art Colleges)
Delight, The Rev. John 1958–61
Doig, Christopher 1976–
Dowsett, Dick 1965–68
Duffin, Peter 1976–   (Ireland)
Duncan, George 1973–77 (Colleges)
Dunlop, Bill 1975–78 (Scotland)

Earnshaw-Smith, Miss Elizabeth 1954–57 (TCCU)
Earnshaw-Smith, Harold 1924–26
Edwards, Miss Mavis 1964–67 (Art Colleges)
English, Donald 1955–58
Evans, Miss Margaret 1958–59 (TCCU)

Fergus, Miss Meryl 1967–70 (Art Colleges)
Fielder, Geraint 1964–69 (Wales)
Fielder, Godfrey 1976–   (Colleges)
Finnie, Peter K. 1961–65 (TCCF)
Fisher, The Rev. Ian 1960–64 (Scotland)
Flanagan, Declan 1974–77 (Colleges)
Foote, Miss M. S. 1946–56
Fox, Miss Adèle 1973–76
Fraser, Mrs. R. M. 1951–52 (Hon. Missionary)
Fraser, Miss Shirley 1971–74 (Scotland)
Freeman, Sid 1973–76 (CECU)
French, Miss Evangeline 1937–39 (Hon. Missionary)
French, Miss Francesca 1937–39 (Hon. Missionary)
Frost, Miss Diana 1974–76 (Scotland)

Gardner, Miss Jo 1963–66 (TCCU)
Garner, Miss Margaret 1976– (Colleges)
Gillies, Sheena 1978–   (Scotland, Colleges)
Gough, Hugh R. 1927
Graham, Miss Anne 1951–53 (TCCU)
Graham, Miss Kitty 1975–78
Green, Andrew 1973–76
Green, Miss Margaret 1949–56
Griffiths, Michael C. 1954–57
Grubb, Norman P. 1929
Guillebaud, Miss Christine 1973–75
Guillebaud, Peter 1965–66 (Overseas students)

Guinness, Howard W. 1932–34, Overseas 1934–37, UK 1937–38

Hamilton, Norman 1976–78 (Colleges)
Handley, The Rev. John 1951–53 (Scotland)
Harman, The Rev. Gordon 1942–45
Harmer, Carey 1970–73 (Overseas students)
Harmes, Miss Elizabeth 1963–67
Harmsworth, Miss D. Madeline 1940–41
Haupt, Miss Mary 1957–60
Henderson, The Rev. A. Roy 1957–60
Herring, Ian D. 1967–70 (CECU)
Hicks, Paul 1973–76 (Colleges)
Hill, Philip 1973–74 (Colleges), 1974–77 (Wales)
Hoare, Brian R. 1962–63 (TCCU)
Hodder, John 1974–78 (Colleges)
Hood, Miss Elizabeth 1973–75
Hooker, The Rev. K. H. 1929–30, 1936–37
Hopkins, The Rev. H. Evan 1937–39
Hornal, Alistair 1977–   (Literature)
Houghton, The Rev. A. T. 1941–44
Howarth, Miss Alex 1978–   (Colleges)
Hutcheon, Miss Christine 1974–78 (Scotland, Colleges)

Innes, The Rev. T. C. 1934–35 (Theological colleges)

Jelbart, Miss Rosemary 1976–
John, Richard 1977–   (Literature)
Johnson, Miss Helen 1976–   (Colleges)
Johnston, Jim 1964–66 (TCCU)
Jones, Miss Angela M. 1966–71 (Therapy students)

Keay, Miss Kathryn 1978–
Keith, Dr. Graham 1978–   (Graduate students)
Kirkland, Jim 1976–   (Overseas students)
Knell, Bryan J. 1969–73 (TCCF)

Lamb, Jonathan 1976–
Lamb, The Rev. the Hon. Roland 1952–55
Lambert, Miss Mary 1964–68 (Scotland)
Lee, Miss Margaret 1947–49 (TCCU)
Lewis, Miss Anne M. 1968–73 (Wales)
Lewis, Miss Brenda 1960–64 (Wales)
Longley, David 1972–74 (Literature)

354

Macaulay, Don 1969–72 (Scotland, ICCF)
McCarthy, David 1978–   (Colleges)
MacGregor, Miss Gill E. 1966–70
Macindoe, Alistair W. 1972–74 (Overseas students)
Mackenzie, Kenneth 1941–45 (Scotland)
McKinlay, Fergus 1972–75 (Scotland, ICCF)
McMaster, Miss Sandra 1977– (Ireland)
McVeigh, Miss Margaret 1972–77 (Ireland)
Maiden, Brian 1969–73 (ICCF)
Mainey, Ian 1977–   (Colleges)
Martin, Miss Anne 1961–63
Martin, Miss Eileen 1971–74 (Therapy students)
May, Dr. Peter 1974–77 (Medical students)
Morrell, Cassels 1976–   (Ireland)
Morton, Miss Rosemary 1966–69
Mynors, Mrs Helen P. 1976–77 (Colleges)
Mynors, James B. 1971–73

Nickless, Dr. Stephen 1978–   (Medical students)
Nicolson, Isobel 1976–   (Scotland)
Nixon, Miss Norah S. 1936–46

Osborne, Miss June 1977–78 (Graduate students)
Overton, The Rev. Tom 1967–71 (Overseas students)

Page, Andrew 1977–
Pantridge, Gavin 1971–75 (Ireland)
Partridge, Miss Dorothy M. 1946–47
Pocock, Peter 1969–70 (Overseas students)
Pollard, David J. 1968–71
Porter, Miss Judith 1977–   (Colleges and RS students)
Pound-Corner, Miss Clare 1973–76 (Overseas students)
Powell, Ian 1974–77 (Colleges)
Pritchard, Miss Heulwen 1973–78 (Wales)

Rainsbury, The Rev. A. W. 1946–51 (Scotland)
Read, Peter 1976–
Rennie, A. M. 1937–40 (Scotland)
Richardson, Miss Fay 1977–   (Colleges)

Richardson, Dr. Stephen 1977–79 (Medical students)
Roberts, Gwilym 1953–55 (Wales)
Roemmele, Michael C. 1964–65 (Scotland)
Rose, Miss Susan 1970–73 (CECU)
Ross, John 1971–74 (Colleges)
Russell-Smith, The Rev. Mark 1977–

Salter, The Rev. John F. 1967–70
Salter, Miss Mary 1974–77
Samuel, Leith 1949–53
Scheuermeier, Miss Esther 1959–63 (TCCU)
Sharp, Miss Diana 1956–58 (TCCU)
Shee, Miss Catherine 1977–
Shell, Robin 1965–69 (TCCF)
Shone, Miss Judy A. 1960–64
Simpson, Roger 1974–77
Sinton, Miss Vera M. 1971–74
Skelly, Miss Violet 1964–67 (TCCU)
Sloan, The Rev. Robert P. 1965–68 (Scotland)
Smith, Miss Joan 1975–78
Smith, Miss Rena 1963–66
Spence, Peter 1977–   (Colleges)
Spink, Miss Jill 1978–
Stalley, The Rev. Michael D. 1965–68 (TCCF)
Steele, William E. 1966–69 (CECU)
Stent, Miss Felicity 1967–71 (CECU)
Stokes, Dr. Keith 1973–76
Stone, Godfrey 1973–76
Strain, Miss Jean B. 1932–35
Stuart-Smith, The Rev. David 1970–74
Sugden, Miss Mary 1949–54 (TCCU)

Taggart, Dr. Charlotte 1953–54
Tattersall, Miss Valerie 1973–76 (CECU)
Taylor, Miss Bridgett 1974–77 (Colleges)
Taylor, Miss Helen P. 1972–75
Telford, Miss Marjorie 1956–59
Thomson, Jeremy 1977–
Todd, W. Noel 1961–65 (TCCF)
Tovey, Alan C. 1969–74 (Wales)
Travers, Miss Veronica 1977– (Therapy students)
Turner, Miss Janice 1978–

Vance, Tom 1970–73 (CECU)
Voke, Christopher J. 1969–72 (CECU)

Wales, Tony P. 1970–73 (Art colleges)
Walker, The Rev. Tom 1964–67

Walls, Andrew F. 1952–57 (Theological students)
Walters, Dr. Gwyn 1950–51 (Wales)
Wardle, Miss Sonia H. 1964–67 (Wales)
Waters, Miss Elizabeth H. 1969–72 (CECU)
Weston, John B. A. 1952–55
Wigg, Miss Hilda 1962–67 (TCCU)
Wilkinson, Miss Joyce M. 1958–60
Wilkinson, Miss Margaret E. 1943–44
Wilkinson, Miss Maureen E. 1967–70 (CECU)
Williams, The Rev. John R. 1960–64
Wilson, Miss Jenny M. 1972–75 (Colleges)
Wilson, Miss Pam 1955–58
Winn, Dr. Susan 1977–
Winter, Miss Tricia 1967–71
Wintle, Miss Ruth 1960–63
Wright, The Rev. Eric J. 1968–75 (Scotland)

Young, Jim 1978–   (Colleges)
Young, Simon W. 1967–70 (TCCF)

Graduate Office Staff
General Secretaries
1924–64 Dr. Douglas Johnson
1965–   Dr. Oliver R. Barclay

Assistant Secretaries
1945–53 Dr. Oliver R. Barclay and Deputy-General Secretary 1962–64)
1946–52 Miss P. Z. Bennett

Universities Secretaries
1953–59 Dr. Oliver R. Barclay
1959–62 The Rev. Robert M. Horn
1962–68 The Rev. John C. Skinner
1968–74 David J. Jackman
1974–   Dr. Ken Wycherley

Women's Universities Secretaries
1956–64 Miss M. S. Foote
1964–67 Miss Judy A. Shone
1967–71 Miss Sonia H. Wardle
1971–74 Miss Gill E. MacGregor
1974–78 Miss Vera M. Sinton
1978–   Miss Susan Brown

TCCU/CECU Secretaries
1947–54 Miss Rosalyn J. Carrick
1954–56 Miss Mary Sugden
1956–60 Miss Margaret Adcock
1960–63 Miss Mary Haupt
1963–68 Brian R. Hoare

1968–73 David R. Elledge
1973–76 Fred E. Hughes

TCCF/ICCF Secretaries
1948–56 Raymond W. G. Turner
1956–67 Arthur M. S. Pont
1967–71 Peter C. H. Seccombe
1971–76 The Rev. Derek L. Williams

Colleges Secretaries
1976–78 Fred E. Hughes
1978–   Norman Hamilton

Theological Students' Fellowship Secretaries
1962–65 The Rev. Robert M. Horn
1965–68 The Rev. David H. Field
1968–71 The Rev. Robert Hope
1971–74 Dr. David Wenham
1974–   The Rev. James B. Mynors

Graduates Fellowship/UCCF Associates Secretaries
1948–59 F. H. Crittenden
1959–64 Dr. Oliver R. Barclay
1964–69 Gordon Landreth
1969–75 Dr. Andrew M. Brockett
1975–   Neil Crosbie

G.F Assistant Secretaries
1946–57 Miss Norah S. Nixon
1973–74 David Limebear

Overseas Students Secretaries
1959–73 F. H. Crittenden
1973–   Bryan J. Knell

Accountant and Administrative Secretaries, post war
1945–68 George E. White
1968–71 Derek R. Nixon
1971–76 Alec G. Povey
1975–   Martin A. Chawner

Senior Office Staff
Adcock, Miss Margaret TCCU Secretary 1956–60
Alexander, David S. Editorial Assistant 1962–71

Barclay, Dr. Oliver R. Assistant Secretary 1945–53; Universities Secretary 1953–59; GF Secretary 1959–64; Deputy General Secretary 1962–64; General Secretary 1965–

Bennett, Miss P. Z. Assistant Secretary 1946–52

Bolton, Miss Ruth. Editorial Assistant 1946–51

Bramwell, Miss Jo. Editorial Assistant 1973–76; Editor 1976–

Brockett, Dr. Andrew M. GF Secretary 1969–75

Brown, Miss Susan. Universities Secretary 1978–

Carrick, Miss Rosalyn J. TCCU Secretary 1947–54

Chawner, Martin A. Administrative Secretary 1975–

Crittenden, F. H. GF Secretary 1948–59; Overseas Students Secretary 1959–73

Crosbie, Neil. UCCF Associates Secretary 1975–

Elledge, David R. CECU Secretary 1968–73

Entwistle, The Rev. Frank R. Deputy Publications Secretary 1973–75; Publications Secretary 1975–

Field, The Rev. David H. TSF Secretary 1965–68

Foote, Miss M. S. Women's Secretary 1956–64

Gladstone, Miss Mary. Editorial Assistant 1951–76; Editor 1976–

Hamilton, Norman. Colleges Secretary 1978–

Haupt, Miss Mary. TCCU Secretary 1960–63

Hoare, Brian R. TCCU/CECU Secretary 1963–68

Holmes, Miss Pat. Editorial Assistant 1958–67

Hope, The Rev. Robert. TSF Secretary 1968–71

Horn, The Rev. Robert M. Universities Secretary 1959–62; TSF Secretary 1962–65

Hughes, Fred E. CECU Secretary 1973–76; Colleges Secretary 1976–78

Inchley, Ronald. Publications Secretary 1936–75; Publications Consultant 1975–77

Jackman, David J. Universities Secretary 1968–74

Jackman, Miss Pamela. Editorial Assistant 1966–67

Johnson, Dr. Douglas. General Secretary 1924–64

Knell, Bryan J. Overseas Students Secretary 1973–

Landreth, Gordon. GF Secretary 1964–69

Limebear, David. Assistant GF Secretary 1973–74

MacGregor, Miss Gill E. Women's/ Missionary Secretary 1971–74

Mills, Miss Sue. Editor 1977–

Mynors, Mrs. Helen P. Colleges Women's Secretary 1976–

Mynors, The Rev. James B. TSF Secretary 1974–

Nixon, Derek R. Accountant 1968–71

Nixon, Miss Norah S. Assistant GF Secretary 1946–57

Pont, Arthur M. S. TCCF Secretary 1956–67

Povey, Alec G. Accountant 1971 – 76

Reeves, Dudley. Editorial Assistant 1961–62

Richards, Miss Clare G. Editorial Assistant 1968–74

Richards, Norman. Editorial Assistant 1957–58

Seccombe, Peter C. H. TCCF/ICCF Secretary 1967–71

Shone, Miss Judy A. Women's Secretary 1964–67

Sinton, Miss Vera M. Missionary Secretary 1974–78

Skinner, The Rev. John C. Universities Secretary 1962–68

Sugden, Miss Mary. TCCU Secretary 1954–56

Thomas, Miss Caroline. Editorial Assistant 1974–76; Editor 1976–77

Turner, Raymond W. G. TCCF Secretary 1948–56

357

Contending for the faith

Wardle, Miss Sonia H. Women's Secretary 1967–71

Wenham, Dr. David. TSF Secretary 1971–74

Wenham, Michael. Editorial Assistant 1971–72

White, George E. Accountant 1945–68

Williams, The Rev. Derek L. ICCF Secretary 1971–76

Wood, Derek R. W. Senior Editor 1976–

Wycherley, Dr. Ken E. Universities Secretary 1974–

Appendix 2

Inter-Varsity Conference of Evangelical Unions: Constitution (1924)

1. That the Inter-Varsity Conference shall be held each year and it shall be open to members of all Universities and associated colleges.

2. That the object of the Conference shall be to stimulate personal faith, and to further evangelistic work among students by upholding fundamental truths, including:-

a. *The divine inspiration and infallibility of Holy Scripture, as originally given, and its supreme authority in all matters of faith and conduct. (2 Tim. iii. 15-16; 2 Peter i. 21).*

b. *The unity of the Father, the Son and the Holy Spirit in the Godhead. (Matt. xxviii. 19; John x. 30; xiv. 26; Romans viii. 9; 2 Cor. xiii. 14).*

c. *The universal sinfulness and guilt of human nature since the Fall, rendering man subject to God's wrath and condemnation. (Romans i. 18; iii. 19, 23; v. 12, 18).*

d. *Redemption from the guilt, penalty and power of sin only through the sacrificial death (as our Representative and Substitute) of Jesus Christ, the Incarnate Son of God. (Matt. xx. 28; Rom. v. 18, 19; vi. 10-12; vii. 34; Gal. iii. 13; Heb. x. 10-12; 1 Pet. iii. 18).*

e. *The Resurrection of Jesus Christ from the dead. (Acts xiii. 30-37; 1 Cor. xv. 3-4, 20).*

f. *The necessity of the work of the Holy Spirit to make the Death of Christ effective to the individual sinner, granting him repentance towards God and faith in Jesus Christ. (John xvi. 7-11; Acts xi. 18; xiv. 27; xx. 21; Rom. viii. 9-11).*

g. *The indwelling and work of the Holy Spirit in the believer. (John xiv. 26; Rom. viii. 9-11, 16; 2 Cor. i. 22; 2 Thess. ii. 13).*

h. *The expectation of the personal return of the Lord Jesus Christ. (Matt. xxiv. 29-31, 42-44; John xiv. 2-3; Acts i. 11; 1 Thess. iv. 16-17; 2 Thess. iii. 5; Titus ii. 11-14).*

3. That there be an Advisory Committee of four (without power of veto) consisting of:-

> Rev. J. Stuart Holden, DD
> Rev. J. Russell Howden, BD
> A. Rendle Short, Esqre., MD, BSc, FRCS
> B. Colgrove, Esqre., MA

This Committee shall have power to fill up any vacancy that may occur in its body by resignation or otherwise.

4. a. That the General Committee shall consist of two representatives from as many Universities as possible, elected by those Societies (where such exist) in the Universities, which uphold the truths for which the Conference stands. These Representatives are to be elected annually before such Conference is held.

b. In a University where a separate Women's Christian Society exists (which upholds the truths for which the Conference stands) one member may be elected by it in addition.

c. That in those Universities where no such Societies exist the Conference General Committee may co-opt one member for each University to represent such Universities.

5. That each year there shall be elected at the Conference an Executive Committee which shall undertake the organisation of the succeeding Conference; members of the retiring and of the new General Committee to be eligible for election to the Executive Committee.

6. That this Executive Committee shall consist of a Chairman, Vice-Chairman, Treasurer, Secretary, and two members to be elected by the General Committee.

7. That a Prayer Secretary be appointed from the Executive Committee to receive from the Unions, before the beginning of each term, brief reports and requests for prayer, and that these be drafted into a letter, copies of which are to be sent to each Union.

8. That all Officials connected with the Conference – including the members of the Executive Committee – shall sign the Basis on election.

9. That Clause 4 shall not refer to any religious body whose activities extend beyond one University.

10. That only those speakers be asked to take part in the Conference whose views are known to be in accordance with the truths stated in this Constitution.

11. That in connection with the Conference no joint-meeting shall be arranged with any religious body which does not substantially uphold the truths stated in the Basis of the Conference.

12. That no alteration shall be made in this Constitution except by the agreement of three-quarters of those present and voting at a Conference General Committee Meeting, and that no less than 14 days' notice shall be given of any such meeting.

Bibliography

I. Chief Printed Sources

The following are recognized as standard histories for the periods and organizations under review.

Balleine, G. R. *A History of the Evangelical Party in the Church of England* (Longmans, 1908; Church Bookroom Press, 1961)

Barclay, O. R. *Whatever Happened to the Jesus Lane Lot?* (IVP, 1977)

Coggan, F. D. (ed.) *Christ and the Colleges: A History of the IVFEU* (IVFEU, 1934)

Downer, A. C. D. *A Century of Evangelical Religion in Oxford* (Church Bookroom Press, 1938)

Elliot-Binns L. *The Evangelical Movement in the Church of England* (Methuen, 1928)

Green, V. H. H. *Religion at Oxford and Cambridge (1160–1960)* (SCM Press, 1964)

McCaughey, J. D. *Christian Obedience in the University* (Story of the SCM, 1930–1950). (SCM Press, 1958)

Mott, J. R. *The Evangelization of the World in this Generation* (SVMU, 1900)

Pollock, J. C. *The Cambridge Movement* (John Murray, 1953)

Reynolds, J. S. *The Evangelicals at Oxford (1735–1905)* (Marcham Manor Press, 1975)

Rouse, Ruth *The World Student Christian Federation* (SCM Press, 1948)

Stoeffler, F. E. *The Rise of Evangelical Pietism* (Brill, 1971)

Tatlow, Tissington *The Story of the Student Christian Movement of Great Britain and Ireland* (SCM Press, 1933)

Warren, M. *The Missionary Movement from Britain in Modern History* (SCM Press, 1965)

Wilder, R. P. *The Great Commission* (Oliphants, 1936)

Wilder, R. P. *The Student Volunteer Movement* (SUM, New York, 1938)

II. Other Printed Sources

(Not included in this bibliography are pamphlets and unpublished

Bibliography

Cairns, W. *Memoirs of Charles Simeon* (Hatchard, 1848)
Cambridge (edited) *Old Paths in Perilous Times* (Marshall, Morgan & Scott, 1913; 2nd ed. IVF, 1932)
Grubb, N. P. *Once Caught, No Escape* (Autobiography), (Lutterworth, 1969)
Guinness, H. W. *Journey among Students* (Anglican Information Office, Sydney, 1978)
Hanna, W. *Thomas Chalmers* (Sutherland & Knox, 1851)
Hennell, M. *John Venn and the Clapham Sect* (Lutterworth, 1958)
IVF (edited) *A Brief History of the Inter-Varsity Fellowship* (IVFEU, 1929)
IVF (report) *Christ our Freedom* (International Conference, Cambridge addresses), (IVF, 1939)
Johnson, D. *A Brief History of the International Fellowship of Evangelical Students* (IFES, 1964)
Loane, M. L. *Archbishop H. W. K. Mowll* (biography), (Hodder & Stoughton, 1960)
Loane, M. L. *Oxford and the Evangelical Succession* (Lutterworth, 1950)
Matthews, B. *John Mott: World Citizen* (SCM Press, 1934)
Moule, H. C. G. *Charles Simeon* (Methuen, 1892; IVF, 1949)
Ollard, S. L. *The Six Students of St Edmunds Hall* (Mowbray, 1911)
Patten, J. A. *These Remarkable Men* (Lutterworth, 1945)
Pollock, J. C. *The Cambridge Seven* (IVF, 1955)
Reynolds, J. S. *Canon Christopher* (Abbey Press, 1967)
Reynolds, Fisher and Wright *Two Centuries of Christian Action at Yale* (Putnam's, 1901)
Russell, G. W. F. *A Short History of the Evangelical Movement* (Mowbray, 1915)
Smith, G. *The Life of Alexander Duff* (Hodder & Stoughton, 1879)
SVMU (edited) *Make Jesus King* (Report of 1896 Students Missionary Conference, Liverpool)
Watson, R. (ed.) *Works of Henry Scougall* (Collins, 1830)
Watt, H. *New College, Edinburgh* (Oliver & Boyd, 1946)
Woods, C. S. *The Growth of a Work of God* (IVP, USA, 1978)

Acknowledgments

In addition to the assistance received from seniors mentioned in the Preface, the author is greatly indebted to the following graduates who have helped from their diaries, papers and memories:

O. R. Barclay
G. Burbridge
B. G. Buxton
Hazel C. Collins
F. H. Crittenden
C. H. M. Foster
A. W. Habershon
Mary Gladstone
T. S. Goodwin
N. Green
N. P. Grubb
H. W. Guinness
J. Hay-Walker
K. H. Hooker

R. Inchley
F. D. Kidner
J. M. Laird
C. M. Martin
T. G. Mohan
Norah Nixon
F. N. Palmer
F. H. Pickering
J. S. Reynolds
L. Sutton
J. P. Thornton-Duesbery
C. S. Woods
M. H. Webb-Peploe

Major assistance was also received from the Editorial Department of IVP; from Dorothy Martin of UCCF's International Friendship Campaign; and from the three secretaries on whom fell the main burden of typing and retyping illegible MSS – Lilian B. Baker, Marjorie Watling and Christine Ward.

Index of subjects

Aberdeen, 26, 37, 46, 61, 63–4, 103, 105
Aberystwyth, 150
Address of office, 162, 171, 198, 339
Adelaide, 175
Advisory Committee, 159, 226, 360
Africa Christian Press, 281, 327
Agricultural Colleges, 250
Agricultural Christian Fellowship, 297
Alliance Club, 238, 310, 311
All Souls Church, 223, 259, 304
Andover College, 19, 47, 48
Art colleges, 249
Association of Christian Teachers, 293, 297
Auchendennan, 228
Auckland, 174, 175
Australia, 173, 174–181

Ballaigues, 278
Battersea Polytechnic, 260
Bedford Square, 171, 237
Belfast, 64, 103, 106, 124, 165, 166
Belfast Technical Colleges CU, 260
Belgium, 176
Bible Churchmen's Missionary Society, 218
Bible research, 210–213
Biblical Research Committee, 210–212, 233, 237, 286, 297, 318, 320, 322
Birmingham, 150–152, 165, 170, 311
Bonskeid, 168, 193, 201, 228
Book Centre, 327, 329
Bookstall Service, 328
Boston, 17, 270, 271, 280
Breakfasts (see also Missionary Breakfasts), 42, 52, 102, 103, 187, 287, 288
Brisbane, 178
Bristol, 93, 103, 105, 165, 224
British College Christian Union, 67
Broadlands, 50, 54
Business Advisory Committee, 158, 159, 166–168, 170, 171, 205, 206, 213, 218, 226, 230, 236, 262, 297, 316, 317, 330
Business Study Group, 297

Cambridge, 13, 14, 54, 183, 185, 201, 278
Camp, 80, 138
Churches – St. Giles, 34, Holy Trinity, 32–35, 56, 90, 93
Daily prayer meeting, 37, 40, 52, 55
Inter-Collegiate Christian Union (CICCU), 37, 49–52, 70–73, 82, 89–94, 135, 140, 160, 221–4, 271
missions, 54–56, 222
open air meeting, 89
Seven, 57, 64
Student Volunteer Missionary Union, 63, 64
Union for Private Prayer, 39, 49
University Church Missionary Society, 40, 49
University Prayer Union, 37, 39, 49
Campus in the Bamboos, 276
Canada, 142–145, 173, 176, 178, 180, 268, 270, 272 (see also Inter-Varsity Christian Fellowship)

Cardiff, 104, 107, 166
Chairmen's Co-ordinating Committee, 232
Change of address and name, 162, 171, 338, 339
of background, 333
of theological climate, 15
Chaplaincies (universities), 245
Characteristics of a student society, 19–22, 242
Children's Special Service Mission, 80, 81, 90, 98, 135, 146, 169, 300, 318
China Inland Mission, 107, 108, 182, 195, 256, 269, 272
Chinese Inter-Varsity Christian Fellowship, 269, 270, 275, 276, 313
Christian, The, 118–120
Christian Dental Fellowship, 297
Christian Educational Fellowship, 292
Christian Medical Fellowship, 232, 238, 289, 297 (see also Medical)
Christian Graduate, 214, 296
Church Missionary Society, 10, 40, 57, 58, 62, 70
City missions, 170
Clapham Sect, 25
College Lecturers Christian Fellowship, 297
Colleges of education, 226, 231, 236, 251–257, 263, 264
Colleges of Education Christian Union, 264, 266
Colleges Christian Fellowship, 267
Colleges of technology, 226, 231, 236, 257–261, 264
Committees (see also General Comm., Executive Comm.), 121, 217, 232, 236
Committees Conference, 232
Conferences, 122, 133, 134, 168, 169, 347 (see also Inter-Varsity Conference)
Constitution, 359
Crusaders Union, 318
Conversation Parties, 33, 34
Council, 232

Denmark, 183
Derby, 170
Digest, 294
Digswell Park, 286
Doctrinal basis, 110–113 127, 133, 156, 255, 359
Doctrine, importance of, 71–75, 109–114, 118–121, 127, 265, 342–5
Doughty Street, 311, 312
Dublin, 103, 104, 124, 125, 165
Dundee, 150
Durham, 116, 150–152, 165, 166

Eastern Lectures, 304
Ecumenical Movement, 69
Edinburgh University, 45, 58–61, 63, 104, 106, 165, 223
medical students, 46, 47, 59
Medical Missionary Society, 106
Missionary Association, 45
Missionary Conference (1910), 69
Theological Association, 45
Educationalists, 291–294 (see also Christian Educational Fellowship)
Elland Society, 31, 32

English Seven, 183
Europe, 176
Evangelical, meaning of, 22–25
Evangelicals, 23, 30–32, 41
Evangelical Alliance, 113, 310
Executive Committee, 123, 127, 133, 143, 206, 218, 227, 230, 254, 269, 285, 303, 317, 360
Exeter, 150, 220
Expulsion of the Oxford Methodists, 29, 41
Europe, 176

Fact and Faith Films, 300
Finance, 138, 139, 156–159, 205, 206, 231, 235–238, 256, 261, 262, 317–320, 338
Finland, 183, 184
Former members, 345, 346
France, 181
Free Church students, 53, 73, 77, 87
Fundamentalism, 246–248, 344, 349

General Committee, 123–127, 133, 137, 143, 188, 360
Ghanian Fellowship, 312
Glasgow, 46, 61, 63, 64, 66, 104, 108, 149, 150, 165, 223
Glasgow Technical College, 259
Graduate-equivalents, 296
Graduates Fellowship, 213, 214, 236–238, 294–297, 305, 306, 345, 346
Conferences, 297
Constitution, 296
Newsletter, 214
Greek New Testament, 22, 28, 34, 42, 52, 76, 77, 94, 95, 211, 212
Guy's Hospital, 40, 46

Harrogate, 347
Harvard, 17, 18, 271, 278
Haystack Prayer Meeting, 48
Henry Martyn Hall, 82, 90, 97
High Church, 14, 28, 53, 73
High Leigh, 103, 122, 133–135, 143, 147, 151, 189
Higher criticism, 15, 24, 73, 76, 344
Historians' Study Group, 297
Holy Club, 14, 27, 28
Hospitality Committee, 303, 308
Hull, 32, 150, 220
Hungary, 176, 183

India, 175, 184, 273
Indonesia, 277
Inter-College Christian Fellowship, 264
International Conference of Christian Medical Students, 289
International Conference of Evangelical Students, 183–186, 269
International Congress of Christian Physicians, 289
International Constitution, 270
International deputations, 182, 272, 279
International Fellowship of Evangelical Students, 181, 270, 272, 279, 313, 329
International Friendship Campaign, 305, 306
International General Committee, 271
International Handbooks, 327
International Overseas Fellowship, 214

Inter-Schools Christian Fellowship, 300
In the Service of Medicine, 289
In Touch, 279
Inter-University Christian Union, 67
Inter-university conferences, 50, 54, 66
Inter-Varsity, 135, 146, 147, 214, 274
Inter-Varsity Christian Union, 122
Inter-Varsity Conference, 13, 98, 103, 112, 115–123, 129, 132, 134, 151, 168, 228, 254
Inter-Varsity Fellowship, 9, 13, 122–127, 137–139, 303
Inter-Varsity Fellowship Trust, 232
Inter-Varsity Missionary Fellowship, 136, 147, 148, 190–195, 241, 242
Inter-Varsity Press, 168, 272, 287, 314–331, 339
Inter-Varsity Christian Fellowship, Canada, 180, 181, 268, 270
USA, 268, 270, 278
Ireland, 228, 240 (see also separate universities)
Italy, 279

Jesus Lane Sunday School, 34–37, 80

Keswick Convention, 62, 66, 68, 80, 89, 90, 92, 98, 138, 218, 308
Kingham Hill School, 210
King's College (London), 166

Lawyers Christian Fellowship, 40, 297
Leaders Conference, 169
Leeds, 150, 165, 170
Leicester, 220, 339
Liberal Churchmanship, 118, 121, 342–345
Liverpool, 170, 225
London Bible College, 300
Londonderry, 104, 109
London Hospitals, 46, 61, 70, 71, 83, 99–101
London Inter-Hospitals CU, 83, 100, 101
London Inter-Faculty CU, 101–103, 124–131, 166, 167, 254, 259
London IFCU Conference, 103
London missionary breakfasts, 102, 103
London University, 61, 63, 64, 70, 93, 101
London Women's IFCU and IHCU, 100, 101
Literature, see Inter-Varsity Press, Publications
Literature Advisory Committee, 330
Literature Committee, 318, 320
Literature Finance Committee, 330
Literature Secretary, 316, 318
Loughborough Engineering College, 259

Manchester, 132, 225
Medical Missionary Association, 63
Medical Prayer Union, 41, 46, 287
Medical section (GF), 288, 289 (see also Christian Medical Fellowship)
Medical students, 40, 46, 47, 110–112, 287–289
Medical conferences, 288, 289
Melbourne, 180
Membership, 248, 249
Merchant Adventurers College, 260
Merger of CECU and ICCF, 266
Methodism, Methodists, 14, 23, 28, 29, 32, 41

Michigan Christian Fellowship, 268
Missionary, 241, 242 (see also Inter-Varsity Missionary Fellowship)
breakfasts, 102, 103, 187
Conferences, 135, 147
Secretary, 188–190
societies (student), 38, 45, 46, 61–65, 165, 167
Volunteers, 191–196
Missions, overseas, 37, 42, 56–65, 135, 147, 148, 327
universities, 54–56, 78, 79, 132, 165–167, 222, 224
Morwell Street, 207, 237
Moscia, 308
Mount Hermon Conferences, 48, 62, 64

Netherhall, Largs, 228
New universities, 44, 337
New Zealand, 173, 176, 181
Nigeria, 274, 275, 281
Northern England, 169, 225, 228, 239, 240
Norway, 176, 182, 183
Nottingham, 150, 170, 220
Nurses Christian Fellowship, 300

Oakhill College, 210, 261
Office, 160–162, 170, 198, 237, 339
Old Jordans, 135, 189
Open air meetings, 43, 89, 99, 166
Organizational growth, 217, 229, 231, 235–238
Overseas students, 302–313
Committee, 307
conferences, 308
houseparties, 308–310
Secretary, 305, 306
Oxford, 13, 14, 27, 30, 40, 41–43, 52–54, 64, 83, 93, 121, 124, 125, 130, 139–142, 201, 269, 289
daily prayer meeting, 42, 43, 52, 53, 98
Inter-Collegiate CU, 52–54, 83, 99, 130, 139–142, 166, 221–223
missions, 222, 223
Northgate Hall, 141, 221
open air meetings, 43, 89, 99, 166
University Bible Union, 99, 121, 124–126, 130
University Devotional Union, 130 139

Pan-African Fellowship of Evangelical Students, 275, 281
Paperbacks, 325
Perth, 175
Philadelphia, 27
Pioneer Camp, 174
Prayer, 37, 39, 40, 42, 43, 140, 141
Prayer bands, 39, 187
Praying Societies, 27, 37, 39, 45
Presidents, 155, 156
Princeton, 19, 243
Portland Road, Brimingham, 311
Publications, 137, 145–147, 167, 168, 177, 207, 211, 281, 316–331, 341
Committee, 217, 233, 236, 237
finance, 317
policy, 320, 341
Secretary, 168, 212, 230, 314

Quadrennial Conversations, 69

Reading, 132
Reformers, 14, 22, 23, 315
Regent's Park College, 201, 269
Regions Beyond Missionary Union, 254

Relations with Churches, 339, 341
Religious societies, 30, 31
Religious tests, 53, 87
Research Scientists Christian Fellowship, 238, 289–291, 297
Royal Commonwealth Society, 238
Russell Square, 43, 162

St. Andrew's, 38, 45, 61, 133, 200, 202, 228, 110–112
St. Deiniol's Library, 211
St. John's Hall, 110, 111, 115, 116
St. Peter's Hall, 201
Schloss Mittersill, 280
Schoolteachers' Prayer Fellowship, 214, 292
Schoolteachers' Christian Fellowship, 238, 292 (see also Educationalists)
Scottish Conference, 168, 193, 202, 227
Scottish universities, 26, 37, 38, 70, 93, 168, 170, 193, 223, 239
Scripture Union, 142, 169, 176, 291, 304, 309, 311, 317 (see also Children's Special Service Mission)
Secretaryship, 124, 128, 129, 160–162
Secretaries, clerical, 162, 163
Secret societies, 17–19
Selly Oak Colleges, 201, 259, 261
Sermons, 32, 33, 52, 221, 222
Sheffield, 150, 170
Singapore, 274, 280
Social Workers Christian Fellowship, 297
Sociologists, 249
South Africa, 175, 176, 184
South America, 276
Southampton, 150, 220
Spain, 76, 281
SPCK, 30
Spectrum, 293
Stockholm, 183
Student Christian Movement, 21, 68–78, 91, 106, 113, 118–121, 124, 130, 131, 140, 175, 215, 343
Press, 67, 118
Student churches, 41, 222, 245
Student Foreign Missionary Union, 61, 64
Student Literature Committee, 330
Student societies, 9, 14–25
Student Volunteer Missionary Union, 47, 48, 57, 61, 63, 64, 66, 67, 69, 93, 94, 187, 188, 192, 215, 216, 233, 242
Swansea, 150
Swanwick, 122, 133, 134, 168, 169, 193, 200, 227, 228, 255, 278, 336
Sweden, 176, 183
Switzerland, 176, 183, 184
Sydney, 173, 174, 179

Technical Colleges Christian Fellowship, 236, 250, 254, 257–261, 264, 266
Thanksgiving service, 348
Theological societies, 45, 46, 110, 111
Theological Students, 209, 240–242, 249, 283–285, 331
Fellowship, 241, 250, 263, 284, 285
Secretaries, 285, 286
Theological tensions, 242
Therapy Students Christian Fellowship, 250, 263
Thirty-nine Articles, 113, 114
Training Colleges, see Colleges of

366

Education
Christian Union, 253–257
Newsletter, 256
Training Programmes, 335–337
Travelling secretaries, 124, 125, 135, 163–165
Tyndale Commentaries, 323, 324
Tyndale Fellowship, 238, 297, 299
Tyndale House, 212, 213, 237, 241, 286, 297–299, 322
Tyndale Lectures, 211, 286, 299
Tyndale Press, 322

UCCF Associates, 296 (see also Graduates Fellowship)
Union of Evangelical Students of India, 273

USA, 68, 181, 268, 269, 278 (see also Inter-Varsity Christian Fellowship)
Universities and Colleges Christian Fellowship, 9, 302, 331, 339, 347
Universities Staffs Christian Fellowship, 214, 297

Vancouver, 173, 175, 177, 178
Vermont, 19
Veterinary Christian Fellowship, 297
Vice-Presidents, 153–156, 193
Vocation Conference, 347
Volunteer Movement, 47 (see also Student Volunteer Missionary Union)

Wales, 170, 228, 239
Watchword, 64, 94, 193
Westminster Chapel, 348
Westminster Confession, 113, 114
Westminster Theological Seminary, 243
Williams College, 19, 22, 48
Women's Colleges, 70, 71, 110, 111, 124
World Student Christian Federation, 68, 175, 184
World Wars, 87–88, 194–198
Wye College, 250

Yale, 18, 278
YMCA, 20, 67, 166, 174, 179

Index of names

Adams, J. R. 259
Adeney, David H. 148, 190, 272, 275
Aitken, John T. 234
Aldis, Arnold S. 182, 183, 235, 254
Aldis, Brian, 199
Aldis, W. H. 185
Alexander, Eric, 349
Anderson, Charles D. 235
Anderson, J. N. D. (Sir Norman), 213, 235
Arana, Pedro, 276
Arndt, W. F. 299
Atkinson, Basil F. C. 89, 95, 234

Bacon, F. D. 158, 170
Baker, Lilian B. 199, 230
Balfour, Ivor, 121
Barclay, Oliver R. 201, 230, 238, 280, 290
Barnhouse, D. G. 222
Barr, James, 344–5
Bassett, Rhoda T. 240
Bazeley, Henry, 43
Beauchamp, Montagu, 57
Bennett, Phyllis Z. 202, 231, 276, 277
Bentley-Taylor, D. 183, 277
Bergin, F. 105
Berridge, John, 31
Bewes, Mrs. Cecil, 156
Billington, J. G. 148, 158, 189
Blackwood, Stevenson, 49, 50
Blair, Duncan M. 155, 160, 233
Bolton, John, 271
Bolton, Ruth, 321
Brainerd, David, 18
Bromiley, H. 181
Broomhall, James, 167, 183, 255
Broomhall, Paul, 162, 171
Brookfield, Ronald W. 214
Brown, Hugh, 145
Browne, Stanley, 346
Bruce, F. F. 210, 211, 235, 286, 299, 325
Bürki, Hans, 277, 280
Burton, Mainwaring, 134, 185
Buxton, Alfred, 80, 83, 98, 194
Buxton, Barclay F. 56, 80, 92, 93, 97, 98, 117
Buxton, B. Godfrey, 89, 95, 115, 117, 120, 184, 185
Buxton, Mrs. Godfrey, 184, 304
Byrde, Louis, 63

Canning, S. 255

Capper, W. M. 235, 288
Carless, Albert, 105, 146, 155, 177
Carus, William, 34
Carrick, Rosalyn, 253, 261
Carson, Herbert H. 240
Cassells, W. W. 57
Cecil, Richard, 41
Chalmers, Thomas, 38, 45
Chapman, Colin, 277
Charteris, Prof. 60, 61
Chavasse, C. M. 140
Chavasse, F. J. 42, 52, 53
Christopher, Alfred, 30, 42, 43
Chua Wee Hian, 280
Churchill, A. W. 168, 185, 205, 316
Clarke, R. E. D. 318
Clee, Mary, 240
Coggan, F. D. 10, 161
Cole, Michael, 240
Cook, Alan, 294
Cook, Christopher, 292
Coote, Algernon, 49
Cowper-Temple, W. 50
Crittenden, F. H. 148, 230, 238, 274, 304–313
Crouch, I. 205, 206
Crouch, Muriel, 235
Cundy, H. M. 292

Dahlberg, Nils, 186, 269
Dale, L. 273
Davidson, F. 211, 323
Davies, D. R. 202
Davies, Elwin, 239
Davies, Mr. and Mrs. 207
De Carteret, J. 151
Dick, R. P. 92, 97
Dixon, P. K. 104
Douglas, J. D. 298, 299, 325
Douglas, Sholto, 50, 51
Drummond, Henry, 58–60, 63
Duff, Alexander, 37, 38

Earnshaw Smith, H. 102, 126, 135, 159, 160, 164, 185, 186, 233, 234
Edmunds, Vincent, 235
Edwards, Jonathan, 18
Elliott, Jean, 279
Ellis, Edris, 170
Enoch, H. 273
Escobar, S. 276

Fairbanks, A. 275
Farish, William, 32, 34
Fleming, Ambrose, 146, 154, 290

Forman, J. N. 47, 62
Foster, Clarence H. M. 89, 95, 117, 128, 157, 160
Foster, Mrs. Clarence H. M. 304
France, Richard, 299
Fraser, Alexander, 106
Fraser, Donald, 63
Fulton, Austin, 109

Gaussen, Louis, 139
Gilbert, T. W. 144
Gillespie, J. H. 166
Gladstone, Mary, 321
Glegg, Lindsay, 158, 159
Glover, T. R. 154
Goodman, G. 134
Goodman, M. 166
Goodwin, Theo. 89, 95
Gordon, D. 278
Gore, Charles, 53, 92
Gough, Frederick, 38, 39
Gough, Hugh R. 132, 135, 138, 143, 144, 164, 170, 222
Graham, Billy, 222, 247
Grant, Lindsay, 179, 180
Gray, Herbert, 92
Green, Bryan, 133
Griffiths, Michael, 277
Grubb, Norman P. 13, 82, 89, 90, 92, 95, 97, 98, 115, 142–145, 164
Guillebaud, H. F. 209, 210
Guinness, Howard W. 129, 144, 159, 164, 166, 173–185, 193, 194, 274

Habershon, A. W. 121, 130
Haile, Peter, 278
Haines, Robert, 179
Hallesby, O. 182–185
Hammond, T. C. 114, 160, 167, 222
Harlow, F. J. 259
Harman, G. H. 183
Harmer, J. W. 292
Harris, Brian, 234, 330
Hart Davies, A. 180
Heim, Karl, 171n, 181
Hill, Arthur, 180
Hodge, L. Stephens, 213
Höeg, H. 185
Hogben, Roland, 195, 196, 256
Holden, Stuart, 159, 160
Hollingworth, Jane, 277
Holmes, John, 278
Hooker, Kenneth, 140, 158, 164, 180
Hooykaas, R. 249
Hopkins, H. Evan, 164, 198

Horan, C. T. 63
Horn, Robert, 241, 286
Hoste, D. E. 57
Houghton, A. T. 203, 204
Houghton, F. 275
Howden, J. Russell, 160
Hunt, Stather, 123

Inchley, Ronald, 168, 212, 230, 281, 314
Ingram, G. 169
Innes, T. 284
Inskip, Thomas (Lord Caldecote), 154
Isaacs, Albert, 38, 39

Jack, Hugh, 109
James, Dorothy, 182, 292
Jeeves, Malcolm, 190
Johnson, J. 277

Kennedy, Alistair, 277
Kidner, Derek, 158, 299, 324
Kinnaird, Lord, 185
Kirk, John, 288
Kiss, Ferenc, 185

Laing, J. W. 170, 171, 206, 213, 229
Laird, John, 150
Lamb, Roland, 224
Lamont, Daniel, 155, 186, 233
Landgren, K. 186
Leeke, E. T. 36
Lehmann, Geoffrey, 159
Lewis, C. S. 198
Liddell, Eric, 107
Liebenberg, Frank, 175
Lightfoot, J. B. 34
Livingstone, David, 39
Lloyd-Jones, D. Martyn, 160, 186, 200–202, 210, 214, 222, 228, 233, 243, 244, 271, 273, 326
Lockett, J. 183
Lucas, R. C. 224
Luther, Martin, 23, 315
Lyall, Leslie, 275

McAdam, W. 259
Macaulay, T. B. 33
Machen, J. Gresham, 243
MacInnes, Miles, 62
MacInnes, Rennie, 63
MacKay, Donald, 290
Mackenzie, K. 202, 239
Maclean, Donald, 210, 233
Maddox, F. Christopher, 148, 191
Manley, G. T. 10, 67, 70, 93–96, 132, 158, 210, 233, 286, 318, 324, 329
Mark, W. H. 39
Marshall, Howard, 331
Martin, Clifford A. 89, 90, 95, 118
Martin, William J. 210, 211, 235, 286, 299
Mather, Cotton, 17
Maurice-Smith, K. S. 117, 121
Maxwell, James, 63
Maynard, A. 40
Millard, A. R. 299
Millard, F. A. C. 98, 121, 176
Milner, Isaac, 32

Milton-Thomson, Mary, 163, 199
Mohan, Talbot, 130
Moody, Dwight, 47, 49, 54–56, 58, 79
Morris, G. F. B. 78
Morris, Leon, 299
Mott, John, 10, 64, 68, 74, 83n
Moule, Handley G. 23, 54, 55, 73, 74, 324
Mowll, Howard W. K. 78, 79, 175, 271

Nicholson, J. B. 174
Nicholson, W. P. 109, 140
Niedermeyer, G. 181
Nixon, Norah, 164, 165, 199, 200, 231, 304
Norris, W. J. 330
Nye, Cyril, 150

Oldham, H. W. 323
Osei-Mensah, Gottfried, 275

Packer, J. I. 235, 243, 325
Padilla, Rene, 276
Palmer, Noel, 13, 97–99, 116, 121, 130, 180
Pettit, W. H. 174
Polhill-Turner, A. T. 57, 64
Polhill-Turner, C. H. 57, 64
Pont, A. 236, 262
Potter, P. H. 82
Price, F. W. 155, 177
Prior, K. F. W. 222
Purves-Smith, G. 59

Rainsbury, A. W. 224, 239
Ramsay, W. 154
Raven, C. 91
Rendle Short, A. 105, 107, 108, 145, 151, 154, 156, 157, 159, 160, 170, 185, 234
Rennie, Alistair, 202, 239
Richardson, J. E. 235, 258, 259
Roberts, Gwilym, 239
Robinson, Godfrey, 324
Rollo, J. 133
Rookmaaker, H. R. 249
Ryle, J. C. 50

Samuel, Leith, 223, 224, 244
Sanders, Keith, 289
Sankey, I. D. 47, 49, 55, 58
Sargent, N. 151
Scott, T. 166
Scorer, C. G. 183, 235
Scougal, Henry, 26, 27, 37
Scroggie, Graham, 142, 160
Shedd, Clarence, 10, 20
Simeon, Charles, 32–34, 38, 51, 56
Simpson, A. R. 59–61
Smith, Stanley P. 57–58
Smuts, Jan, 93–95
Speer, R. 65, 194
Spurgeon, Charles, 61
Sterret, Norton, 273
Stewart, T. Grainger, 60, 61
Stibbs, Alan M. 210, 230, 286, 299
Still, F. 81
Still, W. 208

Stillingfleet, James, 28
Stock, Eugene, 62
Stott, John R. W. 223, 235, 244, 279, 331, 348
Strain, Jean, 158, 163, 164, 182, 255
Studd, C. T. 25n, 57–61, 80, 158
Studd, J. E. K. 54–55, 158
Studd, R. 158
Sutton, L. 89, 96, 115, 117

Tasker, R. V. G. 323–325
Tatlow, Tissington, 68, 73–77, 131
Taylor, Arthur, 108
Taylor, F. Howard, 61
Taylor, Hudson, 58, 61, 157
Taylor-Smith, Bishop J. 102, 134, 150
Thomas, David J. 107
Thomson, J. J. 153
Thornton-Duesberry J. 128
Tinling, J. F. B. 40
Torrey, R. A. 78, 79
Trevelyan, G. 201
Turner, Raymond, 236, 262

Venn, Henry, 31

Walkey, J. 140
Walls, Andrew, 241, 286, 298, 299
Walters, Gwyn, 239
Warfield, B. B. 243
Warren, A. J. 118
Watkin, Prof. Morgan, 108
Watson, D. C. C. 273
Webb-Peploe, H. W. 71
Webb-Peploe, Murray H. 89, 96, 117, 120
Webster, F. S. 52
Wenham, John, 209, 210, 285
Wesley, Charles, 27
Wesley, John, 25, 27, 315
Wesley, Susannah, 27
Westcott, B. F. 34, 36, 72
Weston, John, 278
White, George, 230
White, John, 276
White, Paul, 179
Whitefield, George, 27
Wilder, Robert P. 47, 48, 62, 63, 67, 68, 71, 182, 183, 188, 193, 194
Wilkes, Hamilton, 90
Wilkinson, L. F. E. 135, 147, 148, 170, 188, 189
Williamson, Rutter, 47
Wilmot, A. T. de B. 183, 274
Wilson, Daniel, 41
Wilson, J. R. S. 107
Wiseman, D. J. 235, 324, 325
Wiseman, M. 255
Wisloff, Carl F. 182
Woods, E. S. 119
Woods, Stacey, 268, 269, 271, 280
Woods, Theodore, 92, 96
Wright, James, 35
Wright, Stafford, 210, 286
Wycliffe, John, 22
Wynne, G. F. H. 285

York, E. 140
Young, Stafford, 179